THE TALIBAN ı

ALEX STRICK VAN LINSCHOTEN
FELIX KUEHN
(*Editors*)

The Taliban Reader

War, Islam and Politics

OXFORD
UNIVERSITY PRESS

OXFORD

UNIVERSITY PRESS

Oxford University Press is a department of the
University of Oxford. It furthers the University's objective
of excellence in research, scholarship, and education
by publishing worldwide.

Oxford   New York
Auckland   Cape Town   Dar es Salaam   Hong Kong   Karachi
Kuala Lumpur   Madrid   Melbourne   Mexico City   Nairobi
New Delhi   Shanghai   Taipei   Toronto

With offices in
Argentina   Austria   Brazil   Chile   Czech Republic   France   Greece
Guatemala   Hungary   Italy   Japan   Poland   Portugal   Singapore
South Korea   Switzerland   Thailand   Turkey   Ukraine   Vietnam

Oxford is a registered trade mark of Oxford University Press
in the UK and certain other countries.

Published in the United States of America by
Oxford University Press
198 Madison Avenue, New York, NY 10016

Library of Congress Cataloging-in-Publication Data is available
Alex Strick Van Linschoten and Felix Kuehn.
The Taliban Reader: War, Islam and Politics.
ISBN: 9780190908744

Printed in India on acid-free paper

For Scharlette

CONTENTS

CONTENTS

CONTENTS

CONTENTS

CONTENTS

INTRODUCTION

We can divide the things we may never know about the Taliban's 'Islamic Emirate' of 1996–2001 into two broad categories: that which we won't know because we don't have the information, and that which we won't know because the Taliban's 'experiment' was cut short by international intervention in late 2001.

As a project in the making, there is no solving the mystery of Taliban intentionality. Not only were they engaged in a serious internal conflict until the very end of the Emirate, but the movement itself was in a state of flux. Capturing their goals and intentions in hindsight will only ever reveal a partial picture, one perspective on a set of opinions and processes that had not yet developed or consolidated. Anyone who claims to be able to tell you what the Taliban wanted and what their ultimate goal was during their rule should be viewed with great caution. Similarly, while it is important to understand the history of the Taliban, attempts to deduce what the post-2001 Taliban want(ed) based on what they wanted pre-2001 will in most cases lead to a deeply flawed perspective on the movement and its goals.

Analysts and journalists often consider much of the Taliban's thinking and policy to be static; policies implemented pre-2001 thus 'must' be the same post-2001. Instead of a blueprint, the past offers a roadmap. Groups change as they face challenges, evolve in size and organisational structure, seize power and lose it, and interact in a complex system with other groups. New norms form and old ones dissipate.

The Taliban, much like any other group, is subject to the same processes. Had they continued to rule Afghanistan, instead of being ousted and starting an insurgency, their evolution arguably would have looked different. The movement was removed before it matured. Today it is hard to imagine alternative trajectories that the Taliban could have taken at the time. Reconstructing the past becomes increasingly difficult as senior figures associated with the movement pass away or are killed. This makes the gathering of oral histories and testimony harder, especially in the given context of the continued conflict where even the not-so-recent past remains a matter of political debate. Individuals who share their recollections about the past have to consider the possible repercussions. Still, memoirs are being written and others gather the remnants of their past in other archival projects. They offer small windows into Afghanistan's history and the history of the Taliban.

∞

The Taliban Reader is a collection of statements by those associated with the Taliban movement. The vast majority were published on outlets run by the Taliban, whether newspapers controlled by them in the 1990s or websites in their insurgent guise post-2001. This collection of primary source material fills a hole in the literature and is intended to serve as a reference work for scholars, students and practitioners alike. The material is sorted into broad chronological periods and then, inside each of those, is organised thematically.

In an environment where rumour and supposition often take the place of fact, this collection of Taliban statements is a first step in constructing the foundation on which scholars, academics and students can build their understanding. Reports, articles and even books that rely purely on secondary source materials are commonplace for Taliban studies. Fieldwork is often an afterthought or skipped entirely. This might have been less of a problem if the body of primary source materials was rich and mature following years of collection, but unfortunately this has not been a priority.

A researcher who decides to seek out proactively the kinds of materials assembled in this book will have to overcome several hurdles. The Taliban's website is frequently taken offline, and old articles get purged from the indexes. This means that many statements or online magazines live on only in the private archives of individuals. Books and memoirs are written by members of the Taliban (or those who came into their orbit) but they are sometimes hard to find and rarely make it into university collections, with only a very few (mostly private collectors) purchasing all of them. The language barrier also poses a formidable challenge.

We will return to the need for primary-source-based research, but it would seem self-evident that a rigorous study of history requires such materials in order to begin useful analysis, to begin sifting through the meaning of complex patterns of events. Viewing the full swathe of Taliban output during their most recent activities also allows for the perception of continuities and differences that would otherwise have remained imperceptible. This is particularly the case for highly-politicised subjects, where skipping the commentary might save one from falling for a commonly-held myth. Primary source work should be where research work begins.

Ↄↄ

We first began our formal work in Afghanistan in 2006 with a project that sought to provide access to primary source materials. AfghanWire was a media translation service, a daily newsletter filled with English-language versions of articles published in local media outlets. During that process, we read of the publication of Mullah Zaeef's Guantánamo memoir in one of Kabul's newspapers and began the long process of researching, editing and working with translators to bring that material to a wider audience. Part of that led us down to Kandahar, where the paucity of materials relating to the 1980s war against the Soviets saw us begin a kind of oral history project. We gathered dozens of testimonies from participants, many of whom had never told their stories before.

While working on *An Enemy We Created*, we had several books translated from Arabic and Pashto. Once we were finished with the research, we tried to find a way to make these available to a wider audience. The material would not benefit other researchers or the broader research environment if they just remained on our hard drives. We started *First Draft Publishing* as our formal outlet for these texts. To date we have published five translated titles, with several others in the pipeline.

As part of all of this work with primary sources and documentary evidence, we began collecting documents relating to the Afghan Taliban. We were joined in this endeavour by the journalist and researcher Anand Gopal, author of *No Good Men Among the Living*. Michael Innes helped us structure the process. We collected newspapers, magazines, books and anything else we found lying around that was in need of a permanent home. We asked friends or colleagues of ours to visit poets in the provinces, digitising hand-written collections and transcribing audio cassettes filled with songs.

The digitisation process was slow and difficult. Not only were there implied pressures and concerns that our office would be raided by Afghan government authorities and the archival collection confiscated, but also frequent power cuts and cold winter weather made the work very much a labour of dedication. We used a pre-made book scanner alongside a larger newspaper and magazine tool that we custom-designed and worked with a local carpenter to produce.

Even once the material was digitised, we faced problems when one of the institutional sponsors of our project, the British Library in London, said they would be unable to host materials on account of fears that they would be subject to British government anti-terror legislation.[1]

As we write, the collection is being prepared for online digital hosting.[2] Users will be able to access materials in the original Arabic, Dari and Pashto languages as well as over two million words in translation. Some of those translations correspond to material in this volume.

CR

It is pertinent to ask what the major revelations of the Taliban Sources Project are. Part of the answer to this relates to the missing details in discussions about the Taliban. Anyone who has done any work on the (Afghan) Taliban, particularly if you aren't spending time in the country, has probably realised that the number of useful primary sources is relatively limited. This is starting to change, but compared to most other countries, Afghanistan has a very limited number of resources to start with. So in many ways, the key revelation of the collection is that there *are* lots of details available, and that a more granular understanding of the movement is possible. Discussions of the Taliban have for too long been predicated on an extremely limited set of issues: women/girls, especially in the context of education; cultural destruction / the Bamyan Buddhas; drugs; and bin Laden and international 'jihadism'. This collection helps fill the gaps, showing that for the Taliban those issues were among many other challenges and discussions they faced and held on a day-to-day basis. Reading through the entries, particularly from the early periods of the Taliban, returns some of the real complexity of the day, moving beyond platitudes and displaying Afghanistan as they saw it and experienced it at the time.

More specifically, through interviews and through biographical profiles, as well as through the sheer mass of daily data on ministers and their activities, we can build up far more compelling portraits of the individuals who were the face of the Taliban movement while they were in power. These kinds of portraits (this kind of detail) have never really been part of how the Taliban has been written about. The biographies help illuminate certain questions or settle long-standing debates. For example, there has been a question about whether Taliban intelligence chief Qari Ahmadullah is alive or not. This has relevance in a number of areas, including on deliberations on whom to release from Guantánamo. We have it from the translations now that he is indeed dead, thanks to a martyr's biography published in 2006/7. Similarly, there have been debates about whether certain individuals released from Guantánamo are 'recidivists' or not, and in a number of cases—through martyr bios and interviews with field commanders—we have been able to get new data points to help find answers.

A much fuller picture of the theological/ideological backing that the Taliban consider applicable to the use of beheading, suicide operations as well as their general approach to conflict (i.e. when it is and is not permissible) is also uncovered by this collection. Newspaper editorials and op-eds from the 1990s government detailed the Taliban's consideration of the Islamic basis for a number of issues, and this can be contrasted against the movement's attitudes post-2001, particularly on the issue of government, the role of Islam in the ideal state, the role of religiously-sanctioned violence and some details related to how this is practised. The material is unparalleled in terms of the detail offered. Of course, analysis and explanation must now follow, but with this and other collections becoming available in translation, scholars and students around the world can start to explore their own hypotheses. They can evaluate much of what has been written about the Taliban and their Emirate post-2001 in the light of what they wrote and said at the time. The material that is now available can truly transform our understanding of the Taliban.

From the data relating to professional appointments within the Taliban's government, for example, Anand Gopal has produced a network of Taliban ministry co-memberships. From this, using statistical modelling it is possible to predict with reasonable accuracy which members re-engaged in violence post-2001 and which tried to reconcile—the take-home message being that Taliban decisions to fight or reconcile have less to do with ethnicity or 'ideology' and more to do with their structural location in the Taliban's network of trust and patronage.

◯੨

Research on topics relating to the Afghan Taliban has been due a recalibration for many years. Ideally this will begin with the study of primary sources, and only then can cross-referencing of secondary sources be a useful exercise. We now start to have the data to be sure that we are in a good place to start.

This volume thus aims to help reset the research agenda. We hope that this book will serve as an essential reference work for anyone interested in the Afghan Taliban; remind scholars that there is by now plenty of material worthy of being studied; and stimulate future research and interest in the full collection available online.

There is a great deal of research that remains for scholars of the Taliban and South Asian Islamism. The circumstances in which many discovered the Taliban movement—viewed through the burning ashes of New York's Twin Towers—has meant that of the many millions of words written about the movement, only a small proportion has been based on rigorous research, much less through the assessment and use of primary sources. Commonplace opinions and widely acknowledged 'facts' should be re-evaluated and questioned before we move on to make broader assumptions.

A useful place to start would be the compilation of a cross-referenced chronology of events in Afghanistan for the 1994–2001 period, or, even better, back to the early 1970s. Many accounts of the Taliban during this time are plagued by a lack of attention to dates and time. Biographical details can now be gathered and cross-checked, lifting the Taliban movement out of the shadow of the few public faces and understanding them in terms of the underlying groups and networks they are built on. These groupings reach back to affiliations made during the 1980s jihad against the Soviet Union all through to the positions held during the Taliban's rule.

The sheer volume of material written about the Taliban movement, particularly that produced post-2001 in association with the international military effort, makes it difficult to understand the breadth of the content and its value. For this reason, a comprehensive annotated bibliography of material relating to the Taliban movement would be a boon for researchers, particularly if it referred to print media articles as well. These are laborious tasks that do not require much fieldwork, but rather hours and hours of dedicated desk work. In the end, though, it will be detailed documentation that derails pundits who leap to conclusions. Attention has mostly been directed towards the Taliban's religious and social policies, while other aspects of the movement remain unexplored; economic policies practised by the Taliban were sufficiently different from those of prior governments to merit closer attention, for example. We know a lot about the Taliban's diplomatic interactions with the United States because of the attacks on 11 September, but we know far less about their relations with other countries and organisations. It would be useful to gain more insight into the Taliban's calculations with regard to international investment in natural resource exploitation, for example, as well as a far more nuanced understanding of their relationship with Iran or their Central Asian neighbours, not to mention Pakistan.

A return to ideology is also required, albeit one understood on the Taliban's terms. For the vast majority of discussions about the Taliban, their religious ideology is summed up using the rubric 'Deobandi' without much more supporting detail. Extensive work is needed to understand the Taliban from within their religious education, from the syllabus that most study to the religious argumentation and shorthand employed in discussion among peers. This, again, is where a return to primary source texts will be essential.

For those who can travel to Afghanistan, Pakistan or other places where those associated with the Taliban are currently based, work needs to be done to gather interview material, to compile oral history testimony and to encourage individuals to write up their memoirs.

◌

There is no single Taliban strategy or set of goals. The movement is heterogeneous by nature and continues to undergo considerable changes that see a deepening fragmentation within, all while paradoxically remaining one of the more stable entities in Afghanistan, at least until very recently. There appear to be considerable differences as to the political and military future of the Taliban internally; outright splinter groups have emerged for the first time in the Taliban's history.

The core self-stated goals of the Taliban post-2001 are for justice and a role in the political future of the country. International commentators often voice concern about the revisionist nature of analyses of the Taliban, pointing towards the countless human rights abuses that the movement committed while in power and since their ousting in 2001. These correctly assess that the Taliban are far from being 'modern Robin Hoods' who simply defend their own rights or those of the people; it is nevertheless informative to examine the underlying developments. Local shifts in perception reflect at least a partial reality: corruption and the poor performance of the Afghan government in conjunction with oft-voiced promises and pledges have eroded the credibility of the government in Kabul and the internationals. There is an obvious disconnect between the message and the deed. The Taliban, on the other hand, while employing tactics to sow fear, appear to be consistent, and if not in reality then at least in the perceptions of many. The considerations seem pragmatic for the most part, rather than an explicit subscription to the Taliban's goals and narrative.

To ask the question 'What do the Taliban want?' is already to apply a certain analysis as to who the Taliban are and how to think about them. There are groups within the umbrella term that make up 'the Taliban'—from the field commanders and common fighters to the high-level leaders, from the eastern fighters who increasingly operate and interact with non-Afghan entities to the old senior leadership in Quetta and other places. The emergence of forces nominally loyal to the Islamic State in eastern Afghanistan and elsewhere offers yet another challenge to unity and coherence, one that was accentuated following the revelation of the death of Mullah Mohammad Omar. A political process needs to be understood as engaging elements within this broad grouping and needs to take into account what this engagement means for each particular group in relation to the other parts and interests.

Given that fragmentation is the prevalent dynamic currently, engagement will certainly encourage doubt of those individuals and groups that do participate. This, however, is not a divide-and-conquer strategy in which the goal is to play sections off against each other. There are no sections; sections are shifting and formed and reformed, and alliances easily switched. If the goal is to divide the Taliban—rather than to pull as many as possible over onto the side that is negotiating—then this is likely to translate into a marginalisation of the people whose engagement is sought, to a degree that makes the whole process irrelevant.

The starting positions that all parties bring to political negotiations will often transform—through compromises or otherwise—into something else by the time they are ready for a final agreement. It should not be forgotten, however, that this process can often be generative of new ideas. In this way, part of the answer to the question 'What do the Taliban want?' will be revealed and discovered through the very process of negotiation. Not only will the process reveal what they want, but will also solidify (and to a certain extent, create) who 'they' are.

PART 1

MUJAHEDEEN AND TOPAKIYAAN
(1979–1994)

1979 Soviet Army invades Afghanistan (December)
1988 Geneva Accords signed, providing for Soviet withdrawal (April)
1989 Battle of Jalalabad (March–May)
1989 The last Soviet soldier leaves Afghanistan (February)
1991 Khost falls to mujahedeen forces (April)
1992 Afghan government falls to mujahedeen, followed by civil war
1994 Taliban emergence

The Taliban's roots lie in the religious educational circles and madrassas of southern Afghanistan, which were inspired by the Hanafi Deobandi religious tradition. The movement emerged in 1994, the outcome of deliberations that had taken place among a specific stratum of Afghan society. It was a local expression of discontent, concerned with issues close to home, and at its outset had neither national nor international ambitions. This agenda, however, shifted and changed as time passed, and as those leading the movement themselves changed in reaction to evolving circumstances; all this made the movement quickly swell in numbers. The Taliban were at the head of social circles that previously had no voice and negligible power within the political realities of the day, but soon occupied a position where their opinions and decisions were heard; this inevitably changed the self-perception of the leadership and what they considered to be their mission.

The Taliban pre-2001 were a group that emerged out of a long history, one that technically extended back as long as there were religious clerics, and as long as Afghanistan existed as a country. The past hundred years or so can be taken as the frame for the most recent segment of this story. The religious clergy was not immune to the new ideas of Muslim solidarity and revivalism that swept through other parts of the Muslim world in the early and mid-twentieth century. Where the Deobandi tradition is often considered to be depoliticised, it came about as a reaction to the local political realities in the south Asian subcontinent. The forebears of those who sought to impose order on the chaos of southern Afghanistan during the mid-1990s had become increasingly involved in local politics. This was largely a process of instrumentalisation, but it would set a precedent for later developments. In this sense, the heritage bestowed on the religious students who came to form the Taliban movement presents a particular local brand of mostly rural religious, political and cultural processes. Where religion underpinned much of the movement's identity, it only at times transcended other cultural and political influences.

The relative calm of the early 1970s was disrupted by ideological disagreements and open clashes between Communists and Islamists in Kabul. By 1975, there was a fully-fledged attempt by Islamists to overthrow the government (spearheaded by Hekmatyar and Massoud) and fatwas were issued calling for jihad. Nevertheless, it took the unpopular and disruptive land reforms, along with the strong-arm tactics of the Communist government, to turn the predominantly rural population against it, in particular those living in southern and eastern Afghanistan. Resistance spread throughout the country, and the Communist government under Taraki and later Amin used strong-armed tactics against the traditional rural leadership. Tens of thousands left their homes, crossing the borders to Pakistan and Iran. The resistance, however, would gain much traction and soon the Soviet 40th Army, which arrived on 24 December 1979, saw itself drawn into nationwide war.

Already in the late 1970s the Communist government had tried to subdue parts of the population and to enforce its reforms—disappearances, arbitrary arrests and executions were common—thereby contributing to the establishment of the first mujahedeen fronts that took up arms against the government following the arrival of Soviet troops. In southern Afghanistan, some of the first to fight were members of the religious clergy originally from the districts west of Kandahar city.

Local mullahs, following the call to jihad, converted their madrassas into fronts, leading their students into battle. While the organisation of the mujahedeen fronts was initially hazardous, a distinct meta-structure developed in the first year that would soon be forced under the umbrella of seven officially recognised mujahedeen fronts. The groups of religious students, or 'taliban', would emerge as independent front line groups, embedded into the wider mujahedeen structures.[1] They would come to play a different role than other mujahedeen groups; they were closely associated with the Islamic courts that they operated in Afghanistan during the jihad, dispensing shari'a justice. These developments took place predominantly in Afghanistan's southern and eastern regions.

The experiences of jihad were the single most significant influence on the young religious students' sense of identity. The transformative impact is difficult to overstate. It would inform much of the identity of the group that would later emerge as the Taliban in 1994, individuals who regarded themselves as belonging to one group with a shared identity, separate from those around them.

The experience shaped the Taliban's identity in four ways. First, the trenches created a sense of fraternity, one far more tangible and durable than just growing up with other students and receiving an education at a madrassa or other religious institution. Second, their identity was shaped by witnessing the transformation and disruption of society at large and the sidelining of the old tribal hierarchy; military strongmen or charismatic religious leaders now eclipsed these traditional structures, in part simply due to their presence in Afghanistan instead of being in Pakistan, away from the fighting. Thirdly, their status was elevated by the power that their leaders wielded in the religious courts, which fulfilled an important function throughout the 1980s jihad, in particular in southern Afghanistan. Fourthly, in a blend not uncommon to what would emerge in the mid-1990s in the south, mullahs set up structures that would provide conflict mitigation and pass judgements, issue edicts and fatwas, often primarily concerned with issues that arose between different mujahedeen groups and factions or among the local population.

The overarching principles of the local interpretation of Islam that informed much of the early Taliban's activities and structures—especially the frequently voiced aspiration to transcend tribal and ethnic lines—would also come to play an important role in the evolution of the groups that joined to form the Taliban movement. This sowed the seeds for much of the movement's coherence and appeal, which in turn generated support from the local population.

The departure of the last Soviet soldier from Afghanistan in 1989 and the formation of the mujahedeen government in Kabul were moments of victory and celebration, as well as of sorrow for the losses of the war. Around the country, a tentative optimism was felt, and those who had spent much of the last ten years fighting could take a breath and pause.

The Taliban who had fought against the Soviets did not see themselves as the driving force of future political developments nor as the people to implement what they had fought for, namely an Islamic state. The Taliban waged a jihad as much *against* something as they did *for* something. Their jihad was a defensive one, not an 'offensive' one that would put in place a new government. One should not forget that many of the clergy already regarded Afghanistan as an Islamic state prior to the tumult of the 1970s.

The individuals who would come to form the Taliban in 1994 were largely passive in the years leading up to the formation of the movement, and did not play a significant role in the local power games among different mujahedeen commanders and factions. In particular, the senior leadership of the Taliban, dominated by actual students who had not finished their religious education or were 'village mullahs', went home or turned the fronts back into madrassas in areas where they had fought during the 1980s.[2]

The cessation of government funding from Saudi Arabia and Pakistan meant that many of the groups associated with the Taliban had far less support, having already received significantly less attention during the peak of the jihad. Like the Taliban fronts themselves, support wound down. The Soviet withdrawal had been made possible by an ambitious militia programme that was supported by large amounts of money. With foreign interest dwindling alongside a reduction in Soviet funding, many of the commanders saw their power decline. Looking for alternative sources of revenue, they turned on the population. It was these processes that caused a disintegration of society at large, one which would directly precipitate the Taliban, called upon by their own communities to take action.

The insecurity and lawless atmosphere—known as the time of *topakiyaan*, or men with guns—that developed during the early 1990s in southern Afghanistan was cause for those involved in the 1980s mujahedeen fronts to come together to discuss possible solutions. Most of the mullahs and religious students were at home in their villages, and they began a discussion process that took several months before it led to action.

1

THE TALIBAN FRONTS

[*Mullah Zaeef's account of the 1980s presence of religious students or 'taliban' on the battlefield was not the first time this has been noted. Nevertheless, the pushback from several commentators has underscored the way our understanding of the Taliban movement today is often motivated and shaped by political or social trends of our own time, rather than by a close observation of the primary sources available to us. Zaeef describes the life of but one member of these fronts, but we learn a lot about the kind of life those religious students lived. It was akin to the experiences of the other mujahedeen fighting in southern Afghanistan, but also different in character and tenor.*]

Excerpt from My Life with the Taliban *by Abdul Salam Zaeef, 2010*

I left for Chaman in a bus with nothing but the clothes on my back and one hundred rupees in my pocket. It was the summer of 1983, and the passes were clear so many mujahedeen moved from the camps to Afghanistan and back. I joined a small group that was heading for Kandahar. One of my religious teachers, Salam Agha, was there so he took me with him across the border. We walked all the way, taking the smuggling routes in the middle of the night.

[...]

I knew that the Taliban were fighting in Nelgham under the command of Mullah Mohammad Sadiq Akhund but I was afraid to join them. I had some relatives in that same area, some even fighting with Mullah Mohammad Sadiq, who would inform my family about my whereabouts if I went there. If my family found out where I was, I would surely be dragged back to the camps in Pakistan. Many people talked about the Taliban, even back then. They were respected by other mujahedeen. Some of them even consulted the Taliban courts to settle their disputes or came to seek advice.

Jihad was not just about fighting; in our view, there had to be a strong educational perspective as well as a provision for justice. People came to the Taliban to help them in their disputes. Mawlawi Nazar Mohammad was initially the senior judge, but after he was martyred Mawlawi Sayyed Mohammad Pasanai Saheb took over. A Taliban prison in Pashmol was established along with other holding cells throughout the districts under our control.

Most of the mujahedeen fronts were very homogeneous, with most people coming from the same background, same tribe, same family, or from the same area. The Taliban were different. A group of religious scholars and students with different backgrounds, they transcended the normal coalitions and factions. They were fighting out of their deep religious belief in jihad and their faith in God. Allah was their only reason for being there, unlike many other mujahedeen who fought for money or land.

[...]

☙

I had only been in Nelgham for a few days when Soviet forces and the Afghan army encircled our position. Their artillery fire and air raids turned night to day; the shells and bombs tore apart the land, leaving only ruins behind. There were graves everywhere. I remember the contorted faces of men and women screaming at the countless funerals. The few civilians still living in the area fled, leaving their houses and farms while the Russian airplanes poured bombs like water.

It seemed that the Russian tanks and artillery could attack our position forever while we stayed put. The earth shook for ten days straight. By then we had run out of everything, with just a handful of bullets and one grenade left. The Russians stood firm and held their positions. We decided to retreat and made a run for Zangiabad. It was a rough business and four mujahedeen were martyred during the escape.

There were about seventy mujahedeen in Zangiabad, who had between them three Kalashnikovs, one rifle, one Balazan, one Jaghuri and one RPG, which was not even an original. I had one of the Kalashnikovs and thanked God for it. The Soviet forces had already encircled the entire region and the fighting began in Zangiabad.

In Registan, Rud Panjwayi, Charshakha and from Mushan, the Russians and Afghan government forces strengthened their positions by establishing encircling belts. Planes carried out missions the entire day. Groups of four or six Russian planes would attack our positions. At one point we even counted fourteen planes unleashing hell on the tiny region. Tanks could be heard everywhere, and the hills were blackened by explosions and gunpowder. Everyone who was able to tried to flee. The village of Sperwan and the district centre of Panjwayi were flooded with refugees; several families often shared the same house, with more than twenty people pressed into one tiny room.

After ten or so days the Russians left Panjwayi and moved on Pashmol. Hundreds of mujahedeen and civilians were killed in the battle of Zangiabad and many houses and orchards were destroyed. A few mujahedeen followed the Russians and joined the front in Pashmol. We put up strong resistance there in Pashmol, and fighting continued for almost two weeks. Both sides sustained heavy casualties, and many mujahedeen were martyred. Dozens of tanks were set on fire. Finally the mujahedeen were driven out of the region again.

Among the many mujahedeen and civilians killed in the fighting in Pashmol, two senior mujahedeen commanders, Qazi Mawlawi Nazar Mohammad—the first Taliban judge who preceded Mawlawi Sayyed Mohammad Pasanai Saheb—and another strong mujahed, Mullah Khawas Akhund, were martyred. His mujahedeen kept on fighting, however, not giving an inch of land to the Soviet forces without a battle, moving from village to village, from one region to the next.

The battles of Pashmol and Zangiabad were typical of the war between the Soviets and the mujahedeen. The mujahedeen always had fewer troops, less training and used antiquated weapons, but still we managed to wage a guerrilla war that exploited the weaknesses of the large immobile 40th Army. We established resupply and retreat routes. If the Russians drew too close or if the mujahedeen sustained too many casualties, they withdrew towards Arghandab, Sangisar or Zangiabad, and if they came under pressure in Arghandab they then withdrew towards Mahalajat, Shah Wali Kot and Panjwayi. Later, when the Russians removed their forces, the mujahedeen would return to their original positions. Many times we moved, engaged, fled and regrouped, much like the 'Taliban' do nowadays.

Throughout Afghanistan, the mujahedeen had special cemeteries reserved for martyrs. Many of the casualties of the battlefield could not be treated, however, and often it could take as long as ten to fifteen days until a doctor or medic could treat the wounded. The Russian tactic of encircling the mujahedeen positions made it difficult to transport our wounded out of the area. Wounds would become infected, and thus even small injuries killed many fighters. I remember seeing ten to twelve wounded mujahedeen in the small crowded rooms they used as a base. Those who had attended a medical training course would do their best to treat the wounded.

When the Russians finally pulled out of Pashmol and the mujahedeen and villagers returned to their houses, they found a devastated landscape. The Russian operations had been brutal, and the scenes there belied any traces of humanity.

Even though the mujahedeen had left Pashmol, some civilians had stayed in their houses to protect their livestock. The Russians had killed everything they found. The air was heavy with the reek of decaying flesh, and dead bodies of men, women and children were scattered among the remains of cows, sheep and chickens. The villagers who returned were busy for days, trying to bury relatives, friends and carcasses.

The Russians had established a big army base in the Zheray desert that held DC guns, BM40, BM16, Ouragan and other heavy weaponry and artillery. They would target the villages and houses on the riverside throughout the day and night for no particular reason. When they launched operations they would set the earth on fire: artillery shells would rain down on the houses and villages, and bombs dropped from the sky. They smashed their way through Arghandab, Mahalajat, Zalakhan and towards Nakhunay. When they started their operations they were met by a unified front of several mujahedeen groups, in which the individual fronts supported and reinforced each other. It was always this way: whenever fighting started anywhere in the south, mujahedeen from neighbouring areas would hurry to support one another.

We travelled on foot, each carrying our own ammunition, although later we occasionally found tractors and cars as transport. Back roads and smuggling tracks through valleys and mountains bypassed Soviet or Afghan Communist checkpoints and we sometimes rode motorcycles or horses on longer journeys. The mujahedeen were also very mobile and put their detailed local knowledge of the terrain to use every day. There are hardly any good maps of Afghanistan's south. Not even a satellite picture will tell you where a mountain pass is, or if one route is quicker than another. In this way, local mujahedeen guides were instrumental against the Soviet Union. These wouldn't usually be from your group, but the spirit of cooperation was very much part of the mujahedeen's style. It wasn't difficult to find someone to help with local directions and information.

We fought on regardless of exhaustion, hunger and thirst, walking from Maiwand to Dand, from Shah Wali Kot and Arghandab to Panjwayi and other regions. We would even walk the hundred kilometres or so from Nelgham to Helmand or to Tirin Kot in Uruzgan. We would wear the same clothes for months at a time, surviving on just a loaf of bread or a few dates each day. Many were eager to fight, eager to die, especially young mujahedeen like myself.

We lived off the land and thanked those who donated food and money. People wanted to help just as we wanted to fight. If a commander left somebody out of an operation, that fighter would feel angry and disappointed. Just as normal people are eager to get married, we were desperate for martyrdom. At times you could hear mujahedeen cry out in the midst of battle, but not out of fear. Even though many of our friends were martyred, one after another, we weren't scared. We would have leapt at the first opportunity to run into open fire during battle, if only our commander hadn't reigned us in. It is hard to believe, maybe, but we were happy. From time to time we danced the Atan, such was our elation. At other times we suffered grievously, but it was the true path: if one died, it was meant to be. What a happy life we led! At the end of an operation we would return to our positions and hideouts; we would sit in our rooms, relieved and comforted that we had succeeded in damaging the enemy's military machinery—until the next operation, that is.

Fighting alongside the Taliban meant more than just being a mujahed. The Taliban followed a strict routine in which everyone who fought alongside us had to participate, without exception. We woke before sunrise to perform the *fajr* or morning prayer in the mosque, and afterwards sat together before returning to the camp. We would recite Surat Yasin Sharif every morning in case we were martyred that day.

Some would then leave to strengthen some front or other, or to carry out a raid, while others would tend to prisoners, the wounded or spend some time studying.

Even though a large number of common people took part in the jihad along the Taliban's front, all had to follow the group's basic principles. Apart from dire emergencies during operations or enemy assaults, the mujahedeen were engaged in study. Senior Taliban members would teach the younger seekers, and the senior Mawlawi would instruct other older Taliban members. In this way, a common and illiterate mujahed could become a Talib within two or three years. I carried out both duties on the front; I would learn from my instructor and I would teach others the basics of reading and writing.

We all studied, and so I was able to continue my religious education. People who did not want to study went to fight under other commanders. Not all the fronts worked this in this manner, but we were Taliban and this was our way. We wanted to stay clean, to avoid sinning, and to regulate our behaviour.

I had spent close to a year at the Taliban front under Mullah Mohammad Sadiq Akhund when I was ordered to return to Pakistan. Bur Mohammad, a mujahed known as Mullah Burjan, had been wounded in the leg by a tank shell. He could not walk and it would be difficult and dangerous to get treatment. Pakistan and the International Committee of the Red Cross had established mobile clinics on the border, but it often took weeks to reach them.

At times, vehicles and trucks could only inch forward along the passes and dirt tracks. The mujahedeen, refugees and others would cross the border into Pakistan, and return to Afghanistan by camel. The sick and the injured were transferred in the same way to Chaman. The fighters nowadays have the same options open to them, and mostly take the very same routes that we took to return to Pakistan to recuperate.

The smuggling route was the only way into Pakistan for us. Any male from fifteen and forty-five years old who crossed into Pakistan over the Chaman–Kandahar highway was captured and drafted into the puppet Afghan army. But it wasn't just mujahedeen who would make the treacherous journey through the mountains. For many it was the only way to get in and out of the country. Many civilians, families, foreigners and journalists used the smuggling routes.

I met Mullah Burjan in Nelgham where we started our journey. Roughly thirty years of age, Mullah Burjan was a strong and tough man with a big black beard. From Tangai we made our way through the mountains of Reg on camels. I led our small group of five, moving slowly towards the border. By sunset we were joined by two other mujahedeen from the front near to Mullah Mehrab.

Mullah Khanjaryar was a good mujahed who fought along a small front in Mahalajat. When he was martyred in a battle with the Russians, his brother took his place. Khanjaryar, however, had deviated from the path of his brothers and was running a small arms ring. They were making the crossing with a camel laden with goods. Even though I asked them, they never told me what their camel was carrying.

We eventually reached a place called Do Larey. Only two days earlier the Russians had martyred thirty people and killed seven camels in an ambush in the area. I was convinced that there were Russian forces around and that we would fall into the same trap if we did not prepare ourselves. But we had no weapons with us. There was no other way; another smuggling route would add several days to our journey, and Mullah Burjan was badly injured.

The news of the Russian ambush was extremely worrying to the members of our convoy. We could not return, and Russian troops were waiting in front of us. By then there were about thirty or forty of us travelling together, not one of whom had a weapon. As we walked in darkness towards where the Russians were lying in wait, one of the brothers of Mawlawi Khanjaryar approached me and told me that they had one RPG and five Kalashnikovs loaded on their camel. "We will give you three Kalashnikovs and one RPG", he said, "but we will keep the other two Kalashnikovs for ourselves."

This was good news, I thought, and I told him to hurry up. Our time was running out, and we needed to prepare for what lay ahead.

They stopped their camel and unloaded the weapons, handing us three Kalashnikovs and the RPG launcher. When the people saw the weapons, many sighed with relief. I drew up a plan, telling the men of Mawlawi Khanjaryar's brother that we should split up. I would go with my friends and lead most of the people over one of the smaller side passes, and he and his men would take another pass.

The injured and elderly would follow at a distance, so that they could retreat quickly in case of an ambush and could try to find another way around the Russian forces. This was important as the Russians would often use Roxanas during engagements. These were bright flares that would turn night to day, putting everyone in danger of being targeted.

Just as we were preparing our plan to face the ambush ahead, a convoy coming from Pakistan into Afghanistan was attacked just over a kilometre in front of us. We could hear whistling RPGs and machine-gun fire. The Roxanas created a bright summer day. Helicopters circled in the air, and when the Roxanas were fired, they would sweep down over the ground. We hid under bushes and desert scrub and hoped that the darkness would cover us. Lingering there, we waited until the fighting was over.

We regrouped and proceeded onwards, taking a different route to avoid the ambush site. At dawn we arrived in the mountains of Tangi. At the bottom of the mountains Kuchis had dug wells. We reached the Kuchi camp by sunrise. The village was called Shiin Aka and consisted of some tents and a few houses. Our party split up and went to different houses to rest for the afternoon. The Kuchis were very hospitable, giving us food and water, and we continued our journey at sunset through Naieb Wale to Chaman. Near Bam Bul Tanna we heard of another ambush, so we took a longer way, slipping around it. Arriving safely in Chaman, it was as if nothing had even happened during our journey, and the fear we had felt seemed but a distant memory.

I hurried to bring Mullah Burjan to the clinic, but unfortunately his wound had become infected. Even though he was brought to the Red Cross hospital in Quetta, he soon died a martyr.

There was nothing left for me to do but to see my family. I went to Panjpayi, but the people in the area said that my family had moved to Quetta. I spent the night there, and travelled on to Quetta the following day. It was the summer of 1984 and I had been in Afghanistan for thirteen months.

My family had not heard from me since I had left to join the jihad. But at the time the happiness of seeing each other again was greater than their anger at my leaving without their permission.

2

DESERT ATTACK

[*Abu Ja'far al-Masri al-Kandahari's book tells the story of Arabs who came to Afghanistan to fight in the war against the Soviets. As an Egyptian, he was part of the initially small contingent of 'Afghan Arabs' who organised under the guidance of Abdullah Azzam to support the Afghan mujahedeen parties. Rarer still, Faraj (his real name) was dispatched to southern Afghanistan, where he fought alongside a variety of groups. These included the religious students that Zaeef described in the previous extract.*]

Abu Ja'far al-Masri al-Kandahari / Dr Ayman Sabri Faraj, excerpt from Memories of an Afghan Arab, *2002 (published in Arabic)*

When I learned that the mujahedeen were preparing big interception operations in the desert, I was determined to participate in them. I joined the mujahedeen of Commander Abdul Samad while my arm was still in a cast and tied to my neck. These desert operations were located in the areas of influence of the latter but large numbers of mujahedeen from all the parties came to participate in them. Nonetheless, Abdul Samad was the general commander. The government wanted to enhance its power in Kandahar following the Khosh Ab losses, and was expecting another attack by the mujahedeen on the airport and the city. It was difficult and maybe impossible to deliver supplies to the besieged city with aircraft (in light of the stinger missiles that were in the hands of the mujahedeen). Therefore a land route had to be secured for the military convoys.

The government positioned large numbers of forces from the army and the militias loyal to it in barricaded checkpoints throughout the road linking Kandahar, Helmand and maybe even the Shindand base.[1] Their positions were located on the sandy hills and were close enough to protect the military convoys. The militias included the most evil men who were raised to fight and had no fear, while the army forces featured commandos with black military attire. They were extremely tall, strongly-built, and enjoyed excellent armaments, tanks, mortars, rockets and light and heavy machine guns.

They dug tunnels at the top of these hills but the only factor in favour of the mujahedeen was that these hills were not mined. (Though the presence of mines would not have kept the mujahedeen from storming these positions). Abdul Samad's mujahedeen, led by the daring and courageous Dost Muhammad, moved to an abandoned Kuchi village which contained four or five houses and constituted the winter headquarters of a number of shepherds.[2] We were in the middle of summer, the desert surrounded us from all sides and the heat was worse than that ever witnessed in Egyptian deserts. By noon, we could not walk no matter how thick our shoes were since it was as though we were walking on coal. This heat was only paralleled by that seen in the deserts of the Arabian Peninsula.

Ice reached us from Chaman on a daily basis along with the supplies and ammunition. This was a great luxury to those who were previously in Mahalajat. We stayed two weeks in this position and new posts were gradually starting to emerge next to ours. One of them belonged to the Taliban, i.e. 'the students', and Dost Muhammad and I decided to visit them. They received us warmly and insisted that we have dinner with them on the roof of their post. All the members of the Taliban were young men under eighteen. They were also students of the shari'a and spoke perfect Arabic.

We were joined by Mullah Aziz Mujadidi and I was surprised to learn that Muhammad Rassoul had become one of their commanders. When he saw me, he ran towards me and embraced me with warmth. He insisted on my leaving Abdul Samad and joining him in his new post, but when I explained to him that this might upset the men of Abdul Samad, he decided to stay with me all the time. He would insist that I have lunch with him in his position each day. Muhammad Rassoul loved to repeat the Arabic words he had learned from me in the Karezak position. His looks had somewhat changed since his clothes were clean and his men looked at him with great respect and admiration. Nonetheless, he remained funny and pleasant to be around and he asked me a lot about the former Tunisian pilot Sadiq and was very sad to learn that he had married since he considered that this meant the imminent end of his days in the jihad.

He was always accompanied by Mawlawi Abdullah who was a young twenty-eight-year old man who looked very scary. Had it not been for his great sense of humour, I am sure that no one would have ever dared talk to him or even looked at him. His appearance was that of a typical terrorist or gangster but, truth be told, he was anything but that. He spoke perfect Arabic and loved to chat with me to use the Arabic expressions he knew. He would also try to convince me to leave my commander and join his. I finally gave in to their pressures, since no Arab in Kandahar was ever so welcomed or treated so well, and I promised to go back with them after the desert battle ended.

Mawlawi Abdullah assured me that Mullah Abdul Aziz was unmatched throughout Afghanistan and that he himself was the cousin of Mullah Abdul Samad and used to work under his command until he decided to join Abdul Aziz, which was something very rarely seen in Kandahar. I should, at this point, relate more details about Abdul Samad's men. They were all very young and very fun to work with. They spent their time wrestling and laughing and playing, so maybe the only mujahed in this group worth mentioning was Muhammad Nur. He was a real giant, over two meters high, with huge muscles and an unparalleled power. He was hit in one of his eyes and knew some Arabic. The Afghans used to call him Mullah Nasruddin (a nickname used to refer the town fool) because of his weird voice, the way he talked and his somewhat stupid answers that would make everyone laugh at him. But during the battles, he we was a real lion and went to places that no one else dared to go.

In that same post, we had a mujahed who was over sixty-five years old, who considered himself to be some sort of a leader and gave orders all day long. He called himself *bakhighat bretuna* or the man with the huge moustache, which was true since it was really massive. He would brag all the time about the fact that he was probably the first Afghan mujahed to fight the Russians in Afghanistan. In fact, the other Afghans told me that he fired the first RPG in this long war against the Soviet embassy in Kabul back in 1979. One day, we recorded him talking about his accomplishments in the war without telling him, then we turned the tape on after lunch enabling the whole base to hear his story but to our surprise he was very pleased with this, which proved to me that he was probably truthful.

There were also a number of Arabs, among whom was Abu al-Oussoud the Libyan. He was white, short and skinny and not more than eighteen years old. He was a very modest man with a great intelligence who always forced himself to work more and go the extra mile. One time, he almost died under my supervision since on our way back from Mahalajat with a group of Arabs and when we reached Arghandab, we had to cross a big river. While I was trying to find a car to drive us through this obstacle, an Algerian came to me asking if he could swim in the meantime so I told him it was fine. But as soon as he went into the water, all the other Arabs followed him among whom was Abu al-Oussoud. He was carried by the current and almost drowned, and was saved at the last minute by the Afghans who were with us. I heard afterwards that he met his God in Khost and became a martyr. I hope that Allah took him into heaven as a soldier of Islam and one of his loyal servants.

3

MIRACLES OF THE JIHAD

[*Akbar Agha's book presents himself at the heart of the religious students' networks during the 1980s. This excerpt tells of some of the 'miracles' that he witnessed on the battlefield, and as such this represents a common understanding that was shared by many of the religiously-minded mujahedeen groups. Accounts of miraculous events are a fixed feature of written and oral accounts of the 1980s war. Akbar Agha also offers a brief portrait of some of the ways we can break down even further the organisation of the religious students' groups.*]

Excerpt from I Am Akbar Agha *by Sayyed Mohammad Akbar Agha, 2014*

Talibs were the ones who began the jihad in most provinces, especially Kandahar. For instance, the heads of our front in Tur Taaq were Talibs and most of the mujahedeen as well.

Our front in Nagehan—which was made up of Talibs—was the second biggest after the Tur Taaq front. Then there was a Talib front named after the martyred Qari Azizullah, and then there was Hafiz Abdul Karim's Taliban front. Similarly, there was Mullah Musa Kalim's Taliban front in Zabul, and in Helmand there were the two Taliban fronts of Ra'ees Mullah Abdul Wahid and Mohammad Nasim Akhundzada.

Our front was initially called 'Al-Seria al-Farooqia', Mullah Hajji Mohammad Akhund's front was called 'Haqqania', and Mawlawi Akhtar Mohammad Agha's front was called 'Al-Najia'. There were also fronts led by Mullah Shireen Akhund, Commander Abdul Raziq, Mullah Mohammad Sadiq and Faizullah Akhundzada. The Taliban government was created from these fronts.

These fronts were united and agreed with each other. Most operations were put to a vote and only took place following the assent of all of these fronts. The fact that there were joint groups on operations was a sign of their unity.

There was one joint group in Mahalajat which remained there for years and was led by Mullah Burjan for most of the time. The group was there to assist the Mahalajat mujahedeen. Another could be found in Abbasabad (behind the prison).

Whenever mujahedeen in Arghandab or any other area got into trouble, our joint group was sent to that area. We had courts, too, and all the fronts supported the decisions taken there. The courts implemented *hudood* and *qisas* with this power.

There were some other public non-Talib fronts, but they followed the lead of the Talib fronts. Afghan and Pakistani Talibs would come over to Afghanistan from the Pakistani madrassas for their holidays or when the mujahedeen were under pressure. Their fronts had sections that were devoted to the duty of *Amr bil Marouf wa Nahi min al Munkar*.[1] They didn't permit the use of *naswar*, for example, or cigarettes on their fronts. They carried out their operations in an organised manner following consultation with all parties. They avoided fights among other Muslim groups and encouraged jihad against the Russians. The mujahedeen belonging to these fronts later became the leaders of the Taliban movement.

The Tur Taaq front, the Taliban's first battle and defeat

The mujahedeen thought that 'Tur Taaq', the name of a well-known mountain near Pashmol, would be a good place to set up their front. A base was established there. Expenses and food for the front were provided by the public; most of our supplies were sent from our villages. Mujahedeen came from many different places to join the front. The youth from remote areas gathered together like butterflies with great jihadi enthusiasm. The front gradually started to come together.

Unfortunately, we didn't have many weapons, and even the ones we had weren't a match for the modern weaponry—especially the tanks and war planes—of the enemy. At that time, the mujahedeen weren't familiar with the tactics, strategy and tricks of war that the ten years struggle would teach us.

The red Russian army moved on Tur Taaq, heavily bombing and shelling the mujahedeen base with tanks and artillery. Many of our mujahedeen were martyred and wounded in the face of so much Russian bombing and shelling. The mujahedeen were able to stand firm against a great deal of hardship, but couldn't hold the base. Those who survived scattered away to many different places until a bigger front was prepared—and with it, a bigger battle. I returned to my village and to my home. Our life had become tough, and our house had been searched by the puppets several times. Finally, we were forced to leave.

In 1979, together with the martyred Lala Malang and Amir Mohammad Agha, I received training in how to fire an RPG. We opened a front that was officially registered with the *Harakat-e Enqelab* party. At that time, there were no other fronts (other than that of Esmat Muslim) in the area.

There was a second front led by Mawlawi Akhtar Mohammad Agha. Among the hundred or so people who joined up with this front were the martyred Lala Malang (son of Mawlawi Sadozai Agha), Sayyed Amir Mohammad Agha (who later became influential during the Taliban time), as well as the popular Kandahari wrestlers

MIRACLES OF THE JIHAD

Aminullah Pahlawan and Hajji Sardar Pahlawan (who were martyred in a battle against the occupying army in Registan). The party gave us thirty weapons, and one RPG and a heavy machine gun.

The jihad and the miracle of the mujahedeen

When our small group of mujahedeen decided to move towards Afghanistan, we departed early in the morning from Quetta to Dalbandin. From there, we headed towards Registan. The way to Registan was extremely tough and the weather was still very hot. There was a river at the Naru area near a hill that seemed to be a likely place for planes to bombard.

The mujahedeen caravan stopped there to take a break. The water from the river was bitter tasting; this is something the people of that area had known for years. But the heat, the long route and exhaustion forced the mujahedeen to decide to drink the bitter water. When we drew some of the water, by the power of great God it had miraculously turned sweet. This was clearly a miracle of holy intention, firm faith and the sacrifice of the mujahedeen. This incident was very similar to something that happened to the Prophet Joseph (PBUH) who, when he fell into a well with bitter and putrid water, found that it had turned sweet through God's philosophy. This is something that has remained in my memory.

The mujahedeen stayed at Naru region for two months. Those two months were filled with problems, hunger and thirst. Our affiliate political party—*Harakat-e Enqelab*—once again sent 100 weapons, three RPG launchers, and a heavy machine gun. Also, with the help of our friends, we bought 20 weapons whose magazines held 20 bullets from Iran. After a long break, we moved towards Helmand and stayed in the forest near the area called Falalki. It was a good place to hide. We brought five cars and some other important equipment to the other side of the Helmand river. After a whole night walking, we arrived in Musa Qala.

Talib mujahedeen facing the Red Armies

It was dark and silent and the mujahedeen caravan was moving forward. We arrived in a village called Shaban at dawn. The mujahedeen hadn't even put down their packs when the helicopters and jet planes of the Red Army appeared in the sky. They heavily bombarded our caravan. The helicopters shot at the mujahedeen with heavy machine guns and we also faced artillery fire. One of the cars was set on fire and all the mujahedeen inside were martyred. A bomb hit the second car as well, but only the old grey-bearded driver—a dedicated mujahed man—was martyred. A few of the other mujahedeen were wounded. We received some help from the people of Shaban area at this time, which was greatly appreciated. They helped us move our cars and other equipment.

Finally, the mujahedeen caravan reached Musa Qala. This was the seventh day following the capturing of Musa Qala, where Mullah Mohammad Nasim Akhundzada was leading the mujahedeen. News spread that a large military force of the Red Army was approaching Musa Qala. Mullah Mohammad Nasim Akhundzada asked for our assistance. We remained there for a few days before deciding to move on. We left a heavy machine gun with Mullah Mohammad Nasim Akhundzada to borrow from us.

[...]

Order and virtue of the mujahedeen on our front

We tried our best to keep some sort of order to our front and to our daily duties. We registered all the weapons that we distributed to the mujahedeen and tried to keep them in good shape. Everyone was responsible for their own weapon. We held training sessions and gave five cartridges to use at the range to practice their aim. If we weren't in a battle or training, none of us carried weapons around with us.

We organised a schedule of duties. Mujahedeen were required to pray their five prayers each day and anybody who violated this was assigned an additional two-hours of work or duties.

Nobody was allowed to fire a single shot without the express and prior permission of the commander or head of the front. Violations were subject to punishment. We consulted each other for any decision that needed to be made concerning the front, major or minor. We had a meeting to calculate our accounts at the end of each month and helped the families of the mujahedeen who were extremely poor if we could.

It was extremely important for us to be honest in our financial dealings. The use of drugs was completely banned for our front. Teenagers weren't able to be part of our front, either. No mujahed was able to travel into the city (or to stay there) without our prior permission. When the mujahedeen were sent to Quetta on jihad-related matters, each person was given 250 kaldars to cover their transportation. We had rented a house in Quetta for mujahedeen and for our injured. Later on we also bought a car.

We had some cars at our front as well which were used to transport mujahedeen from one location to another and to carry weapons and military equipment. We tried to provide everything that was necessary for the mujahedeen on our front to make their jobs easier. Later on we bought land near Nazar Jan Bagh and divided it up for mujahedeen to build houses. We provided construction materials and daily labourers. We bought cars and motorcycles for our leaders and for those with disabilities. We also sent some of them on Hajj.

[...]

Miracles of the jihad

During the first days and nights of the jihad, mujahedeen were very committed to great God and had only good intentions. Nobody thought about position, power and wealth, so it was an obvious truth that divine light would be seen on many martyrs' graves, and when one would get close to the grave, there would be nothing there. Secondly, most martyrs naturally smelled very good, without using any perfume. This was a good smell that was different from any other smell in this world. I have personally smelled that smell, and it soothes human beings. Also, it was a miracle that the bodies of most martyrs would stay untouched in their graves, and their bodies were undisturbed despite several injuries, because most of the mujahedeen were far from their homes and according to shari'a law they had to be buried wherever they were martyred. According to shari'a law, it is respectful to the dead to take not take the body to another location. Sometimes, when relatives of a martyr would come and insist on taking their martyr to their home, they would go and exhume the martyr; we would notice that despite the passing of a long time, the martyr was still lying sound in the grave.

Also, we can point out victories of small numbers of mujahedeen against large numbers of the armed forces of the Red invaders as miracles of the mujahedeen, similar to the Badr fighters and Talut people, because the mujahedeen fought against a superpower equipped with various types of weapons, artillery, tanks, war planes and helicopters, with only very old weapons, and few of them. Still, the mujahedeen would succeed as the Badr fighters did and as Talut's small group of fighters defeated a big army of Jalut [Goliath] with the power of great God. The holy war of the Afghan mujahedeen was the proof of this verse of holy Qur'an: 'A small group would succeed against a large group with the order of God, and God is with those who are patient.' Also during the jihad, there was an abundance of everything. All the deserts that used to be dry were filled with water, and older people said they had never seen that before. That was the bliss and miracle of jihad and the mujahedeen. The dreams of any mujahedeen in custody would mostly become true, because they would sleep according to shari'a. The messenger of God (PBUH) has said about this that revelation has ended now and after him it would be in the form of *mobashirat*. One of his companions asked the prophet what *mobashirat* was, and he replied that *mobashirat* was the delivery of good news through dreams. That is how the dreams of every detainee would become true.

Another miracle of the jihad and mujahedeen was that mujahedeen's prayers would be heard quickly. It happened several times that if somebody treated a virtuous mujahed badly, that person would get in trouble one way of the other. That was the time when mujahedeen were under severe pressure everywhere. Most soldiers were trained to treat detainees equally badly regardless of their innocence or guilt, goodness or badness, age, reason of detention, knowledge or lack of knowledge. One day a soldier told me that if he argued with a detainee and the detainee was killed in the dispute, it would not be a problem, but that if he got killed, he would be a martyr. He asked me if that was true, but I said that he would not be a martyr, but merely a cruel person. I told him that he could see what type of people the detainees were. Most of the political detainees were clerics, people who had memorised the Qur'an and people who were readers of God's words (the Qur'an). I told him that he could see how religious they were, because they would be busy performing prayer, reciting and memorising the Qur'an. Also, there was a madrassa where religious teaching and studying took place. Most of the detainees would fast outside of Ramadan month as well and would perform *tahajud* prayer. I should mention that most of the detainees would somehow get released before completion of their sentence. That was only as a result of prayers and virtue. There were even detainees would not be happy upon their release, because they would not have the opportunity to pray and worship as much as they could in the prison.

4

SOVIET ANDREI

[Gumnam's Kandahar Heroes *was the second of two popular accounts of the mujahedeen published by someone from Kandahar. This except tells the story of a Soviet prisoner who converts and joins the cause of the mujahedeen. These kinds of stories were rare, but their strangeness is one reason why they are told so often when discussing the events of the 1980s with participants today. The Afghans in the story were religious students or scholars, moreover, so the story has relevance to what would later come together as the 'Taliban' movement.]*

Excerpt from Kandahar Heroes *by Mohammad Tahir Aziz Gumnam, 1995*

I asked the hero commander Mullah Mohammad Ismael Akhund how the exchange of Lala Malang and the Soviet happened. The hero said that one of the heads of our front was getting ready for an operation around Kandahar International Airport but he suddenly felt that somebody was lying in wait for them. He suddenly gave the order for everyone to hide from the enemy and secretly started to watch out for the enemy. They discovered that a Soviet soldier was looking for something. The mujahedeen changed their movement patterns into an encircling formation and as soon as the Soviet entered the circle the mujahedeen all stood up and arrested him. He was then brought to Sher Surkha by the mujahedeen.

Hajji Mullah said that when I saw the Soviet captive he had completely lost his mind. I gestured to assure him that he was with friends. I assured him that he was completely safe. This Soviet called Andrei was 22 years old and he was from Moscow city.

We took the Soviet Andrei from Shir Surkha to Zelakhan and the next day we took him to the centre of the front in Chenarto with four motorcycles.

Chenarto was considered the nucleus of our jihad and was home to three hundred always-ready mujahedeen who were in state of readiness night and day.

Chenarto had a very strategic location, and staff for management and logistics were placed there as well. Chenarto centre has a good religious madrassa, logistics stores, a medical clinic and all other necessary equipment.

31

Local cases and complaints were taken care of under the supervision of Chenarto Justice Council. In short, Chenarto was a strong trench in that neighbourhood, and that's why we brought Soviet Andrei to the big trench.

Hajji Mullah said that he gathered all the mujahedeen and ulemaa of Chenarto and I told them that I knew that Andrei was a Soviet, non-Muslim and that he was our enemy, but I thought this enemy should be kept alive for the moment.

"We can kill him near the airport later on. Killing him will never be a problem for us, but my point is that the Soviets are engaged in a war with us, not just on the military side, but also a war of attrition. This means that they have hit us one by one and caused troubles among our own people. So we should give them a problem as well among their own people. We should show Andrei that Islam was so holy that we even treat our enemies well and with an open mind. We should install the rays of Islam into his heart with love, dedication, passion and through our good behaviour. We should show him that Islamic civilisation is based on purity, affection and nobility because Our Prophet his Excellency Mohammad (PBUH) did not force people to convert to Islam but rather had them accept Islamic beliefs with great respect, ethics, passion and dignity.

"He showed the values of Islam to people in practice. He placed the glory of Islam as a shining light so that the people themselves could become lovers of Islam."

My point was to make it clear that Andrei should be washed with Islamic love from insight so that he would carry out Islamic matters for us in the Soviet Union.

"Leave Andrei on his own for the time being," I said. "Treat him well and with love." I left Andrei in Chenarto for few days and returned to Zelakhan.

Hajji Mullah said that the Chenarto mujahedeen treated Andrei very well and added that Andrei started to learn the language slowly. Andrei noted that the mujahedeen woke up early in the morning, took ablutions and worshipped the only Allah and then recited the holy Qur'an. He also saw the Talibs studying in the Islamic religious madrassa.

Andrei thought about what all of this meant. He must have realised he was lucky not to have been executed already. He came to the Islamic soul cruelly and amidst murder, but they are now treating me well, with friendship and honour, so how much must the greatness of Islam be that I am receiving this respectful treatment?

As Andrei dealt with the internal struggle between Islam and blasphemy, the great month of fasting came, and all the mujahedeen were fasting and Andrei as well together with them. The mujahedeen provided him with breakfast and lunch but he didn't eat and waited with the mujahedeen until they broke their fast.

Hajji Mullah said that, "I went to Chenarto on the fifth day of Ramadan. When Andrei saw me he ran towards me, embraced me and told me as he was crying, saying, "Ikhlam, in his word, Mullah Sakheb, I... mukhalman"... [Andrei was saying that he accepted Islam in his Russian pronunciation and using the few Pashto words he'd learnt.]

I told Andrei that, "You are free. You don't have to accept Islam." Andrei started screaming and said, "No... no. I like Islam." He was crying. The generosity of the mujahedeen had transmitted the rays of Islam into his heart. I was sure that Andrei had really accepted Islam from his heart and I saw that my original plan had come to fruition.

Andrei converted to Islam during this fasting month and we gave him a new name, Abdullah. Then we circumcised him and I asked Mawlawi Faiz Mohammad to teach him the principles of faith.

Abdullah fell in love with Islam so much that within the same month he had memorised four chapters of *shorout u-salat* [an Islamic book about prayers]. He also memorised Yasin [one of the Qur'an's suras or chapters] and all his prayers were conducted as part of the collective sessions. He also learned how to read and write Pashto a little.

Hajji Mullah said that his interest really increased and all the mujahedeen became fond of him. When I saw him after Eid he was very happy. He had learned more Pashto and he told me:

"Hajji Mullah! When you arrested me and told me that you were my friend, I thought it was a trick. I thought you were my death but now that I know that in this world, the only real humans are the Muslims.

"Islam is a kind religion. Socialism and Communism are paths of force and coercion. I am a Muslim. This is my homeland. I am a mujahed. Hajji Mullah is my brother..."

Hajji Mullah said that they had a group that was responsible for people's complaints, and they assigned Abdullah as the commander of that group. Abdullah took his religious education in Quetta, Pakistan and carried out his job properly.

5

MARTYR HAJJI MULLAH MOHAMMAD OSMAN AKHUND

[*A large part of* Kandahar Heroes *is taken up with telling the stories of certain individuals that Gumnam has deemed representative or important in terms of their status among the mujahedeen. This particular vignette is similar to many of the martyr's portraits that the Taliban would continue during the time of the Islamic Emirate and onwards into the present day. (See source 67 for an example of this.) Note that the portrait is as much factual as it is about the values that the particular figure can be said to have embodied. Thus we learn about the kinds of military engagements that Mullah Mohammad Osman Akhund took part in, but we also learn about his character. For these kinds of portraits, character is at least as important as the specific achievements that he made.*]

Excerpt from Kandahar Heroes *by Mohammad Tahir Aziz Gumnam, 1995*

During the days that the *Kandahar Heroes* book was about to be finished, I was getting ready to publish it. Untimely I was informed that Hajji Mullah Mohammad Osman Akhund's body had been found. I left everything else and went to Kandahar.

I knew Hajji Mullah Mohammad Osman Akhund: this great martyr brother of ours was from Kariz Bazaar. I also knew that Hajji Mullah Mohammad Osman Akhund had joined the Islamic Movement of the Taliban and I knew that he had gone to the Shindand fight and that he had lost his life in this battle. His younger brother, Hajji Mohammad Omar Akhund, who was known as Omar Khan, had taken many efforts to find his brother, but Hajji Mullah Mohammad Osman Akhund was not found. It was as if he had been turned into water and was absorbed by the ground. The last time his group saw him was 17 April 1987. This was the same day that Mullah Janan was wounded and Hajji Mullah Mohammad Osman put him on his back. This incident took place in Ab-e Khurma area on the front line. This was the night when the enemy assaulted the Taliban fronts.

Mullah Janan Akhund was seriously wounded in the first phase of the operations and Hajji Mullah Mohammad Osman Akhund had put him on his back; he wanted to take him to the back of the front. There was only a ditch between the two fronts. Hajji Mullah Mohammad Osman Akhund lost his way and entered the enemy's side. He had continued until dawn when he suddenly found himself in front of an enemy checkpoint. Hajji Mullah Mohammad Osman Akhund, who was very tired, put Mullah Janan on the ground and asked them to let him pray since it was the time for the dawn prayer.

Hajji Mullah Mohammad Osman Akhund took his ablutions and started to pray. Those cruel men opened fire on both of them after the prayer and threw them in the ditch. The day of their martyrdom was 18 April 1987. The Taliban had waited a long time for Mullah Mohammad Osman, Mullah Janan and one other Talib who was missing. But they waited in vain, since Hajji Mullah Mohammad Osman and Mullah Janan were martyred far away from their trenches. All the parts of Ab-e Khurma that were controlled by the Taliban were asked but nothing was found about these two Taliban and this issue remained a mystery.

Martyr Hajji Mullah Mohammad Osman was the son of Mullah Jan Mohmmad Akhund and was from the Noorzai Afghan tribe. He lived in the sixth district of Kandahar city. He was 45 years old when he joined the Taliban movement.

Hajji Mullah Mohammad Osman was an innocent, chaste, bright and well-known individual. Wondrous Allah had put many great qualities in him. He was patient, honest, generous and humble. He had devoted his life to serving the public. He had done a lot of service in the path of Islamic Jihad after the ominous Saur coup in 1978.

Hajji Mullah Mullah Mohammad Osman Akhund was a kind mujahed brother. He would get sad at everyone else's sorrow and shared in the pain of each.

The areas around Kariz Bazaar, especially the residents of Etefaq Mosque, are all in debt to him for his favours.

Kariz Bazaar was the last line of the Communist trenches and the first line of the Islamic trenches. Kariz Bazaar was a cradle of grief between the two forces and this cradle was set in motion between the night and day like clockwork. [...]

Kariz Bazaar was, in other words, a place of death and in this uneasy environment any grief could come. Hajji Mullah Mohammad Osman was the first individual who would become aware of it. He would make his chest a shield to any grief in Kariz Bazaar and he would carry the countrymen's problems in the difficult times and places.

Most of the services of Etefaq Mosque were done by Hajji Mullah Mohammad Osman. Hajji Mullah Mohammad Osman Akhund was the chief Mullah of Etefaq Mosque. Hajji Mullah Mohammad Osman Akhund taught religious subjects to most of the youths and children of Kariz Bazaar.

Hajji Omar Khan, his younger brother, was first a mujahed of Hafiz Abdul Karim Haqqani's front and later he was a mujahed and ally of Mullah Shireen and Mullah Azizullah Akhund's Islamic front.

MARTYR HAJJI MULLAH MOHAMMAD OSMAN AKHUND

He made many sacrifices for Islam and for the freedom of the homeland. Hajji Mullah Mohammad Osman was a virtuous, Sufi and quiet person, and he would always praise the Prophet. Hajji Mullah Mohammad Osman Akhund was a real Muslim; he possessed a clear conscience and in the last days of his life he received the honour of memorising Jalalain-e Sharif by Hajji Mullah Abdul Wadud. I would sometimes be honoured by getting to meet Hajji Mullah Mohammad Osman Akhund. He was a bright and spiritual person. He would talk about Sufis and Gnostics. He was a Sufi and he was following Bayazid Bustami, Abul Hassan Kharqani, Wais Qarani, Hassan Basri and Ibrahim Adham.

There is a proverb saying that everybody knows how to preach, but Hajji Mullah Mohammad Osman Akhund's mouth was different. All these martyrs of clear faith are close to Allah, but Hajji Mullah Mohammad Osman Akhund's martyrdom was a bright torch on this world and there is a living proof for our claim, so let's see how great Allah rewards his sincere creatures in return for their sincerity.

We thought that Hajji Mullah Mohammad Osman Akhund was lost to the Taliban and friends. After Ab-e Khurma, Shindand and Herat were captured by the Taliban, Hajji Mohammad Omar Khan travelled in that direction as well.

Hajji Mohammad Omar Khan searched desperately in the deep ditches and high hills of Ab-e Khurma and he became aware of an unexpected fragrance while doing this. He followed the fragrance and finally he found the two fragrant and bright martyrs after five months separation. One of them was Hajji Mullah Mohammad Osman and the other was Mullah Janan Akhund.

Hajji Mullah Mohammad Omar Akhund said that he thought the two martyrs were asleep. Their holy bodies were fresh and clean. Their skin was still fresh and blood was flowing from their wounds despite five months having passed.

Hajji Omar Khan said that Hajji Mullah Mohammad Osman was lying face up and his eyes were closed. The hair of his beard had fallen on his chest and also his hair had grown. The hair of his beard that had fallen on his chest was not swept off despite the fast winds in Ab-e Khurma.

Despite the hot weather of Ab-e Khurma, their wounds' blood didn't stop either. So when over a period of five months neither the wind can sweep off the hair of their beard nor the hot weather can stop their blood, then who could deny the greatness and miracle of the martyrs.

Hajji Mullah Mohammad Omar Akhund said that they brought Hajji Mullah Mohammad Osman Akhund to Kariz Bazaar and thousands of people saw him sound and Kandahar city was the witness of these Taliban martyrs.

Hajji Mullah Mohammad Omar Akhund said that jihad was their professional and Islamic mandate. He added that they have seen many strange and great things from martyrs during jihad.

We have seen lights above martyrs' shrines and Martyr Mullah Mohammad Osman Akhund was a cordial and humble person. Great Allah has done a big favour and kindness to him.

Hajji Mullah Mohammad Osman Akhund was celebrated by a huge number of the people of Kandahar with special respect and a big crowd attended his funeral. People at Kandahar's Taliban cemetery again saw Hajji Mullah Mohammad Osman's body sound, fresh and fragrant.

This bright martyr was buried in the western part of the Taliban cemetery and beside Zahir Shahi canal. Many of the Central Council authorities and Kandahar's people were present at the burial ceremony. May Allah do more favours to him with his great blessings. The following poem was written on his shrine:

Don't die in a way that you cry and people laugh
Die in a way that you laugh and people cry

6

THE MEN WITH GUNS

[*This brief bridging passage is included as an excerpt to hear first-hand some of the problems that were the reality for citizens of southern Afghanistan during the post-Soviet, pre-Taliban period. There is much to be written about the precise weighting of reasons why and how the 'Taliban' movement emerged in 1994, but an overwhelming part of this is the historical moment that the 'students' seized, riding a tide of dissatisfaction with the status quo, supported by communities who had had enough of predation and disruption to their lives. Zaeef describes some of the practical ways that this affected his life.*]

Excerpt from My Life with the Taliban *by Abdul Salam Zaeef, 2010*

In Kabul, fighting soon broke out between Massoud and Hekmatyar. Massoud had demanded full control of the city but Hekmatyar—as Prime Minister—didn't accept this. The old Communist party splits between Khalqis and Parchamis were being played out again, and while alliances were never clear, the Khalqis sided with Hekmatyar while the Parchamis seemed to support Massoud. Soon the fighting reached Kandahar, where rival commanders clashed in the city. Ustaz Abdul Haleem, a commander of Sayyaf's faction, had taken the provincial police department, but Mullah Naqib's forces turned it into rubble. Abdul Hakim Jan was the commander at that battle, which lasted just one day before Ustaz Abdul Haleem fled. Most people in the building were killed, but some escaped towards Sarpoza and to the main base of Ustaz Abdul Haleem.

The Taliban didn't involve themselves in these disputes, and in any case most had returned home by now. Mullah Mohammad Omar turned our old mujahedeen base in Sangisar into a madrassa. I briefly considered staying there as well, but without any work it would be difficult. I decided to return to my wife and children. I had married in 1987 and we had moved in with my father-in-law in Deh Merasay. My wife had given birth to our children by then. I discussed our situation with her and my father-in-law and we decided that I should start to look for work.

I had never worked in my life, had no money to start a business and didn't know what to do. My own family was living in Pakistan; they could help me to find work or start a business, but I did not want to leave Afghanistan. I had heard there was a foreign organisation operating along the Salawat-Panjwayi road where people had found work, so the next morning I went to register with them.

I was given a shovel to dig water channels along the road and started work straight away. Everyone there was given 250 Afghanis and seven kilos of wheat per day. It was the first time I had worked and I wanted to make a living for my family, so I enthusiastically took to the task. The other workers stopped digging as soon as they were left alone or when no one was watching them. They sat down and chatted amongst themselves, and even told me to stop digging. I shouldn't bother doing any work, they said, if no one is watching. And even when they're watching I could apparently get away with looking busy and not really doing anything. Work hours were from eight in the morning until one in the afternoon.

[...]

The next day I took my son to see a doctor in Kandahar city. Ustaz Abdul Haleem and Mullah Naqib were still fighting when we passed through the area near the prison. A group of shaggy, dirty-looking men stopped us and told everyone to get off the bus. They ordered us to start digging trenches. I told one of them that I had my six-month-old son with me who was ill. "We are on the way to the doctor," I explained, "and his mother is not with me." But the man just shouted at me, telling me to get to work and not talk about things I wasn't asked about. If I spoke one word more, he said, he would riddle my body with thirty bullets. He cursed me, and asked why I didn't want to help the mujahedeen. Shame on this kind of mujahedeen! They brought a bad name and embarrassment to the whole jihad!

I did not know anyone on the bus, so I gave my son to an old man saying, "Brother! Take this child to the driver, and when I am finished with the work they force me to do I will come and get him. If anything happens to me, the driver knows my village and will bring the boy back to my wife."

We were in between Mullah Naqib and Ustaz Abdul Haleem's areas of control. Many travellers had been martyred or had disappeared while they were held up and forced to dig trenches. On many occasions innocent passersby would be shot by one side or another, and they would be thrown into the ground disrespectfully, without consideration for the proper religious burial rites and without informing the family to alert them of the death. I had not yet reached the place where I was supposed to dig when someone put his hand on my shoulder and said, "Oh Mullah Saheb! What are you doing here?"

I told him that I had been commanded off the bus and forced to work. Without replying he turned to his friend and shouted, "Mother-fucker! Don't you know what a Ghazi looks like? You've been taking them off the bus. Look, my son! This is Mullah

Saheb. He is a Ghazi from the Russian time. You should know him!" He told me to get back on the bus. The man who had forced me off the vehicle apologised. "My son! How could I have known who this father of mine is?" I was glad to be spared this work and got back on the bus. Only a couple of minutes further down the road the bus was stopped again. We had reached Hindu Kotai and now it was the turn of Mullah Naqib's men. One of them got on the bus, looked around and got off again. He said nothing. Another man got on carrying a bag of fruit. He was one of Mullah Naqib's men and worked at the checkpoint.

When the bus drove off I turned to the man. "Brother! How much did you pay for this bag of fruit?" I asked. He laughed and explained. "We take commission from the trucks that transport fruit on the highway." I asked him how many bags of fruit they took from a truck. "Ten bags," he said. "You must be responsible for the vehicles' security till they arrive in Pakistan then," I said. I had presumed that they accompanied the vehicles all the way until Pakistan. "No, brother. They travel only till Hazaraji Baba without fear. After that, Lalai controls the road and his men take their own commission," he replied. Hazaraji Baba was only three or four kilometres away from Hindu Kotai. Trucks must have been losing most of their load travelling through the checkpoints.

In the evening I returned home from the city together with my son. I told my family that I thought that Afghanistan was no longer safe for them. Even though the district administrator of Panjwayi was Moalem Feda Mohammad, a good man and a mujahed, nonetheless travelling to the city had become a dangerous and troublesome business. Moalem Feda was strict and did not allow any thieves, gamblers or wine-drinkers in his district, and had always been helpful to us. But how long would he be able to defend his district?

Once, during the days of Eid, Ustaz Abdul Haleem had come to Panjwayi with his men. They held dog fights and were corrupting the people. When he first arrived his men got into a fight with the district security personnel even before they had started to gamble and stage their dog fights. Soon the mujahedeen of the district gathered together and turned his pleasure into grief. Several of his men were killed or injured but Ustaz Abdul Haleem managed to escape.

So I took my family and we fled to Pakistan. We avoided all the main roads and used smugglers' routes and back roads to avoid the criminal gangs that were holding up travellers, robbing them and raping their wives all over southern Afghanistan. There was no security and there was no law. Gangs of former mujahedeen, thieves and thugs were bleeding the people. No one was holding them accountable and travel had become dangerous and expensive.

I was relieved when we arrived in Pakistan without incident. My cousin Obaidullah in Sumungali near Quetta gave us a room to stay in. The money from Hajji Bahauddin soon ran out, and once again I found myself in a difficult situation. I first opened a small shop with the money I borrowed from my cousins, but it made hardly any money. Nevertheless, I rented a small house and began to study and teach again.

Soon I began to forget about Afghanistan. I started to develop land, borrowing money to buy small plots on which I built houses. It took several months, but once the houses were ready I sold them off for a profit, paid back the money I had borrowed and bought another piece of land to develop. My portfolio of houses grew and the financial situation of my family improved. I worked hard and used every waking minute to work or study.

Business was good and soon I was able to leave for Peshawar to focus on my Islamic studies and finish my education. It was there that I started to develop and cultivate an interest in politics.

PART 2

ISLAMIC EMIRATE OF AFGHANISTAN
(1994–2001)

1994 The Taliban take Kandahar (November)

1996 The Taliban take Kabul (September)

1997 Taliban forces enter Mazar-i Sharif but are later pushed out (May–July)

1998 Al-Qaeda attacks in Africa lead to Cruise missile strikes on Afghanistan (August)

1999 The Taliban take Mazar-i Sharif (October)

1999 International financial sanctions placed on the Taliban government along with an air embargo (November)

2001 Taliban forces destroy the Bamiyan Buddha statues (March)

In 1994, a small group of Taliban mobilised against criminal gangs west of Kandahar city. This early group was local, reacting to the situation in its area. It mobilised around a blend of local culture and a literalist interpretation of Islam to try to impose order on a chaotic situation. At the time, there was little concern for anything beyond immediate and local circumstances.

Several groups around Kandahar province started to root out rogue commanders at roughly the same time. This loose network formed of friends and relatives who had studied, worked and fought together would join to form the Taliban movement. As the movement gathered momentum, it advanced from Kandahar province to Zabul, on to Helmand and Uruzgan, capturing Herat in September 1995 and Jalalabad and Kabul in September 1996. The five years that followed saw the Taliban struggle to conquer central and northern Afghanistan and consolidate their hold on the country and its diverse population while imposing highly conservative social policies. The Taliban's unprecedented rise was due to their widely resonating promise of security and justice. Their sustained military campaign was in part enabled by external support by the government and security apparatus of Pakistan and the arrival of madrassa students from across the border.

The group of students and former mujahedeen fighters that banded together in mid-late 1994 were predominantly based in Kandahar province, but the network

43

extended further to refugees in Pakistan and local village mullahs. Discussions were often about the immediate situation, one seen as a function of the failure of the mujahedeen commanders to translate the victory against the Soviet army into a united government and peace. The small groups took action, therefore, to mean first ridding their villages and stretches of road of the rogue commanders. Once action was taken and the first commanders defeated, events developed rapidly. Local communities flocked to the Taliban and within weeks Kandahar province, including Kandahar city, the second largest city in Afghanistan, came under the Taliban's control.

What was initially a few dozen became one hundred, two hundred men. A key moment came when they had to decide to split their forces: one half moving east and the other west. The question of intent is important here: to what extent did the movement intend to expand outside Pashtun areas? Or to what extent were they following the old mujahedeen plan from the late 1980s?[1] With the benefit of hindsight, it seems to have been a combination of factors: momentum was spurred by Pakistan's provision of support in the form of transportation and materiel, but also from other Afghan factions, coupled with a feeling among those who participated that they were engaged in 'good work' in terms of their provision of security and justice.

The Taliban's offensive was stopped outside Kabul where their forces remained caught in a stalemate with Hekmatyar and then Massoud's troops. They moved into the Jalalabad/Nangarhar area to the east in the second week of September 1996, and it was at this point that the movement 'inherited Osama'. Despite some claims to the contrary, bin Laden and the Taliban knew very little of each other—they had not fought together during the 1980s, and Mullah Mohammad Omar even seemed unaware of developments in the Arab world relating to bin Laden and the ideology he had begun to represent.

Aside from the issues over bin Laden, the Taliban were facing serious bureaucratic problems: the more they expanded, the more they were expected to offer some form of governance or at least an expanded version of their sparse 'security and justice' agenda. They were not bureaucrats, however, nor did they possess the capacity needed among their ranks. In order to fill positions and satisfy the increasing demand, the Taliban relied on bringing back old civil servants who had worked in previous administrations. Not all of these agreed with the Taliban's various stances, whether religious, social or political. The rapid expansion of the movement, the lack of a coherent plan or understanding of how to create or govern a country, paired with the large intake of a diverse set of individuals, translated into increasing internal strife, conflict and turmoil amongst the Taliban's ranks.

The Taliban were, at the beginning of August 1998, in the middle of an increasingly large-scale war with various forces in the north of the country.[2] The government that had formed in Kabul and Kandahar, meanwhile, was facing growing internal difficulties bringing its own personnel under control as well as keeping peace and security in the area it had taken.

Their military campaign had stalled in the north and the Taliban had shown themselves to react as ruthlessly as other mujahedeen factions in their military campaign conducted in the central region of Afghanistan; they had closed off all access points there, which caused a severe famine for the local, predominantly Hazara (also shi'i) population, in an effort to subdue them. Furthermore, the northern front line saw widespread atrocities carried out by all those involved.

Each new territory meant the acquisition of a fragile network of brokered deals and conflicts within local communities, fuelled by the Taliban's at times rigid application of social policies, much of which was derived from their understanding of the workings of Pashtun communities in rural southern Afghanistan. This changed internal dynamics significantly and over-extended the limited abilities of the Taliban's bureaucracy.

Interviews with former officials involved in the Taliban's administration at that time unanimously state that there were two priorities back then: the ongoing jihad (i.e. bringing the rest of the country under their control) and—for some—starting to make Afghanistan under the Islamic Emirate function as a 'real' country.

On 7 August 1998, two near-simultaneous bombs struck American embassies in Tanzania and Kenya. Bin Laden's threats and statements had found an outlet. This was a serious issue for the Taliban movement at the time: the 'political' Talibs—some had already voiced their concern over the presence of bin Laden—were worried that the United States would now use bin Laden as a scapegoat for any future attacks on the United States; and others, who weren't sure whether bin Laden was responsible, said that if he was it would be a catastrophe for the movement. The subsequent cruise missile strikes on 20 August offered conclusive proof of their position. Bin Laden was, they believed, a strategic liability for the movement and they sought to convince Mullah Mohammad Omar of this.

In 1999, the United Nations imposed a sanctions regime (resolution 1267) which targeted the Taliban and al-Qaeda, making no distinction between the two. Coupled with a failed attempt to encourage the Taliban to expel bin Laden from Afghanistan brokered by Saudi Arabia, the embassy bombings were a turning point for the movement's international relations. The Taliban's social policies had already started to provoke considerable international condemnation, and the isolation that resulted meant that many in the leadership started to turn inward.

An op-ed published in *Shariat* newspaper in November 1999 entitled 'Ways of protecting the Islamic Movement from veering off the course' lists ten 'ways the movement can remain pure'. It can serve as a way of highlighting some of the ways that the Taliban sought to remain balanced as the composition of the state and the citizens under their rule changed, and as more responsibilities fell on their shoulders.

We can note some of the fears that afflicted the senior leadership: the need to protect the purity of the movement; the results of fragmentation and disunity; the need for good advice; and the sense that the long-term work of governing and developing a country was different from the things they had previously been involved in. This article is notable in how openly the criticisms are stated, though it makes the case that debate and freedom of thought should and can benefit the movement and not cause disunity and disintegration.

The senior leadership sought to balance the demands of loyalty to God and their beliefs with the challenges of ruling over a country. In retrospect, it makes sense that they chose to take the path of least resistance, keeping as much as possible the same, and changing structures slowly, feeling their way as they went. How much of this can be understood as a deliberate plan is doubtful. Often it appears that the Taliban improvised and simply reacted to circumstances arising.

By 2001, relations between the Taliban and the international community had deteriorated to the point where suspicion and mistrust characterised interactions. Even internally, the Taliban had not managed to provide an interim solution to the country's problems. The United Nations had nominally taken on the responsibility for the provision of emergency food aid—unwilling simply to pull out of Afghanistan—and the second year of drought had further devastated conditions for the broad mass of Afghans around the country. There were 1.15 million people internally displaced by mid-2001, and international assistance organisations had slowly been isolated and restricted throughout 2000 and 2001; this had taken place in part on account of Taliban intransigence and pressure, and in part as 'principled' withdrawals of funding or programmes in the face of the Taliban's social policies.

NASCENT STATE (1994–1996)

THE BEGINNING

[This is an excerpt from a book written by an Arab fighter who wished to tell something about the Taliban's Emirate government. As part of his fascinating account, he included a verbatim transcript of a radio broadcast made by Mullah Mohammad Omar in which the early days of the Taliban movement are described in detail. It is one of the only places where we get to hear a quasi-oral history account of the movement's founding from this key figure.]

Excerpt from The Giant Man *by Husayn Ibn Mahmud, 2005*

He gathered with him the students of the religious schools and (study) circles, for this purpose, in the summer of 1994, and they started the work by helping some of the businessmen and field leaders. He, along with a small group of students of the Shari'a sciences and Afghan Mawlawees in Qandahar, began pursuing some thieves that stole a convoy from some travellers and abducted some women near Kandahar. Then the students, and at their head was Mullah Muhammad 'Umar, captured the thieves' weapons and found some of the women killed. Then the thieves fled from them away from Kandahar. Then the people of that area removed its governor, who was a follower of Rabbani—the ruler of Kabul at that time—due to his inability to hold the thieves accountable, and they appointed Mullah Muhammad 'Umar as an amir over them. He then announced the implementation of the shari'a in Kandahar, which was pleased with him and with his followers from the students of shar'i science.

And this is the story of the beginning which Amir Al-Mu'minin narrated and which came from his tongue in a recording which was broadcast by the radio (station) 'The Voice of the shari'a' in Kandahar, which was the official radio station of the Islamic Emirate. He—May Allah protect him—said,

'I used to study in a school in the city of Sanj Sār in Kandahar with about twenty other of my fellow students. Then corruption took over the land, murder, looting and robbery reached alarming proportions, and control was in the hands of the corrupt and wicked ones, and no one imagined that it was possible to change this condition and rectify this situation. And if I too thought that and said to myself, "Allah burdens not a person beyond his scope,"[1] then this verse would have sufficed me, and I would have left the matter, because nothing was in my capability. But I trusted upon Allāh (with) the pure trust, and whoever trusts upon Allah with this type of trust, his hope will never be let down. People may be wondering: When did the movement begin? Who was behind it? Who finances it? And who directs it and manages it?

And I say: The beginning of the movement was that I folded my books in the school in (Sanj Sār), and I took another individual with me and we walked by foot to the area of Zanjāwāt. And from there I borrowed a motorcycle from a person named Surūr, then we went to Talūkān. This was the beginning of the movement, and remove any other thoughts from your minds.

We began visiting the students in the schools and the study circles in the morning of that day, and we went to a study circle in which approximately fourteen individuals were studying, then I gathered them in a circle around me and said to them, 'The Religion of Allah is being stepped on, the people are openly displaying evil, the People of Religion are hiding their Religion, and the evil ones have taken control of the whole area; they steal the people's money, they attack their honour on the main street, they kill people and put them against the rocks on the side of the road, and the cars pass by and see the dead body on the side of the road, and no one dares to bury him in the earth.'

I said to them, 'It is not possible to continue studying in these situations, and those problems will not be solved by slogans that are not backed up. We, the students, want to stand up against this corruption. If you want to truly work for the Religion of Allah, then we must leave the studies. And I will be honest with you, no one has promised to help us even with one rupee, so that you will not assume that we will provide food for you, rather we will request food and help from the people.'

I said, 'This is not the work of a day, nor a week, nor a month, nor a year, rather it will take a long time. Are you able to perform that or not?'

And I used to encourage them and say to them, 'This evil one who is sitting in his centre like a black cauldron due to the extreme heat—and those days in the summer season were very hot—is openly waging war against the Religion of Allah, and we claim that we are from the People of the Religion of Allah, and we are not able to perform any action to support to His Shari'a.'

I said to them, 'If we conquer an area, we will defend it, then do not complain that there is no studying or a lack of money and weapons, so are you able to perform this action or not?'

Then no one from those fourteen accepted to perform this action, and they said, 'We might be able to perform some of the duties on Fridays.' So I said to them, 'Who will perform them the rest of the days?'

I make Allah as my witness that this is the truth, and that I will testify to that in front of Allah, Azza Wa Jall, on the Day of the Gathering.

This movement was the result of a pure trust (in Allah) because if I had gauged the rest of the schools and (study) circles according to this (study) circle, I would have returned to my school. But I fulfilled the oath I had taken upon myself for (the sake of) Allah, Ta'ālā, and he treated me with what you have seen. Then I went on to another study circle in which there were about seven students, so I presented the matter to them just like I presented it to the students of the first study circle, then all of them got ready for action.

All of those ones were one nation, there were no differences between them from being young men and old men, or children and young men, or male and female, but this work was based upon Wisdom from Allāh, Ta'ālā, so he placed me in a test since the beginning of it. Then we travelled on this motorcycle to the schools and study groups until 'Asr prayer, until fifty-three People of the True Trust (in Allah) were ready. Then I returned to my school and said to them, 'Come tomorrow morning', but they arrived at one in the night to Sanj Sār, so this was the beginning.

The work started before (even) twenty-four hours had passed on the idea. And one of my friends led the people in prayer, so when he led them in the *fajr* prayer, one of the followers said, 'This night while I was sleeping, I saw the Angels entering Sanj Sār, and their hands were soft, so I asked them to wipe me with their hands for blessings.'

And the next morning at ten o'clock, we asked for two cars from Al-Hāj Bishr, one of the businessmen of the area, so he gave us two cars: a small car, and a large cargo truck. Then we moved those students to the area of Kashk Nukhūd, and others joined us. And when the numbers became many, we borrowed weapons from the people, so this was the beginning of this movement, until it continued.'

MESSAGE OF THE SUPREME LEADER OF THE ISLAMIC MOVEMENT OF THE TALIBAN

[*Mullah Mohammad Omar, speaking in 1995, describes the context that led to the formation of the Taliban movement as well as some of the goals as formed thus far. He connects the lived reality described in the previous two sources to his religious training and belief, holding up tyranny and opposition as a lens through which the current reality could be understood.*]

Tolo-ye Afghan, 25 May 1995

Dear religious scholars, jihadi commanders, tribal elders, intellectuals, the elderly and my Taliban brothers!

Salam 'aleikum. Everyone in this country and the whole world knows about the terrible crisis that Afghanistan and the people of this country have gone through in the past seventeen years. There is no need to go into the historical details of all those events. But under the current circumstances it is the religious duty and obligation of every single Muslim in this country, especially those who have a good understanding of the Islamic faith, to leave their houses and villages and abandon all business and activities. It is time that they take up arms and join their Taliban brothers in the pious struggle that they have started and fully participate in this struggle. It is time to start their jihad. It is time that they make all kinds of sacrifices for the protection of the Islamic faith. The brave Afghan nation has not only beaten the Soviet Union with the help of Allah and their Islamic spirit, but they have indeed destroyed a great oppressive imperial regime which was known as the Warsaw Pact throughout the world. This nation has defeated the tanks and the armies which were trained on the soil of Europe to come and fight here. This nation has raised the cry of Allah-u-Akbar in Moscow and wherever its puppets were. This mujahed nation taught the people of Moscow an unforgettable lesson. *Insha'allah,* as long as they remember that lesson they will never dare to talk about Communism again. The label of Communism has now indeed become a matter of shame around the world. The whole philosophy of

Communism has no followers any more. The forces of Communism have been defeated all around the world. All this was possible with the help and the blessings of Allah Almighty. But unfortunately there were a few puppets of the Communist regime in our country. Some people in our country were influenced by this philosophy and they were able to infect the minds of a few others. It was because of this philosophy and the actions of its followers that our courageous nation once again fell into crisis.

There was a time when some people in this country laughed at the philosophy of jihad and they made fun of the mujahedeen, committing a great sin due to their ignorance. The importance and significance of jihad is evident from the Qur'an. So to reject it or to make fun of it is indeed a great sin. It was because of such a situation and the presence of such people in our society that we decided to do something about it and fix things once and for all. We asked the religious scholars for their advice and received a shari'a-based decree from them. In the light of this decree from our religious scholars, we started our armed resistance to the corrupt regime in Kabul. We started this movement for the protection of the faith and the implementation of the shari'a law and the safeguarding of our sovereignty. We started this movement in order to rescue our people from the crisis they were facing and to bring a long-lasting peace and security to this country. The Afghan nation knows us. They know we are their brothers who stood by them in their jihad. They know we are the ones who fought with them in the trenches and on the battlegrounds. We are the ones who made sacrifices during the jihad. But despite all this there are individuals and groups who are continuing to spread false propaganda against us. We went to all these corrupt leaders and begged them to stop the intimidation of their people and put an end to the crisis in the country. We begged them to stop fighting. But despite all our pleas these power-hungry individuals didn't listen to us and continued to brainwash the world about the Islamic movement of the Taliban. But Allah is our witness; we will not be ashamed to stand in front of him on the Day of Judgement. We know we are on the right path. We also call upon Muslims to prepare themselves for sacrifice in the way of this pious cause. Anyone who fights for the cause of Islam is our brother. We do not choose our friends and enemies on the basis of their language or race. Anyone who believes in our cause is welcome to come and join us.

If you look at the History of the Islamic faith, the Prophet Abraham (peace be upon him) made the first sacrifice. Then the religious students at the time of the Prophet Muhammad (PBUH) also made great sacrifices. Now it is our turn to work for the cause of Islam and not refrain from any sacrifices. Our wish was the implementation of the law of the Qur'an and it still is. We are fighting so that our countrymen can have a peaceful and prosperous life. We are not afraid of dying in the way of this cause. The nation knows that we have faced many tyrants in the past and will continue to do so in the future. You also know that we have not plotted with any outside power for any personal gain or interest. Our friends and supporters are all those pious people who do not have any material wishes. These are the people who stood up to the Russian aggression and fought bravely. These are the same men who have done nothing against the nation during the crisis of the past few years. I would like to insist once again that we started this struggle in the light of the decree by the religious scholars, and we still continue to stand by that decree. If anyone would like to advise us on the progress and activities and goals of our Islamic movement then we are ready to listen to them and act upon their advice in the light of Islamic teachings. I hope that all the oppressive tyrant forces of the world are defeated and Islam and the Muslims come out victorious. May Allah help us.

9

OH PROUD PEOPLE OF THIS COUNTRY!
GET TO KNOW THE TALIBAN MOVEMENT!

[Looking back, it is easy to forget just how unexpected and indeed unknown the Taliban were when they first started, even among local communities. Rumours ran rife about how they were funded by the United States and were secretly working against Islam. It is for this reason that newspapers of the time are filled with exhortations and explanations encouraging people to give the Taliban an opportunity to prove themselves, or simply introducing their goals and trying to assuage any doubts or push back against rumours. Each article ends with a call to support the Taliban alongside the claim that they are the only group genuinely working for the good of the people.]

Tolo-ye Afghan, 7 June 1995

Afghanistan is a country where 90 per cent of the population follow the Sunni sect of Islam. The people of this country have high moral values and strictly believe in and follow the Qur'anic law. It is because of these pious values that Afghanistan has always remained a thorn in the eyes of the enemies of our faith. The imperial powers have always been busy plotting against the people of this country and have always devised plans to divide the country. They have always made plans to undermine the Islamic brotherhood of the Afghan nation. By doing so they actually wanted to threaten the Islamic faith and undermine the interests of the Muslim people all around the world. It was because of such plans and ambitions that the Soviet Army shamefully invaded Afghanistan and came in with all the tanks and cannons they had at their disposal. They thought it would be a walk in the park and that they could suppress the Afghan nation and achieve their goals. They spent years fighting this nation and brought down all manner of tyranny and terror upon the Afghans. But they still couldn't suppress the will of the Afghans and finally they had to leave in an even more shameful way. The Afghan nation fought back bravely and resisted the Soviet oppression. They used their chests as walls of steel and stopped the Soviets from achieving their goals. The Afghan nation made a great number of sacrifices in this jihad. Millions of people died for the cause of Islam. There will hardly be a family in this country that has not lost a loved one to the Soviets. The Afghan nation fought so they could kick the Soviets out of their country and implement Islamic law in this country. They fought so that they could live according to their faith and their wishes. There came a time when they achieved that and were able to defeat the Soviets. They managed to drive the Red Army out of their land. The whole purpose of the fourteen years of jihad and the sacrifices made during that period was to establish a government which worked according to Islamic law. This was why millions of people laid down their lives. This was the reason why millions of other people left their homes and villages and migrated to other countries. The day the Soviets left Afghanistan the whole country was joyful. Everyone thought this was the moment they had waited for. They thought this was the moment they had fought for and that now they could live in a peaceful and prosperous country in accordance with their faith and their beliefs. But the enemies of the faith had not given up on their plans to destroy the Muslim umma. They couldn't win militarily so they resorted to other tactics.

After being kicked out of Afghanistan and being embarrassed in front of the whole world, the enemies of the faith came up with a different plan this time. They continued with their enmity towards the Afghan nation but through different means. This time they used some faithless puppets to achieve their goals. These were so-called Afghans and Muslims who never really cared about their homeland and the interests of their people. So the enemies of the faith used these puppets to destabilise the situation in the country and undermine the glorious victory of the Afghan nation. These internal puppets took directions from their Communist backers and started a new crisis in the country. Their actions and wicked politics led to an internal conflict that was even more disastrous for the Afghan nation than the fight against the Soviets. As a result a power-hungry group managed to come to power in Afghanistan. This group cared about nothing but its own interests and ways of prolonging its power. Their stubbornness led to a civil war that plunged the country into further crisis. This was a disastrous time for Afghanistan. Many more innocent Afghans were killed and millions were forced to flee their homes and villages once again. The whole nation was facing a terrible disaster but the leaders in Kabul hardly cared. Their carelessness led to the blood of many people being shed for no reason all around the country. The leaders in Kabul were directly responsible for the misery the Afghan nation was facing. The beautiful land of Afghanistan was stained with the blood of its own people. But the thugs in Kabul had no shame and they didn't stop their pursuit of power. Those Afghans who had lived abroad as refugees for many years were also excited to return to Afghanistan after the Soviets were defeated. But they were disappointed to see that the country had fallen into an even deeper crisis. They came back to see that the whole country had been turned into small kingdoms. There was a checkpoint every hundred metres and the Afghans were humiliated in their own country. They had to pay the thugs and robbers to make their way across and reach their own homes and villages. But they soon realised they couldn't stay there for longer. They had to flee again with broken hearts and wishes unfulfilled. They knew they had to leave again because the honour and dignity of their mothers and sisters was not safe in Afghanistan. Because of this internal conflict, the country fell into such a crisis that people started to lose their moral values. Rape and homosexuality were common in areas that were controlled by thugs and illegal militias. Everywhere there was widespread looting and robbery. No one was safe and people were completely fed up with the situation in the country. Everyone was looking for a change and for a way out of the crisis.

It was at this time that a way out of this disaster appeared. As a result of the prayers of this oppressed nation and the blessing of Allah, the Islamic movement of the Taliban emerged in Afghanistan. The religious scholars and students of this country had fully participated in the jihad against the Soviet Army. After the defeat of the Soviets they had put down their weapons and had gone back to their normal lives. Most of them were in their madrassas and were continuing with their religious education. They were not interested in the political process or government-making and didn't want a share for themselves. The religious scholars and students, however, were well aware of the crisis the country was going through. They finally came together and started to think about how they could put an end to this crisis. They reached a conclusion. They decided that in order to end this crisis they had to take up arms once again and start a new jihad against all the thugs and looters in the country. They concluded that the only way to bring down the corrupt and unjust regime in Kabul was to topple it militarily. Therefore a decree was issued and the Islamic movement of the Taliban emerged on the scene.

They first decided to try and negotiate with the corrupt regime in Kabul. They invited the rulers to talk to the Islamic movement. They asked the rulers to give up on power and stop their tyranny. They asked the rulers to follow Islamic rules and principles and put an end to all the immoral and un-Islamic activities that had become common around the country. But this had no effect. The arrogant rulers in Kabul didn't listen to the message from the Islamic movement and didn't give up on their illegal rule. As a result the Islamic movement of the Taliban decided to take up arms and start a jihad against the regime in Kabul. They started their struggle with honesty and sincerity and only wanted to fulfil the wishes of the Afghan people. They started their struggle for the implementation of Islamic law in the country and the welfare of the people of this country. They had no personal political ambitions or agendas and didn't care about power and authority. Their ambition was to safeguard the national interests of Afghanistan and bring the country out of civil conflict and allow people to live peacefully and in accordance with their faith and beliefs. It didn't take them long to reach many parts of the country and establish an Islamic system of governance in areas which came under their control. They achieved quick victories because the people of this nation were with them and knew that this movement was a purely Islamic one which only fought for the sake of Islam and the motherland. A complete implementation of law and order was established in all areas that came under their control and people were once again able to go on with their lives in a peaceful manner. The Islamic movement of the Taliban put an end to all immoral and un-Islamic practices in these areas and strictly punished those who had usurped people's rights. They also punished those who had looted and robbed, and had shed the blood of innocent Afghans. Since the arrival of the Islamic movement of the Taliban there have been no reports of any corruption or injustice at all. No one has been killed or looted. No one's honour and dignity has been disrespected. People are happy with their lives and the general situation in their areas. They are once again hopeful about their future and the future of their children.

Pure Islamic law is being implemented in the areas which they control and the population is fully satisfied with this. The constitution of the Islamic movement of the Taliban is the Qur'an. They follow it themselves and implement it in its true spirit. The leadership of the Islamic movement of the Taliban are no different from the ordinary people of this country. They don't go around with an entourage of body-guards. Their houses and offices are not guarded by armed men. They are simply a part of the general population in this country and cannot be differentiated. They live in the humblest way possible. This humbleness is a sign of the time of the Caliphate when the friends of the Holy Prophet Muhammad (PBUH) used to rule. Any ordinary Afghan who wishes to see the supreme leader of the Islamic movement of the Taliban, Mullah Mohammad Omar Mujahid, does not need any sort of appointment to do so. He can simply walk into his office and see him whenever he wishes.

If you go around the country and talk to ordinary Afghans they will tell you that they are very happy with the current situation. They are hopeful and really believe they now have a future in this country. There is a general sense of satisfaction among the people. This is something which didn't exist for many years. People didn't know what the next day would bring them. Now they are hopeful and satisfied. The nation is praying for the victory of the Islamic movement. They know that the only ambition of this movement is the implementation of the Islamic laws and the ways of the Holy Prophet Muhammad (PBUH). Any group which has such high moral values defi-nitely enjoys the blessings and the help of Allah Almighty. Such a pure Islamic move-ment has emerged after hundreds of years. It is therefore compulsory for the Afghan nation and the whole Muslim world to support this movement and join their cause. It is an obligation for all of us to help this movement and not refrain from making any sacrifices for the cause of this movement. We call upon all Afghans to pledge their support towards the Islamic movement of the Taliban. It is their movement and it is fighting for their welfare and their future. This movement has no personal political ambition. It is therefore important that the people of this country try and help this movement and make it possible for them to achieve their goals.

10

SIMPLE LIVES

[*Akbar Agha's retrospective account of the Emirate is unusual among former senior associates for offering criticism and a negative picture of the movement (in parts). Here, however, he speaks of how the new government sought to distinguish itself from some of the previous other governing groups. Just as with the martyr portraits from the 1980s, the focus is on how they have different values and how this affects how they treat other people.*]

Excerpt from I Am Akbar Agha *by Sayyed Mohammad Akbar Agha, 2014*

The Taliban were very humble people who led very simple lives. Most of them—especially those who were committed Talibs and who had some knowledge—were very virtuous and would not betray the movement. Those who were stationed in government institutions were very committed to their duties and would take care of the work of the people very quickly.

If someone in a government institution didn't do the work that they were supposed to on behalf of the people, then there was a place for them to report this. There was no corruption at all. If anyone was found taking a bribe, then when caught the Taliban would blacken their face and take him around in public.

The people mostly dealt with the Taliban's judges. This might be true for other countries as well, but during the Taliban's time the court decisions were made very quickly. They would not send plaintiffs away and they wouldn't take bribes. Of course, there were some people provoked by foreigners among the Taliban who would crack down on the former mujahedeen. Those were mostly new and young Taliban and very few of them were from the older generations. Those were not virtuous people and they collected so much wealth. They now have fancy houses abroad and the Taliban leadership was not happy with their actions.

Meanwhile there were also those among the Taliban who could barely meet their own basic financial needs and who had no access to health, but who would never consider dipping into the *Beit ul-Maal* for their own purposes. In their offices they

61

had simple furniture and wouldn't even sit on chairs. They were living the village life, sitting on mattresses around the edge of the room as was common in many parts of Afghanistan. They ate the same food as any other family and their equipment was simple as well, just as if they were living in the desert. They didn't change their clothes all the time and remained with their simple ways as before. They didn't change their clothes to go to work. They didn't wear suits, only *shalwar qamis*. They weren't embarrassed by wearing old clothes and consider a turban one of their only required items. They didn't let people with shaved faces or long hair work together with the Taliban. They all grew their beards and the young men who didn't have beards weren't allowed to work together with the Taliban. Even a leader or a minister would travel using public transport despite having a good car.

11

FOR THE IMPLEMENTATION OF ALLAH'S LAW

[This article states the Taliban goals alongside a brief explanation of their origin story (which in 1995, at the time of writing, was still taking shape). Practical considerations are at the forefront (peace, security and the disarmament of militias) but these are quickly subsumed into the wider and more important cause of bringing Islamic law to the country. This, the author believes, holds the promise of a lasting solution.]

Tolo-ye Afghan, 7 June 1995

Our proud nation and this country have a 5,000-year-old glorious history. This is something we can be proud of. This is something our future generations can look to and take pride in. But unfortunately during the last sixteen years this wonderful nation of ours was a victim of war and it resulted in the destruction of our beautiful country. The flames of war engulfed our beautiful country and burnt our nation and everything that we had. It reduced this country to ruins.

[...]

Then, with the grace of Allah, the light of justice and equality rose in this country. The Islamic movement of the Taliban emerged and the whole political and security picture of the country started to change for the better. It is because of this Islamic movement that a number of menaces have been eliminated now and the country is on its path to a better and a more prosperous future. Wherever the forces of the Islamic movement of the Taliban have reached, they have put an end to all kinds of corruption and injustice. No one is suffering at the hand of another person any more. There is general and open justice which is available to all the people of this country and which serves all the citizens of this country.

The Islamic movement of the Taliban has come forward to achieve specific goals and they are fighting for a specific cause.

One of their goals is to bring permanent peace and security to this country. They have been able to do so in areas which have so far come under their direct control.

The people in these areas are extremely happy with the law and order situation in their areas and are continuing with their daily lives without any problem whatsoever. Islamic law has been implemented in these areas and all sorts of immoral and un-Islamic practices have stopped. This is something that the people of Afghanistan have always wanted and this is the kind of government and regime which they have always wanted to establish.

Another important thing that the Islamic movement of the Taliban has achieved is to disarm illegal militias in areas under their control and confiscate all illegal weapons. This has resulted in an improved security situation in these areas. Everyone in the areas under the control of the Islamic movement seems to be happy. People go and resolve their issues and differences in Islamic and shari'a courts. Their arguments are heard and decisions are made without any sort of prejudice or injustice. This has greatly improved the general atmosphere in the country and people are once again hopeful about their future.

The Islamic movement of the Taliban is also working hard to revive the education sector. The people of this country should come forward and help the Islamic movement in this great cause. This is a purely Islamic movement and is above any kind of ethnic or linguistic prejudice.

The only cause for which this movement is fighting is the implementation of Islamic law in this country. The Islamic movement is only interested in the welfare of the Afghan people and the rebuilding of this war-torn country. They have proved it to the Afghan nation and the whole world that they are sincere in their cause. Standing against this Islamic movement and taking up arms against it and killing the innocent Taliban is indeed a great crime and injustice against this nation. Anyone who does so will be punished for it in this world and the hereafter. All those who oppose this Islamic movement will one day have to face Allah and answer for their actions and decisions. So it is the duty of every Muslim to stand beside this movement and support it with their lives and their property. They should support these brave sons of this land. All the people of the country should come and join us so that we can prevent all sorts of injustice and corruption in this country. Only then will we be able to wipe the tears of our widows and orphans and fulfil the wishes of our martyrs. Only then will the people of this country be able to live and work in a peaceful and dignified way.

12

THE AIM OF OUR JIHAD IS TO IMPLEMENT ISLAMIC PRINCIPLES

[This news report records the summaries (and sometimes exact words) of a number of different clerics from within the nascent Taliban leadership. Obedience and unity are so often cast as essential precepts for the Taliban that it is rare for written accounts or sources to divulge some of the diversity within the movement, acknowledging that different groups brought different perspectives on the priorities for the movement. Thus we hear from northerners as well as those from the south, Sunni as well as Shi'i.]

Tolo-ye Afghan, 2 August 1995

Dear readers,

A number of respected religious scholars have been visiting Kandahar in recent weeks. They have been holding meetings with the leadership of the Islamic movement of the Taliban and have been reporting about the latest military and political situation in their districts and provinces. Due to the deep interest of our readers in these visits, we are giving a brief report about a number of religious scholars who have come to Kandahar recently.

Al-Haj Mawlawi Mohammad Sadiq Sahib of Ghazni province held a huge gathering of religious scholars in the Khirqa Sharifa Mosque in Kandahar. During his speech Mullah Sadiq talked in great detail about the current political and military situation in the country. He said the peace and prosperity of the human race was dependent on the establishment of an Islamic regime all around the world. He said Islam was the only prescription which could cure all our social ills and menaces. He said it was the obligation of every Muslim to spread the message of Islam around the world. He said Islam brought a message of peace and brotherhood for all humans. He said we should only follow the commands of Allah and spend our lives in accordance with the teachings of the Prophet Muhammad (PBUH). Mawlawi Sadiq said Islam did not allow us to discriminate against our fellow brothers and countrymen. He said all human beings were equal and the only thing that made them better than others was their piety and their sincerity. Mawlawi Sadiq said the people of Kandahar had sacrificed for the sake of Islam throughout history and had defeated the enemies of their faith on a number of occasions. He said the people of this historical region had always stood against tyrants and had never bowed their heads to oppression. He mentioned the battle of Maiwand as an example. He said during the battle of Maiwand the infidel British army attacked the Muslim people of this region and wanted to defeat them and usurp their freedom. The British thought it would be business as usual and that they would easily [beat] the Afghan army. They had completed underestimated the commitment of the Afghan people to their motherland and to their freedom. They did not know that the Afghan people were ready to sacrifice everything they had for protecting these values, which they cherished more than anything else. During the battle the Afghan army fought with courage and the spirit of sacrifice. They defeated the mighty English army and completely shattered it on the battlefield of Maiwand. It was a huge embarrassment for the British Empire and it proved that the Afghan people would stand like a wall made of steel in front of any aggression against their freedom and their motherland. During the battle a number of Afghans, both men and women, lost their lives. But they left behind a proud history and a message of sacrifice and courage for their cause of freedom.

In another gathering which took place in the Hazrat Jee Baba Mosque, Mawlawi Ahmadullah from Kabul province spoke about the current situation in the country. He said there were three golden principles of Islam which were important for the establishment of an Islamic system in the country. He said the first system was that of *qisas*. He said according to this principle anyone who commits murder should be executed. He said this principle was a guarantee to the lives of the people in a society and was important because it would stop anyone from committing murder. He said if this principle is properly implemented in society, then no murders will take place. Another golden principle was that of *zina*. According to this principle the dignity of human beings will be protected in society. Anyone who commits adultery should be punished according to the principles of Islam, and then as a result no one will commit such a crime again. The third golden principle was that of jihad, and it meant that Muslims should struggle and fight for their freedom and protection of their faith. Jihad is an obligation for all Muslims in the light of this golden principle of Islam. He said the Muslim nation should rise as one and stand united against any aggression which undermines their identity and their faith. He said the people of Afghanistan should fight against anyone who prevents the establishment of an Islamic system in the country. He said it was our duty to work and strive towards our aim, which is the implementation of the Islamic principles in society. He said the people of Afghanistan should not refrain from making any necessary sacrifice for the sake of their faith. They should stand with the Islamic movement and work for a prosperous future.

Respected religious scholar from Logar province, Mawlawi Mohammad Yousuf, spoke at the Akhund Baba Mosque in Kandahar. He said the secret of success for all the Muslims around the world is to hold on to the rope of Allah and never deviate from the right path. He said as long as Muslims stand together and act according to the principles of Islam, they will be successful both in this world and in the hereafter. But as soon as Muslims deviate from the true path and ignore the teachings of Islam, they will face many troubles and will be isolated and defeated. He said in the past our leaders did not care about their faith and their identity and they deviated from the right path. As a result Allah punished us and brought an aggressor to our land. This aggressor was the Soviet Union. During those years the people of Afghanistan paid a heavy price and suffered great losses. It was a punishment from Allah because our leaders had gone astray. But then the Muslim people of this country decided to stick to their faith and the principles of Islam. And it was because of this commitment to their Islamic faith that a jihad was started all over the country against the Soviet aggressors. Allah kept his promise and helped the people of Afghanistan during those hardships. The mujahedeen put their trust in Allah and fought with bravery and courage. They did not refrain from making any sacrifice for their freedom and their faith. They started a holy war with empty hands and soon Allah gave them great victories. This was a golden period in the history of jihad and the whole world was shocked by the success of the mujahedeen. During the years of jihad the people of Afghanistan made numerous sacrifices for the sake of their faith. They gave their lives so that future generations could live in peace. They sacrificed their lives so that the flag of Islam is kept high. But after the Soviet Army was defeated, the leaders of the jihad once against lost their way and forgot the aims and purpose of the jihad. They forgot what the people of Afghanistan had fought for in the first place. They forgot what the people of Afghanistan wanted and put their personal ambitions first. They did not care about the sacrifices of the Afghan people and worked for their personal luxury. They became power hungry and tried to usurp the rights of others. As a result Afghanistan was plunged into a bloody civil war which took the lives of thousands of innocent people. Allah punished us again for going against the principles of Islam. As soon as we deviated from the right path Allah brought down misery upon us. We should have learnt our lesson but we didn't. Fortunately, we now have the Islamic movement of the Taliban which has emerged from within the people of this country. This movement belongs to the Afghan nation and works for the welfare of the Afghan people. The aim of the Islamic movement of the Taliban is to establish a purely Islamic system in this country. This movement wants to implement the principles of the Qur'an because that is the only way towards success and peace and stability in this country. Mawlawi Yousuf said the Islamic movement of the Taliban did not strive for personal gains or power and did not have any foreign agenda. It was a purely Islamic and Afghan movement and the people of Afghanistan had fully supported it and welcomed it with open arms. Mawlawi Sadiq said the people of Afghanistan were fed up with the regime in Kabul and wanted to get rid of it. This regime had committed atrocities against its own people and had forgotten the aims of the jihad against the Soviet Union. He said the regime in Kabul was not committed to peace in the country and did not want to give up power willingly. He said this regime had blocked all efforts for the establishment of an Islamic regime in the country and hence it did not deserve to rule the people of Afghanistan any longer.

Another religious scholar from Logar province, Mawlawi Fazal Ahmad, spoke at the central mosque in Kandahar. He said the issue of the hijab for our Muslim sisters was explained properly in the Qur'an and in the hadiths of the Holy Prophet Muhammad (PBUH). He said it was compulsory upon all Muslim sisters to wear the hijab and respect the principles of Islam. Their success and their dignity is hidden in acting according to the teachings of Islam. He said the Western media should not spread false propaganda against the Islamic movement and should not make fun of Islamic principles. He said the niqab was not a violation of women's rights but in reality it guaranteed the protection of a woman's right and her dignity. He said that Muslims should not come under the influence of foreign ideologies and should stick to their Islamic roots. He said the West wants the Muslim people to leave the path of Islam and the Qur'an and follow their ideology. This was a plot by the enemies of Islam to confuse the Muslims of the world and turn them away from the true path. Hence the Muslims should be careful about their plot and not let the enemies of their faith succeed.

Mawlawi Mohammad Akram from Nangarhar province spoke at the Akhundzada Mosque. In his speech he said Islam guaranteed justice and equality. He said according to Islamic principles anyone who commits a sin should be punished and justice should be provided to the victim immediately. He said any delay in providing justice is against the teachings of Islam. He said any land where the true principles of Islam are implemented is guaranteed to enjoy peace and stability. He said it was a blessing from Allah that the Islamic movement of the Taliban had emerged in the country. He said it was an obligation upon all the Muslims of Afghanistan to join the Islamic movement of the Taliban and work for their cause. He said the Islamic movement of the Taliban worked in accordance with the teachings of Islam and hence everyone could expect it to bring peace and stability to Afghanistan. He said everything the Islamic movement did was inspired by the teachings of the Holy Prophet Muhammad (PBUH). He said this movement did not have any personal aims and ambitions and hence did not strive for power or any other worldly gains. The aim of the Islamic movement was to give the people of Afghanistan the chance to [live] their lives according to their beliefs. It struggled so that the future generations of the proud nation can live peacefully like any other nation in this world. He said the people of Afghanistan should not listen to propaganda by the enemy and should have no doubts about the origins of the Islamic movement. He said this movement was made up of the sons of this land and belonged to the people of this land.

Mawlawi Shams-u-Rehman from [Wardak province] spoke at the Grand Mosque in Kandahar. He said he had travelled to many parts of the world and had seen most of the Islamic countries for himself. He said most of the Islamic countries, despite claiming to be Islamic, did not implement the true teachings of the Shari'a and the Qur'an in their affairs and in their laws and constitution. He said the people of this country did not enjoy true freedom and their leaders were mostly corrupt and incompetent. He said most of these countries confused pure Islamic laws and principles with a number of other laws which were influenced by Western and non-Islamic ideologies. As a result the governments in these countries did not deliver justice and badly failed to serve their people. Their leaders cared more about their personal luxuries and did not know the pains and grievances of their people. They lived comfortable lives and were completely out of touch with their people. Mawlawi Shams-u-Rehman said the people of Afghanistan should be thankful to Allah for the Islamic movement of the Taliban. He said this movement had brought peace and stability to all the areas which had so far come under their direct control. He said the people of Afghanistan had never experienced such peace and stability before in their history. He said the aim of the Islamic movement was to establish the principles of the Qur'an in this land. This was also the ambition of the Afghan people and this is what they fought for and gave sacrifices for. He said it was time the entire Afghan nation stood up to the corrupt regime in Kabul and threw them out of power. He said he had never seen such happiness among Muslims anywhere in the world before, but now that the Islamic movement has emerged people have found a new hope. He said any nation which does not deviate from the right path and stick to their Islamic identity will be peaceful and prosperous. He said the success of human society was in sticking to the principles of Islam. He said it was Allah who gave pride and success to a nation and it was Allah who brought shame and misery upon a nation. We should therefore stick to the principles of Islam and not go astray. As long as we act according to what the Qur'an has taught us, we shall not fail in this life and in the hereafter.

Mawlawi Mohammad Saqib who had come from Kabul spoke at the Shah Mosque in Kandahar. He said it was evident from human history that the religious scholars were most capable of leading a nation towards peace and prosperity. He said it was a blessing from Allah that the Islamic movement of the Taliban had emerged in Afghanistan. He said the Afghan nation should grab this opportunity with both hands and listen to what their religious scholars told them. He said the religious scholars had the knowledge and the understanding to feel the pain and grievances of the people and find out solutions to human miseries. He said the Prophet Solomon chose knowledge among all of Allah's blessings. So he was given knowledge and that knowledge enabled him to become the leader of the entire world. So the religious scholars are people of knowledge and they know best how to lead human society and serve the people. He said the Islamic movement of the Taliban was led by respectable religious scholars and all their actions were in accordance with the teachings of the Qur'an. He said this movement struggled for peace and stability in Afghanistan and wanted to serve the people.

Mawlawi Mohammad Muslim Haqqani had come to Kandahar from Baghlan. He was speaking at the Moi Mubarak Mosque. He said with the blessing of Allah the Islamic movement of the Taliban had reached Baghlan province too. He said since the arrival of the Islamic movement to the area the whole security picture had changed. He said the Islamic movement of the Taliban had brought peace and stability to Baghlan and people were now happy and continued their daily lives without any fear. He said Allah had blessed the Islamic movement with the opportunity to work for the welfare of the Afghan people and now it was time for the Afghan people to put their trust in this movement and join their cause. He said Afghans should not waste this golden opportunity and come forward and sacrifice everything they have for the cause of the Islamic movement. He said the people of Kandahar were lucky to have the Islamic movement and its leadership and they should never let this movement or its leadership down. He hoped that this light of Islam will soon spread to all parts of the country and the Afghan people shall once again live in peace and prosperity.

Also, Mawlawi Azam Gul, who came from Paktika province, spoke at the Haji Musa Jan Mosque. He said our mothers and our sisters should follow the teachings of the Qur'an and take care of their hjiabs. He said the hijab was a part of their Islamic identity and they should not compromise this at any cost. He said the Islamic movement of the Taliban was working for the implementation of the teachings of the Qur'an in society. It was therefore an obligation on all Muslims to come forward and help this movement in its cause. He said that Allah will grant success to anyone who joins the Islamic movement of the Taliban and works for the implementation of the Islamic government in this land. But he warned that anyone who opposes the Islamic movement will be doomed and destroyed. No one should try to prevent the Islamic movement from implementing the teachings of the Qur'an in this land. He said anyone who does so will ultimately fail and this peaceful movement will in the end succeed in bringing a lasting peace and stability to Afghanistan.

13

THE MUSLIM PEOPLE OF KANDAHAR WILL SUPPORT THE ISLAMIC MOVEMENT OF THE TALIBAN UNTIL THEIR LAST BREATH

[*This is an account of one of the early support meetings where—as in previous accounts—the new movement would have to explain itself, its goals and introduce members of its leadership. Different goals were presented depending on the audience. For this local meeting, practical considerations were placed alongside broader attempts to counter corruption or implement an Islamic system.*]

Tolo-ye Afghan, 26 April 1995

The residents of Kandahar city gathered in the central mosque of the city on 22 April 1995 to announce their full support of the Islamic movement of the Taliban. The meeting was attended by religious scholars, tribal elders and ordinary people. It started with recitation of verses from the Qur'an, and was chaired by Mawlawi Abdullah. First to speak was Mawlawi Abdul Wadood. He said the Taliban movement had emerged to rid our society of corruption and evil. He said it is the best Islamic alternative to the current corrupt system. He said the Taliban movement was based on justice and it conducted all its business and affairs in the light of the Qur'an and the hadith. He said the people of Kandahar had nothing to do with people and groups whose actions were against the shari'a. Wakeel Lal Mohammad and Abdul Hadi Arghandiwal also addressed the gathering. They were followed by another speaker, an Afghan migrant who had just returned from the United States. He said the so-called government of Mr Rabbani was actually run by his Communist friends, Mr Nabi Azimi and Baba Jan. He said it was obligatory for all Muslims to fight this corrupt government.

Next to speak was Mullah Mohammad Akhund. He said whoever fights the students of the Qur'an (the Taliban) will lose out in this world and the hereafter.

Ghulam Jan Natiq Ja'fari also addressed the gathering and read out his poem. He spoke on behalf of the Shia community and pledged his full support towards the Taliban movement.

Then Mullah Amir Khan Muttaqi spoke on behalf of the Taliban High Council. He said it was a matter of joy and pride that so many people had gathered here for one single cause. He thanked the people of Kandahar for showing their support towards the Taliban movement and promised them that the movement will continue their jihad for the honour and dignity of the people and for bringing peace to the country. He said the Taliban movement had started to implement Allah's will and to solve the issues the nation was facing. He said the people of this country had waited a long time and had hoped that their issues would be solved with the fall of the Communist regime. But unfortunately that didn't happen. The Taliban movement therefore started their struggle with the support of the people and the decree of the religious scholars. Addressing those who criticised the movement and had doubts about its intentions, Mullah Muttaqi said people should go and study the history of the Taliban and the religious scholars. He said the Taliban movement did not act upon anyone's orders. The only thing they obeyed was the shari'a, and the shari'a does not follow any other law. He also said it was not in the blood of the Afghan people to take orders from foreigners. He also said the Taliban movement was not against the opening of schools. He said it was the corrupt and Communist ideologies that the movement was against. He said such ideologies were against the faith and were a menace for an Islamic society. He also said the Taliban movement were looking into their financial capabilities and trying to fund the restoration of schools and religious madrassas. Mullah Muttaqi emphasised that the Taliban movement was not settling any personal scores with anyone. He said all the people and the leaders and the jihadi commanders were our brothers. He said the movement would embrace anyone who worked for the implementation of the shari'a law and the safeguarding of national interests.

Next to speak was Mawlawi Dost Mohammad from Farah province. He said it was a matter of great joy and he was thankful to Allah Almighty that the religious scholars had decided to stand up for the protection of the faith and implementation of the shari'a. He said this was the secret to the success of the Muslims. He said it was unfortunate that some leaders and armed commanders had misused Islam. They had brought shame on to the faith with their actions and deeds. He said there was a real danger that the motives and ambitions of the jihad would not be fulfilled. But now that the Taliban movement had emerged, that threat had disappeared. He said the Taliban movement not only demonstrated the strength and greatness of the Islamic faith to the world but also fulfilled the wishes of the people and protected the motives of our jihad. He said the Holy Prophet (PBUH) had told us to stop evil with our hands wherever we saw it. It was in the light of this hadith that the Taliban movement had started their struggle. The meeting ended at around midday. But before that a resolution was presented. It was approved unanimously.

14

CUSTOM TAX STARTS, FOLLOWING THE REQUEST OF TRADERS AND THE DECREE OF THE RELIGIOUS SCHOLARS

[*The Taliban's early years are often portrayed as being primarily concerned with matters of public and private morality, with the exercise of power and the imposition of their new system. Interviews such as the one below display the far more mundane business of trying to build a working state. Mullah Dadullah, who would later rise to even greater prominence within the movement, talks here about how, early on, they began a rudimentary taxation of imported goods. Note that this was a continuation of the policies imposed by the previous government(s). Where the Taliban didn't have ideas or innovations of their own, they were often willing simply to use what had been present before.*]

Tolo-ye Afghan, 28 June 1995

Dear readers,

Following our series of interviews, we have talked to Haji Mullah Dadullah Akhund this time. He is responsible for customs in Kandahar province. We invite you to read this interview here.

Question: What was the reason behind your decision to start collecting tax on imported goods? How did you reach this decision?

Answer: After the forces of the Islamic movement took control of Kandahar province, they initially did not have any sources of financial income. The number of Taliban forces was increasing rapidly. The Islamic movement had to come up with a way of facing the financial burden of their activities. Hence a meeting between the religious scholars and our national merchants took place in the provincial capital. In the meeting it was decided that from now onwards all imported goods will be taxed so that the financial issues of the Islamic movement are resolved at least to some degree.

Question: Please tell us about your achievements in the past month. Also, can you please tell our readers how much income you have generated during the past month?

Answer: We started working under difficult circumstances. Yet so far we have been able to carry out our duties according to the rules and regulations. According to latest figures we have deposited around one and a half billion Afghanis into the bank so far.

Question: Do you also tax goods which are imported via air?

Answer: Yes, we have an office at Kandahar International Airport. All goods that are imported to Afghanistan via air are also taxed. Usually there are three to four flights a week which bring these taxable goods.

Question: What about other provinces which are under the control of the Islamic movement? Do you have offices there too? Do you tax imported goods in other parts of the country as well?

Answer: We do not have any central offices in other provinces, but we do have branches in all the provinces which are under our control. They are also regulated by us and are connected to our central province. So yes, all goods which reach other parts of the country are also taxed accordingly at the local level.

Question: Can you tell us if you have prevented any smuggling into the country? Do such things happen or not?

Answer: Yes, unfortunately such things do happen. There are people who try to smuggle goods either into or out of the country. We have carried out operations to prevent this and were able to confiscate goods and arrest people on a number of occasions. The things which we usually catch and confiscate include drugs, ranging from opium, hashish to other items. Some people have also tried to import expired medicine into the country. During our operations in different parts of the country we were able to prevent the import of such hazardous medicines and have arrested those responsible for such acts.

15

A TALIB DOES NOT WANT ANYTHING ELSE

[This poem finds artistic expression for the goals and aspirations of the new movement. This vision of the ideal group places heroism, group loyalty and taking action for what is right at the head of its cause. It is the ideal-type expression of what the movement sought to become, and how they sought to be considered by others.]

Abdul Ahmad Mohammayar
Tolo-ye Afghan, 21 June 1995

A Talib does not want anything. He has no other goals.

All he wants is the honour of Islam. He wants his faith to be respected and to be practised.

He loves Islam, he loves his faith, and he is completely addicted to it and will do anything for it.

For him it is like an addiction. He is so used to it now that he isn't concerned with anything else in this world.

This is the army of Islam. It is a pious army and is fighting for a great cause.

It is made up of great men. Each of them is like a mountain. Each of them is an example of courage and bravery.

This army is ready to sacrifice anything for this great cause. It doesn't worry about life and death.

But it has a goal. The goal is to put an end to tyranny and oppression in this land. The goal is to free the oppressed and help the helpless.

This army has come out to fight the tyrants of the time and they are committed to crush him and destroy his rule.

They have made their decision: they will crush the enemy in a shameful defeat and kill it once and for all so that it never dares to return.

This whole army is a wonderful example of the spirit of sacrifice. They have given their all and will not stop from doing so again.

They have a great ambition: the ambition to rebuild their beautiful country once again and live in it peacefully.

The nations and the tribes living in this land are all happy about this wonderful new time.

They are happy about the emergence of the Islamic movement of the Taliban and are looking forward to supporting and joining it.

Now it is time to free all the helpless people from the claws of the tyrant rulers of this time

Their tyranny and their oppression must end now. This nation has suffered a lot and cannot bear it any more.

All these great men have been brought up in the cradle of courage. They are men with great courage and strong hearts.

These great men have been taught the lesson of bravery and championship. They have not forgotten that lesson one bit.

The Islamic movement of the Taliban is a movement with a great ideology behind it. It has emerged for a great purpose.

It will eventually succeed in eliminating all the enemies of the faith and will protect their faith from any kind of aggression.

The Islamic movement of the Taliban is not about any race or ethnicity or tribe. For this movement it doesn't matter whether someone is a Tajik or a Pashtun.

These things are meaningless for the Islamic movement of the Taliban. It considers all the people living in this country as one and equal. There is no division or difference.

The Islamic movement of the Taliban wants to bring all these tribes and all these ethnicities together under one single flag and under one single banner.

It wants to encourage and develop the spirit of unity and the spirit of brotherhood among the different tribes and ethnicities in this country.

Oh people, listen to me. Now is the time when these long dark nights will finally come to an end. These dark nights will be turned into bright light once again.

This will happen. It will happen because the Islamic movement of the Taliban has emerged and is fighting for this very purpose.

This pious movement has a new message for the people of this country. It is the message of a new peaceful and prosperous life for everyone who lives here.

The people clearly want to live in such an environment of peace and prosperity.

All the people of this country love the forces of the Islamic movement of the Taliban and have accepted them.

They consider them as their own and support them in this pious cause, the cause of faith and welfare of the people.

A TALIB DOES NOT WANT ANYTHING ELSE

Mohammadyar is extremely happy about the emergence of the Islamic movement of the Taliban in his beautiful land.

But at the same time he also wants the rest of the people in this land to love and to respect this great movement of faith.

16

IT IS AN OBLIGATION FOR ALL RELIGIOUS LEADERS AND THE PEOPLE TO DO JIHAD AGAINST THE OPPRESSORS

[*This interview with a respected scholar reveals some of the ways in which the religious establishment were firmly brought in as instigators and encouragers of the general population. It wasn't enough to wait for people to support the Taliban of their own accord; religious scholars issued numerous pronouncements like this to encourage participation, no matter what that meant in practice.*]

Tolo-ye Afghan, 24 May 1995

Dear readers,

We have carried out an interview with the country's renowned religious scholar Mawlawi Enayatullah. He is also known as 'Ghbargi' Mullah. This interview was conducted by Radio Sharia. We invite you to read it here.

Question: In your opinion, what should the religious scholars and the Taliban and ordinary Afghans do under the present circumstances, where a part of the country is under shari'a law while others parts of it are still ruled by corrupt tyrants?

Answer: It is an obligation for all religious scholars and the Taliban and ordinary Afghans to do jihad against the tyrants and try to stop their horror and injustice with all force, using all means at their disposal. This is not only the duty of the religious scholars and the Taliban. It is obligatory for every ordinary Muslim living in this country. If they cannot physically participate in the jihad against the corrupt rulers, then they should do so with their voice and their words, or at least work against it within their hearts.

Question: A number of religious scholars and jihadi commanders, including yourself, have come to Kandahar. Can you please tell us about the purpose of your visit?

Answer: We have come and gathered here because the injustice and tyranny of the corrupt rulers have reached an all-time high. We have participated in the jihad alongside our Taliban brothers in the past. And we have come here to join them against the corrupt rulers once again. We will not refrain from any sacrifice in this way and will stand by our brothers of the Islamic movement of the Taliban at all times and in every battleground. We will not stop our jihad until the moment when this nation sees the end of all tyranny and injustice and until the true wishes of the people of Afghanistan come true.

Question: What is your message for this oppressed nation?

Answer: My message to my people is that they should keep their promise which they made to Allah. It is a promise we all make even before we are born. In order to implement the law of the Qur'an in this land it is an obligation for all Muslims of this country to support their Taliban brothers and join them in their struggle. They should not refrain from making any sacrifice for the cause of this movement and should give their lives and their property for the achievement of their goals and ambitions. I also call upon the people of Afghanistan to pray for the success of the Islamic movement of the Taliban. This is a movement which will ultimately put an end to all terror and injustice in this country and will free this country from the rule of the oppressors. The people of Afghanistan should understand that it is only the Islamic movement of the Taliban that can bring true peace and prosperity to this country. They can bring a true Islamic system and can give people a peaceful environment to live in.

17

IN THE DICTIONARY OF ISLAM, MARTYRDOM DOES NOT MEAN DEATH

[Part of the participation implied by the previous source was to serve in the nascent armed forces associated with the Taliban. Their army was volunteer-based, and as such it wasn't a professional force but rather one that could rely on a steady stream of volunteers to step into the face of danger. Early on, therefore, the vocabulary connecting service to the idea of martyrdom became a common feature of the movement's lexical universe. Note that this was merely a continuation of trends that had been amply developed during the 1980s war, which didn't necessarily have anything to do with the religious students or Taliban groups themselves. But they were quick to employ its imagery and justifications in order to help bring about their 'revolution'.]

Tolo-ye Afghan, 14 June 1995

There is no doubt in the fact that good governance and leadership can only come with competent and committed leaders. These are the qualities of people who are committed to their cause and strive hard to achieve their goals. In order to implement the law of the Qur'an in its true sense, it is important that a society is led by someone who is committed to his faith and has all the qualities of a good leader for a Muslim people. It is such leaders who have the ability to bring positive change in society. These are the people who can read the nerve of their society and understand the mentality and the temperament of their people. Such are the leaders who can really bring about a revolution and guide a society onto the right path. Such leaders also have the quality to attract the younger generation and impress them with their qualities. They are a kind of role model for the youth of the nation. They inspire the youth to follow them and give them the spirit to stand up for their true cause and struggle to achieve it.

A revolution which is led by a group of pious and committed people is sure to reach its goals. True change in society can only come when the leader plays a serious and leading role in the process. Such a leader is also expected to have all the qualities which he wishes to see in his people. Of course it takes everyone to step forward and play their role in this process, but the role of the leader is always crucial. For a true leader, life and death in the way of Allah and for the sake of his cause does not matter. What matters are the ambition of his people and the will of Allah. These are the goals for which he strives in life and is even prepared to accept death for it.

These true leaders are never afraid of death. In fact they preach to others not to fear death in the way of Allah and for the sake of their true cause. The happiness and the excitement that they feel about their cause is evident from their faces. It is evident from their speech and from their actions. When they stand in front of their people and talk about their cause, they attract the attention of their people. There is a clear sense of honesty and commitment in what they say to their people. One can clearly see it in their faces, that they wish for martyrdom for the will of Allah and for the sake of their cause. Such great leaders stand by their word. They do what they say. They practise what they preach.

Martyrdom is a pride for a Muslim. We should remember that in the dictionary of Islam martyrdom does not mean death. In fact it is the complete opposite of death. Martyrdom in Islam means eternal life. Allah has clearly mentioned in his book that martyrs are alive. They have succeeded in this life and also in the hereafter. They have achieved their goal and have fulfilled their dream. They will have a special place in paradise where they shall live forever. It is natural that a Muslim dreams of martyrdom. He knows about the rewards that come with it. It is also natural for a Muslim to praise the martyrdom of his fellow Muslim brother and also wishes the same for himself. No true Muslim would like to lag behind in this great cause. Martyrs are people who have sacrificed their lives for the will of Allah and for the sake of their faith. They have shed their blood for the sake of implementing the law of the Qur'an in the land. Since a martyr dies for the sake of Allah, therefore it is only Allah who can reward him for his courage and his sacrifice.

As martyrdom is not considered death, it is therefore not advisable to mourn it. Muslims are advised not to cry over the martyrdom of a fellow Muslim. They should not feel sadness and grief. In fact they should be pleased about the fact that a fellow Muslim succeeded in this life and the hereafter. Relatives of a martyr should indeed take pride in their sacrifice and ask Allah for its reward and for forgiveness. They should realise that a martyr only returns to where he actually belongs. His true place is in paradise where he is much closer to Allah. A martyr is someone who writes his destiny with his blood. He is someone who leaves a great example of commitment and sacrifice for his people. He travels his journey in an exemplary way and lights the way for others to follow. He seals his name with his blood in the book of achievers and winners. They are like a candle that burns in the darkness and they will enlighten us for the rest of history. They are people who brighten our eyes. Martyrs are people who have always stood up against oppression and tyranny and have fought the evil of imperialism throughout history. They have sacrificed their lives so that their people can live in freedom and with dignity. They have shed their blood to protect the Islamic faith and to implement the law of the Qur'an in the land. A martyr lives for his people and his faith and also dies for the sake of his people and for the will of Allah. There can be no greater life than this. There can be no better death than this. They do not care about personal gains or glory. They do not think about gains and losses. They do not fear death. They do not fear those who oppress innocent people and prevent the implementation of the law of the Qur'an. They stand up against the enemies of faith and fight them with courage. A martyr is someone who believes in the freedom and independence of his people. He is someone who cannot be ruled by force or be oppressed. Martyrs strongly believe they have the right to live according to their faith and their beliefs. They demand the same rights for their people. A martyr believes in only one law, the law of the Qur'an. He wants to live according to this law and will never ever accept any other principles to live by. Martyrs are living examples for the rest of us and they set examples for us. They are alive and will be remembered by history.

18

WHAT DID A MARTYRED TALIB WANT?

[This source describes the idealised journey of a volunteer fighter, one who eventually succumbs in the midst of battle. This was part of the omnipresent ideological recruitment drive that characterised the movement at this time. It is important to remember, too, just how embattled the forces associated with the Taliban were in those early days. It was by no means a certainty that they would prevail over the forces associated with Rabbani / Massoud or Hekmatyar. Indeed, at many times it seems like they were on the point of being pushed back and defeated.]

Mullah Ameer Khan
Tolo-ye Afghan, 9 May 1995

I am talking about the Talib who was trained and educated by his teachers with great difficulties and sacrifices. I am talking about the Talib whose parents had sent him to the madrassa with great hopes. I am talking about the Talib who was loved by his friends and they had great expectations of him. I am talking about one who was the dearest at home. He was loved by all his villagers and he had found his way to everyone's heart. He had fallen in love with his books. They were his best friends. He would never be separated from his books. His teacher at the madrassa would work hard with him and make sure he was getting the best education. His parents and siblings would wait for him at home eagerly. They would welcome him with joy when he returned. Their eyes would glow at the sight of him. He loved his books and his studies so much that nothing else in the world would attract him or distract his attention from them. He didn't wish for any other blessings on earth.

That Talib finally had to abandon his books. He took leave from his teacher. He went home and packed some clothes and took some money for his journey. He left on a journey that not many have returned from. He joined the convoy of those who wouldn't be able to return to their houses and their studies. Before leaving home he put henna on his hands. He coloured his hair red as well. He had never prepared so much for a journey before. But this time it was a special occasion for him. It was a special journey that he was going on. He left home walking on his own feet. But he was brought back on the shoulders of other men. In the past when he returned the children at home would be joyful and would celebrate. This time they welcomed him with cries and screams. In the past when he returned he used to put on clean clothes. He would talk to his mother and father and tell them interesting stories. But this time he was not able to change his clothes. He couldn't say a word either. In short, he left for good. He left without seeing his dreams come true. It was not just his dreams that didn't come true. The dreams and wishes of his parents and siblings were also left incomplete. His books were left abandoned too.

But the question I want to ask is why did all this happen? He didn't want any position or money or power. He didn't have any personal enmity with anyone either. He never troubled anyone in his own life. So why did he have to leave like this? He didn't want any of the above-mentioned things. If he wished for them, he would have tried to get them long ago. He would have gone for them.

It is clear that the Talib died for the sake of the Qur'an. He sacrificed his life in the way of Allah. The Talib died for the protection of the faith and the implementation of the Islamic system in this land. He was martyred for the love of shari'a in his heart. He died while protecting the property and dignity of his Muslim brothers and sisters. He died because he wanted to rescue the oppressed from the tyrants. He died because he wanted to rid his nation of thugs and looters. The Talib died for the protection and honour of his Islamic faith. But it is unfortunate that some shameless people still have doubts about him and his motives.

19

POLITICS AND GOVERNMENT IN THE LIGHT
OF ISLAM

[*While Islam has some guidance about the shape of a system in accordance with its core tenets, its scholars and various legal traditions do not agree on the shape and form of an Islamic government, just as there is no universally accepted shari'a law. Accordingly, there have been various attempts to find or represent the most ideal system. Each group tries to find the solution in whatever school of thought or context it is educated and immersed. For the Afghan Taliban, this meant the Hanafi legal tradition and Deobandism as they understood it, combined with whatever changes had happened as a result of the 1980s war (and the politicisation it had brought).*

This source offers an outside perspective. Written as a multi-part op-ed in a prominent broadsheet newspaper, it is framed as if offering advice. As we shall see later, this was one of the external tools open to those outside the leadership to try to shape the direction of the movement. July 1995 was a period of considerable turmoil and a long-term perspective must have been hard to come by. This article reminds the senior Taliban figures that there are some secure principles on which they should model their rule: the idea of service, transparency above all, reform of what has failed, merit-based appointment and so on.]

Tolo-ye Afghan, 26 July 1995

As we discussed in the previous issue, the word 'politics' means to manage something. It can be the management of a government or a country in today's social science terminology. The purpose of politics in today's society is to elect a group of people who can come forward and run the daily affairs of a state and its government in the light of a set of rules that have already been agreed upon by the people of that state and preserved in the form of a law or a constitution. So these elected people are brought into power by the people of that particular state and then are responsible for the daily management of the affairs of state and are answerable to the same people who elected them or brought them to power. So we can say that these elected representatives are actually holding office to serve people, listening to their problems and demands, and finding the most appropriate solutions to these problems within the framework of the country's laws and the constitution.

Hence these elected people are not rulers and should not behave as rulers. They are servants of the people and they will only fulfil their duties properly if they listen to their people and serve them properly.

As we said earlier, politics and the management of a country's affairs should always take place within the framework of a law or a constitution. Without the presence of such a law or a constitution, there will surely be anarchy and mismanagement in the country. If one person or official does not obey the law of the country, then it will have negative impact on the very structure of that country or that society. It will create confusion and unrest in the society and its daily working will be disturbed. It is therefore important that all the people within a society, especially those who are tasked with running the affairs of a government or a country, operate and work within the framework of the law and the constitution.

The very purpose of politics is to bring reform in society. Politics should be a means of improvement, service, reform and coordination. It should enable a country to make fast and smooth strides on the road towards progress and development. If this basic purpose is not served, then surely politics or politicians are not doing their work properly. All politicians are expected to perform their duties in accordance with the country or society's laws and principles. An Islamic society is based on the principles of Islam and the Qur'an. Anyone who comes forward to serve his people in an Islamic society should have the required basic understanding of the Islamic principles which will enable him to work and serve. Unless he has that basic understanding of the Islamic faith, he is surely going to fail in his duty. The Qur'an is a law and a complete code of conduct for an Islamic society. It provides all necessary guidelines for the management of a society. It takes into consideration all the matters which are crucial in the affairs of a society. As long as the leaders of an Islamic society act according to the basic principles of the Islamic faith, then they are surely going to succeed in their affairs and be of best service to their people. But if they deviate from the principles of Islam and do not act in accordance with the prescribed principles, then they will fail and will be held responsible on the day of judgement. Islam says that when you are entrusted with power and authority, then you should not become arrogant and should not misuse that power and authority. Instead you should use it to serve your people in the best possible way. You should try to reach out to your people, talk to them and try to understand what their needs and their demands are. You should not consider yourself above the people whom you are supposed to be serving. You should in fact consider yourself their servant and make sure that no one's rights are usurped and that you do justice to your position in the society. A politician should try his best to be a role model in society and set an example. He should first of all look at his own affairs and make sure that he fulfils his duty with honesty and also behaves and acts in accordance with the country's laws and regulations. He should be sincere in his affairs, should not lie, and should not work for personal gains and ambitions. Instead he is supposed to prefer national interests over his personal interests all the time. He should act and behave in exactly the same way that he wants other people to behave. Politicians' affairs should be transparent and people should have the right to ask them about their official actions. A politician should always be ready to come forward and answer the needs and demands of his people. Since the purpose of politics is to bring reform and improve society, therefore a politician bears more responsibility than anyone to serve this purpose. He should make sure that when someone comes to him and complains and if his complaint is legitimate, then he should be provided with immediate justice. He should make sure that he does not ignore issues and matters which can have an impact on the lives and businesses of people. He should act in the best possible way, always making sure that the law of the land is preserved in all the decisions that he makes. He should not do personal favours and should always decide on the basis of merit. If a politician is found guilty of misusing power and usurping the rights of someone else, then he should immediately present himself to the court and people should have full right to come forward and ask him about his affairs. He should not be given, nor should he expect any concessions in his favour. He should consider himself equal to everyone else in society, and the same law should apply to him as to everyone else. Politics of corruption and self-interest always lead to anarchy in society. A society where people's lives and property are not safe will surely move towards destruction. Such a society can never move towards progress and equality. Societies in which different laws apply to the rich and the poor cannot survive for too long. Equality and social justice are one of the basic pillars of a successful and peaceful society. Unless such equality and justice are provided, the people of a society can never feel safe about their future. The Qur'an provides a clear explanation of how justice should be provided in a society. According to Islamic principles, everyone in the society is equal and should have access to the same services and is bound by the same law. Wealth and authority do not make anyone immune from punishment if he commits a crime. The life of some great Muslim leaders provide a good example of how they considered themselves as equal to their people and always presented themselves in front of the court or jury when there was a complaint about the way they ruled or how they provided justice or made decisions on important issues.

On the other hand, the purpose, definition and responsibilities of a government are also very clear and simple in Islam. According to Islamic principles, a government should always be formed in the light of Islamic principles. One of the most important duties of a government is to implement the law of the Qur'an in the land. A government in a Muslim country is responsible for making it possible for the people to live according to their faith. It is the government's responsibility to ensure that the pure and true law of the Qur'an operates in the land. No other law should be used in the land in the presence of Islamic law. No other system should be experimented with in the presence of an Islamic principle. An Islamic government ensures the welfare, security and progress of that human society. An Islamic government is always based on the golden principles of equality, justice, accountability and transparency. Unless all these golden principles are implemented in a society, you cannot call a society a truly Islamic one in nature. It is the duty of an Islamic government to bring peace and stability to the country and the society. It is the responsibility of the Islamic government to allow people to live peacefully and continue with their lives in accordance with faith. It is also the responsibility of a government to ensure that no member of the society is living under any kind of external or internal threat. The security of peoples and their lives and property is one of the most important and fundamental duties of an Islamic government. It is also the duty of an Islamic government to put an end to all sorts of tyranny and injustice in society. People should not fear anyone because of their power or wealth or authority. People in a society should only be subject to the law of that society and not the will of any other individual or group or even the government if the government is acting above the law. It is the responsibility of an Islamic government to make sure that an oppressed person is rescued from the terror and cruelty of a tyrant. A leader in an Islamic government can only implement laws which are in accordance with the teachings of Islam. No law should be acceptable which is in direct contradiction of the Qur'anic teachings. If any such law is being imposed by force and without the will of the people of the country or the society, then the people have every right to stand up for their rights and oppose any such law or move.

An Islamic government should also be free of corruption. The hands of those who are responsible for running the affairs of a country should always be clean and they should be respectable and acceptable people. They should not have a history of usurping people's rights and should not ever have acted on personal favours and against the interests of the country or the society. Leaders should be answerable to their people, and people should have the right to ask their leaders about their wealth and their income. This example has been witnessed in the past and some of the most prominent figures in Islamic history have willingly come before the people and presented their accountability.

Another important responsibility of an Islamic government is to work for the protection of the Islamic faith and the Muslim people all over the world. An Islamic government should prepare the people to stand like a wall in front of any aggression and be prepared to make any sacrifice for the protection of their Islamic faith and identity and the preservation of their rights and their land. An Islamic government should never leave its people to the mercy of others and should not ignore their call for help and support. We have witnessed over the past centuries that the enemies of Islam and the Muslims have never stopped conspiring against them. They have time and again come up with different plots and agendas and have attacked the Muslims. They have killed innocent men and children and have grabbed their land and their property. They have never stopped spreading their poison against Islam. We are even witnessing this trend in this age and day. We can see that the whole of the Western world seems to have come together and conspired against the Muslims of the world. Wherever you go around the world you will always see that it is the Muslims who are being killed and persecuted and thrown out of their lands. Their resources are being taken by force and their faith is being targeted deliberately. Under such circumstances it is the responsibility of all Muslim leaders around the world to come together and work together for the protection of their faith and their Islamic identity.

It is also the responsibility of an Islamic government to work for the unity of the Islamic world and resolve all the internal differences between the Muslims of the world. Under the present circumstances we can see that the Islamic world is deeply divided. We can see that the leaders of the Islamic world are busy with their luxurious lives and their worldly comforts and seem to have completely forgotten about the pain and the misery of their people around the world. Muslims are suffering aggression around the world. They are being targeted for no reason. It is a shame that our leaders are not even aware of the grave danger which is posed to the Islamic world and Muslims by our enemies. They do not understand the bitter truth that some people can never be friends, no matter how honest we are in our affairs with them. Our leaders seem to have relied completely upon the fake promises of the Western world. We are in this crisis today because we have stopped living our lives according to Islamic principles. We are facing this desperate situation because our leaders have forgotten to rule in accordance with the teachings of Islam. But they should know that it is only the Islamic system that can guarantee the provision of justice to people in a society. It is only an Islamic system in which the lives and properties of people can be safeguarded and they can live freely in accordance with their faith and their beliefs. So it is time for us to return to our roots. It is time for us to repent and to give up on all the non-Islamic ways of living and all the laws and regulations which come from sources other than the Qur'an. We can only succeed if we stick to our basic Islamic principles in life. If we do not do so, we shall lose our identity and with it we shall also lose the ability to defend ourselves against aggression. It is time for the Muslim world to realise the importance of unity and come together by putting all their internal differences aside. Otherwise we shall continue to suffer. Otherwise the blood of the weak and the oppressed will continue to be shed and no one will be held accountable. We should sort out our lives and we should also sort out our affairs. We should make sure that we consider the basic Islamic principles in whatever we do in our lives. If we do not change now, we shall continue to suffer from war and aggression and atrocity. The shari'a law and an Islamic system are our way towards success and prosperity in this world and the hereafter.

20

WHO SHOULD BE THE CALIPH AND WHAT SHOULD HE DO?

[Just as there were articles written about how the movement should be structured and behave, so were there also commentary pieces on the leadership and its role(s). This source explains some of the ways new caliphs were installed in the past, before placing this all in the framework of the present military and political situation.]

Tolo-ye Afghan, 7 June 1995

Allah says in the Qur'an that all those people whom he has bestowed with power on earth should pray regularly, give charity and work for the promotion of virtue and prevention of vice. Religious scholars say that all those people who have power on earth and are elected as leaders or kings are, in a way, the representatives of Allah. Their duty is to work according to the will of Allah and try to implement his law. If this is not the case, then such a person cannot be the caliph of the Muslims.

There are two things that are very important in the life of a Muslim. These are his prayers and worship, and the caliphate. At the time of man's creation, Allah nominated Adam (peace be upon him) as his caliph on earth. Allah says clearly in the Qur'an that Adam (peace be upon him) has been nominated as his caliph. Allah also says that he gave knowledge to Adam (peace be upon him) and taught him the names of all the things on earth. Thus he was made the caliph of all the people.

If we look at our history, all the prophets who were made caliphs of Allah on earth were people of knowledge. Consider the examples of Adam, and Moses, and David and Muhammad (PBUH). These were men who believed in justice and provided justice.

There are two ways in which a new caliph can be elected and installed. He can either be elected by a joint decision by the religious scholars of the time. This decision can be taken by men who are known to be just and honest. The election of Abu Bakr (May Allah be pleased with him) took place in this way. Another way to elect a new caliph is when the previous or outgoing caliph puts his hand on someone and chooses him as his successor. The election of Omar Farooq took place in this way. Apart from this there can be no other way to elect a new caliph. Also, no person can individually come forward and announce himself as a caliph. The election of Abu Bakr (May Allah be pleased with him) happened as a joint decision of the companions of the Holy Prophet Muhammad (PBUH). It happened before the burial of the Holy Prophet (PBUH). One of the reasons for his early election was that the whole burial had to be organised and conducted properly.

After the withdrawal of Soviet forces from Afghanistan, the religious scholars and ordinary residents of Afghanistan expected an Islamic government to be established and the shari'a law implemented. Unfortunately this didn't happen. The problems of the people were not solved and the situation in the country deteriorated even further. It was for this reason that the religious students, the army of the Holy Prophet (PBUH) started their jihad so that all the issues in the country could be resolved. The people of Afghanistan know well that only the religious scholars and the Taliban can truly implement the shari'a law and can fulfil the wishes of the people of Afghanistan. The so-called regime of Rabbani and Masood can never do this; nor can their Communist backers solve the problems of the people of Afghanistan. The enemies of Afghanistan should understand that the people of this country, especially the religious scholars and the Taliban, will never allow them to implement their wicked plans in this country. With the help of Allah we will do everything in our power to implement the Islamic law in this country one day, *Insha'allah*.

21

MULLAH MOHAMMAD OMAR AKHUND

WE ARE TRYING TO PREVENT ANY CONFLICT IN THE COUNTRY

[*This coverage of a meeting in Kandahar is unusual in providing details of some of the early suggestions for different possible leadership formulas for the Taliban movement. It is often assumed that the senior leadership implemented a clear strategy from the beginning, but improvisation and a lack of long-term clarity were more the order of the day. As we read in this source, they were also mooting a shura- or council-based model for all the people of Afghanistan. This is similar to what eventually happened, minus various key details, but the fact that it was raised at this early meeting helps trace the outlines of the evolution of their thinking on political structures for the country.*]

Tolo-ye Afghan, 7 June 1995

A meeting of the Taliban High Council, headed by the supreme leader Mullah Mohammad Omar Mujahid, was conducted at the 2nd Corps Commander's office on 2 June 1995. The meeting started with the recitation of verses from the Qur'an. First to speak was the supreme leader of the Islamic movement of the Taliban, Mullah Mohammad Omar Mujahid. He talked in great detail about the ongoing political and military situation in the country. He said that the Islamic movement of the Taliban was trying its best and making all sorts of possible efforts to prevent any potential conflict in the country. Mawlawi Abdullah Zakeri and a number of other participants presented a number of suggestions during the meeting. These suggestions were discussed and considered by the members of the meeting. As a result, a five-member commission was authorised to work on them. This commission included the governor of Khost province, Mawlawi Ehsanullah Ehsan; the mayor of Kandahar, Haji Mullah Mohammad Abbas Akhund; the military commander of the Islamic movement, Mullah Mohammad Akhund; Haji Mullah Mohammad Sadiq Akhund and member of the High Council Haji Mullah Mohammad Ghaus Akhund. Afterwards, it was suggested to form a grand Islamic shura for all the people of Afghanistan. All the participants liked the suggestion and it was decided that further necessary steps would be taken and ways and means would be considered for the formation of such a grand Islamic shura. It was also suggested that all conflicts and rifts in the country should be resolved through peaceful negotiations between the parties involved. This suggestion was also liked and accepted and it was decided to take necessary steps to implement it. The meeting ended with prayers for the implementation of full shari'a law in Afghanistan and other Islamic countries around the world. [...]

22

THE SECRET OF OUR SUCCESS LIES IN OBEDIENCE

[At the beginning, the Taliban ruled through consensus. They brought their Pashtun background with them and tried to find agreement and cooperation in whatever they did. At a certain point, when they grew beyond the confines of certain small rural areas and started to impinge on the territory of other provinces, or when they ran up against groups that had had almost two decades of experience with political organisation (i.e. Hizb-e Islami), they introduced a new organising concept: obedience. This was luckily a strong part of previously-existing Islamic guidance, but the emphasis that they placed on loyalty and obedience was extreme. They saw the disunity of the early 1990s as the anti-model to what they were trying to do, and this source explains other reasons for why they were so keen to avoid internal strife.]

Mohammad Akbar
Tolo-ye Afghan, 21 June 1995

If we look at human history, it is evident that justice has always fought against evil. This struggle began with the beginning of life and will continue as long as there is life on earth. It is a never-ending struggle. Although there have been periods when evil seems to be winning and has gained ground, yet it is also evident from human history that justice has always prevailed and that the final victory has always belonged to those who are on the right track and struggle for the right cause. At the end of the day, evil has always lost this battle and has escaped shamefully.

History teaches us that everyone who has sided with evil faced a disastrous end. They were buried under the ground or drowned in the seas. They might have triumphed momentarily but have never gained anything on a permanent basis. On the other hand, those who side with justice and truth have always succeeded. They might go through a lot of difficulties and make a lot of sacrifices. But those who stand their ground firmly and are committed to their true cause have always gained what they wished.

One reason why evil will never succeed is arrogance. Those who side with evil are arrogant people and are unaware of where they have come from and who their true creator is. They reason they were shamed and destroyed throughout history, but it is because they disobeyed their true creator. They deviated from the path that was advised and neglected the message that came to them. It was because of this disobedience and negligence that they lost direction in life and wandered. At the end of it all, they were defeated and were taught a lesson that history will never forget. Allah sent prophets (peace be upon them) throughout history and they brought a message to different nations. Many people accepted the message and were saved. But there were many more who rejected it. When the prophets (peace be upon them) asked them for obedience and submission to the will of Allah, they ignored it and said they would not accept a new ideology. In fact they laughed at this message and made fun of the prophets (peace be upon them). They disobeyed, and that was the reason for their failure and destruction. So it is evident that success lies in full obedience and submission. It comes with patience and discipline.

The Holy Prophet Muhammad (PBUH) has said that Islam comes with social unity. Social unity comes under the emirate. An emirate can be established when there is obedience. So in order to succeed in life and in order to be able to serve Islam and live according to the faith, it is important that we consider the above three golden points. It is with the help of these three golden principles that we can treat many social evils.

If there is obedience and submission, then there won't be any prejudice or racism or hate in society. Instead there will be love and prosperity and respect and happiness.

With submission and obedience, there is a general rule of law in society. People respect each other's rights and no one breaks the law. No one deviates from the path and principles defined in that society. Many other social illnesses are also cured if people avoid crossing the red line.

There is justice and equality all around. Everyone is the same in front of the law. The only preference one can have over another individual is because of how pious he is. In such a society all the norms and all the principles are in accordance with the shari'a law and everyone is happy. In such a society everyone's rights are defined and respected and well known. No one feels insecure and no one fears another individual.

In closing, I would like to insist once again that the secret of our success lies in our submission and our obedience. We obey our leadership and we submit to the will of Allah. We are successful because we are united and because we have patience. We are successful because we resist evil and stand our ground firmly.

23

THE CURRENT CIRCUMSTANCE AND THE
RESPONSIBILITIES OF THE RELIGIOUS SCHOLARS

[*The Taliban movement changed the place of religious scholars in society in a significant way, but it was accelerating a trend that had begun a decade or two earlier. This source comments on the role of the ulemaa and the basis for their pre-eminence. As 'heir of the prophets', their role is described as a great responsibility.*]

Mohammad Musa from Wardak province
Tolo-ye Afghan, 13 April 1995

Our great nation of Afghanistan has been the birthplace of some of the greatest Islamic scholars in history. They have done a great deal of work for the faith and nation. Their valuable literature is a great service to the country and their name is written in our history books in golden lines. The new generation of young religious scholars has a responsibility to follow the footsteps of these past religious authorities, and serve their faith and country in the future. Fortunately our younger generation has not forgotten their forefathers and their achievements. They are increasing their knowledge and applying their experience in the service of the nation and are doing wonderfully this far. The young religious scholars know their responsibilities well and are not refraining from fulfilling them.

It is a fact that the religious scholars have a special responsibility to awaken the minds and thoughts of society and make sure there is justice and welfare in society. Here, I want to point out a few responsibilities which the young religious scholars need to fulfil in the cause of serving their nation and their faith.

Religious scholars are the teachers of Islamic principles and shari'a law. Allah has bestowed upon them the sacred duty of protecting the faith and working for its propagation. They are obliged to serve society in the light of Islamic principles. They should make people aware of shari'a law and its implications. They are the heirs of the prophets. They are the leaders and imams of their people. Other people in society should follow them and look up to them for guidance, and Allah has declared them as the guides of society. Ordinary people should follow the ways and lifestyle of religious scholars in all aspects of their lives. The schools and other learning centres of society are successful only if they have great religious scholars in them. As the head in our body is one of the most important organs and performs some of the most vital functions, so the religious scholars have similar importance in society. It is because of the efforts and teachings of these religious scholars that a society can progress and succeed.

The Islamic movement of the Taliban has emerged for the welfare and protection of the people of Afghanistan. They are serving the poor and the helpless and are trying to rescue them from the misery and tyranny that have been brought upon them. It is true that the guidance and leadership of the religious scholars play a vital role in the success and welfare of society. There is a hadith which says that religious scholars are the heirs of the prophets. Their duty is to teach and implement Islamic laws and principles in society. It is because of their guidance that a society becomes happy and prosperous.

Allah has sent prophets time and again so that societies can be rescued from destruction and misfortune. They have worked for the promotion of virtue and prevention of vice. They guided people in their respective societies towards the right path. But once the process of sending prophets was complete with the last Prophet, Muhammad (PBUH), Allah bestowed this responsibility upon the religious scholars. It is a pious and important duty indeed. So it is the duty of the religious scholars to work for the propagation of the faith on earth. Allah has said in the Qur'an that there will be a group of people among you who will invite people to do good, and will ask them to promote virtue and prevent vice. These are the people who will be safe from the wrath of Allah.

It is clear that this group of people are the religious scholars. They are the true heirs of the prophets. They have the responsibility to promote virtue and prevent vice on earth. They explain to their people the principles and orders that are part of the shari'a. They cleanse society from corruption, injustice and atrocity. They rescue society from doom and destruction. They work for the establishment of peace and calm in society, which is the right of every individual. They try to fulfil their duty, bestowed upon them by Allah, in the best possible way. They please Allah by working for this pious cause.

So it is the duty of every single Muslim to support the Taliban movement and play their role in the implementation of shari'a law and the establishment of an Islamic government in the country. The Sufi poet Rahman Baba puts this as follows:

The religious scholars are the light in this world
They are the guidance for all humanity
If the chemist is looking for the best match
The friendship of the religious scholars is the best chemistry

RESPONSIBILITIES OF THE RELIGIOUS SCHOLARS

In the companionship of the religious scholars one turns into gold
Even if he is a stone or a grain of sand in the desert
I, Rahman, will keep the company of the religious scholars
Whether they are young, middle-aged or elderly

24

WE ARE NOT RACISTS, NOR ARE WE
NARROW-MINDED

[*The more the Taliban were exposed to groups different from them (whether this meant local Afghan groups from around the country, or international diplomatic representatives), the more they found that they had to justify their existence and push back against what they saw as a propaganda campaign. A key charge levelled at them was that they were uneducated and that they discriminated against other groups. (Note that the author interprets 'racism' to mean not following Hanafi precepts.) This article attempts to push back against some of these criticisms for a local audience, though as we shall see, this need to justify themselves has persisted up to the present day.*]

Mullah Rafiullah Nomani
Tolo-ye Afghan, 24 May 1995

If we look at the history of mankind, we will find that there has always been a struggle between justice and injustice. This struggle continues even today in our time. It will indeed continue right until the Day of Judgement. You are also aware that throughout history, at all times and reigns, those who stand by injustice and tyranny have plotted against those who stand by justice and the truth. They have spread all sorts of propaganda and have made all sorts of accusations. Despite all the allegations and the propaganda, it is an evident fact that the Islamic faith is the true and the only source of success and prosperity for all humanity.

In the recent past Afghanistan has suffered a great number of difficulties, which you all have witnessed with your own eyes. There is no need to go into the details of this recent unfortunate history of our nation. When the Communists first came to power they started a wave of propaganda and allegations against the Islamic faith. Sometimes they would say that Islam is an old and outdated ideology and the Muslims are backward people. Sometimes they would say that Islam is racist and the Muslim people are all narrow-minded. They would also try to argue that women have been oppressed throughout the history of the Islamic faith and they have never been given their rightful place and status. They would argue that a man is allowed to have four wives at a time according to the Islamic faith. But then a woman is not allowed to have more than one husband at the same time. They would say that man and woman are equal in all aspects and so discrimination is a cruelty.

If a man with a healthy brain thinks about these stupid allegations he will understand that it makes no sense at all. The Islamic faith provides proper answers to all these questions and allegations. These answers make complete sense to the mind. Not just that, but all the commands of Allah and all the hadiths of the Holy Prophet (PBUH) are full of secret blessings for mankind.

According to research by scholars, it is now clear that the population of the world contains four times more women than men. In other words there are four women in this world for each man. Now imagine what will happen if a woman was allowed to have more than one husband. Even right now it is difficult for all the women to find a man as a husband. If one woman takes more than one man as a husband, then it is clear that a large population of women will remain unmarried in this world. This will surely result in a huge social disaster.

Let me try to explain this with the help of another example. Imagine four people pouring in their share of water into the same cup. Once the cup is full, no one will be able to separate their share of water. It will be impossible. Now the same can happen if a woman has more than one husband. It just won't work. When this woman has children, it will be difficult to find out which one is the true father. Also, she can either have male or female children. Some men will prefer to have male children and others would want female ones. How would you resolve such a situation? On the other hand, if one man pours water into four different cups he won't have to worry about anything. He can use the water from any of the cups he wants, as all of them belong to him.

So, as mentioned earlier, the enemies of the Islamic faith have always plotted many things and in many ways against the Muslim umma. They have used propaganda and false allegations. When the mujahedeen came to power in Afghanistan, all the nation hoped that now it was time for the establishment of an Islamic regime in the country and that everyone would be able to live according to their beliefs. But unfortunately the wishes and dreams of the people of this country were squashed and all the commands and the principles of the Islamic faith were violated. It was because of this that the religious students closed their books and picked up the swords of their fathers and grandfathers. They put on the shroud of courage and bravery and sacrificed themselves in the way of Allah. With the help of Allah Almighty they were able to bring many areas of the country under their control and managed to establish a system in accordance with the teachings of the Qur'an and the hadiths of the Holy Prophet (PBUH) and the writings of the Great Imam, Abu Hanifa.

Now that we have achieved these wonderful things, there are people who call us racist and narrow-minded. They call us racist because we won't listen to or practise any other way than the way of the Great Imam, Abu Hanifa. Real racism is when someone sees justice and knows that a particular group is right and just, but would still block their way. We have never turned our backs on the just cause and will never do so in the future.

They call us narrow-minded because we have shut down some places where evil practices took place. Public baths for women are among such places. We have done this in order to protect the honour and dignity of the women. It is against our culture and tradition and against the teachings of the Islamic faith that women go to public baths. We have given women all the rights which are given to them by the Islamic faith. So we are not narrow-minded because we are acting in accordance with the teachings of the Islamic faith. The Islamic faith is a broad-minded faith and anyone who puts these labels next to our names is indeed racist and narrow-minded.

25

LEAVE US ALONE

[*A common complaint against the international community during the early years of the movement was that they were seeking to interfere in Afghanistan's domestic affairs. This source argues that the Taliban have every right to apply the shari'a as the defining system for the country's rules and calls on the international community to stop meddling: 'leave us alone and mind your own business'. In some ways, this is an accurate summary of a prominent strand of Taliban thinking on foreign policy, particularly once naive expectations of acceptance by the international community had been refuted.*]

Tolo-ye Afghan, 7 May 1995

All the Muslims of the world took part in the Afghan jihad for fourteen consecutive years. Many people migrated. Around a million and a half people were martyred for the sake of their religious obligation. All these sacrifices were made so that we can implement the law of our creator in this land, the law of the Qur'an. He gave us the strength to stand up to oppression and fight for our freedom. So why did I waste my chance? Why did I waste my right? Why did we not come together and agree on implementing the shari'a law at the end of all these sacrifices?

There is no reason to be sceptical of the shari'a law. Chopping off someone's hand or stoning someone is for the sake of society. Such harsh punishments are prescribed for those who oppress others and usurp their rights. It is for those who transgress. We all witnessed what happened when there was no shari'a law in the country. The last few years are a good example of the disaster a society faces without a strict code or law. We saw in the last few years that there were tyrants and warlords every half kilometre in this country, and they had made life difficult for the ordinary citizen. They didn't care about any ethics or any law or any culture. No one could stand up to them and no one dared to try and stop the barbarism they had started in this country.

So the shari'a law is our natural right. We decide what kind of a system we want for ourselves and our society. We saw what happened in this land when this natural right was taken away from us. The tyrants had blocked our way towards a society where we could live under our preferred system. But then we also saw the great change that came after the true sons of this land decided to put an end to the crisis in this country. We saw the sudden and amazing change when the pious Taliban decided to start a jihad against the tyrants who had turned our lives into hell. They stood up and took up arms and we saw that wherever they went, there was peace and stability and a general sense of happiness and satisfaction among the people. There was no injustice and no cruelty any more in any of the areas that came under the direct control of the Taliban movement.

So this wasn't just a coincidence or a mere chance. Every single person, even an idiot, understands the clear reason behind this sudden but positive change in society. Everything changed because the Islamic movement of the Taliban was able to implement the shari'a law. The situation improved because they were able to rule according to the teachings of the Qur'an. So this clearly shows what kind of a system can bring peace and stability in this country. It also explains what sort of a system the people of this country want for themselves. It is unfortunate that our natural right and our demand for the shari'a has been misinterpreted and misunderstood by many, even some of our own people. It is unfortunate that some individuals and groups are continuing with their armed resistance against the Islamic movement of the Taliban and are blocking the way to full implementation of shari'a law in this country. They want to usurp this basic right of our people. These groups and individuals continue with their false propaganda against the Islamic movement of the Taliban.

There are many things that they point towards and criticise in the Islamic movement of the Taliban. But one issue that they raise more than any other is that of human rights. They accusation is that the Islamic movement of the Taliban does not respect human rights. They have made a lot of noise on this issue recently. This is very strange as well. Allah Almighty says there is life and prosperity behind such punishments. They are prescribed so that society can be cleansed of all the evils and menaces that mankind has developed. But these thugs call this inhumane and against the will of Allah. They do not have any idea what they are saying. They do not understand the teachings of the hadith. They are talking rubbish.

Allah has clearly defined the responsibilities of men and women in this book. A woman has been given the important and crucial responsibility of making a family and looking after it. She is responsible for bringing up the children because she can do it better. She is not obliged to go out and work and earn. She is not made for any other type of harsh labour either. On the other hand a man's responsibilities are completely different from those of a woman. He is supposed to go out and work and earn bread for the family. He is the one who should be doing the harsh labour. It is his responsibility to look after the wife and the children and provide for them. He is made for such work, both physically and mentally. If a man starts doing housework then he won't have time for his outdoor responsibilities. So he should rather stick to his outdoor duties and leave the house in the control of the woman.

So it is our right to decide how we live in this society. Any accusation from the outside world is interference in our internal affairs. This should not happen. They should rather take the blame for making weapons which are against humanity. They also disrespect and violate human rights by killing thousands of people. So we ask all those who accuse us of violating human rights to stop pointing their fingers at us and to look at their own record. Leave us alone and mind your own business. If you really are so concerned about human rights, then you should destroy all your atomic bombs. Stop bothering us.

26

MESSAGE FROM MAWLANA RASHID AHMAD LUDHIANVI

[*Pakistan's role in the formation and day-to-day rule of the Taliban movement has been a mainstay of commentary on the 1990s government. Much of this has focused on the ways that the formal Pakistani state contributed to the Taliban, through training, diplomatic support or financial aid. It is important to note, therefore, that counsel via informal means was equally important, even if it complicates our understanding by not being sure how every piece fits into the context of the formal Pakistani state apparatus. Mufti Rashid Ahmad Ludhianvi was a very prominent cleric who frequently advised the senior Taliban leadership. This religious-cum-political advice was eagerly taken, in part because senior figures had a feeling of inferiority for having not completed all of their religious studies. Ludhianvi was thus well placed to have a strong influence on the movement and he wrote various articles, speeches and pamphlets which we know Mullah Mohammad Omar found important. In this source, he offers support to the Taliban in their early days, reaffirming what he sees as their important role in the Afghan political configuration.*]

Tolo-ye Afghan, 24 August 1995

The most senior cleric in Pakistan, Mawlana Rashid Ahmad Ludhianvi, has sent a message of support and congratulations to the Islamic movement of the Taliban. In his message, the grand Mufti has congratulated the Islamic movement of the Taliban on recent victories against the enemies of Islam and Afghanistan. The grand Mufti has also mentioned the landing of a Russian plane in Kandahar and the arrest of the crew. He has also criticised Rabbani's puppet regime in Kabul. We are publishing his message here for our dear readers:

In the name of Allah, the most merciful, most beneficent.

First, let me convey my message of peace and support to the supreme leader of the Islamic movement, Mullah Mohammad Omar Mujahed, and to the entire Taliban High Council and the movement itself. I am extremely pleased to be communicating with a group of pious and dedicated Muslims who have started a holy war for the protection of their faith and their motherland. The entire Muslim world is proud of the achievements of the Islamic movement of the Taliban and are looking up to this movement as a source of inspiration. If we read the Qur'an, we will find out that whenever a nation loses its direction and strays away from the right path, Allah brings upon them difficulty and hard times. And whenever people lose their contact with Allah, then they come under the leadership of people who are tyrants and oppressors. Allah always gives us what we deserve. We should therefore always stay on the right path and pray to Allah to grant sincere leadership.

The people of Afghanistan and the entire world Muslim world are extremely fortunate to have witnessed this golden period under the leadership of the Islamic movement of the Taliban. I have no doubt in my mind that the entire movement and its leadership have no other agenda or ambition than serving the people of Afghanistan. The Muslim people of Afghanistan have made sacrifices for the sake of their faith and their motherland throughout their histories. They have given everything they had to protect their faith and their future generations. The defeat of the Soviet Army in Afghanistan was indeed great news for the entire Muslim and non-Muslim world. The whole world should therefore be thankful for the courage and bravery of the Afghan people. Had it not been for the sacrifices of the people of Afghanistan, the Soviet Army would have succeeded in its imperialistic plans and it would have been extremely difficult for the Muslims of Afghanistan and the world to live their lives in accordance with the teachings of the Qur'an and the Sunnah.

So the Afghan people did not just fight their own war. They fought a war for the defence of the entire Muslim world. They did not just defend their land but the whole Muslim world from infidels. The sacrifices of the Afghan people will not and should not be forgotten by the world. Afghans have been a peace-loving nation and have always wanted to live peacefully and in harmony with other nations in the world. Unfortunately they have been oppressed time and again by the tyrant armies of the world, and have not been allowed to live their lives according to their beliefs.

They have faced the invading armies of Alexander and Genghis and then the British and most recently the Soviet Army. But the brave and courageous Afghan nation has never bowed down to oppression and has never compromised on their faith and their sovereignty. They have stood up like a wall in front of all oppressors and have fought for their rights and their freedom. They have given their blood and their lives and their property and everything else. Such examples of sacrifice are very rare in human history. Afghans had to lose their homes and villages and their livelihoods. They lost their loved ones and faced extreme hardships living as refugees in neighbouring countries. But all these hardships did not bother them and they were never deterred from defending their country and their faith. They fought against all the superpowers with extreme courage and the whole world has witnessed their commitment to country and faith.

At the end of all these sacrifices the Afghan people deserved to get what they wanted. They deserved to live in an environment of peace and stability and live their lives in accordance with their faith. They deserved to have the opportunity to bring up their children in the light of the teachings of the Qur'an. They should have been given the chance to bring up their future generations with the true values of Islam. They should have been allowed to stick to their Afghan values and identities. But unfortunately this did not happen. A group of brainwashed individuals tried to change the country overnight and thought they would succeed in rooting out the Islamic identity of the Afghan people. Unfortunately they didn't study the history of this country and its people thoroughly. They did not know that the Afghan people will never at any cost compromise on their faith and their freedom.

The Soviet Union thought they could simply introduce a puppet regime and install it in Kabul by force and then they could do whatever they wanted. They sought the help of their puppets in doing so and so came up with a plan to introduce Communism in Afghanistan. They thought they would succeed in transforming the entire identity of this nation. They were wrong, of course. The Afghan people had rejected and resisted such plans in the past and there was no reason why they would bow down to Soviet oppression this time. They completely rejected Communism and its puppets in Afghanistan and started their holy war against the Soviet Army. They made numerous sacrifices but successfully defeated the Soviet Army and defended their land. They came out victorious in yet another battle against the infidels.

After the defeat of the Soviet Army the Afghan people thought they would be able to live peacefully and would never have to face any terror and tyranny again. The Afghan people put their trust in their leaders, the same leaders who led them during the years of the jihad against the Soviet Army. They thought these men would stick to the promises which they had made to the Afghan people and would serve the men and women and the widows and the orphans of this country. The Afghan people had stood by these leaders and had fought for them and had made sacrifices for them to come to power. They thought their so-called leaders understood the pain and the misery of the Afghan nation and would therefore do everything in their power to heal the wounds of the Afghan nation. They considered these leaders as their own and thought they could trust them with the future of their children.

But unfortunately these so-called leaders had other plans of their own. They had forgotten the promises they had made to the Afghan people. They had completely forgotten the purpose of the jihad. They did not remember the sacrifices of the Afghan people. They changed their lives and their world and their lifestyles. After coming into power they became corrupt and blind. They did not care about the miseries of the Afghan nation.

These so-called leaders started a bloody civil war which took the lives of thousands of other innocent Afghans. The Afghan people continued to suffer at the hands of the same people whom they had trusted and obeyed during the years of the jihad. These so-called leaders started working for their personal gains and ambitions. They turned their guns on each other for the sake of power and wealth. No one cared about the hopes and ambitions of the Afghan people. No one cared about the sacrifices the Afghan people had made. Everything changed from bad to worse. People lost hope in their future and there was no hope and no light. While these corrupt leaders fought each other for power and luxury, the Afghan people continued to die and suffer. They once again had to pack up in the middle of the night and leave their homes and villages and flee to neighbouring countries. Many were unfortunate and could not do so and were caught up in the bloody civil war and lost their lives. The beautiful city of Kabul was also reduced to rubble.

But Allah listened to the cries of the Afghan people. It was time someone had to stop all this atrocity and war and destruction. It was time someone listened to the cries of the orphans and wiped the tears of the widows. The Islamic movement of the Taliban was a blessing from Allah and was established in order to put an end to the misery faced by the Afghan people. A group of pious religious scholars came together and decided to change the destiny of this nation. They decided to take matters in their own hands and put things right. These men emerged from within Afghan society and were the sons and brothers of this nation. They understood the pain and suffering of the Afghan people very well. They started their pious struggle against the tyrant regime in Kabul and have so far gained some wonderful victories all over the country.

We here in Pakistan have no doubt in our minds that the regime in Kabul does not represent the people of Afghanistan and does not stand for the values and the traditions that the Afghan people believe in. Over the last three years the corrupt regime has only worked for their own personal gains and ambitions, while the Afghan people have continued to suffer throughout this period. We truly believe that the people of Afghanistan have stood behind the Islamic movement of the Taliban. This movement is made up of the Afghan people and has been started to serve this country and put an end to the ongoing crisis in the country. The Afghan people also understood this reality very well and that is why they have made sacrifices for the cause of the Islamic movement.

The only ambition of this movement is to establish an Islamic government in Afghanistan where the true and pure laws of the Qur'an can be implemented and people can live according to their Islamic values. That is exactly what the Afghan people want and that is what they have fought for and made sacrifices for. The Afghan people do not want any other regime or ideology or government. They are pure and pious Muslims and would spend their lives according to their faith.

Anyone who thinks otherwise is mistaken. It is time for the Western world to stop its propaganda and accept the Islamic movement of the Taliban as a reality in Afghanistan. The enemies of Islam and Afghanistan should stop their evil plans and stop destabilising this country further. Russia should also stop supporting the regime in Kabul and should listen to the demands of the Afghan people. The landing of a Russian military plane in Kandahar and the arrest of its crew is a serious matter. It proves that Russia is still interfering in the internal matters of Afghanistan. It also proves that the corrupt regime in Kabul is depending on foreign military aid which it uses against its own people. This is a direct aggression against Afghanistan's sovereignty, and the international community should take note of this. Russia should be asked to explain its action in Afghanistan and should be held responsible for the ongoing crisis in this country.

To conclude, let me once again convey my message of peace and support towards the entire Islamic movement of the Taliban and congratulate them on their amazing victories recently. *Insha'allah*, the flag of Islam will soon appear all over Afghanistan and Allah will bless the Afghan people with a truly Islamic government. I pray for your success in this great cause.

27

OBEDIENCE TO THE AMIR

[*These are some extracts from Mufti Ludhianvi's* Obedience to the Amir. *It is unclear exactly when the text was written, but it was probably in 1998 or 1999. Ludhianvi had visited the Taliban movement and Mullah Mohammad Omar inside Afghanistan and came away with extremely positive impressions. He wrote his short text (in Urdu) primarily as advice for members of the Taliban movement, and Mullah Mohammad Omar is known to have handed out Dari and Pashto translations of the book to visitors, saying that this is what they should read in order to understand the Taliban. The text is divided into eight sections and is more a series of proscriptions rather than prescriptions. This format is something that was mirrored in the 2006 version of the* layeha *or 'rules' (and subsequent versions), clearly modelled on Ludhianvi's short book. This is not a text where ideology or doctrine are mentioned much. This is a functional guide to the management of the organisational identity of the movement. The key theme or goal to which Ludhianvi guides and encourages the reader is unity. This, he argues, is the key way that the Taliban can distinguish themselves from the mujahedeen groups. This principle of unity is emphasised throughout the book. The various precepts and advice that Ludhianvi offers all return to the need to keep control of the movement and to concentrate power in the figure of the Amir, Mullah Mohammad Omar. Section 2 focuses on this point and included citations of (and commentary on) forty hadiths that justify the need to obey the amir. The final three sections (6, 7 and 8) relate to advice, how the amir should seek counsel, and how those giving advice should in turn behave.*]

Excerpts from Obedience to the Amir: An Early Text on the Afghan Taliban *by Mufti Rasheed Ludhianvi, 1998/1999?*

Section 1
Maintaining internal consensus and unity and avoiding differences and splits

The Taliban have implemented a supreme and sacred system in the land of the martyrs, the ultimate authority of which is the God of the martyrs and mujahedeen. This same authority has given so much attention to establishing the maintenance of consensus and unity as a duty and has rendered the propagation of difference as reprehensible and most unfortunate. The relevant instructions are:

The foundations of religion are incompatible with differences

'Allah set that religion for you which was brought to you by the prophet Noah, the same which was sent to you through the prophets Abraham, Moses and Jesus. They carried the instruction to you that you must hold fast to this religion and never oppose it.' (Qur'an 42:13)

Two important issues have been shown in this ayat:

1. The instruction to maintain consensus and unity is so important and great that it has been delivered to the most honourable prophets and their peoples. The whole value of the shari'a is linked to this instruction.
2. The foundations of religion are impossible without consensus and unity.

This shows that if someone through his deeds or words gives rise to dissent, then in reality he is acting against Islam and is showing defiance to Islam.

Power and grandeur are lost through difference

'And obey Allah and His Apostle and do not quarrel for then you will be weak in hearts and your power will depart, and be patient; surely Allah is with the patient.' (Qur'an 8:46).

Several issues are shown by this: Benefits

1. Your power will dissipate from internal difference, through which the enemy will unexpectedly lose his fear. As an ultimate consequence of this Islam will be destroyed.
2. The secret formula for maintaining internal consensus and unity in any social endeavour is that if you face something which is counter to your opinion, nature or advice, then you should put on a show of patience.
3. If this patience seems to you like an effort and a burden, then trust in God's company, the God of the patient. Tell yourself that this divine company is no ordinary treasure.

The instruction of God's messenger:

From Bukhari, Muslim and Ahmad:

'If a decision of your amir seems unpleasant, then show patience.'

Avoiding the stinking thoughts of party manoeuvring, tribalism and bigotry

'And hold fast by the covenant of Allah all together and be not disunited, and remember the favour of Allah on you when you were enemies, then He united your hearts so by His favor you became brethren; and you were on the brink of a pit of fire, then He saved you from it, thus does Allah make clear to you His communications that you may follow the right way.' (Qur'an 3:103)

Benefit: in this too some aspects are worth noting.

1. This ayat is fully applicable to the Taliban and therefore the Taliban should read the text of this ayat again and again. There was a time when the Taliban were divided into various groups and there was no possibility of them working together. But God was kind and under his name and his plan all the groups united under the amir and became as one and indistinguishable from each other and freed from the dirt of organisational difference and were cleansed of group prejudice and hatred and were bathed in sweetness and love. In this way the idols of party manoeuvring, ethnicity and bigotry were broken and all memory of barbarism were erased.

2. If at any time the devil tempts you, dwell on the words 'jal-allah' and think how can I do the bidding of the wretched Satan rather than the bidding of God?

3. To maintain sweetness and love it has been commanded that the great blessing of unity be discussed and God be thanked for this, for from one blessing one progresses to another blessing.

If you are thankful, then more blessings will be showered upon you.

And discuss this and debate upon issues that unite you and avoid bringing divisive issues into discussion.

The demon of tribalism, clannishness, regionalism and factionalism is injurious to both this world and religion. In this regard, certain actions are obligatory.

1. Every member of the movement should pay particular attention to the fact that the heart and mind should be kept free of any form of prejudice. If involuntarily such a thought comes to mind, it should never be translated into words.

2. If some action provokes such suspicion, then recite three times 'God protect me from Satan', turn to your left and say 'thoo, thoo' and believe that this action has been undertaken in good faith based upon authority. Tell yourself that at the most this is an error of the amir in his striving, which will not be considered a sin for him, rather he will be rewarded.

3. Remember that harbouring suspicion is a major sin and a precursor to other major sins. Harbouring suspicion can destroy any social endeavour. It is a grave misdemeanour to harbour suspicions about your amir, based upon rumours or scruples and without shari'a-based reason.

The secret formula for avoiding every error

'Do not become like those people who after the arrival of the clear instructions divided themselves with differences, as for those people the day will be a great torment when some faces are made white and some faces are made black.' (Qur'an 3:105, 106).

Benefit

1. This ayat, just like the first ayat, applies one hundred percent to the condition of the Taliban. Taking into account the place and situation, this ayat is so important for the Taliban that it has the potential to protect them from every mistake and to warn them of any danger. Likewise if the Taliban fail to pay attention to the lesson of this ayat, then they will be vulnerable to every danger.

Every office member of the Taliban movement should fix this in his mind that there were other mujahedeen before them upon whom God bestowed the treasure of jihad in the way of God. As a result of this the Soviet Union was destroyed. Allah granted them force, suzerainty and power. But they did not value this and instead of implementing Islam they succumbed to internal differences. Not only did the wretched results render them infamous throughout the world, jihad, which is a sacred duty in Islam, also got a bad name.

If those to whom the Taliban's sacred movement is entrusted do not learn a lesson from the fate of the previous people, then listen, their fate will be no different from the fate of the previous people, rather it will be worse than their fate. From those people's differences, only the section of jihad was affected. But if the Taliban fall prey to differences, it will bring a bad name on the whole of Islam. Islamic affairs and the sacredness of God's name and his system will be trodden underfoot.

Dissent is the work of polytheists

'Do not become polytheists—those people who have brought splits in their religion.' (Qur'an 30:31, 32)

Benefit

1. This shows that in the Qur'an indulging in difference and divergence is the work of the polytheists.

It is a shame that the matter has been turned upside down. Now the infidels and polytheists observe the instruction of the Qur'an to maintain strict unity and consensus. Despite the differences arising from their varying colours, races, languages, temperaments, interests, concerns, in their confrontation with the Muslims they are united and of one mind on every front. Meanwhile the Muslims have neglected this instruction and have descended to tearing each other apart and destroying Islam.

OBEDIENCE TO THE AMIR

Maintaining consensus and unity is very dear to God

'Allah holds dear to him those people who follow his path and maintain unity while they fight, as if they were a single edifice. (Qur'an 61:4)

Benefit

Who can deny the importance of that action which renders someone dear to Allah?

Section 2
Obedience to the amir

This testament is so important and great that it is appropriate, even important, to describe it as the summary or essence of this guidance.

Acting upon this testament will be the guarantee of the welfare of the Taliban Islamic movement, in this world and the next. Closing every door to difference will keep the spring of familiarity and love flowing between the leadership and the most junior member of the Taliban.

Oh God's brave mujahedeen, selfless Taliban, the Qur'an, hadith and common sense show that in organisational matters, in anything which involves a collective task, obedience to the amir is as important as air and breathing are to staying alive.

Come, self-sacrificing army of Mohammad!

Obedience to the amir is the order of obedience which distinguishes either the highest office holder or the most junior member as sincere and faithful.

This is the criterion which distinguishes jihad, the supreme act of worship, from discordant politics. It was on this scale that the sincerity of the rightly guided caliphs' governors, ministers and commanders was weighed. It is through this pulse that the doctor diagnoses a disease.

This is that same secret which in the first century made Islam honoured in four-sixths of the world and won for it power, majesty and reverence. It is that true brightness which made Rome and Persia and their great powers scatter before a few humble hut dwellers. It was this which made the tallest, most robust and strongest abodes of the infidels and polytheism come tumbling onto the ground with a crash. Every member of the Taliban movement, whether he be a member of the shura, or a provincial governor, or a soldier on the battlefield, or someone following orders in an office, must act with this in mind, that any deficiency occurring in the obedience to the amir is tantamount to a deficiency in Islam.

Any weakening of the spirit of observance of obedience to the amir weakens the implementation of God's system. Therefore God has linked obedience to the amir to obedience to God and his prophet.

28

VISITORS FROM LONDON

[This source offers an intriguing glimpse into the ways that the Taliban were part of a broader international dialogue, even by August 1995. A delegation of Muslims meet with Mullah Mohammad Omar; we hear from their representative and their concerns are outlined before the Taliban leader responds. It is relatively unusual to have such a full account of a meeting like this, with specific details of speeches that were made.]

Tolo-ye Afghan, 24 August 1995

A delegation of Muslims from London travelled to Kandahar and met with the supreme leader of the Islamic movement, Mullah Mohammad Omar Mujahed. The meeting took place at the governor's office in Kandahar.

First of all a few verses of the Holy Qur'an were recited. Then a member of the delegation spoke on behalf of his friends and explained the purpose of his visit to Kandahar. He first thanked the leadership of the Islamic movement for providing the delegation the opportunity to come to Kandahar and meet the leadership of the Islamic movement. He said he had brought a message of support and friendship from all the Muslims in the UK. The leader of the delegation said the Islamic movement of the Taliban was a symbol of peace and prosperity and had given hope to all the Muslims around the world. He said the entire Muslim umma was going through a difficult time and it required a strong and sincere leadership to face the challenges of the new world. He said Muslims all over the world were looking up to the Islamic movement as a source of inspiration. He said he was truly impressed to see how the Islamic movement had managed to implement shari'a in its true sense and make it possible for the people of Afghanistan to live their lives peacefully in an Islamic environment. He also said the Western media were busy spreading false propaganda against the Islamic movement, but that the Muslim world had now seen the true faces of these enemies of Islam and were not going to be fooled by what they were trying to show and say about the Islamic movement.

Other members of the delegation also spoke and mentioned the problems and threats faced by Muslims all over the world. They showed their solidarity with the people of Afghanistan, Kashmir and Palestine. They said the Islamic movement in Afghanistan gave inspiration to Muslims in other parts of the world and proved that even in today's world and under the present circumstances it is possible to establish an Islamic government and run a country in accordance with the principles of Islam and the Sunnah.

Members of the delegation said they were concerned about the future of their children in the non-Islamic world and wanted to be able to live in an environment where they can bring up their future generations in accordance with the teachings of Islam. They said the Western world had never accepted the Islamic movement as a true representative of the people of Afghanistan and was trying to undermine the success of this movement. Members of the delegation expressed their fully-fledged support towards the Islamic movement and said they would try to spread the message of the Taliban movement all over the world. They said they will go back to their countries and tell their people about the impressive performance of the Islamic movement in bringing peace and stability to Afghanistan.

Then the supreme leader of the Islamic movement, Mullah Mohammad Omar Mujahed, spoke. He thanked the delegation for their visit and said the Islamic movement will always welcome their Muslim brothers from all over the world to come to Afghanistan and see for themselves what was really happening in this country. He also thanked the delegation for their support and asked the members to go back to their countries and their cities and spread the message of peace and Islam. The supreme leader said the Islamic movement of the Taliban was a true representative of the people of Afghanistan and had emerged from within the Afghan people.

He said the Western world and some enemies of Islam were spreading all sorts of false propaganda about the Islamic movement. The supreme leader said the Islamic movement of the Taliban has nothing to do with any foreign government or agency and was purely made of Afghans. He said it's true that some non-Afghans were present in the ranks of the Islamic movement, but these people had come to Afghanistan voluntarily in the spirit of Islamic brotherhood and wanted to take part in the holy war against the enemies of Islam and Afghanistan.

The supreme leader said the people of Afghanistan had accepted the Islamic movement of the Taliban because this movement was made up of their own sons and brothers. He said the people of Afghanistan sacrificed their lives and their property for the sake of Islam and fought a number of superpowers. They wanted to establish an Islamic government in this country, but some corrupt leaders hijacked the whole process of jihad and started to act in their own personal interests. He said the corrupt regime in Kabul had done nothing for the people of Afghanistan except looting and killing them. He said the so-called leaders siting in Kabul were only bothered about their own personal gains and interests and were not even aware of the pain and misery of the Afghan people.

The supreme leader said he completely understood the concerns of the Muslims living in the West and realised that the future of their children was at risk. He said the Islamic movement wanted to establish an Islamic system not only in Afghanistan but all over the word. The supreme leader said the establishment of such an Islamic government was the sole aim and ambition of the Islamic movement. He said the Muslims of the world should come together and be united and stand behind their true sincere leaders and work for their prosperous future. The supreme leader said that jihad is an obligation upon all Muslims when their faith and their land is under threat and that they should participate in the jihad sincerely. He assured members of the visiting delegation that their concerns will be assessed and the Islamic movement will continue to serve the Muslims of Afghanistan and the world.

BEGINNING GOVERNMENT (1996–1998)

29

SPECIAL ANNOUNCEMENT OF AMIR UL-MU'MINEEN FOLLOWING THE TAKEOVER OF KABUL

[*This was one of the first formal orders Mullah Mohammad Omar issued following the fall of Kabul. It is interesting to note how practical the instructions are. There was no time for high-minded discussions of who the Taliban were or what they stood for. Rather, the concerns of the present moment reigned.*]

Shari'at, 28 September 1996

After destroying the roots of corruption and cruelty in the capital of beloved Afghanistan, Kabul, Amir ul-Mu'mineen Mullah Mohammad Omar Mujahed has released the following decree:

1. After this, a pure Islamic government will rule over Afghanistan.
2. All Afghan ambassadors in foreign countries are suspended and have no official authority. All foreign countries must protect Afghanistan's money and other properties and prevent ambassadors from making financial transactions.
3. All citizens of Kabul are asked not to evacuate their families from the city. Those who have evacuated the city should return to their homes because the Taliban will protect their life, property and honour.
4. Demining agencies must clear all routes leading to Kabul from mines and solve the problems for commuters to the city.
5. All national traders must start importing food items and fuel to Kabul city to prevent any problems for the residents of the city.

30

NEGATIVE RESPONSES TO THE ISLAMIC GOVERNMENT'S OBJECTIVES

[*From the moment the Taliban took Kabul, the amount and tenor of the criticism levelled at them took on a new dimension. As such, they were often reduced to a defensive position, trying to justify their existence in the face of withering international commentary. This article deals with the way the discussion around women's rights was part of this atmosphere.*]

Shari'at, 14 October 1996

The mujahedeen of the Islamic movement of the Taliban entered the historic city of Kabul on 27 September. First of all, an Islamic regime was announced, security was established and an amnesty was announced to all residents of capital. Those laws of the former administration which were in contradiction with Islamic values were abolished and the residents of Kabul were asked to obey all Islamic regulations. Women were asked to stay in their homes and those women who walked in the bazaars were required to wear the Islamic hijab. Also, it was announced that those women who worked for the former administration would receive their unpaid salaries at home.

All these achievements were achieved without any loss of life, property and honour of people. For the first time in years, the opportunity for the establishment of a pure Islamic regime and fulfilment of dreams of one and a half million Afghan martyrs was provided. The residents of Kabul performed prayers, gave alms to the poor and expressed their happiness about the collapse of the former regime under which their lives, properties and honour were not protected.

The infidels, above all the West, who are sworn enemies of Islam and Muslims and have not spared to plot to destroy Islam and defame Islamic movements started negative propaganda against the Islamic regime and attempted to give a false impression of Islam to the world. They try to show to the world that the Taliban are against human rights and women's rights, that we have banned women from working and education and consider these actions against human rights. They have launched such an extensive campaign against the Taliban that they have convinced people around the world that the Taliban are unique in their not respecting women's rights and that everything else is all right in the world. These un-Islamic propagations of the West are so intense that now a number of Muslims also unknowingly echo these claims.

The issue of women's rights under the Islamic government got so much attention because the Special Envoy of United Nations, Dr Norbert Holl, travelled to Kabul repeatedly and each time put the issue of women's rights as an important and key concern in discussions with officials of the Islamic government. He asked the Islamic government to lift bans on education and work for women and asked us to allow women to work and study jointly with men as in the previous regime.

These conditions are one hundred percent against Islamic principles and the values of Afghan society. Dr Norbert Holl was only concerned with these rights for women and stressed these issues as if he was the UN representative of women's affairs. All these efforts distorted reality, since he showed no concern about the lives of 25,000 widows who have lost their husbands during the civil war in Kabul. Dr Norbert Holl not only interprets the bans imposed by the Islamic government on women incorrectly but he also ignores other efforts of the Islamic regime for the empowerment of human rights. He has threatened that if Taliban don't lift the bans on women, the United Nations will stop all humanitarian aid projects in Afghanistan.

Before we analyse the nonsense spouted by Dr Holl regarding women's rights from a diplomatic point of view, it is important to explain the details of the Islamic government's limitations on women. The High Council of the Islamic Government has announced that the limitations on the education of women are imposed because of improper conditions in the country; once the conditions improve, necessary decisions regarding lifting of these bans will be taken.

In addition to that, the Taliban movement has announced their respect for all members of society including women and men. These decisions and restrictions by the Islamic government are not only in agreement with Islamic instructions but also indicate respect for rights of women and human rights. In the context of human rights, education of women is not considered as important as the protection of honour and the integrity of women. Also, there are many other issues such as security, peace and the elimination of corruption which are a higher priority than having education for women.

The Taliban have maintained security and the properties of individuals are protected. Now no one can steal the vehicles of the United Nations in territories under the Taliban's control, while it was the case before the takeover of Taliban. Dr Holl must understand that the Taliban have achieved what the United Nations and its partners and collaborators failed to achieve in Afghanistan. Is bringing peace and security to the country not considered to be the empowerment of human rights? Is the protection of society against corruption and immorality not considered a necessity? Is the protection of honour and dignity of women from the sleazy eyes of voyeurs not considered respect for human rights? Is the establishment of a strong government with the people's support an empowerment of international standards or is it breaking them?

The answer to all these questions is a resounding yes. We advise Dr Holl not to generalise and summarise everything under the rubric of 'education for women' and to ignore all other achievements. If Dr Holl is really concerned about the rights of women, he must advise his organisation to recognise the Islamic regime of the Taliban and cooperate in the construction of separate schools and educational centres according to Islamic principles for women and pave the way for the education of women.

The biased and irresponsible remarks of Dr Holl indicate that the UN is not concerned about the rights of women and only wants the Islamic movement to deviate from its key principles. The Islamic movement of the Taliban is decisive in its stance and will never compromise its Islamic principles due to threats. The United Nations must realise that as an independent and neutral organisation, it doesn't have the right to interfere in the implementation of Islamic and Afghan principles in our country, otherwise it would face a strong reaction from the Afghan people.

31

THE WAY OF DELIVERANCE

Q&A WITH MAWLAWI ABDUL ALI DEOBANDI

[Articles in the Taliban's newspapers often took the form of an interview. This source queries a prominent Deobandi scholar on a number of divergent topics, and the excerpt chosen relates to marriage in a non-Muslim country.]

Extract from a weekly religious advice column in a Taliban newspaper written by Mawlawi Ali Deobandi

Tolo-ye Afghan, 31 August 1997

Question: if a person wants to marry a woman, but he cannot find a witness or someone who will take them through the marriage ceremony, what is he to do?

Answer: What is he doing in such a country where there are no Muslims and no one to perform the wedding ceremony? Why did he go to such an unbelieving country? In marriage, a mullah must be brought who will, in front of others, loudly repeat Qur'anic verses and both sides must repeat the vow of marriage in the presence of witnesses. If a Muslim goes to America and wants to get married to an American and there are no Muslims to take part in their wedding ceremony, this Muslim man can marry the American woman and should explain to the woman what the wedding ceremony is about and then find two unbelievers. As this Muslim man and American woman go through the process of accepting one another, the man will say in front of the witnesses, 'I accept you as my wife,' and the wife returns the acceptance by accepting him as her husband. These are the words of the ceremony. He does not need a mullah, but the witnesses are necessary. The man has to give the gift to the woman that is specified.

A Muslim brother thus can marry an American or a girl from London. But if the woman is Russian or Japanese there is no legal marriage with these (as they are not people of the Book).

32

SPEECH BY MULLAH MOHAMMAD OMAR

[*This incomplete transcript of a meeting held by Mullah Mohammad Omar in Kandahar in 1997 offers a glimpse into the way he offered advice. His focus on the need to do things properly, on the need to serve without 'negligence and inattention', would become ever prominent in his public pronouncements as the years passed.*]

Tolo-ye Afghan, 14 December 1997

'The service of God and religion cannot be done with negligence and unwillingness. The Taliban are focused on the nation. They should separately pay attention to the poison of nationalism.'

The highly respected Amir ul-Mu'mineen

Amir ul-Mu'mineen received a number of commanders and government officials in his office. According to Bakhtar News Agency, the highly respected Amir ul-Mu'mineen, in his meeting with a number of commanders, made some astute comments to them:

'God's religious service cannot be done with negligence and inattention. Serving God Almighty one day with enthusiasm is better than anything else. The Taliban are the investment of the nation. Do not get involved in the poison of tribalism, and in this way you will be saving society from the sickness of this disease. The amount that people try to gain power is the amount that they debase themselves. The faces of the mujahedeen should be dazzling and their souls should be unblemished, not wanting anything to do with what is *haram*, and they should be avoiding illegitimacy.[1] Those who have slaves should look like a white-skinned person among the Ethiopians. One cannot trust life for one hour; we are seeing the caravans of the martyrs. We must turn to our intentions and ask God so that we can serve in a better way. Our name, our titles, our aim is huge, so it is necessary to improve our invalid past. And we should completely improve and annul it. Really the Muslims are on the brink of passing away. Or else what is new about applying the shari'a?'

137

33

THE GROUP

[Even in 1997, as this source shows, the Taliban seemed to be stuck in a cycle of need-ing to introduce themselves to the nation, over and over again. Not only did they feel they had to push back against criticism, but they sought to explain what they saw as the positive aspects to their movement. Sacrifice, for example, was considered to be of great value.]

Tolo-ye Afghan, 26 October 1997

Like many countrymen, I was unemployed. A Talib entered the room, and upon seeing him I realised that I knew him. He started talking to me and addressing me as 'Ustad'.[1] When I recognised him, for his bravery, I said, 'I am not worthy of the word Ustad.' This Talib was much younger than me. It was a good period of his life; he was young and must have had many wishes, like the wish to study, the wish for a good life, the wish to get engaged and be married. But he had put all that behind and he had come out to serve his religion and the country.

While talking to me, I grew to understand that someone was waiting for him or that something was on his mind. Later he told me, 'Let me tell you that my group is going to the front.' We said goodbye to one another and he set out. He left me as I said to myself: look at this youth; despite leaving everything behind, he is in a hurry to go. He has had a haircut and wears his clothes as if he is going for a picnic. He knows well that he is going to his death. Really, death for him is living. He knows that martyrdom in the way of God Almighty is perpetual life because of serving God and being of service to the people. To give your spirit is to gain a higher spirit; leaving behind family and friends is praying and he is earning pride for them. These people who are now happy for their group and who are going to the fighting line are not seeing it with the eye that they used to see it before; those places used to be called the war front, the battle grounds and such names. There, the people were troubled: they did things without considering the security implications or the oppressed and inno-cent human beings' honour or their property getting looted.

Now the group is a security organisation. The organisation is in love with the goal and remains loyal to it. Being part of the group means carrying out the order and giving your life to offer security for others. The war front is also a distance between what is legitimate and what is not, what security is and is not, and what is right and what is invalid. It is a line of the wishes of martyrs; it is the line of something that is correct. This line is the bloodied line against the jihad against the Communists—yes, the line that was hidden by civil wars and illegitimacy.

Today, with the sacrifice of the youth, that line is lit once again: the line of being ready to die for something. The group and the war front represent a great wish. It is true: when someone's wish is big, his personality will also be big in order to prepare for greater sacrifice.

Those humans before us have all gone. But those who turned their death into martyrdom—he who gave his life for the goal and whose blood was shed in a sacred way—their wishes are written on walls and in rivers, in graveyards and on the minarets and their names are forever written in gold. Every group can change a human into a hero.

34

ONLY THE ISLAMIC EMIRATE CAN BRING COUNTRY-WIDE PEACE

[*This op-ed article makes a case for why the Taliban are the best rulers for Afghanistan, asserting that they are the logical choice and not just the de facto choice (given their increasing territorial control).*]

Dari commentary

Tolo-ye Afghan, 9 October 1997

Recently some countries of the region and the world (through their media) have begun tricking and making deafening noises about the situation and affairs of our country. Through their media output they talk about the formation of an authority to their liking and a leadership (made up of this person or those persons of the present irresponsible groups who are just in-name) and presenting such information to their listeners. We say that the power that can bring country-wide peace in the country should have the following conditions:

1. The movement must be Islamic.
2. It should be able to apply the edicts of the Islamic shari'a.
3. It should have a capable Islamic army who can control the whole country.
4. An Islamic powerful army with sincerity, particularities, that is loyal to the people and to dear Islam.
5. Continuous Islamic attempts for the implementation of nationwide peace.
6. Continuous struggle for the great jihad and for thrashing the rebellious dissenters and the unbelieving forces.
7. In general, authoritative characteristics and total responsibility in its affairs for defending the country's independence, national sovereignty, territorial integrity and national honour vis-à-vis the rebellion of the dissenters and foreign occupiers and to stand against any kind of foreign conspiracy and plot.

Thus only the Islamic movement of the Taliban of Afghanistan, headed by the Islamic Emirate, has the above characteristics and is a certain power to bring country-

141

wide peace with the required courage and dedication to action. So in more than two-thirds of the country the shari'a of the Prophet (the peace and blessings of Allah be upon Him) is completely implemented.

Under the present conditions, when the country—from the point of view of politics—is in a stormy situation, leaving the issue of implementing peace to this or that group or party with their completely irresponsible forces and questionable dedication to the territory of Afghanistan, all this is something which is not comparable to the national tradition of Afghanistan nor to the tradition of Islam.

The Taliban Islamic movement of Afghanistan, with its power to implement the Islamic shari'a, is a certain force that implements peace and security in the country and is of the opinion that any attempt at solving the problems politically should be done by Afghans within our country and through Afghan dialogue. Most important of all is that the decision should be within the framework of Islamic shari'a. Otherwise any other political and military problems will be against the wishes of the Afghan people and will face obliteration and total shame. Bringing about such a political make-up by others will fail from the start and will be defeated, God willing.

35

OPENING A LIBRARY FOR JIHADI RELICS

[Considerable care was taken to construct a narrative of history in which the 1980s jihad was connected to the present-day struggles. In this way, the Taliban saw themselves as part of a longer trajectory. (We can, of course, trace this back—as many did—all the way to the example of the Prophet Muhammad). This source shows the ways that jihad was brought into the centre of their self-conception, with the construction of a museum to preserve documents and artefacts of the 1980s conflict and, presumably, that of the present day.]

Tolo-ye Afghan, 9 March 1997

A library of relics from the time of jihad was opened next to a public library in a special ceremony. Bakhtar News Agency reports that the ceremony was organised for this library. The librarian, those interested in books and some intellectuals, workers and a number of journalists took part. At the start of the ceremony some verses from the holy Qur'an were recited and after that the Chief Justice of the Islamic government of Afghanistan and the acting deputy for the high court, respected Mawlawi Jalilullah Mawlawizadah, was there to open the library by cutting the ribbon.

He spoke about the need for such libraries and for the collection of relics from the time of jihad. He thanked those who have put together these artefacts and asked those responsible for this library to do their best to maintain and preserve these objects. After that, Mawlawi Zakiullah Ashrafi, the head of the public library, respected Mawlawi Rahimullah Zurmati, the publication deputy of the Ministry of Information and Culture, and respected Al-Haj Mawlawi Abdurrahman Ahmad Hotaki, deputy of finance and administration in the Ministry of Culture and Information and responsible for publishing the weekly *Shariat* newspaper, all of them in turn spoke about this library and the value of such artefacts.

They said this library should be extended to house more such relics. They said the collection of such items was a service to the true Islamic culture and regarded the idea of such a library as a valuable step. They asked the writers, intellectuals and the

Muslim people of Afghanistan to send any printed books, magazines and newspapers, their annual collections—all of which represent the time of jihad—to this library in order to make this library fuller and more valuable.

The ceremony ended with a prayer for the implementation of the aims of the Islamic government of Afghanistan, the strengthening of peace and for the progress of genuine Islamic culture. This library, in addition to newspapers and magazines, has 60,000 relics from the time of jihad which are ready for those interested to come and browse through.

36

GREAT AND HISTORIC POETRY-READING CONTEST HELD AS AN INITIATIVE OF *SHARIAT WEEKLY*

[*Poetry and song (in a particular context) were very important to the Taliban, from senior leadership down to the lower ranks. If we can talk about a cultural legacy that the Taliban were part of, this was a significant aspect. Contests and grand gatherings were a long-standing feature of Afghan society, so there wasn't anything particularly path-breaking in the Taliban's version of these traditions. Rather, it is instructive to read how they sought to sew the binding energy of this literature into the fabric of the movement.*]

Shariat, 27 March 1997

An honourable poetry-reading contest was held in the Intercontinental Hotel on 8 March 1997 by *Shariat Weekly* on the occasion of spring's arrival and given the provision of security in the country. The *Shariat Weekly* reporter reported that the contest began at nine o'clock in the morning and several ministers, heads of governmental offices, clerics, poets, people of literature and journalists attended.

The contest began with recitation of few verses of the great Qur'an by Qari Fazlur Rahman Saraji. After that, the Deputy Minister of Culture and Information and administrative and financial affairs and Director of *Shariat Weekly*, Al-Haj Mawlawi Abdurrahman Hotaki, welcomed the guests and said in his speech that before everything else he would pray for the spirits of the martyrs of the incident in Jalalabad and asked Allah to grant patience to the families of the victims. Respected Hotak said that when the Taliban laid down their books in the madrassas and put their pens in their pockets to ensure an Islamic system, the territorial integrity, political and national sovereignty of their homeland, they not only kept the trenches of jihad hot with their blood and sacrifices, but also rolled up their sleeves for the cultural construction of the country. In a very short time, they have provided a lot of services in this regard.

After that, the message of the head of the Supervisory Council of the Islamic government of Afghanistan, respected Al-Haj Mullah Mohammad Rabbani, was read to the participants by the director of Radio, Television and Afghan Film: Mullah Mohammad Eshaq Nizami. In one part of the message, it said, 'Dear respected brothers, you know that literature is a crucial part of intellectual culture, and nations and ethnic groups are known by their culture and literature, but it is beautified with beautiful literature and culture.'

After that, respected Qari Noor ul-Haq recited a few verses of the Qur'an and prayers were offered for the martyrs of the Nangarhar incident. The report adds that respected poets then presented their poems reflecting their messages about their love of the Lord's shari'a, presenting images of security in the country and the season of spring flowers.

37

HISTORIC POETRY-READING CONTEST
OF *SHARIAT WEEKLY*

A GREAT EXAMPLE OF THE ISLAMIC MOVEMENT'S
PROMOTION OF POETRY AND LITERATURE

[This op-ed makes the point that poetry is part of Afghanistan's national wealth and heritage. It refutes (as speakers at the conference seemed to have done) the criticism that the Taliban are a movement without culture.]

Shariat, 27 March 1997

Our suffering nation has experienced so much pain in all aspects of its life over almost two decades at the hands of the Communists and their masters, unprecedented in recent history. Russians and their puppets not only were after the underground wealth our country's mines, but also were trying to remove Islamic belief and culture from our minds; many of the Muslim believers and cultural people who opposed their false beliefs were put in the hell-like prison of Pul-e Charkhi. It was as a result of the Communists' brutality and terror that many of our powerful writers and poets were forced to migrate from their homeland and live wandering across foreign countries, due to their hatred of the Communist regime and their uncompromising actions.

Also, the other oppression that the past regime had against our nation is that they spread ethnic, linguistic and regional discrimination against our cultural people and people of literature as well. Some of our writers—instead of carrying out their Islamic mission and serving their nation with their pen and thus working for their culture and literature—committed themselves to writing propaganda against their brothers, their tribe, language or region and wrote such things that never look good with the holiness of the pen.

Now that the flag of the Islamic system flies in Kabul, thanks be to God, and the bloody colour of millions of our martyrs, widows, orphans and handicapped shines, the Islamic government that feels responsibility for all justified demands of the nation is trying to serve the oppressed nation sincerely and rescue them from this darkness and fatal condition. In addition to other aspects of life, they have started tireless efforts to rebuild our culture.

The scientific seminar on 4–5 March 1997, and the great and beautiful poetry-reading event on 8 March 1997, held as an initiative of *Shariat Weekly*, are good examples of these efforts. The pages of our cultural history are full of poetry-reading events anyway, but such a poetry-reading event where our people could participate free of differences based on colour, language, region, tribe has not been seen, even occasionally.

This poetry-reading event joined those hearts and minds that were distant from each other and inspired national unity against the foreigners who were the enemies of our faith, culture and soil. Also, this poetry-reading event and other cultural activities of the Islamic government totally belied the accusations that had been levelled against the Islamic movement through propaganda. The poetry-reading event showed that the Taliban not only value cultural activities, but that they are also representatives of Islamic culture, and that they would make efforts in this regard more than anybody else.

We had many poets and writers who were disappointed by tough conditions in the past and the obstructive actions of past regimes. This poetry-reading event spread the spring's tulip pink colour on the dry lips of those poets. Also, many hidden talents became known. This poetry-reading event showed some of the poets—those who clung on to the butterfly, flower, pine trees and nightingale, candle and butterfly and some old historic phrases—that the situation has changed now. We are in the midst of a revolution and Afghanistan faces streams of blood; we do not have anyone in our society who has not been harmed.

Therefore, it was necessary that our poets used their talent in the service of their religion and nation and that they stood up to their Islamic and human mission. They should reflect the unfulfilled wishes of the martyrs, the sighs of widows and the cries of orphans in their poems. Today's poets should move their minds away from natural views, mountain bottoms, river sides and imaginary flying and paint a picture of their nation's pain and the ruined country in their poems, as well as introduce the traitors of religion and the homeland to our people. If they do so, the Islamic government will extend their encouragement of culture towards them.

38

MESSAGE OF THE HEAD OF THE SUPERVISORY COUNCIL TO PARTICIPANTS OF THE POETRY-READING CONTEST

[Mullah Mohammad Rabbani's message to the conference (read out on his behalf) continues the theme of literature being a key aspect of a nation's culture and heritage and that the pen is a way of joining on the path of 'jihad, martyrdom and sacrifice, heroism and bravery'.]

Shariat, 27 March 1997

All praise be to Allah. Dear respected knowledgeable people, grammar specialists, writers and mujahedeen: *al-salaamu 'aleikum*. We are grateful to Allah, who with his mercy and blessings brought light to the eyes of our Muslim, heroic nation for the sake of the sacrifices of our current and former sincere and heroic mujahedeen. Life has started in their bodies with the new spring once again, and they are committed to rebuilding their destroyed homeland. They have rolled up their sleeves and have started moving towards their destination.

We are grateful to God that our lovers of literature and culture are making a large gathering and poetry-reading contest on this occasion. This is a constructive and fortunate beginning. On the one hand, it reinforces our dying culture and literature; on the other hand, it increases the commitment of our nation. Such actions encourage our brothers who have migrated to work on rebuilding the homeland. In addition, they inspire our political mujahedeen brothers who are chasing the corrupt, bandit groups when they see movements towards the building of the country. This is proof of the revived security around the country, because it shows that there are knowledgeable people who make use of their sacrifices for the good of Islam and our homeland. Our zealous brothers!

You know that literature is a large part of intellectual culture; nations and peoples are known by their literature and culture, but beauty is added to it through art and fine culture. Islamic culture is richer and finer than the rest of the cultures in the

149

world, and it has endured through several centuries. This is especially true of our Afghan Islamic culture, which has kept its fine features even though it has received many blows from enemies.

Our enemies—who wanted to ruin everything we had—had hoped to destroy our culture and literature as well, but great God had not intended it to be so and paved the way for the language of your pen once again, so that you would not just rebuild and make it shine, but completely turn it towards the beautiful path of Islam and Islamic shari'a. With the beginning of the Islamic jihad in Afghanistan, poetry, writing, connection, separation, competitors and strangers have changed the forms, and mujahedeen poets are separate from that process now. They are following the path of Islam and jihad, martyrdom and sacrifice, heroism and bravery.

Sincerely wishing you success, reconstruction of our country and prosperity for the Islamic nation: your brother,

Mullah Mohammad Rabbani

39

THE RESOLUTION OF THE FRONTIER TRIBAL-WIDE JIRGA

[*This resolution was issued in part to satisfy the senior leadership's desire for international recognition (in whatever shape) and also as a result of their ongoing discussions with tribal elders across the border in Pakistan. The Taliban sought both to court this tribal order as well as to supersede it, at least in Afghanistan. They realised that the tribal system was part of the fabric of society, but they also aspired to a system that rose above: the Islamic shari'a, as they conceived it.*]

Tolo-ye Afghan, 29 October 1997

1. All tribes consider the Islamic Emirate of Afghanistan as the culmination of the past eighteen years of holy jihad and as a government that is in accordance with all international principles.
2. All the tribes in one voice call on all Islamic and non-Islamic countries to officially recognise the Taliban's Islamic government.
3. In an Islamic government where Islamic shari'a is the law of the land, a murderer is hanged for his actions and a thief's hand is cut. Those caught in fornication are stoned, the shari'a hijab is asked for, and there are separations between men and unrelated women and such like. The ulemaa and tribal leaders and elders strongly support such a government and its holy shari'a system.
4. Any who oppose the Islamic government—in the light of Islamic principles—are called rebels. Therefore, anyone who in the tribal area makes any programmes against the Islamic Emirate of Afghanistan will face the opposition of the Free Tribes and we will make them leave the area.
5. The tribal jirga in Afghanistan condemns any kind of illegitimate interference in Afghanistan's internal affairs, and calls upon the interferers to stop their illegitimate interferences very quickly.
6. The Free Tribes consider Afghanistan as their second home and will defend the borders of their home with all their power.

7. The representative of the eight agencies' ulemaa and tribal leaders are asking the leaders of the Taliban of the Islamic Emirate never to bring any change to their present shari'a system because of any foreign interference and to stand firm with their present policy.

40

YOUR LETTERS, OUR RESPONSES

[*The question-and-answer format of the letters page is always an interesting opportunity to read some of the day-to-day concerns of citizens. This source contains three disparate comments. In the first, a woman questions (with pure logic as well as Islamic reasoning) the way the hijab and burqa are imposed on citizens. The second (written by a mullah) calls on readers to take advantage of the beneficial situation that the Taliban have brought. In the third, a university student complains about the bakers' neglect of hygiene.*]

Shariat, 6 March 1997

1st LETTER: Dear respected employees of *Shariat Weekly*, may God grant you success in your daily tasks. Dear brothers, you would definitely agree with us that during the time of the Russians and Communists, Afghan sisters took part in jihad beside their hero brothers and they have gone through hard times like their mujahedeen brothers because of the Communists. Since then, Rabbani's time was not any better for them. When the Islamic movement of Taliban was established and prevented insecurity, oppression, prostitution, looting, theft and other illegitimate actions, God is witness to the fact that we became so very happy after hearing this good news. We prayed each moment for the Taliban's arrival in Kabul to end the ongoing savagery. All praise be to Allah, that moment for which we were praying has arrived. Now that Kabul is under control of the Islamic movement of Taliban, shari'a is enforced, prostitution is prohibited and sisters have gained their Islamic position, I can say that Taliban brothers brought us great respect and honour. They freed us from oppression and savagery. The truth is that in the past, everybody's life, property and honour were at risk. I should also add that enforcement of the Islamic shari'a is the duty of the Islamic movement of the Taliban and covering the sisters in hijab is part of it as well.[1] Not observing the hijab is an instance of 'vice' and the Taliban have a duty to prevent any vice from happening. However, we would like to remind our brothers in the Taliban that many corrupt and bad systems have ruled here and have affected the minds of our citizens in Kabul. Therefore, if the Taliban used advice, philosophy and some flexibility, it would have better results. We admit that each new process has natural shortcomings; we are praying that God will resolve our shortcomings. All praise be to Allah, we are all Muslims; our ancestors were Muslims and we have sacrificed our heads for our honour and chastity. Nahida, who jumped from the fourth floor of Macrorayan, sacrificed herself just for her honour, and we are Afghans, whose example of zeal and modesty is unprecedented around the world. Therefore, the hijab and covering ourselves is dear to us just like our faith. We understand that Islam has ordered us to observe hijab, but it has not specified the use of a special design or white, black or green colour like the Afghan burka or Arab and Iranian hijabs. The purpose is to observe the hijab fully and we have the option to choose the method of cloth to cover our entire body. Are the black veils that we use *haram*? The colourful burkas are even worse and call attention to themselves. Meanwhile, we all know that Afghans face financial difficulties in general and the Afghan burkas are very expensive. Even the cheapest burka is 300,000 Afghanis, so how can we afford this? We hope that our respected clerics would explain the Islamic responsibilities in this regard. Also, using philosophy, mercy and kindness while presenting Islamic advice are considered important principles. Respected brothers, the Taliban should observe the principle of philosophy and mercy while implementing this duty on the sisters. The Messenger of Allah has said about this: 'Ease up and do not be tough on people. Give good news to people and don't make them flee.' These actions will increase hatred in our sisters' hearts. It has also been seen that some people who are not related to any official authorities beat up women and threaten them. Those who are aware of Afghan culture and traditions understand what consequences beating up somebody's woman and honour can have in the Afghan community. To this end, I would like to remind my Taliban brothers that I am not opposing hijab and, God forbid, I am not a follower of any other thoughts either. My only desire and demand is that the path of philosophy, advice and ease should be chosen. Your sister, Hosna

RESPONSE: Dear sister Hosna, Please accept our good wishes as well. We have published your letter and hope that it will draw the attention of the relevant authorities of the Islamic government of Afghanistan, and that the Islamic Government Centre for Fatwas will respond to your query.

2nd LETTER: Dear countrymen, it is obvious that whatever the Taliban of the right path say, they implement it in action. They are not like those oppressing elements who would say one thing and do another. In other words, [those who] show that they are talking about the Qur'an and words of the Prophet, but in their actions they take advantage of those words for their personal interests. They explain the Qur'an and words of the Prophet to the public, but use it as a screen to cover their awkward actions. The Taliban of the Islamic movement promise our people that they will fulfil all the wishes and demands of this war-shattered nation in accordance with the shari'a, that they will take care of our widows, that they will wipe the tears of our orphans and that they will appreciate and value the blood of our martyrs whom history will never forget. Every single citizen of this homeland now values and appreciates the sacrifices of the Taliban and even those opposed to the Islamic government like Rabbani, Hekmatyar, Dostum and Khalili admit the fact that this is a movement of true Islam. A representative of Hekmatyar's *Hezb-e Islami* in Pakistan stated that: 'Yes, we and our leaders now believe that the Taliban movement is in fact a holy movement; however, we used to say that it was created by Pakistani intelligence; we did not find any evidence to show that ISI helped this movement. Now that an Islamic government is established by the Taliban, Pakistan recognises it officially. We also said that this was a programme of the Americans, and once the Taliban captured Kabul, they were going to bring Zahir Shah back to power. When the Taliban captured Kabul, none of these things happened; therefore, we now believe in the holiness of the Islamic movement of Taliban, but we engaged in war against them for personal issues. We are also sure that we cannot win on the battlefield, but we are under pressure from foreign governments who say that we need to fight.'

The Islamic government would like to inform all those who are opposed to it to give up unnecessary vice and surrender their weapons to the Islamic government and benefit from Amir ul-Mu'mineen's general amnesty decree. They should take advantage of this opportunity. If not, the past has shown what the consequences will be. At that time, they will not be able to do anything. Respectfully, Mullah Abdul Qayyum Atef

RESPONSE: Dear brother Mullah Abdul Qayyum Atef, We have published parts of your long letter and hope that you will be happy with it. Please keep up your cooperation with us.

3rd LETTER: To *Shariat Weekly* office, Hello to you all. I hope that you will publish my letter in your honourable publication. As we note in Kabul city, most of the employees of bakeries do not make ablutions or wash their hands in the early morning before starting their work. Therefore, the blessings and goodness go away from the bread. Today, now that Mohammadi shari'a is enforced over three-quarters of the country, we would like to ask the authorities of the Department of the Promotion of Virtue and the Prevention of Vice to follow up on this issue and pay special attention to negligence by the bakers so that they would perform their religious duties on one hand and observe cleanliness in serving their countrymen as they should. Respectfully, Ahmad Shah Ramez, Student at the Language & Literature faculty of Kabul Pedagogy Institute

RESPONSE: Dear brother Ahmad Shah Ramez, Here we have published your letter hoping that the relevant authorities will read it. We look forward to having your cooperation in the future as well.

41

THE MARTYRS ARE HERE

[*This is a rare instance of a poem written by a woman being included as part of the corpus of published poetry in a prominent newspaper. Hanifa Zahed writes of the clash between Communists and atheists on the one hand and the 'followers of the holy Qur'an' on the other.*]

Hanifa Zahed

Tolo-ye Afghan, 9 October 1997

Come to the Polygon area, the martyrs are here
   our dears who disappeared are here

The Communist savagery brought their skulls
   O Afghan, your innocents that bring your heartache are here

Those who suffered the cruelty of imprisonment
   our famous leaders of the Caravan are here

These are a memorial to the Russians, Khalqi and Parchami
   buried alive are Charkhi prisoners here

When heaven would tremble with the clanging of their handcuffs
   the followers of the holy Qur'an are here

O human rights of the world, watch attentively
   come and see those who devoted themselves to the shari'a here

Their clean consciences couldn't accept atheist laws
   humans who devoted themselves to their holy abode are here

The nation that kept this investment of the country
   the ulamaa of the madrasas, universities are here

They kept the mysteries of righteousness in others' hearts
   those who had colonialism in their throats are here

Revenge will be taken from the enemy by the righteous youth
  those Afghans over whose bodies wheels were run

Zaheda, why are you bringing out these pains from your heart?
  These are the spoiled guests of God Almighty who are here

42

ON BECOMING THE 'ISLAMIC EMIRATE'

[*This transcript of an interview between Mutawakil and a BBC correspondent reveals the extent to which many larger decisions about the political direction of the country were unclear or the product of improvisation. The name of the country changed from republic to Emirate, yet the precise contours of what that meant were still not defined.*]

Tolo-ye Afghan, 29 October 1997

In connection with this change, the BBC correspondent had a phone interview with the adviser and secretary to the Islamic Emirate of Afghanistan, respected Wakil Ahmad Mutawakil, on 27 October 1997, and we present the text of that interview.

Q: Respected Mawlawi Saheb, why has the 'Islamic Nation of Afghanistan' become the 'Islamic Emirate of Afghanistan'?
A: There is nothing new here. During our previous history such names were also adopted and were forcefully applied.

Q: Can you say which authority made such a decision? Was it done on the basis of an order from Amir ul-Mu'mineen, or was it adopted by some gathering of the ulemaa?
A: Before it become official, an announcement was issued to the esteemed ulemaa and high officials of the government and it was in consultation with them that the decision was made and then a decree about the change was circulated.

Q: Don't you think a greater authority is needed for such a change, like consulting with the people or calling for a bigger meeting (Loya Jirga)?
A: The name of Afghanistan has not been changed. Instead of the Islamic nation of Afghanistan, the word Islamic 'Emirate' of Afghanistan has been substituted. I said earlier that in the history of Afghanistan such name changes have happened and most rulers were called 'Amir'. In this short time of our lives we have seen Afghanistan has been sometimes called the Republic and other times different names. The word for Nation is an Islamic word, [but] the word that is closer to the name of Amir ul-Mu'mineen is the word 'Emirate'.

Q: What will be the political consequences of this? Does it mean that in the future there will be no elections or parties?

A: The future of Afghanistan is in front of the people and the people's vote will be used. There is no doubt about this. But I can say in clear terms that all future changes will have a connection with the sweet and sacred religion of Islam. If you do some research on the history of Afghanistan, you will find many examples of it.

Q: Mawlawi Saheb, does changing the name of Afghanistan into Emirate not mean that in the future only the orders and edicts of the Amir ul-Mu'mineen will be implemented? It will not be a government where the views of all the people will be required and will have a constitution.

A: Yes, it will be like that. Everyone's actions will be assessed according to shari'a and then the Amir ul-Mu'mineen will be issuing his orders. The orders of the Amir ul-Mu'mineen will be in accordance with the wishes of the people. This, however, does not mean that the orders that will be given will be contrary to the wishes of the people.

Q: How will the people's votes or wishes to be taken into consideration?

A: This is not a difficult issue. Before, we had different departments and organs to run the government and they had their shuras. There are educated persons and ulemaa who are present in Afghanistan. There are also many other ways to solve such issues.

43

INTERVIEW WITH MULLAH MOHAMMAD OMAR

[*This excerpt of an interview with the Taliban leader continues the theme of uncertainty about the specifics of policy combined with a strident certainty as to the correctness of the overall approach. If something is currently unsatisfactory, he says, that's not to say that they don't wish it otherwise or that they're making efforts to correct the problem. On the question of the political system under which the country will be administered, his comments leave the door open for some of the opposition groups to surrender and be absorbed into the movement.*]

Shariat, 30 April 1997

Question: Regional countries, especially our northern neighbours, are concerned about the victories of the Islamic movement of the Taliban and see the military advancements of the Islamic government as a threat to them. What is your Excellency's response to them?

Response: When the objectives of jihad and the wishes of the martyrs were not fulfilled following the victory of jihad in Afghanistan, and the jihad's objectives were betrayed on a daily basis, the Islamic movement of the Taliban emerged as the result of an Islamic and national uprising in order to fulfil the objectives of jihad and rescue our beloved country from destruction. Therefore, our movement rests firmly on the principles of Islam. Islam is not a threat to anybody. Concerns and anxiety that our northern semi-independent neighbours show are the result of provocation by our old and defeated enemy (Russia). They are scaring their puppet governments so that the Russians would be able to pave the way for their presence in Asian Muslim countries. If that is not the case, Turkmenistan is our neighbouring country as well, so why do they not consider our victories as a threat? With regard to Iran, I would like to say that we have always looked at them as a Muslim brother neighbour, but we do not understand why they have chosen a hostile policy against us. They support our opposition. I would like to say in a few words that there is no threat posed to anybody from our side and there is no reason to be concerned.

161

[...]

Question: Following the decision of the Islamic government's administrative council, several government employees have been laid off. Since they are the intellectual wealth of our country, what is your decision about their future?

Response: Due to the erroneous policies of past regimes, many unnecessary offices and positions were created. These unnecessary offices required expenses. For some work, several ministries were created—for example, the Ministry of Public Profits, Ministry of Rural Rehabilitation and Development and the Ministry of Urban Development—while the Ministry of Public Profit can do the work of all these ministries on its own. Therefore, in order to resolve such big and only-on-paper inflation, it was deemed necessary to bring some reforms. Still, very few employees should have been laid off, because the offices that were eliminated existed only in name, but did not have an actual physical existence. Still, if some employees have been dismissed, we are working on ways to provide them with job opportunities. The first thing is to launch projects where such employees could work. Thousands of our countrymen will be able to work on the pipeline extension project from Turkmenistan through Afghanistan. Meanwhile, there is a need for government employees in the provinces; therefore, they could be assigned to the provinces. We will not fail to take all efforts to find them so that they can be assigned there.

Question: The salaries of government employees are very low compared to what is needed for daily expenses. Have you instructed the Islamic government to solve the problems of these employees by increasing their salaries, or found some other way?

Response: All our countrymen know that due to the destruction caused by war, our economic system and currency's value have been seriously damaged and have brought about these problems. We are trying our best to solve the problems of all our people, especially government employees. Although the government's economy is very weak, we have doubled the food allocation for the government's employees in order to decrease their problems to some extent. In this series, we have distributed food to them in many provinces. Also, we have helped many of our poor people in the capital through the Red Crescent Society. We are going to work further to solve the problems of government employees, but we need some time. Once God helps us to finish the war, the rest of will be easy afterwards.

Question: Our country's educational institutions—especially Kabul University—has many problems and fewer than 50 per cent of university students can afford to continue their education. What is your opinion about the extensive campaign to draw on the assistance of foreign Islamic countries in order to solve the problems that exist in our universities? And what measures have you undertaken to solve this problem?

Response: We have given special instruction to the Ministry of Higher Education on this matter, to begin working on solving the problems of educational institutions; we have sent delegations to the universities of the Islamic world and other countries in order to seek their assistance. We will not shy away from any assistance we can provide. Herat University is operational; for Kandahar University, we have approved another faculty of agriculture in addition to the faculty of medicine. We have started Nangarhar Medical School, and Kabul University as well just resumed its operations. We are going to continue our efforts in this regard, because the university is our intellectual wealth and the main hub of our country's development, so we will never forget about it.

Question: Women's education seems necessary in some of the branches in order to solve the daily problems of Muslim women. What is your opinion about providing a shari'a-based educational system for women as soon as possible, and what is your decision in this regard?

Response: The holy religion of Islam has valued knowledge more than any other religion. Also, learning shari'a knowledge has been mandated for male and female Muslims. However, since our country is currently in a state of emergency and war, and given that our economy is very weak, too, therefore we have some problems in the field of education. But once these problems are solved and the Islamic system is ensured across the whole of Afghanistan, all these things will be done.

[...]

Question: During the past regimes, especially during Rabbani's time, many public properties were distributed to some people for political considerations. What is your view about this matter, and what is your decision about this going forward?

Response: The physical wealth of Afghanistan—including forests, land, mines and transportation means and other government-related equipment and tools—are considered public property. Also, weapons and military equipment are part of this public property. That is why the Islamic government is collecting weapons as well as returning the rest of the public properties all over the country. After collection, they are kept in safe places. In addition, anything that is given to anybody from the public property is illegal and in violation of the shari'a principle. It will be taken back from them and returned as public property to the government treasury. We pay special attention to protecting the government treasury and we have even prohibited the cutting of forests in this regard. We have prevented anybody's transgression against the public wealth very strictly.

Question: What is your view about the participation of jihadi parties in political power and struggles in the future, similar to political parties that compete to gain political power in other countries?

Response: Political groups are formed based on tribal, linguistic, regional and some other false prejudices, and they cause disunity and hostility in the country. Such groups that bring about disunity do not have any place in Islam. In the Islamic system, all Muslims are brothers of one another and all of them are equal before the law; they have equal rights and responsibilities. The Islamic government's and the Islamic movement's bosom is open to all sincere believers. It was as a result of disunity between these jihadi parties that civil war broke out after the Islamic revolution and Muslims fought with each other and ruined the country. If they were in one group, had one plan and platform, we would never have seen this destruction. Sincere and true mujahedeen from the jihadi parties still make up a major part of the Islamic government. Others can also come and stand beside us in one line and serve Islam, the country and our Muslim countrymen sincerely. This verse of the Qur'an is enough to make a life based on Islamic principles: 'If you fought over something, refer to Allah [his book] and his messenger [his hadith].'

[...]

Question: In the end, if you have any message for our countrymen, please go ahead and present your message. We wish you a long life and further success in the path of serving the truth.

Response: My message to our countrymen, wherever they are, is to start correcting their own and their family's beliefs and actions. Their words, external and internal behaviour should be in compliance with Islam. In addition, they should take part in the correction of their communities and people in their communities. They should stand beside their Islamic government sincerely and fulfil their Islamic and national responsibility in the enforcement of a shari'a-based system and the reconstruction of the country. They are all like my head and eyes. No one can violate their rights in any way. No matter who the person they have complained about is, even a minister, the courts will hear them and will make a just decision. God willing, from now on all Afghans will share in every aspect of this country and no one will be deprived of any of their shari'a rights. In the end, I ask Allah to grant everybody the strength to serve on the path of Islam honestly.

44

THE MINISTRY FOR THE PROMOTION OF VIRTUE AND THE PREVENTION OF VICE

[*Akbar Agha once again brings a certain amount of criticism to bear against the activities of the group that was to many emblematic, al-Amr bil Ma'rouf wa al-Nahi 'an al-Munkar ('commanding right and forbidding wrong'), which was promoted to the level of a ministry in early 1996. The ministry operated outside the control of the main council of ministers in Kabul and answered only to Mullah Mohammad Omar. This gave it the flexibility to tackle the wide range of tasks allocated to it, though it also meant that it was largely unaccountable. While the Taliban movement struggled with the precise way to implement the instruction to 'command right and forbid wrong', all those involved in the government note that it was an important duty and a key part of how they envisioned their role in society. In this way, we can see the tension between the practicalities of rule and their ideological agenda. Finding a balance between these two would occupy the leadership until the very end. This excerpt echoes complaints and gentle suggestions from other Afghan sources at the time.*]

Excerpt from I Am Akbar Agha *by Sayyed Mohammad Akbar Agha, 2014*

The Ministry for the Promotion of Virtue and the Prevention of Vice has recently come under a lot of criticism. The minster of this administration was one of my mujahedeen during the jihad period. His virtue and fear of God were known to me and he was a knowledgeable person. His name was Mawlawi Mohammad Wali and he was from Siachoy village of Panjwayi district of Kandahar province. He was martyred in the bombings. Two of his brothers were martyred in the war against the Russians on our front.

There are a few reasons for the criticisms of the Ministry for the Promotion of Virtue and the Prevention of Vice. There were some negative points, but also some positive things. This kind of institution was not new in the Islamic world: it has been active in Arab-speaking countries for a long time. But it was new in Afghanistan, and had strict rules, which seemed to be difficult for Afghans to follow.

The minister was also not especially professional, starting slowly and introducing things gradually until people became used to the new rules. An indication of his unprofessionalism was that he set up *pataks* for prayers and would make everyone pray regardless of whether they were sick or hadn't even done their ablutions. Many people (including myself) told him that they should perform their duties like the Saudis do, only asking the shopkeepers to shut their shops during prayer time and guiding people to perform their prayers. Other people in the city usually had to work with the shopkeepers, and when the shops were closed they would come and perform the prayers.

In some provinces, uneducated people were assigned to this administration. Most of the things that the Ministry for the Promotion of Virtue and the Prevention of Vice implemented were necessary, but they should have been introduced gradually. Anyway, the ministry was good from an Islamic perspective and Muslims need it, and there is no question about whether it should have existed in the first place as some people have said.

45

ALL OF OUR EFFORTS ARE FOR THE PROMOTION OF VIRTUE AND THE PREVENTION OF VICE

[*This interview with a senior figure within the Amr bil Marouf at the time was pub-lished in Sangar newspaper (the outlet of the Ministry of Defence). Qari Abdul Wadood outlines why he sees the Amr bil Marouf group as necessarily being at the core of the Taliban's agenda. Note that the injunction 'to promote virtue and prevent vice' has a strong and clear eminence in the Islamic tradition (particularly stressed in the Qur'an and subsequently in the hadith literature). It was not a Taliban innovation to raise it to this centrality.*]

Sangar, 7 September 1998

It is a fact that one of the main objectives behind starting the Taliban movement was the implementation of the Qur'anic system in society and the transformation of all aspects of our social life to be in accordance with the supreme shari'a laws of the Prophet. In other words, the purpose of the Islamic movement was the promotion of virtue and the prevention of vice. Fortunately, the Taliban Islamic movement has taken considerable measures for the realisation of these objectives and so far has achieved great successes. These views were expressed by Qari Abdul Wadood, the head of the investigation and supervision branch of the Ministry of Vice and Virtue during an interview.

He noted that: 'After its excellent performance and the special attention of His Excellency Amir ul-Mu'mineen, the department of Vice and Virtue evolved and became a ministry. From the very beginning, the Islamic Emirate utilised very effec-tive methods of work. Tremendous efforts were made to remove all those bad things from our society which were made common by the regimes of the past. Instead, we tried to strengthen the moral foundations of society and synthesise the life of our people in accordance with the principles of the Islamic shari'a laws of the Prophet Muhammad. Luckily, the faithful people of Afghanistan have worked fully with us in the implementation of these principles, because they have waged jihad at a cost of one and a half million martyrs and many other sacrifices for the sake of the realisation of their ideals. After their effective participation and full coordination, we are successful in our mission. The faithful people of our country are witness to the fact that due to the striking and brilliant achievements of the Islamic Emirate, now our society is advancing towards a complete and exemplary Islamic system.'

Regarding the order of the Amir ul-Mu'mineen about the regularity of prayers, respected Qari Abdul Wadood said: 'Prayer is one of the main pillars of religion. It is necessary for the faithful to offer it on time and regularly in order to achieve the rewards in this world and the world hereafter. It was because of this reason that the Amir ul-Mu'mineen issued the special order in this regard. First of all, we sent our representatives and taskforces to explain the importance of this order to all departments, ministries, organisations, local residential areas, mosques and common people. We gave various tasks and responsibilities to the imams of the mosques. Fortunately this programme has been successfully implemented. With the help of the special delegates and imams, the people are now in the process of learning the proper way of prayers.'

About those persons who just use the name of the Vice and Virtue Ministry and cause trouble for the people, he said: 'We will never allow anyone to cause any kind of trouble and torture to our faithful people. Our investigation and supervision officials keep a close eye on the performance of all staff members and don't let them violate the rules. We want to implement the principles of the Islamic shari'a. We will not allow anyone to violate these principles. However, on some occasions it has happened that some opportunists have abused the name of the Vice and Virtue department and have caused trouble and problems for the people. We have issued special announcements and taken various effective measures for the exposure of this kind of people.'

46

MULLAH MOHAMMAD OMAR AND THE APPLE

[*The Taliban's newspapers were fond of including educational or morally instructive stories among their pages. This tale emphasises the rewards of abnegation and the benefits that will accrue in the hereafter. This is a prominent theme in the way the Taliban saw the world.*]

Shariat, 2 November 1998

There is an account of Omar's bravery telling how he never gave into greed.[1] Instead, he strived with utmost bravery to revive the kingdom of the Rashidun Caliphate which existed almost a century ago. There is a story that one day fruit bought from the public funds was being distributed among the needy. Omar's son grabbed one of the apples and started eating it. When the Amir ul-Mu'mineen saw his child, he suddenly snatched the fruit from his son with a force that hurt the child's hand as a result. His son started crying and went to see his mother.

His mother immediately bought some apples with her money and offered them to her son. The Amir ul-Mu'mineen returned home and asked his wife where she had bought the apples. The wife answered him by asking why her son had been hurt for just one apple that had been bought out of the public funds. The Amir ul-Mu'mineen responded: 'I don't want to miss out on the rewards of judgement day because of a single apple. I also don't want my name to be struck off the list of virtuous and honest people.'

ISOLATION AND RETRENCHMENT
(1998–2001)

47

THE RESPONSIBILITIES OF AN AMIR
AND HIS OFFICIALS IN THE ISLAMIC SHARI'A

[*This source continues the discussion about the role and proper activities for an amir. Once again, obedience from his subjects / 'faithful' is repeatedly stressed, as are the obligations on the amir to shape a proper shari'a environment. This included managing the* Beit ul-Maal *or national treasury, appointing appropriate people to positions of leadership and so on.*]

Tolo-ye Afghan, 4 February 1998

Speech by Mr Mawlana Moeenuddin Abu Fazl on the occasion of Eid ul-Fitr

Respected scholars and authorities of the Islamic Emirate, may peace be on you. First of all, I would like to congratulate you on the happy Eid ul-Fitr, and congratulate the people of Afghanistan for the peaceful coexistence which has prevailed in the country for a long time. Almighty God has given us a legitimate Amir ul-Mu'mineen whom Afghans didn't have as of yet. Almighty God gave us peace and prosperity when we had the worst conditions of security and peace, and when law and order were not present at all. Brutalities, cruelties, corruption and other evils have been replaced by justice, piousness and chastity. The movement of the Taliban and the Islamic Emirate of Afghanistan gave a very respectable name to the people of Afghanistan, which had [previously] become a notorious stain on the face of all Afghans. The Taliban replaced the Eid of evildoing with the Eid of the Islamic shari'a, and the notorious criminal leaders have been replaced by pious and sincere ones. Those who tried their best to sell every square foot of Afghan soil, and those who destroyed the country and were inexperienced and ignorant, and power- and money-loving leaders, all these have now been replaced with people of respect and honour. Almighty God has now given the people of Afghanistan experienced, loyal and educated personalities. We wish all the blessings of Almighty God for the people of Afghanistan. Dear listeners and respected countrymen, my speech on this sacred day to all Afghans is as follows:

1. Muslims will have a general amir, a leader for all Muslims, and all the people under his rule will accept and obey him as the Supreme Leader. Muslims will all obey the order of the amir and the Emirate and they should work for the collective cause of the Emirate. On the other hand, the amir should also be a true Muslim, sincere and conscious of his responsibilities.
2. What does a legitimate amir, a leader, mean in terms of the performance of the obligations on his shoulders?
3. What are the rights of the amir for civil servants and the people of the country?
4. If someone disobeys the orders of the amir, then what will be his or her punishment by the Emirate and how should people behave towards that person? Plus, what will be the punishment for the person on the Day of Judgement? And if someone favours or helps a rebellion, then what will be the punishment? And to what extent does rebellion endanger the cause of the Emirate itself?

Now pay close attention to the main point. Respected Muslims, this is the issue of our religion and faith. The selection of a single amir is the duty of Muslims, and thus obeying the legitimate amir is essential and obligatory for every Muslim. In our Hanafi jurisprudence of Islam, if someone has the resources to do the essentials, then that becomes obligatory for him or her. The Friday prayer is obligatory, Eid prayer is essential, the defence of the Islamic state is obligatory. The implementation of Islamic laws and regulations are obligatory for every Muslim. All these things work for the same cause, which is the selection and obedience of the orders of a single amir, the Amir ul-Mu'mineen. Similarly, it has been mentioned in our Islamic books which state that: 'the prophecy was for the purpose of protecting the religion and to manage the business and politics of the world in a better way'. In the same way, the amir and the Emirate have been established for the same purpose. And for this reason the selection of a pious amir is the obligation of all Muslims. Although some religious scholars say that it is a religious [duty] as well as something that needs the wisdom of the people, some scholars have a different perspective when they say that it only requires a religious perspective. A well-known Arab poet whose name is Afohi Audi says in one of his poems: 'those people who don't accept a single amir for all Muslims and bypass the orders of the Emirate have departed from their obligation and are committing great sins'.

With regard to such people, the Prophet Muhammad (PBUH) says that it is as if those people who have not accepted the amir of their time and haven't obeyed his orders are helping non-Muslims against the Emirate or Islam.

Now I draw your attention to the second point, which is about the importance of a single amir, the leader of Muslims, and the Emirate, and which duties have to be performed by the amir and the Emirate. The duties of the Islamic Emirate—in other words its importance in social issues, national issues and international politics—are profound, and we cannot mention [all of them] here.

THE RESPONSIBILITIES OF AN AMIR

Accepting the amir and the Emirate in general means nine things:

1. Obedience of religious laws
2. The implementation of shari'a law in order to protect society from corruption and cruelties
3. Ensuring complete peace, so that the people of our country travel back and forth for their business without any issues
4. The implementation of the rule of shari'a for the purpose of protecting the rights of the people
5. The protection of borders and soil where there is a danger from enemies
6. The collection of revenues for the *Beit ul-Maal* which will be used for the development of society and for the betterment of the people
7. The use of funds from the *Beit ul-Maal* for the needy, and to solve the problems of the people
8. The selection of pious leaders and experienced personalities for all government positions
9. The supervision of all position-holders and analysing their day-to-day activities

The first right of an amir over his officials and public is that as long as he issues decrees and instructions according to Islamic shari'a, everyone is obliged to obey him. According to Islam, obeying the amir is a highly compulsory obligation and stopping doing this is considered one of the biggest sins as described in [our] religion. Opposing the amir and thus not obeying his orders is not only a great sin but it also is very dangerous for the economy, security and the domestic and foreign interests of the country. For this particular reason, Prophet of Allah Hazrat Muhammad (PBUH) has called the obedience of the amir as being essential and rewards it like obedience to the Prophet. He has stated that disobedience of the amir of the time is like disobedience of the Prophet Muhammad (PBUH). Obeying the amir is not only obligatory from the viewpoint of Islam but in many ideologies, governments and civilised societies, obeying the head of state is considered to be the highest obligation for the citizens of those countries.

The second right of an amir who abides by the Islamic shari'a law is that the members of the public and his state officials must devote their lives to making any kind of help, assistance, cooperation and sacrifice in order to support the amir. They should confront the enemies of the amir in every possible way and means (like with their tongue, heart, life and property or possessions) so that the amir enjoys a conducive environment in order to fulfil his duties and responsibilities that almighty Allah has assigned to him with greater ease and correctness. For all these reasons, it is obligatory for the citizens of a country to confront, kill and get rid of any elements that rebel against the amir and consequently pose a threat to the security and stability of the country.

The third right of an amir over his public is that they remain sincere well-wishers when it comes to suggesting and advising the amir. If the amir issues an incorrect or inappropriate decree, one opposed to the shari'a law, members of the public and officials should draw the amir's attention to it. It is also the responsibility of the amir to listen carefully to such advice and bring any required changes. This had been the practice of the caliphs of Islam: in his very famous sermon, Hazrat Abu Bakr Siddiq (May Allah be Pleased with Him) said to the people, 'O people! I am the follower of the instructions of Almighty Allah and his Prophet. I am not perfect so do extend your help if I intend to do good work but I lose my direction and divert from the righteous way... do put me back on track.'[1] Hazrat Omar Farooq (May Allah be Pleased with Him) used to say the following: 'the dearest among the members of public to me is he who points out my shortcoming and mistakes to me'.

But this advice and reminders to the amir should always remain within the boundaries of ethics and good manners. It should come from good intentions and should be done by a person who has the capability and knowledge to do so. Members of the public and state officials must not conduct their dealings with the amir of the time based on hypocrisy and ill-intentions. Abdullah ibn Omar (May Allah be Pleased with Him) asked a few people at the time of the rule of Marwan Ibn Hakam, 'Do you speak the truth and what is right when you are in the presence of Marwan Ibn Hakam, and if he does anything against the Islamic shari'a law do you criticise it and register your objection?' The answer was no. These people further added that 'we swear by the name of Allah that Marwan Ibn Hakam does things at times which are against the instructions of Islam but we all praise him for what he says and when we leave the court we slander him and speak out against him'. Hearing this, Abdullah Ibn Omar (May Allah be Pleased with Him) said that 'without any doubt your actions are nothing more than pure hypocrisy'. The Prophet Muhammad (PBUH) has said that 'If you come across the followers of a religion who could not call a cruel person cruel, go far away from the followers of that religion.'

The sixth right of the amir over his public and officials is that as long as he abides by the Islamic shari'a law, he should remain the amir of the state or country.

The last point is in case someone rebels against the Islamic amir; the instruction of the shari'a is that the first step should be to give the person appropriate advice. But if the advice does not bring any reform and correction and the person engages in rebellious activities and starts killing people, in such a case he should be confronted and killed. Muslims are obliged to extend their full support to the amir of Islam with all possible means and ways. They must pursue the rebels, rout them from their shelters and hideouts and, if possible, kill them. The Holy Qur'an instructs us about the subject in the followings words: 'If one group of Muslims retaliates against another Muslim group, you must fight against the rebel group until they bow to the instructions of Almighty Allah and surrender to the Islamic Emirate and repent.' The Prophet of Islam, Hazrat Muhammad (peace be upon him) says that 'If someone approaches you and seeks the position of an amir and his intention is to break you into groups and damage your unity, although all of you have a consensus over another amir, do not let this person go—kill him.'

48

ACCOMPLISHMENTS OF THE TALIBAN ISLAMIC MOVEMENT AND ITS AIMS

[*This text was posted on a website affiliated with the Taliban movement in the late 1990s. It is unclear to what extent the Taliban exactly controlled the management of this website (it seems to have been managed from abroad, but the texts seem to be translations of official positions). It is one of the more specific enunciations of the period, so it is worth reading for this level of detail alone.*]

Taliban website, Late 1990s

A. Restoration of Full Security for Citizens
B. Pursuance of Honest and Sincere Negotiation
C. Support for the UN and OIC Peace Efforts
D. Respect for UN Rules and Principles
E. Search for Mutual Respect and Friendly Relations Towards All Countries
F. Establishment of a Credible and Accountable Islamic Regime
G. Protection of Human Rights and Liberties
H. Restoration of Women's Safety, Dignity and Freedom
I. Observance of the Islamic Hijab or Veil
J. Women's Education in the Islamic State of Afghanistan
K. Establishment of Representative Government on the Basis of Islamic Shari'a
L. The Islamic State Lends Full Support to the UN Agencies and NGOs
M. Efforts to Combat Production and Consumption of Illicit Drugs
N. The Islamic State is Against all Forms of Terrorism
O. The Islamic State of Afghanistan Intends to Rebuild the War-Torn Country

Thus, when the Taliban Islamic movement took the reins of political power in Kabul on 27 September 1996 and formed the Islamic State of Afghanistan, the city was in shambles, the treasury was empty, the administration was crippled, the infrastructure was ruined, and city services, such as healthcare, sanitation, water, electricity, telephone and transportation, were almost non-existent, opportunities for productive and gainful employment did not exist, food and grain were in short supply, hyperinflation was out of control, and economic dependency among families was widespread. In simple words, for the overwhelming number of people who were not in one way or another attached to the regime of Mr Rabbani or his self-styled commanders, life was brutish, difficult and extremely painful. The Taliban, from the very first day of their rise, were determined to put an end to this dismal situation. Thus, after taking Kabul, they began the difficult task of rehabilitating Kabul and the rest of the country. In the pursuance of this noble objective with the help of God, The Almighty, they have succeeded in bringing about a number of drastic changes, some of which are briefly discussed in the following.

A. Restoration of Full Security for Citizens

The Islamic State of Afghanistan disarmed hundreds of large and small groups of bandits and self-proclaimed commanders who were killing, raping and robbing the citizens in the city and its surroundings.

A working judicial system has been put in place in the areas under the Taliban administration. Life, property, children, personal rights and dignity of the people in these areas that one could aptly call 'the liberated areas' are protected in the framework of the holy Islamic Legal Code, i.e. the Islamic shari'a, regardless of race, language, tribe, or regional origin of the persons involved. Property rights of individuals and legal entities enjoy full protection in the Islamic courts. Properties taken away by force or deception from people by the state or by individuals are returned to their original owners. Checkpoints and looting posts erected by self-styled administrators and commanders have been eliminated from roads and highways. Roads have been opened for free movement of persons and goods.

B. Pursuance of Honest and Sincere Negotiations

As a second important step towards restoring peace and tranquillity in the country, the Islamic State of Afghanistan is committed to giving priority to sincere, honest and constructive negotiations with those who still resist the restoration of a united Afghanistan. The Islamic State of Afghanistan strongly believes that the continuation of war and armed conflict in Afghanistan is not only detrimental to the interests and well-being of the Muslim people of Afghanistan, but also seriously endangers peace and security in the neighbouring countries and the region. In line with this stance, the Islamic State of Afghanistan has repeatedly asked the neighbouring countries to stop their financial and arms assistance to the opponents of the Islamic State, and to use their influence on these groups to bring them to the negotiating table.

Unfortunately, so far, the opponents of the Islamic State, gathered around the former Communist militia leader Rashid Dostum and their foreign supporters, have failed to reciprocate these good, peace-seeking intentions of the Islamic State of Afghanistan under the leadership of the Taliban Islamic movement. By contrast, every time they have received a new shipment of arms or money from their foreign supporters, Dostum and Masood have tried to gain territory by force and have let cannons scream instead of allowing peace to raise its voice.

C. Support for the UN and OIC Peace Efforts

From the very first day of their rise against vice and corruption, the Taliban Islamic movement of Afghanistan has lent serious and genuine support to the peace-making efforts of the United Nations and the Organisation of Islamic Countries. We have always welcomed the UN Special Envoy for Afghanistan and his staff, as well as representatives of the OIC, with utmost respect and interest in Kabul and Kandahar. We have provided them with conveniences they needed to travel inside Afghanistan. The leadership of the Islamic State of Afghanistan has never failed to search for possible venues for peace and negotiations by persuading the opponents to lay down their weapons and return to the negotiating table. We have sent high-level delegations to all of the preliminary meetings organised so far by Dr Norbert Holl.

D. Respect for UN Rules and Principles

The Islamic State of Afghanistan considers itself to be a faithful member of the United Nations. As one of the oldest members of the world body, the Islamic State of Afghanistan respects and adheres to all rules and principles ratified by the UN, provided they do not contradict the teachings of the Islamic shari'a. The Islamic State of Afghanistan considers all international treaties to which Afghanistan has been a legitimate party as valid, and promises to fulfil its obligations in this respect, in so far as the principles laid down in Islamic shari'a support and confirm such obligations.

Regrettably, as a result of the current domestic conflict, as well as a certain degree of negligence and indifference on the part of the UN, today the Afghan UN representation has been given to a group of self-seeking and war-mongering individuals who not only do not represent the Afghan people, but use this position to conspire, in cooperation with the enemies of Afghanistan, against the self-determination right of its innocent and oppressed people.

The Islamic State of Afghanistan is hopeful that this injustice done to the people of Afghanistan is soon corrected and the Afghan representation at the UN is returned to its designate representative and his staff, who are present in the city of New York.

E. Search for Mutual Respect and Friendly Relations Towards All Countries

Based on the condition of respect for the sovereignty and territorial integrity of Afghanistan, the Islamic State of Afghanistan wishes to develop and maintain friendly relations with all countries in the region and in the world. The Islamic State of Afghanistan is anxious to participate in efforts aimed at maintaining peace and resolving conflicts in the region and the world. Based on tradition and recent experience, the Islamic State of Afghanistan has great respect for the sovereignty and territorial integrity of the nations, whether adjacent to or far from Afghanistan.

In pursuing this basic principle, the Islamic State of Afghanistan rightfully expects that other nations too refrain from interfering in the internal affairs of Afghanistan. In cases where the goodwill and good wishes of the Islamic State of Afghanistan are reciprocated with hostility and bad intentions regarding the sovereignty and territorial integrity of Afghanistan, the Muslim people of Afghanistan reserve the right to defend themselves and their country in any way they see appropriate.

F. Establishment of a Credible and Accountable Islamic Regime

Since the arrival of Islam to the two sides of the Hindu Kush mountains over 1,300 years ago, Afghanistan has always been, and will always remain, an Islamic country. Except for the relatively short but bloody period of the Communist reign, the political regime of the country has been based on the teachings of Islamic shari'a. Islam always provided the fundamental legal code or the set of laws upon which the political, economic and judicial systems of the country were founded. During this century, these laws twice underwent some modifications: once during the time of King Amanullah in 1921, and for a second time during the reign of the former King Mohammad Zaher Shah in 1964.

After liberating Kabul in September 1996, the Taliban Islamic movement declared all non-Islamic laws and regulations passed and practised during the Communist regime to be invalid, and reintroduced the set of laws that were in place during the time of the former King Mohammad Zaher Shah. At present, the Islamic State of Afghanistan runs its affairs on the basis of these laws and the constitution passed in 1964. To adapt the constitution to the present situation, the chapter dealing with the status of the king has been removed. Furthermore, to eliminate government waste and inefficiency, the Islamic State of Afghanistan has reduced the number and size of government ministries to what existed during Daud's regime.

G. Protection of Human Rights and Liberties

By restoring security and applying the uniform rules of the Islamic shari'a, for the first time since April 1978 the Islamic State of Afghanistan is providing equal protection and justice for all. As a result of the introduction of shari'a, arbitrariness in resolution of disputes, nepotism, discrimination on the basis of tribal, linguistic, religious orientation or regional affiliation have been eliminated. Individual property rights have been restored, confiscation of private property by the state or by those attached to it has been stopped. Freedom to engage in legal economic activities and freedom of movement have been guaranteed.

H. Restoration of Women's Safety, Dignity and Freedom

Being highly concerned about the well-being of its female citizens, the Islamic State of Afghanistan soon introduced measures to put a stop to the miserable living conditions under which women lived in Kabul. After the Communists took over in Kabul, they began to exploit women for the purpose of advancing their political and social agendas. In spite of war conditions in the country and with no work in the offices, the Communist regime forced a large number of women to attend government offices only for their amusement.

The Islamic State decided to pay the salaries of these women at their homes, so that they could stay home and take care of their families and children. The purpose of this policy is to help revive the Afghan family and household as the foundation of Afghan society, a foundation that was intentionally destroyed by the Communist regime.

The Islamic State of Afghanistan is determined to provide educational and employment opportunities for the women of Afghanistan, as soon as the security and financial circumstances under which the Islamic State operates allow such a step to be taken. In the meantime, the Islamic State of Afghanistan will try to acquire the resources and build the facilities that would make the separate education of women possible.

I. Observance of the Islamic Hijab or Veil

The enforcement of the code of the Islamic hijab by the Islamic State of Afghanistan is fully consistent with the Islamic beliefs of Afghans and the traditions of Afghan society. Wearing a veil is common among women all over Afghanistan. Islam and Afghan tradition attach the greatest importance to the honour and safety of women in society.

To comply with the Islamic code of the hijab, as well as to reduce the degree of threat to the personal safety of women, the Islamic State of Afghanistan is asking women to observe the Islamic hijab and cover their faces in public. This is a measure undertaken for the simple reason of protecting the honour, dignity, and personal safety of the women in Afghanistan.

J. Women's Education in the Islamic State of Afghanistan

Based on the holy teachings of Islam, the Islamic State of Afghanistan considers education as the pillar of a healthy and prosperous individual and social life. The Islamic State is determined to provide educational opportunities for all Afghans irrespective of gender, race, tribe, language or regional affiliations.

Unfortunately, today conditions for the implementation of a sound, effective and Islamic educational programme for the women of Afghanistan are non-existent. Over 90 per cent of school buildings have been ruined by the war. Qualified teachers have left the country. School books are full of Communist propaganda and indoctrination. Because of past abuses of the educational system for the purpose of propagating atheist ideology and ideas, the great majority of Afghan fathers and mothers have lost faith in schools and secular education. Last but not least, In spite of its deep desire to activate the school system in this country, the Islamic State of Afghanistan has been facing great difficulties in securing the financial and physical resources needed to provide security for the schools, reconstruct school buildings, print new books, acquire the necessary materials and pay for qualified and dependable teachers.

The limited amount of resources at the disposal of the Islamic State are being used to finance a war that has been imposed on Afghanistan by the brazen and open intervention of countries such as Iran, Russia, Uzbekistan and India. Intervention by these countries, and the resulting terrorist activities launched against the innocent men and women of Afghanistan by groups affiliated to these countries, have made the task of providing security for schools and public buildings, particularly girl's schools, extremely difficult.

K. Establishment of a Representative Government on the Basis of Islamic Shari'a

The Islamic State of Afghanistan adheres to the principle of a representative government based on the teachings of Islamic shari'a. Government in Islam is open to all groups living in Islamic society, irrespective of their race, language, region, ethnicity, tribal affiliation and religious orientation within the Islamic faith. Discrimination by government and in government on any pretext is strictly prohibited in Islam. Government posts in an Islamic society are to be given to those who are the most virtuous members of society. Leaders of an Islamic state serve as role models and set examples. Thus, these leaders are chosen on the basis of their merits and virtues, not on the basis of their party or other kinds of affiliations.

Members of the current caretaker administration in the Islamic State of Afghanistan have been chosen by the ulemaa of the country. These members represent all ethnic, religious and jihadi groups who have struggled to free Afghanistan from the tyranny of atheism and fascism. When circumstances change, and an appropriate environment more conducive to political dialogue is created, the Islamic State will take further steps towards solidifying the representational foundations of the Islamic State.

L. The Islamic State Lends Full Support to the UN Agencies and the NGOs

The Islamic State of Afghanistan has paid special attention to cooperation with UN agencies and the NGOs operating in Afghanistan. The Islamic State has provided full support and protection to the legal activities of the NGOs in the territories under its control. The security forces of the Islamic State have safeguarded the life and property of all foreign citizens working in Afghanistan, including UN officers and personnel, foreign reporters, teams and delegations of other international organisations and states visiting the Taliban-controlled areas. The security of highways and air traffic made possible through security efforts of the Islamic State of Afghanistan have facilitated the movement of humanitarian international assistance across the liberated territories.

M. Efforts to Combat Production and Consumption of Illicit Drugs

The Islamic State of Afghanistan has declared the production and shipment of illicit drugs throughout its territories as illegal and prohibited. Consumption of narcotics and alcohol has been prohibited and is punishable on the basis of shari'a. The Islamic State has made serious efforts to curtail and eliminate poppy and hashish cultivation and production in areas under its control.

Nevertheless, the Islamic State of Afghanistan is concerned that as long as there exists a lucrative market abroad, and as long as the economic situation of the Afghan farmers is such that it provides drug dealers with the opportunity to exploit their poverty, the problem of illicit drug production and trafficking will continue to be a difficult and costly fight for everybody concerned.

Thus, the Islamic State of Afghanistan asks the United Nations and the world community to design, among other measures, a programme of reasonable incentives for Afghan farmers, and farmers of other drug-producing countries, to stop them from engaging in this activity.

N. The Islamic State is Against All Forms of Terrorism

The Islamic State of Afghanistan has not and will not support acts of violence and terrorism under any name or in any form in any part of the world. The Islamic State of Afghanistan firmly believes in peaceful ways of resolving conflicts at national and international levels. The Islamic State of Afghanistan is fully aware of the delicate geopolitical location of the country in the region, and is thus interested in friendly relations with all countries on the basis of the principles of mutual respect and non-interference. Based on this stance, the Taliban Islamic movement has put an end to the paramilitary training activities of foreign groups, run under the sponsorship of the Rabbani regime and its affiliated political parties in different parts of Afghanistan, now under Taliban control. The Islamic State of Afghanistan is seriously determined not to allow Afghan territory to be used in the future by terrorists or any other organised groups for the purpose of launching terrorist activities against other countries. The Islamic State of Afghanistan announces its readiness to cooperate fully in joint international efforts aimed at combating terrorism in all its shapes and forms.

O. The Islamic State of Afghanistan Intends to Rebuild the War-Torn Country

The Islamic State of Afghanistan is earnestly determined to begin the process of national reconstruction. To accomplish this goal, the Islamic State of Afghanistan appeals to all international agencies, such as the World Bank, the IMF, the United Nations as well as private entities, to consider taking part in the grand task of rebuilding Afghanistan. To facilitate this process, the Islamic State of Afghanistan is ready to provide the necessary guarantees regarding legal aspects of the projects being considered.

To speed up and to provide a conducive environment for the reconstruction of Afghanistan, the economic policy of the Islamic State of Afghanistan has been designed to promote a market economy based on the principle of free enterprise, and to encourage private investments and undertakings. The Islamic State of Afghanistan attaches great significance to the role of private foreign capital and expertise into Afghanistan.

49

WAYS OF PROTECTING THE ISLAMIC MOVEMENT FROM VEERING OFF COURSE

[*It would be an overstatement to suggest that criticism was a regular feature of the Taliban's newspapers, but the occasional article did get published, either because the charges were so mild and couched in defensive apology or because the author was sufficiently well-known. This source is one of the strongest lists of failings, albeit not going as far as arguably one might have in 1999.*]

Shariat, 11 October 1999

It is a well-known fact that every Islamic movement comes into being based on good objectives and sacred plans initially. But as time passes it deviates from its route and goes in a different direction due to the laziness of individuals. But the origin and source of the Islamic movement are two fundamental principles of Islam, i.e. the Qur'an and hadith. Within these two principles, clear paths have been laid out for believers, and by following them Muslims can save themselves from all kinds of deviation and mistakes. We are going to mention some fundamental points which explain how the Islamic movement can remain pure.

1. First and foremost, everything should be done to please Allah Almighty. It is not just about instilling this in the minds of the workers, but utmost care should be taken to ensure it. It needs to be promised with full sincerity and determination that Allah's pleasure is initially and lastly our ultimate objective, and we have joined the movement for the sake of the same. This work can only be maintained with the same exclusive sincerity and dynamism. And so if the effort to please decreases, then it is rendered soulless; we saw this practically proven when the mujahedeen entered Kabul, and there was a decrease in effort to please Allah. That was the reason we faced its terrible consequence. It meant a compromise with the forces of untruth.

2. The disease of flattery and compromising with untrue ideologies and thoughts should not arise among the workers of the movement. They most definitely

need to pay attention to this disease, because naturally the people of untruth use different ways to put fear in the hearts of people of the truth. This is why if the movement does not prevent these efforts forcefully and freely, it would not take long for the workers to get affected by the tactics that are nothing less than fatal poison for the movement.

3, Attention should be paid to seekers of wisdom and understanding, to protect the movement from lack of planning; wisdom and acting on the advice of the seekers of wisdom and understanding are as necessary as protecting it from getting compromised. Like other movements, an Islamic movement should progress gradually. If we put this evolution and policy behind us, the movement will fall into an abyss, just like a disobedient horse. And we already saw the consequences of this in the recent past.

4. Religion should be protected from unbalanced ideas. The [unclear] of the movement should maintain a correct and balanced vision and should not be replaced by a frozen and unbalanced interpretation. Religion should be introduced to the workers as an all-faceted guidance system, in order to show them that Islam does not mean just worshipping rituals but there is ample space for progress, science and technology. God forbid if secularism originates as a reaction to our religion, just as it happened against the monasticism and Christianity of the priests and popes.

5. Workers should be protected from frigidity of thought. Workers should not get a feeling of inadequacy in the battle of thoughts, just as in a practical battle. If those workers develop a freeze in their thoughts, then the movement itself cannot travel the right course. They should be allowed to roam freely in the landscape of reflection, so that they can freely and optionally commit themselves to the objectives of the movement. If someone joins the movement to obtain some material benefit and does not have an ideological affiliation with it, then they surely will become opponents of the movement if they do not obtain their material benefits. We are examples of this ourselves, but the fact is that such actions cause the decline of the movement.

6. Freedom of thought and opinion should be used properly. Difference of opinion among movement workers is bound to arise, because this is a natural consequence of human thought and strategy. But this difference in opinion should not lead to disintegration and mental segregation. It is true that freedom of thought and speech is a basic right of every human being. If this right is used properly, it makes the movement healthier and increases its power of initiative. However, if it is used improperly, it causes the disintegration of the movement and of the right way to be modest and humble in non-specialised affairs where general opinion is sought. Discussions and conversations should be conducted sincerely and patiently to get a productive result. But if a decision is made in the end, one should stop insisting on one's opinion. [Arabic] 'Everyone is responsible for themselves' [Pashto] is a course fatal to harmony in a movement.

7. One needs to develop passion for [Arabic] 'preventing evil and enjoining good'. [Pashto] We should not allow the faith interest in [Arabic] 'counselling each other to truth and advising each other to have patience' [Pashto] to go down, and instead should create the circumstances to increase it. We should start the work of [Arabic] 'preventing evil and enjoining good' [Pashto] from our own selves. One should clean one's mirror first and then use the accusing finger.

8. The correct concept of following the amir should be kept in mind. The workers of the movement should fully realise that it is their duty to listen, obey and advise their leaders, and this has two important aspects. 1: that they should completely obey the amir in good deeds and should love and respect him. 2: that they should become the means of protection for the amir from all kinds of ideological, practical and every other type of aberration.

9. Frustration and pessimism should be stopped. The activists of the movements who have called the work a duty in their lives should never become victims of helplessness and a sense of failure. They should not be trapped in the tricks of the ego and the devil. He should think that maybe there is some shortcoming [unclear] in his actions or behaviour. If his inviting people to the cause does not give any tangible results, then there is surely a solution to my aforementioned shortcoming.

10. The inviter should not associate success with tangible results. If his work does not bring any result, it does not mean that he should stop the work. Instead he should say that he is doing the work of winning support to the best of his ability, and if that does not give any clear and solid results, [it doesn't matter because] the results are in the hands of Allah and the Muslim's job is to utilise his resources, and that is it.

50

WE SHOULD USE SOFT LANGUAGE WHILE ENFORCING THE PROMOTION OF VIRTUE

[This article criticising the Amr bil Marouf group's activities was published in Herat, where stronger criticism was often to be found (given the foreignness of the Taliban to the life and culture of the city's people). Once again, however, the criticism is couched in Islamic arguments and practical entreaties, rather than simply stating that the activities of the Amr bil Marouf are generating resentment in how they are carried out.]

Etefaq-e Islam (Herati newspaper), 20 December 1999

In contrast with the other so-called Islamic countries, the promotion of virtue and the prevention of vice in our Islamic society is not the duty of only the Department of Promotion of Virtue and Prevention of Vice. It is every faithful Muslim's duty to make every effort and sacrifice towards uprooting corruption and eradicating vice.

It is fortunate that great efforts are being made to promote virtue in most parts of Afghanistan because of the attention being paid by and the wisdom of the responsible officials of the Emirate. However, it should be categorically stated that no force or pressure should be used in furthering this great and sacred aim, which is one of the priorities of the policies being carried out by the Islamic Emirate of Afghanistan.

As ordered by the Almighty God, we should first give sound advice to the people to pursue good and to practise tolerance. We should, before everything else, propagate these values in the mosque. We should first enlighten people's minds and invite Muslims using soft language to make efforts to observe the shari'a and the rules of the Islamic system with love and affection.

To this end, our dear compatriots also have the duty to help the responsible officials of the Department of Promotion of Virtue and Prevention of Vice and strengthen the pillars of the Islamic system. They should not allow a small number of corrupt and extremist elements to benefit from the bloodshed and sacrifices made by hundreds of thousands of our compatriots.

It is important to emphasise once again that all those individuals who are trying to promote virtue and want to eradicate corruption and extremism in society should not even for a moment use force instead of advice and nice language, to avoid negative consequences after corruption has been eliminated. The eradication of one vice should not create another. This would be a place of great misfortune if we were satisfied with only apparent obedience in the expectation of the kindness and mercy of the Almighty God.

51

OUR MADRASSAS NEED VARIOUS REFORMS

[*The improvement of religious schools was, paradoxically, something that the Taliban's senior leadership seemed to have a great deal of time to hear about. This article offers a collection of complaints, from calling attention to fraud, changes to the curricula and the lack of specialisation of students.*]

Shariat, 15 July 2000

Thanks be to God, since the establishment of the Islamic Emirate, due attention has been paid to the management of the mosques and madrassas. But nothing can be free of flaws. The management and administration of these religious seminaries and mosques also have some flaws. This emergence of this kind of difficulty is quite natural and no one is free of some kind of weakness. Nor can we blame others exclusively. However, it is wrong if one becomes indifferent and deliberately ignores these problems. In our opinion, the following are the important flaws:

1. A large number of seminaries which have hostels have been built in the capital and provinces. The managers of these seminaries have prepared long lists and every month they receive billions of Afghanis for expenditure. In many places it has been witnessed that the real numbers of students are much lower than that which is being shown in the list. We should pay full attention to the Emirate's problems and try our best to prevent every possibility of fraud.

2. Keeping in mind the present situation of the country, it is necessary to close the hostels of those seminaries which are located in villages. The money which is saved from this should be added to the salaries of teachers. It will help them to perform their duties in a better way.

3. Curricula and other teaching resources have an important role in the field of teaching. The teachers must pay attention to this area. Concerned officials should also pay due attention and provide the books, stationery and other necessary teaching materials on time.

4. The present curricula must be implemented in accordance with the requirements of the present time, and in this connection the scholars, educationists and specialists must be consulted. These curricula leave a deep impact on the education and training of our new generation. We should fulfil our duty in this regard.

5. Another problem is the lack of specialisation. At present our students study a combination of different subjects to the level of grade twelve. But they are unable to specialise in any of these fields. So it is important that the subjects must be separated at the level of grade ten and the students should be given a proper chance to select the subjects of their choice.

52

BLIND MEMORISERS OF THE HOLY QUR'AN WILL HAVE THE RIGHTS OF GRADE THREE EMPLOYEES

[*This short article confirms and illustrates the value that Mullah Mohammad Omar placed on religious education and its institutions. The full corpus of the Taliban Sources Project contains many mentions of occasions when the Taliban leader visited a school for an inauguration or to celebrate the turban-tying ceremonies of graduation.*]

Shariat, 5 March 2000

On the basis of order number 3 issued by His Excellency the Amir ul-Mu'mineen, blind memorisers of the Holy Qur'an will have the rights of grade three employees. Salaries will be paid to them from the budget of the Islamic Emirate of Afghanistan. The management of this matter is the duty of the Ministry of Education.

Regards,
The servant of Islam
The Amir ul-Mu'mineen Mullah Muhammad Omar Mujahed

53

MARTYR FRIEND

[*This poem serves as a reminder that despite the political and military activities of the Islamic Emirate, there was an ongoing cultural life and expression through poetry. This particular poem merges traditional tropes of moths drawn to a flame (an image that represents love) with themes closer to the Taliban's agenda, like sacrifice and devotion.*]

Mullah Abdul Wali Halimyar, excerpt from Poetry of the Taliban, 1998

He, on the edge of taking leave of life,
On the edge of the path of continuous silence,
He who would win hundreds of breaths,
By giving out one breath,
Yes,
At the cost of a free independent life,
The youth who got love's inspiration from a butterfly, he slept beside the burning light,
He got burnt, he did business with his head.

54

EVEN IF OSAMA LEAVES THE COUNTRY, THE LINE OF AMERICAN EXCUSES WILL STILL REMAIN LONG

[*This op-ed takes aim at the policies of the United States (and by extension the United Nations, who had just levelled sanctions against the Taliban's government). This reflects a common idea at the time—one that seems to have gained currency with Mullah Mohammad Omar—that bin Laden was just one demand among many by the United States. Even if they handed him over and complied with US demands, the argument runs, more requests would follow. In the end, the movement would be forced to compromise on their national character and religious beliefs to meet all these demands; and thus perhaps now, the article suggests, the better policy is to refuse to hand over bin Laden.*]

Shariat, 31 October 1999

Ever since the Islamic system has taken over in Afghanistan and the dreams of the Eastern and Western colonial countries have been frustrated, a flame of fire consumes the body of international colonialism; and since that day, it has been busy making excuses, plans and pulling tricks in order to, God forbid, bring an end to the Islamic Emirate of Afghanistan. Their interference in the affairs of the Islamic Emirate of Afghanistan have even crossed the limits of disgrace. They are finding such [insignificant] excuses against the Emirate, and the top one is the presence of Arab mujahed, Osama bin Laden. The United States of America wants the Islamic Emirate of Afghanistan to hand over Osama for trial [unclear]. The United States has not hesitated from exerting all kinds of pressure, in contravention of international guidelines, on the Afghan nation of mujahedeen with regard to Osama. They imposed economic sanctions on this oppressed struggling nation, the very nation due to whose sacrifices they [the US] roam about with proud eyes and call themselves an unrivalled power in the world.

Despite all this, the Islamic Emirate of Afghanistan took appropriate, efficient and [unclear] steps to address the American demands and anxiety, and from the very first moment the Emirate presented various methods for a reasonable resolution of the issue, took appropriate steps and proved that the Emirate truly wanted to solve the Osama issue through dialogue and harmony, and believed that reason should not give way to emotion.

For example, as a first step, the Islamic Emirate declared to the whole world that if anyone thought Osama was a criminal, they should come to the Supreme Court of Afghanistan along with documentary evidence and testimonies, and the Emirate granted full powers and authority to the Supreme Court. But no one was there, no evidence was presented to the Supreme Court and not a single applicant appeared. The second step the Islamic Emirate took was that it put Osama under total restrictions and took away all sorts of communication resources from him. The Americans still remained unconvinced. In order to get rid of the prevailing critical situation and put an end American excuses, the Islamic Emirate suggested that religious scholars from Afghanistan, Saudi Arabia and three more countries should sit down and decide the fate of Osama, but the United States did not [pay attention] to even this suggestion of the Esteemed Amir ul-Mu'mineen. The fourth proposal of the Islamic Emirate was that since the United States did not have any proof and documents to prove Osama guilty, and the US itself had said that Osama was not guilty but rather 'under accusation', the Islamic Emirate was ready to work in harmony with the United States to adopt a course which would satisfy the US with regard to what they call the Osama threat and that meant that the Islamic Emirate was ready to cooperate with the US in taking any course of action that it deemed satisfactory in protecting that country from what it called the Osama threat. Still, the United States [rejected] such flexibility and concessions offered by the Islamic Emirate and has, proverbially, shoved its feet into one shoe and keeps repeating its earlier stances.

Americans should give consideration to Afghan culture, national pride and their religious and national traditions and should chart a course of action which guarantees the protection of the aforementioned values. But it seems the cause of American enmity with the Islamic Emirate of Afghanistan is not just Osama, and could it be that America 'holds half a bowl under another bowl' [a proverb, meaning 'has underlying objectives']. If this was the case, the United States would still be creating a hue and cry that the Islamic Emirate should expel Osama from Afghanistan. But when news sources reported on 30 October 1999 that Osama bin Laden had written in a letter to the Esteemed Leader of the Faithful that he wished to leave Afghanistan, instead of waiting for more details about the letter, US authorities very quickly and very ignorantly asserted that [this wouldn't lead the United States to offer official recognition to the Islamic Emirate]. It is clear from this remark by James Rubin that even if Osama got out of Afghanistan, they would still formally not recognise the Islamic Emirate and neither would Osama's departure put an end to their pretexts. Based on James Rubin's comments, we can say that Americans do not consider Osama's departure from Afghanistan a solution either, therefore we wonder about what the solution could be.

In the end, we hope once again that the US will act with tact and wisdom and it must understand that even [unclear] death cannot force Afghans to leave their religious and national traditions, not to mention economic sanctions. This is not the time to solve issues through force. It would be better if solutions to every issue could be found through understanding and dialogue in a friendly atmosphere.

55

INSTEAD OF TACKLING THE REAL CULPRITS, THE UN SECURITY COUNCIL THREATENS OTHERS

[*This article considers the Taliban to be victims in an international conspiracy with the United Nations at its head. The movement were subject to sanctions as of 15 October 1999, and they sought to push back against what they saw as favouritism and discrimination by the international community. Note, too, that this article was published in the context of negotiations that were ongoing, an attempt to find some compromise solution between the Taliban and their internal opposition.*]

Shariat, 7 May 2000

Following its views and expressions about Afghanistan, it has become clear that the UN Security Council is not interested in the peace and security of the world at all. Its statements, announcements, communiqués and press releases all show that it is working for accomplishment of a particular ideology. It has always been under the control of a particular superpower. Under the garb of the UN, it works for the interest of a particular power. It seems that it has forgotten and ignored the UN charter's article which guarantees that it is an independent, impartial and non-aligned organisation. This organisation does not work for the interests of a particular nation, ethnic group, language and a country. It has been guaranteed in its charter that this organisation respects the values and traditions of every nation and country. Unfortunately, the UN always ignores the implementation of these principles about Afghanistan. This organisation has a double-standard policy for the Islamic Emirate of Afghanistan. In other words, the UN turns a blind eye towards facts and realities.

At the moment, the Afghan conflict has two sides and parties. One party is the Islamic Emirate of Afghanistan which enjoys 100 per cent of the people's support and controls over 95 per cent of the territory, including the capital of the country. It has established a government which consists of a cabinet and other branches and departments. The other party consists of rebel militia groups which have no legal status. They have been rejected and shunned by the people; even they have no postal address or a bank account inside the country. The 4–5 per cent of territory under their control is subject to anarchy and disorder. Every day, reports of internal fighting come out of the area. Despite this superiority of the Islamic Emirate over its rival groups, still both are considered to have an equal status. In many cases, even the smallest opposition group is given more importance than the Islamic Emirate. This group has been formally recognised and receives every kind of financial and military support. It clearly shows that the UN is afraid of the establishment of an Islamic system in Afghanistan. It is unable to tolerate the Muhammadi laws of the shari'a.

Last night's threat made by the UN explains this very well. Last night once again the so-called UN Security (insecurity) Council threatened the Islamic Emirate that if it started fighting, more sanctions would be imposed to punish it. Ironically, they never give this kind of threat to those groups which are fighting against the Islamic Emirate. In fact, every time attacks are launched by these groups, fighting is imposed upon the Islamic Emirate. They force the Islamic Emirate to take up arms for self-defence. So every time the opposition groups launch an attack, it is the Islamic Emirate which is subject to sanctions and threats. This will definitely lead us towards suspicion and lack of trust about the impartiality of the UN as an international body. Another irony is that this time also the opposition has launched the attacks. But the UN has been silent and on the contrary started to criticise and threaten this Islamic Emirate. It wants to make an impression that neither do the opposition groups belong to a warring party nor do they participate in any fighting. This kind of unilateral judgement will definitely reduce the trust of the people of Afghanistan in the UN as an international impartial organisation.

In fact, the UN tries to torture and punish the people of Afghanistan further. It seeks hollow excuses for the imposition of more sanctions. If the UN really wants peace and an end to the fighting, it must prevent foreign interference in the domestic affairs of Afghanistan. Apart from this, it must remain impartial and avoid the sprinkling of salt on the wounds of the people of Afghanistan. Is Lakhdar Brahimi unaware of the interference of the two plus six or US, Russia and the six neighbouring countries and the support which they provide to the opposition groups? The countries which are calling for peace in Afghanistan in fact fan the flames of war. The UN should not make judgements which are based on partiality and must avoid the policy of double standards. Otherwise it will lose even the little trust that remains.

56

MESSAGE FROM THE ESTEEMED LEADER OF THE FAITHFUL ON INTERNATIONAL WOMEN'S DAY

[*This lengthy message seems to have been part of the occasional efforts taken by the Taliban's government to convince the international community that they could play by the same rules and standards, that there were more shared values than differences between the two, and that this position stemmed from the very top of the organisation. Mullah Mohammad Omar speaks directly to Afghanistan's women and attempts an explanation for the movement's policies.*]

Shariat, 8 March 2000

Pious, honourable and respected mothers and sisters!

Greetings of peace to you, and the mercy and blessing of Allah be upon you! May Allah grant you rewards in this world and the hereafter for all the laments, pain, problems and troubles which have troubled you and all other countrymen for twenty years and made them tough in the testing furnace. This is because our country is, as someone said, 'aflame in the fire of its own skin'" over periods of history, which means that this has been a battlefield for the aggression of invading forces through centuries due to its geographical location and natural resources. And as you know, many skulls of unjust aggressors have rolled here. Their expectations and wishes have been left unfulfilled. The unjust invasion of the defeated Soviet Union, those countless problems and troubles it brought our countrymen face-to-face with, and then the humiliating defeat of the Soviets: you saw all these. After the defeat of the Soviet Union, when a government in the name of Islam and the mujahedeen was established in the country and the country's widows, orphans, the disabled and healthy mujahedeen and all compatriots, in fact the whole Islamic world, tied a lot of hopes to it, expecting a prosperous, thriving and peaceful country and the complete implementation of the Islamic shari'a ... unfortunately these hopes were left unfulfilled and became dust in dust, due to the greed of some deviant and self-serving persons. You remember whatever you, the countrymen, saw and heard during this tragedy word-by-word. You are all the countrymen who saw that our fellow citizens experienced intolerable troubles and grief and those too from people who were our own compatriots and carried the label of 'mujahedeen'.

Upon seeing such countless injustices, evils and shameful acts, especially sensing the danger to the honour of you honourable ones, the sense of honour of your honourable Taliban sons and brothers and pious mujahedeen exploded into flames. In order to get rid of these pressures, laments and pain, they rose up with a commitment to offer their lives. They obtained a shari'a-based fatwa, and started a jihad against evil. After undertaking a lot of tiring work and troubles, and by losing [many] valuable souls, all praise is due to Allah, the country was protected from division and disintegration. The Islamic shari'a, which was the wish of all citizens of the country and the blessed martyrs (may Allah have mercy on them), was implemented in all its meanings, security was established, and the lives, property and honour of the countrymen became secure. The pillars of the Islamic system and government became firmly established, and with empty hands the work of reconstructing and developing the country started from scratch. Praise is due to Allah, a lot of work has been done until now and we hope to progress even further with the blessing and assistance of Allah Almighty. We should not lose hope over occasional acts by some appointed officials.

Due to this blessed system, you are also competing equally with your counterparts in the world and are observing International Women's Day with full confidence, satisfaction and a peaceful atmosphere. I admit that we still have many problems and our country is beset by political, economic and many other troubles. There is fighting going on in a part of the country with the incitement and open interference of the country's enemies. The anti-Islamic countries of the world have become our enemies because we have fully implemented the Islamic shari'a and on account of our firm stand on our national traditions and customs. They impose economic sanctions on us, carry out bad propaganda against us and instil sedition against us. Despite all these problems, the territorial integrity and sovereignty of the country, national independence and freedom, and the complete implementation of the Islamic shari'a, and the protection of our honour and dignity are important and worthy of pride, more than anything else.

One can face problems with high spirits, firm resolve and trust, complete patience and seriousness. Putting up with troubles is particularly easy for a believing nation that trusts in the blessing and mercy of Allah Almighty and deems this worldly life a path and means to make the everlasting life in the hereafter prosperous. You know that many nations in the world are facing so many problems and troubles that make our problems pale into insignificance. Some people's flesh is cut with [knives] by cruel invaders. Some cannot find the dead bodies of their relatives due to natural disasters, earthquakes, floods and tsunamis. It is incumbent upon you and us that we express gratitude over the blessing of Allah Almighty, act as the slaves of Allah Almighty with love, sincerity and complete discipline in order that Allah Almighty may lift the troubles and increase his blessings upon us. You know how much evil propaganda is circulated against us by the world of infidels in regard to women's rights; and to them human rights are only those corrupt Western traditions and culture in which women are insignificant, honourless and serve as [unclear]. Muslim women feel disgust about that position and seek thousands-of-times protection from them from Allah Almighty. Evil-intentioned infidels without a conscience are not as worried about and do not assist our poor, hungry, thirsty sisters in [meeting] basic needs [like] food, drink, clothing and shelter as much as they do selfish propaganda.

My demand is that by protecting your piety, dignity and high status with patience, sobriety and tolerance, you should put dirt in the mouths of the infidels and bury their dirty and foul-smelling culture in a grave of rejection forever. Rear the new generation in such a manner that they are pious Muslims, clever, intelligent and honourable Afghans. I promise and assure you that I will take urgent steps, within my means and by trusting in Allah Almighty, with regard to the education and upbringing of the new generation according to the demands of the implemented Islamic system. And I shall work ever more to fulfil and protect all your shari'a-based rights as further [measures] beyond the earlier decrees and observations. I will not spare any inconvenience to myself and efforts in ending the economic problems and all the troubles of life. I hope you will make powerful prayers for me. Hoping here for the blossoming of the country and the bright future of fellow citizens!

The servant of Islam,
Mullah Mohammad Omar

57

CONSTITUTION

[*The Constitutional Commission was the Taliban's response to the question of the nature of their state. External actors had, following Mullah Mohammad Omar's appointment as Amir ul-Mu'mineen, offered advice as to the various directions this could take. A Pakistani religious political party close to the Taliban—the Jamiat-e-Ulemaa-Islam under Maulana Fazlur Rehman—even drafted a constitution for the Taliban to use in October 1996, reportedly following a request from Mullah Mohammad Omar. By June next year, the head of the Supreme Court, Nur Mohammad Saqib, told one journalist that the Taliban had no need for a constitution, 'because shari'a is the only constitution'. Indeed, the refrain that the Qur'an and/or shari'a could function as a constitution was repeated in the Taliban media throughout their years in power. An October 1997 news report states that the Ministry of Justice had recently started work on the constitutional review, but it seems this was an independent attempt from what became the official constitutional commission. Mullah Mohammad Omar issued a decree on 20 June 1998, in which he tasked Nur Mohammad Saqib (the Chief Justice) and the Supreme Court with reviewing the terms of the constitution (along with all other laws). They were still busy preparing the new document in May 1999, and in fact had never formally issued the completed draft for official approval by the time their government fell in late 2001. The full text offers an interesting historical glimpse into the Taliban's thinking about the nature of the state, the role of the judiciary and other related issues as conceptualised towards the final years of their rule.*

The 1964 constitution and that drafted by the post-1992 interim mujahedeen government formed the basis for the Taliban's efforts, and it is interesting to note how many similarities exist. Centralisation remains a key point of emphasis for the Taliban, as in the 1964 version; there is little leeway given to anything that might lead to fragmentation or too much independence from the decrees of the central government and its leadership. Despite a good deal of renaming of terms and positions, the Taliban's constitution also has a broadly similar vision of the key institutions of the modern Afghan state: a strong leader, a strong Supreme Court appointed by the leader, and a council of ministers to run the ministries. Many articles in the Taliban's document make reference to a general principle whereby everything 'must conform to shari'a principles'. In this way, the drafters of the document left certain offices or articles vague and subject to interpretation by the judiciary and leadership. They also made reference to particular documents (like an Education Law) that in some cases did not yet exist or had not been formally approved. The repeated statement that so-and-so was valid 'except when it is in contradiction to the Islamic shari'a' was presumably a safeguard allowing flexibility to the judiciary and to Mullah Mohammad Omar in taking decisions. One area which the constitutional draft is notably vague is as to the manner of appointing or installing the leader or Amir ul-Mu'mineen. This may have been a concession to the fact that there is considerable debate in Islamic political thought over this question, or this may simply have been an oversight.]

Introduction

In any country or government, the basic law—or in other words [the basic fundamentals], [the basic message] or [the constitution]—has a great value and its implementation is certain.

But in a real Islamic state and government, the basic law and other laws and verdicts should match the complete Islamic shari'a.

Accordingly, his eminence, the Amir ul-Mu'mineen, stated on 20 June 1998, within the 18th decree to implement the legitimate system in the country, that the clergy has to study, under the supervision of the Supreme Court, all laws and verdicts implemented in the country and must delete all illegitimate and non-denominational articles.

Based on that, good clergy were brought from all over Afghanistan to the city of Kabul. Their names and signatures are included in the final chapter of the constitution; and then they conducted a shura assembly presided over by Haj al-Mawlawi Nur Muhammad Saqib, the chief judge and chief of the Supreme Court, to complete the work in the palace of ruling.

This assembly started work on 2 July 1998. On the first days, the work was on the basic law, where the basic laws of Afghanistan in different governmental eras and different situations were demonstrated before the honourable clergies. All articles of the law were discussed in detail, based on the Islamic shari'a fundamentals and laws. Articles which match the Islamic shari'a were approved; as for other articles that do not match the shari'a or the Islamic denomination, they were modified or completely deleted. In some sources, new legitimate articles were included, based on requirements.

After consecutive meetings which lasted for many days, work was successfully completed and the basic law of the Islamic Emirate of Afghanistan was arranged and approved and was named the constitution of the Islamic Emirate of Afghanistan, which matches and totally complies with the shari'a and the Al-Hanafi denomination.

Once again the Supreme Shura Council of the Islamic Emirate of Afghanistan approved this constitution (basic law) on 23 June 2005.

CONSTITUTION

Chapter One: General Principles

Article 1: Afghanistan is an Islamic Emirate, a free, independent, unitary and indivisible state.

Article 2: The regime in the Islamic Emirate of Afghanistan is founded on the Qur'anic verse 'ruling is but for God'.

Article 3: Islam is the religion of the Afghan nation.

Article 4: The Hanafi jurisprudence is the official set of religious guidelines of Afghanistan.

Article 5: The Islamic shari'a is the only source of lawmaking in the country, governing all aspects of individual and social life of people in the light of life constructive teachings of Islam. Laws and resolutions should not be, in any way, contrary to religious provisions and foundations.

Article 6: The Islamic Emirate of Afghanistan is founded on the basis of politics, social life, culture and economy and according to Islamic basics. Law-making methods in Afghanistan and the reorganisation of life are set on the basis of the Qur'an, the sunna and the Hanafi jurisprudence.

Article 7: Work in the Islamic Emirate of Afghanistan is given to the right people, and piety is the first condition for eligibility.

Article 8: Political, social, cultural and economic orientations are implemented according to the provisions of Islamic shari'a.

Article 9: The Islamic Emirate of Afghanistan considers the call to kindness, the propagation of virtue and the prevention of evil the responsibility of all Muslims. It is a dual duty of the Emirate and the people, and its conditions and limits are regulated by Islamic religious law.

Article 10: Education of the Muslim individual and family, the creation of an integrated Islamic society, seeking the unity of the Islamic nation, and the expansion of Islamic instructions to the greatest possible extent are the primary duties of the Islamic Emirate of Afghanistan.

Article 11: Pashto and Farsi are the official languages of Afghanistan. The necessary benefit to laws, resolutions, documents, offices, books, teaching materials, means of mass communication and the teaching of literature and languages is drawn from each of these languages accordingly. The Emirate is responsible for their development.

Article 12: The Islamic Emirate of Afghanistan develops, through offering and applying specialised programmes, the teaching of the Arabic language, which is the language of the Qur'an, Islamic knowledge and sciences.

Article 13: The Islamic Emirate of Afghanistan reinforces the teaching of Arabic (religious) books in private and public schools, following the country's senior scholars' old method.

Article 14: The calendar in the country shall be based on the pilgrimage of the holy prophet (peace be upon him). The Hijra lunar calendar is prevalent in the Islamic Emirate. Friday is a public holiday. Other holidays are regulated by law.

Article 15: The administration in the Islamic Emirate of Afghanistan is central, and Kabul is its capital.

Article 16: The flag of the Islamic Emirate of Afghanistan is rectangular, it is white, and its length is the equivalent to one and a half times its width. The definition, size and insignia are regulated by law.

Article 17: The family is the basic unit of Islamic society. The Emirate regulates laws, provisions and necessary programmes on the basis of Islamic rights and ethics, in order to facilitate matters associated with the family and its composition, and preserving and reinforcing the existence of family ties.

Chapter Two: Fundamental Rights and Duties of Citizens

Article 18: All the people of Afghanistan, without any discrimination or privilege, have equal rights and duties before the law, taking into consideration the Islamic provisions.

Article 19: Freedom is a natural right of human beings, unless it affects the freedom and dignity of others, public utilities, general security, public interest, or Islamic principles and provisions. This right is regulated by law.

Article 20: Innocence is the original state; the accused person is innocent until he is convicted by the authorised court with a final verdict.

Article 21: No act is considered a crime unless determined by the provisions of the Islamic shari'a and the laws implemented before committing the act.

Article 22: No one is judged but in accordance with the decision of the authorised court. No one is punished but in accordance with the provisions of the Islamic shari'a and in conformity with the laws adopted before committing the accused act,

Article 23: No person can be pursued or arrested except in accordance with provisions of the law.

Article 24: No one can be detained except with a warrant by the authorised court and according to provisions of the law.

Article 25: A crime is a personal action. The prosecution, arrest and detention of an accused and the execution of the penalty cannot affect another person.

Article 26: It is prohibited to acquire a confession, testimony or statement from the accused or any other person by force, threat, torture or enticement. Any statement, testimony or confession obtained from an accused or of another person by means of compulsion is invalid.

Article 27: No person, even with the intention of acquiring testimony, can resort to torture or order the torture of another person who may be under prosecution, arrest, or imprisoned, or convicted to punishment.

Article 28: Every accused person can defend himself or seek an advocate to defend his rights or to defend him in accordance with provisions of the law.

Article 29: No citizen of Afghanistan can be extradited to a foreign state under the allegation of being accused of a crime.

Article 30: Any person suffering undue harm by government action without a reason is entitled to compensation, which he can claim by appealing to court. The Emirate cannot claim its right without the order of an authorised court, unless in situations stated in the law.

Article 31: No Afghan citizen can be sentenced to deprivation of citizenship except in accordance with provisions of the law. No Afghan citizen can possess dual citizenship. The status of the tribes on the border is to be regulated according to law.

Article 32: Confidentiality and freedom of correspondence and communication, whether in the form of letters or through telephone, telegraph and other means, are immune from invasion. The Emirate does not have the right to inspect personal correspondence and communication unless authorised by provisions of the law and by the authorised court.

Article 33: A person's residence is immune from invasion. No one, including employees of the Emirate, is allowed to enter or inspect a private residence without prior permission of the resident or holding the warrant by the authorised court or methods indicated in the law.

Article 34: Freedom of expression and statement, within the Islamic shari'a limits, is inviolable. Every Afghan citizen has the right to express his thought through speech, writing, illustration or other means, according to the provisions stated in the law.

Article 35: The citizens of Afghanistan have the right to demonstrate for legitimate purposes, unarmed and peacefully, and avoid harming people according to the provisions of the law.

Article 36: Property is immune from invasion. Nobody's property shall be confiscated without provisions of the law and the order of an authorised court. The authorised court will inspect complaints regarding obligatory property acquisition.

Article 37: Work is the right of every Afghan citizen if he possesses legal eligibility. Employer–employee affairs are fairly regulated by law. Forced labor is forbidden even if it is for the Emirate. This prohibition does not contradict applying provisions set to regulate collective activities to provide public welfare.

Article 38: The Emirate is obliged to provide compulsory intermediate level education and to expand and develop specialised education and public secondary school level, free of charge by the state.

Article 39: The education of women is regulated within the limits of the Islamic shari'a by a special law.

Article 40: No one can exploit his rights and position to serve as a tool for others to misuse public utilities.

Article 41: Preserving the gains of jihad, defending the borders of the Islamic Emirate and preserving the laws of the people are the responsibility of all citizens of Afghanistan. All citizens of Afghanistan are obliged to perform military service in accordance with the provisions of the law.

Article 42:

A. The total consideration of Islamic provisions in individual, family and social affairs, and obeying the provisions of the constitution and the Emirate, adhering to public law and order, and protecting the utilities of the Islamic Emirate are the duties of all people of Afghanistan.

B. Promoting non-Islamic beliefs is prohibited, and those who violate this—locals or foreigners—will be tried according to the shari'a.

Article 43: It is obligatory to care for the Islamic veil.

Article 44: The citizens of Afghanistan have the right to establish private religious schools.

Article 45: The establishment of public schools and special courses, especially establishing factional schools, is linked to government authorisation.

Chapter Three: Islamic Shura [Council]

Article 46: The Islamic Shura is the limited power whose members are selected as follows: three members from the first-class provinces; two members from the second-class provinces; and one member from the third-class provinces. The quorum is completed with the presence of the Amir ul-Mu'mineen.

Article 47: The Islamic Shura members have the leaders' characteristics.

Article 48: The work system and the activity of this Shura are organised by internal regulations.

Article 49: The Islamic Shura has a chairman, a vice chairman and a secretary general. The chairman is chosen by the Amir ul-Mu'mineen from the members of the Shura.

Article 50: Duties and authorities of the Islamic Shura are as follows:

1. approving laws;
2. monitoring the legality of the Emirate administration's procedures;
3. making decisions in disputed matters;
4. approving plans, formations, and the normal and developmental budget of the Emirate;
5. making decisions regarding war and ceasefire in cooperation with the Supreme Shura of the Supreme Court and the Cabinet under the presidential authority of the Amir ul-Mu'mineen;
6. approving treaties with other countries in cooperation with the Supreme Shura of the Supreme Court and the Cabinet;
7. approving government policy;
8. questioning the government;
9. protecting the values and goals of jihad;
10. approving taking zero-interest loans from other countries and international organisations;

11. informing the council, which is formed of the chief judge, the prime minister, and the chief of the Islamic Shura, whenever the Amir ul-Mu'mineen desires to abandon his post, and then an immediate session of the Islamic Shura is to be held with the cooperation of the chief judge and the prime minister, who will make the decision;

12. after the death or resignation of the Amir ul-Mu'mineen, especially in the case of not recommending anyone as a new Amir ul-Mu'mineen, the chief judge will take the responsibility of the Emirate issues; and

13. permitting foreigners to establish legitimate companies of heavy industries.

Article 51: Whenever accusing a member of the Islamic Shura, members of the Cabinet, the assistance of both councils, or a member of judiciary of a crime, the official in charge has to inform the chief concerned about the matter, and after obtaining the permission of the chief concerned, the accused is to be put under legal custody. In the case of committing a crime, the official in charge has the authority to put the accused under legal custody or to arrest him without obtaining the permission of the chief concerned.

Chapter Four: Amir ul-Mu'mineen

Article 52: The Amir ul-Mu'mineen is at the top in the Islamic Emirate of Afghanistan, and he performs his duties according to this constitution's laws and other laws on executive, judicial and limited matters.

Article 53: The Amir ul-Mu'mineen has to be a Muslim who follows the Hanafi denomination, possesses Afghan nationality, and his parents have to be of Afghan descent.

Article 54: The Amir ul-Mu'mineen is the first decision-maker in the state within his legal authorities.

Article 55: The duties and authorities of the Amir ul-Mu'mineen are as follows:

1. acting as the supreme commander of the Islamic Army of Afghanistan;
2. appointing and dismissing the prime minister and the ministers;
3. assigning some of his authorities to someone else;
4. approving the appointment of the ministers who were chosen by the Islamic Shura Council after they were nominated by the prime minister, and then announcing them;
5. appointing the Supreme Court's chief;
6. appointing members of the Supreme Court after consulting the Supreme Court's chief;
7. appointing and dismissing the judges;
8. approving the retirement of senior military and civilian officials according to provisions of the law;

9. appointing ambassadors abroad and convoys to international committees and accepting the letters of credence;
10. granting honourable titles, medals and decorations according to provisions of the law;
11. announcing war and ceasefire after getting the Islamic Shura's approval;
12. representing the Islamic Emirate of Afghanistan on the level of countries' presidents in the international assemblies;
13. signing laws and legislative decrees;
14. signing contracts and treaties with other countries after being approved by the Islamic Council;
15. reducing and pardoning penalties in accordance with legislative decrees;
16. approving the normal and development budget of the Emirate;
17. forming the normal session of the Cabinet;
18. granting Afghan nationality according to provisions of the law;
19. giving formal permission to print and disseminate banknotes according to the Ministry of Finance's suggestion; and
20. declaring a state of emergency and ending it according to provisions of the law and after getting the approval of the Shura.

Article 56: The salary of the Amir ul-Mu'mineen is to be specified and his disposition of public property and rewards are according to provisions of the law.

Article 57: The Amir ul-Mu'mineen or relatives cannot purchase governmental capital or public property or stand to benefit from the government.

Article 58: In the absence of the Amir ul-Mu'mineen, the Emirate's issues will be supervised by the person to whom duties are being assigned.

Article 59: The Amir ul-Mu'mineen has the same legal responsibilities as other citizens.

Article 60: This speech is to be read in the name of the Amir ul-Mu'mineen.

Chapter 5: The Government

Article 61: The government is the supreme executive and administrative power in the Emirate. It is made up of the prime minister and the ministers. The number of ministers and their duties are regulated by law.

Article 62: The prime minister must be a Muslim and a follower of the Hanafi sect. He must be born to Muslim parents.

Article 63: An appropriate pay is to be allocated by the law to the head and members of the government.

Article 64: The prime minister, in his capacity as the head of government, has the following jurisdictions:

1. representing the government;

2. acting as the first commander in giving orders at government level, according to provisions of the law;
3. heading the council of ministers to work as a unified entity;
4. transferring some of the jurisdictions to a minister;
5. signing agreements and pacts at government level;
6. supervising the administration and regulating the works of the ministries and the autonomous administrative units within the government; and
7. appointing, granting rank, putting into retirement, and dismissing the government's employees, in accordance with provisions of the law.

Article 65: Duties and jurisdictions of the government are:

1. implementing the country's internal and external policy in accordance with provisions of the law;
2. regulating the works of the ministries, the autonomous administrative units and the attached departments;
3. taking the necessary procedures in executive and administrative matters in accordance with the laws, drafts and amendments of the Islamic Shura;
4. preparing and drafting the regulations and the rules of government;
5. presenting, regulating and adjusting the Emirate's budget and submitting it to the Islamic Shura;
6. presenting and implementing the programmes of the economic and social development and initialling procedures for rebuilding offers;
7. monitoring and supervising matters related to banks and government securities, in addition to preventing inflation;
8. regulating matters related to internal and external borrowing in accordance with the directions of the Islamic Shura;
9. maintaining security and public order throughout the country;
10. conducting agreements and pacts with countries and international organisations in accordance with the law;
11. carrying out the required procedures for eradication of administrative and ethical corruption;
12. implementing the hijab in accordance with the shari'a;
13. creating available opportunities for developing the moral, scientific and cultural personality of citizens, in accordance with the high Islamic values and directions;
14. spreading Islamic brotherhood and national unity and strengthening the spirit of cooperation and solidarity among the people;
15. establishing, strengthening, educating, developing and organising an Islamic Army in a proper way consistent with the guidance of the Amir ul-Mu'mineen;
16. regulating the issues concerning the martyrs' families, ailing people, orphans and widows;
17. regulating issues related to the return of refugees and seeking facilities to accommodate them;

18. being accountable, in its capacity as the executive power in the Emirate, for its actions before the Islamic Shura and the Amir ul-Mu'mineen;
19. being assigned to implement the irrevocable sentences issued from the courts;
20. presenting, regulating and implementing the education system in accordance with Islam;
21. protecting the Emirate's properties and personal properties against wrongful behaviour;
22. attracting unconditional aid from foreign countries and organisations to rebuild a new Afghanistan;
23. spreading and developing preventive and curing medicine in order to protect and improve public health; and
24. approving the hiring of foreign experts.

Article 66: Ministers are appointed or dismissed upon recommendation of the prime minister and are subject to the approval of the Amir ul-Mu'mineen.

Article 67: Members of the government are not permitted to abuse their position for personal benefit, and they should not be given favourable treatment.

Article 68: The duties and the rights of the Emirate's employees and workers are regulated through law.

Article 69: Solving crimes and apprehending culprits are the duties of the police. Investigation, surveillance and filing lawsuits are done by the attached department in accordance with the provisions of the law.

Chapter Six: The Judiciary

Article 71 [no Article 70 as received]: The courts are independent in issuing their verdicts, and they are authorised to ensure justice and issue verdicts based on the shari'a.

Article 72: The verdicts issued by the courts should be implemented, except the death sentence verdicts that should be ratified by the Amir ul-Mu'mineen prior to their execution.

Article 73: Trial sessions shall be open, whereas the cases during which the trial sessions are secret shall be specified by the law. The issuing of verdicts shall be public in all cases. The courts shall mention the reasons for the verdict while announcing it.

Article 74: The head of the judicial authority shall be appointed by the Amir ul-Mu'mineen, who should take into consideration the qualifications of such a person. The deputies [of the head of judicial power] and the office heads shall be appointed by the Amir ul-Mu'mineen in coordination with the head of the Supreme Court, taking religious commitment, knowledge, fear of God, and the professional knowledge of the judicial and legal affairs of the country into account.

Article 75: The judges are appointed upon the nomination of the head of the Supreme Court and the approval of the Amir ul-Mu'mineen.

Article 76: When a judge commits a crime, the Supreme Court shall hear his statements. After hearing them, the Supreme Court can recommend the Amir ul-Mu'mineen to depose the judge. If the suggestion is ratified by the Amir ul-Mu'mineen, the judge shall be deposed from his position.

Article 77: Neither any law nor any figure can exclude a case or issue from the jurisdiction of the judicial authority and assign it to any other authority.

Article 78: The budget of the Supreme Court shall be prepared by the Supreme Council of the court. The budget proposal shall be submitted by the government to the Islamic Shura to obtain its approval.

Article 79: The laws of the state's administrative employees are applicable to the employees of the judiciary force.

Article 80: The jurisdiction of the judiciary includes the cases in which individuals or the state are either the defendant or the plaintiff, according to legal provisions, in addition to other [normal] legal cases.

Article 81: The replacement, promotion, retirement or acceptance of resignation of judges shall be by the Supreme Court, according to provisions of the law.

Article 82: The head and members of the Supreme Court cannot, while they are in office, practise any commercial activity with the Emirate.

Chapter Seven: Administration

Article 83: The Islamic Emirate of Afghanistan's administration is divided into three [as received] directorial units: states, districts, sub-districts and civilian divisions which are administered and funded by the government.

Article 84: The administrative units are formed under the proposal of the government and after the guidance of the Islamic Shura and approval of Amir ul-Mu'mineen.

Chapter 8: Economic System and Financial Affairs

Article 85: Individual property and Emirate properties are the basis of the economic system of the Islamic Emirate of Afghanistan. The Emirate leads, encourages and protects the economic growth of the country in both sections through programmes regulated by law.

Article 86:

A. The Emirate is responsible for keeping Islamic assets for growth and strengthens the Treasury and its payments.
B. The collection and distribution of *zakat* [alms] and the one-tenth tax are regulated according to Islamic provisions in an independent regulation.

C. The cancellation of all usury transactions and zero-interest loans is the task of the Emirate.

Article 87: All the resources of the country are to be used by the Emirate for economic improvement and self-dependence to eliminate retarding growth and to increase public living standards by formulating and implementing economic and social programmes according to the Islamic shari'a.

Article 88: All affairs associated with unclaimed, underground [unaccounted for wealth] minerals, forests, pastures, and basic energy sources, historical monuments, communication facilities, great dams, frontier entrances, transportation networks, heavy industries, media stations, airports and other [facilities] are to be regulated through a special law in consideration for the country's higher interests and in accordance with the shari'a provisions.

Only the citizens of Afghanistan and the Islamic Emirate of Afghanistan have the licence and the right to establish a public press and distribute publications in accordance with the law.

The investment of private sector capital is to be regulated to utilise the woods and pastures, energy sources, and in the field of buying and selling intelligence devices according to the law.

Article 89: Foreign bank branches and institutions are regulated in accordance with the law and Islamic principles.

Article 90: Any change in banking methods and affairs and related amendments in accordance with Islamic economic provisions are the responsibility of the Emirate.

Article 91: The Emirate is to expand and strengthen the activities of the cooperative, productive and distribution institutions by related administrations and in accordance with Islamic provisions.

Article 92: Financial and technical aid are provided by the Emirate through its authorised institutions for the villagers, farmers and cattle keepers to reclaim and expand agriculture, to increase the kinds of crops and cattle, to help in creating modern ways of planting, to reclaim fallow lands, to expand roads and to pay attention to irrigation affairs according to the law.

Article 93: The Emirate encourages and protects individual—local and foreign—investments in the fields of industry, trade, construction, aviation, transportation, agriculture and services to develop the national economy according to the law.

Article 94: Real estate acquisition for individuals and diplomatic missions is regulated by law.

Article 95: The Emirate defends all kinds of public and private legal properties. Every citizen is a legal owner of what is gained and the legal work [entailed]. Individual legal ownership is immune from invasion. Acquisition of a property is according to the law and by the order of the authorised court. The acquisition is to be fairly made in return for paying an advance value, only for the purpose of providing a public utility, according to law.

Article 96: The standards, amount and type of fees and harvest [tax] in the Islamic Emirate of Afghanistan are determined according to shari'a law and social justice. The citizens of the Islamic Emirate of Afghanistan and foreign individuals are to pay the fees and harvest to the government according to the law.

Article 97: The Emirate is responsible of taking necessary actions through the concerned institutions in order to preserve natural wealth and take a reasonable benefit of its resources and prevent environmental pollution to the extent possible.

Chapter Nine: Foreign Policy

Article 98: The foreign policy of the Islamic Emirate of Afghanistan, in light of the valuable Islamic instructions, aims to perform an efficient role in building and spreading humanitarian values, social interests, political freedom, territorial integrity, international security and international cooperation.

Article 99: The Islamic Emirate of Afghanistan respects the regulations of the United Nations, the Organisation of the Islamic Conference, the Non-Aligned Movement, human rights and other accepted regulations which do not contradict the fundamentals of Islam and the country's interests.

Article 100: The Islamic Emirate of Afghanistan, based on respecting the reciprocal rights according to the Islamic shari'a, wants to strengthen and expand its relations and build good relations with all countries, especially those that supported the oppressed Afghan people during the legitimate jihad.

Article 101: The Islamic Emirate of Afghanistan, based on the rights of its neighbours, wants to increase the level of cooperation with its neighbouring countries and seeks to strengthen Islamic brotherhood and unify the Islamic nation.

Article 102: The Islamic Emirate of Afghanistan, based on the Islamic shari'a, respects the rights of all world nations and condemns any kind of violation against their rights and any prevention of their freedom.

Article 103: The Islamic Emirate of Afghanistan, in order to protect human rights for all members of the humanitarian community for the sake of their freedom, stands beside the legal causes of nations and demands solution to infighting in a peaceful manner based on Islamic fundamentals and fair balance. It also condemns the methods of pressure by force.

Article 104: The Islamic Emirate of Afghanistan defends programmes of disarming the superpowers and removing weapons of mass destruction.

Article 105: Citizens of the Islamic Emirate of Afghanistan living abroad are under the Emirate's protection and the Emirate shall defend their legitimate rights.

Chapter Ten: Miscellaneous Powers

Article 106: Any amendment, modification or deletion of the constitution is made on the proposal of the Amir ul-Mu'mineen, the Council of Ministers, the Supreme

Shura of the Supreme Court, or a number of members of the Islamic Shura. It is validated after the approval of the Islamic Shura, the Supreme Shura Council of the Supreme Court, and the Council of Ministers.

Article 107: The entering-into-force of this constitution completely brings to an end all main regulations of previous regimes and deems them null and void.

Article 108: The interpretation of this constitution is the prerogative of the Islamic Shura.

Article 109: The provisions of laws which were issued prior to the implementation of this constitution are considered valid unless they conflict with the provisions of the Islamic virtuous religion, and the values of this constitution.

Article 110: The implementation of this constitution that has been arranged in ten (10) chapters and one hundred and ten (110) articles is announced starting from the date of its declaration and published in the official gazette.

58

SHARI'A COURT PUNISHES THREE CRIMINALS

[*This source gives a flavour of some of the events taking place in the country's judiciary at the time. Punishments are allocated for events involving the 'possession of spirits'.*]

Tolo-ye Afghan, 6 July 2001

A shari'a court convicted two Arabs and one Afghan, assigning the punishment of thirty-nine lashes to each. Bakhtar news agency reported that four Arab citizens, now residing in our country—al-Akh al-Qital, Masab al-Sharif, Haidar and Hashmat— and an Afghan, Abdullah, contacted the secondary court. They informed the court that there was an Afghan, Saif al-Shara'i, who was possessed by spirits. In order to free him from the possession of the spirits they beat him. But during the beating he died. Therefore they came to the court to be duly punished according the principles of the Muhammadi shari'a. The matter was presented to His Excellency the Amir ul-Mu'mineen, who suggested the formation of a special tribunal for the assessment of the matter. After a comprehensive analysis, the tribunal released Hashmat and Haidar and condemned al-Akh al-Qital, Masab al-Sharif and Abdullah to be lashed thirty-nine times each. Their imprisonment was suspended until the heirs of the deceased contact the court in this regard. All three were lashed thirty-nine times in the court-yard of the High Court.

PART 3

INSURGENCY (2001-)

2001 Al-Qaeda attacks the United States (September)

2002 Hamid Karzai elected as interim president (June)

2004 Presidential elections (October–November)

2005 Parliamentary elections (September)

2009 Obama administration reveals new strategy for Afghanistan and begins their 'surge' (March)

2009 Presidential and provincial elections (August)

2011 Burhanuddin Rabbani assassinated in Kabul (September)

2014 Presidential election (April–September)

2015 First 'Islamic State' groups announced inside Afghanistan (January)

2015 Taliban announce that Mullah Muhammad Omar died a few years earlier (July)

2016 Mullah Mansour, the replacement leader of the Taliban, is killed in a drone strike (May)

After the attacks on the World Trade Center and the Pentagon, the Islamic Emirate of Afghanistan found itself in complete isolation. The Taliban leadership reiterated a number of solutions, offering to try bin Laden before an Islamic court in Afghanistan on the eve of American airstrikes, or a week later offering to hand him over to another Islamic country for trial. It also condemned the attacks in an official statement.

The United States, however, expected a unilateral surrender of bin Laden to US law enforcement authorities, with President Bush calling on the Taliban to hand bin Laden and other al-Qaeda leaders over and close down foreign-fighter training camps.

On 22 September, the Northern Alliance started to launch coordinated attacks on Taliban positions in the north after the arrival of covert CIA team 'Jawbreaker' in Afghanistan. The US government was approaching senior Taliban leaders they deemed more amenable, trying to split the movement along moderate and radical lines, but to no avail.

In the run-up to Operation Enduring Freedom, opinions among the Taliban leadership were split: some were convinced that the US would soon attack, while others—including Mullah Mohammad Omar—did not think that the US would choose to go to war over bin Laden. On 7 October, the US launched operations with coordinated airstrikes on multiple targets throughout Afghanistan. Kandahar city and province were bombed throughout the night; Kandahar was not only the spiritual capital of the Taliban movement, but also the place of permanent residence of Mullah Mohammad Omar. Bin Laden, along with much of the core leadership of al-Qaeda, had relocated by mid-November from Kandahar to Tora Bora, while the Taliban leadership had stayed in Kandahar, with more and more regional and field commanders joining Mullah Omar.

When held against the north, the US lacked allies on the ground in southern Afghanistan to engage the Taliban forces. It was also considerably more difficult to get American boots on the ground. Many previously exiled mujahedeen commanders recognised the opportunity to reassert themselves in Afghanistan. Gul Agha Sherzai, the pre-Taliban governor of Kandahar, prepared for his return by dispatching a group of tribal elders as early as 9 October to persuade the Taliban to stand down.

In early November, Gul Agha Sherzai, with a hurriedly assembled ragtag militia of some 1,500 fighters and the help of an American special forces team, entered Afghanistan and started to march behind a heavy moving curtain of airstrikes on Kandahar. The city came under siege, and by the end of November rumours had spread about the Taliban leadership negotiating with Mullah Naqib and Hajji Bashar for a possible handover.

The city fell on 7 December, and even though US forces and their Afghan allies tried to block retreat routes to Pakistan, some 2,000 Taliban fighters managed to slip past them, finding refuge in Pakistan's border provinces.

The ongoing conflict in southern Afghanistan even after the fall of the Taliban's forces left ample place for bandits and rogue commanders to operate, while family members of the Taliban and tribal elders fell victim to abuses by the new interim government, being alienated and sidelined in the process. This in turn led them to contact the Taliban leadership that was regrouping in Quetta, Pakistan. The lack of political reconciliation and a political process that allowed for holistic participation meant that parts of society re-aligned with the Taliban. This gave the fledgling resurgent movement a contact network and footholds into local communities throughout 2002.

In the first eighteen months after being ousted from power, the Taliban movement faced the danger of fracturing. In early 2002, a group of Taliban led by Mawlawi Nabi Mohammedi's son broke away from the main movement and revived a group called Jamiat-i Khudam ul-Qur'an, but they were later re-absorbed.

As early as April 2002, Taliban propaganda reappeared in the form of leaflets or night letters left in school buildings; these called on the population to resist the new Afghan government and its foreign allies. As in the 1990s, the Taliban began to communicate with local communities via these simple messages, printed or even sometimes handwritten, addressed to the general population or to individuals. The earliest instances, however, are most likely the product of free agents who acted autonomously within the general outline of the Taliban movement.

By mid-2003 the Taliban leadership had regrouped in Quetta. Mullah Mohammad Omar announced the founding of a new Taliban leadership council, the *rahbari shura*, often referred to as the Quetta shura. The shura had initially ten members, then twelve, eighteen and eventually thirty-three. The initial council members were responsible for assigned regions, in a regional command structure. The individual commanders had re-established initial contacts within Afghanistan; they were often approached by Afghans from within Afghanistan, and communities that had been strong supporters of the movement in the past were quite quick to re-establish links.

With their consolidation of power and an established base in Pakistan, the leadership set out to establish a shadow government, mirroring government positions by appointing district chiefs and province governors, as well as revitalising their legal system. As in the 1990s, the Taliban focused on two key areas: security and justice.

In 2003, they established roaming courts. These were initially reactive bodies, holding session for specific issues and events. The courts increasingly expanded their outreach into areas under Taliban control, settling disputes, civil and criminal cases. The increasing provision of government-type services and the acceptance of the local population in sync with the Taliban's ability to enforce their justice system was a strong indicator of the progression of the conflict. The Taliban's provision of services was often even used by communities not directly under their influence: it outperformed the government justice system in its track-record of caseloads, as well as in terms of minimal corruption.

The insurgency campaign grew increasingly violent. During 2003 the Taliban began a targeted assassination campaign, killing ulemaa, government employees, tribal elders as well as Afghans, denouncing them as spies and collaborators, in what looked like a re-run of the mujahedeen's campaign in the 1980s jihad.

While the Taliban were increasingly successful in Kandahar and southern Afghanistan, they continued to face problems of unity, with another group, Jaish ul-Muslimeen, breaking away from the Taliban over the progression of the insurgency. As with Khudam ul-Qur'an, the group was later re-absorbed. Central to the problems of fracture within the movement was the organisational structure of the Taliban, modelled on the mujahedeen fronts that fought against the Soviet Union. In contrast to that time, the funding structure of the movement post-2001 was increasingly diverse, facing up to the problem that individual commanders could operate completely independently from the central authority of the *rahbari shura*. In other words, the very structure that lends the Taliban their strength, allowing for flexible and proactive insurgency, can be understood at the same time to be one of its potential weaknesses.

Disagreements continued to cause rifts within the *rahbari shura* in Quetta and beyond. Nevertheless, in October 2006 Mullah Mohammad Omar announced the formation of the Majlis al-Shura, a body with thirteen members, mostly well-known Taliban commanders. Around the same time Haqqani was appointed overall military commander, effectively replacing Dadullah and Osmani who had openly fallen out. Dadullah had been criticised by many Taliban for his decapitation campaign and violence against the Afghan population, and Mullah Mohammad Omar was reportedly dissatisfied with his performance in Kandahar the previous summer.

In March 2003, Ricardo Munguia, an engineer who had been working with ICRC in southern Afghanistan, was assassinated. The assassination marked a shift in the Taliban's attitude towards aid workers who were regarded as legitimate targets, together with anyone who supported the government in Kabul. This triggered an exodus of foreign aid organisations from the more dangerous parts of the country.

The presidential and provincial council elections held at the end of November 2004 and September 2005 respectively were a milestone achievement for 'project Afghanistan' and passed without the violence that many commentators expected. It is unclear why the Taliban did little to prevent the elections. Speculation varies from Pakistani influence to the Taliban wanting a representative partner with which to negotiate. Local voices believe that the Taliban were still consolidating their efforts at the time, and were simply not prepared to conduct widespread operations to disrupt the elections.

While the Taliban had employed propaganda as one of their main strategies, the period 2003–6 saw the movement focusing on their strategic communication. The Taliban increasingly used a diverse range of media to broadcast their message, producing VCDs and DVDs, cassettes, as well as setting up websites and radio stations. Video and audio footage was widely available. The quality of the products as well as the construction of the message improved and became sophisticated, taking the grievances of the population and integrating them in a greater historical and religious context, playing on national, cultural and religious themes. This included the first rollout of their *layeha* or rulebook, in which they attempted to offer a degree of transparency to how they functioned.

Military operations came to be determined by their communication effects and carried out to make public statements rather than for any specific military objective. The growing losses sustained by the attempt to fight more traditional battles with foreign forces and their Afghan allies directly translated into a focus on soft targets that would achieve a greater effect on public debate and influence the opinion of local communities.

Mullah Mohammad Omar's twice-yearly Eid statements became much-anticipated occasions, and the length of messages increased to match the interest. Few believe that Mullah Mohammad Omar was necessarily the sole author of the documents, but as a representative statement of what the Taliban stood for they were seriously read and considered by diplomats, researchers and journalists alike.

PART 3: INSURGENCY (2001-)

The big event of 2009—both for the Afghan government, their foreign allies, and for the Taliban themselves—was the 20 August presidential elections. Throughout the whole time between January and August, the Taliban's official spokesmen and websites were extremely non-committal as to how they saw the upcoming elections, as well as what their plans were. This mirrored the Taliban's off-and-on stance during the 2004 and 2005 elections. Some statements were very forthright and claimed that the Taliban would shut the elections down in a fierce campaign, while in other places the message was less clear.

One reason for the lack of clarity was probably the desire to see what the broad mass of Afghans (especially those living in the districts) thought about the elections. In the previous elections, the Taliban had mostly taken a back seat in the face of a strong public desire to come out and vote. For this round, it became apparent that ordinary people were not much concerned with voting and that the Taliban could mount a large campaign, but that it probably would be a wasted effort as nobody would be voting anyway.

The Obama administration instituted a review of its Afghanistan strategy, culminating in a decision to double-down on the military's approach, coupled with a plan to engage the Taliban politically. As a US troop surge decided upon in the review reached its peak, Taliban operations were constrained in certain parts of the country. A parallel political process—always threatening failure—took on more importance during those years, and messaging was increasingly directed outwards to a foreign audience. Following the withdrawal of most of these surge troops, the Taliban regained the upper hand in some areas. Needless to say, a lot of this had occurred by default or as a result of government weakness rather than through Taliban strength.

The problem of organisational instability reared its head once again, provoked by the increasingly public political overtures between the Taliban and the US and the rise of affiliates of the (Iraq/Syria-based) Islamic State group.

International meetings increased prior to the troop withdrawal, cementing the international commitment to funding the Afghan state, though without much acknowledgement that this could not serve as a long-term solution. By late 2016, the international community remained occupied by a series of events that had little to do with Afghanistan (continuing turmoil in the Middle East, ongoing refugee flows, Brexit and the US presidential election), throughout which the Taliban continued their slow de facto increase of territorial control, while at the same time being subject to internal fragmentation and discontent.

SHOCK AND AWE (2001–2003)

59

HIS EXCELLENCY AMIR UL-MUMINEEN'S ORDER

[*This was one of the final formal announcements issued by Mullah Mohammad Omar. Anis was a quasi-independent newspaper that ran a series of issues in the final days of the Taliban government's presence in Kabul.*]

Anis, 19 September 2001

All the infidel powers of the world have united against the Islamic Emirate of Afghanistan and the mujahed Afghan nation and—God forbid—want to collapse the pure Islamic system that has been enforced in Afghanistan. The heroic and mujahed Afghan nation have not bowed their heads to foreigners at any time and have always made sacrifices and referred to God Almighty for assistance. Therefore, the public and all offices of the Emirate are ordered that—in addition to being ready for making sacrifices—they need to hold Qur'an-recitation sessions in their mosques and they need to ask God Almighty for the humiliating embarrassment and defeat of the infidel powers. Meanwhile, all imams of the mosques are ordered to start reading Qunoot Nazila after the *fajr* prayer as ordered by the instructions of the Prophet.

60

TALIBAN RESPONSES TO 11 SEPTEMBER

[These two passages represent the official diplomatic position of the Taliban movement in the days following the attacks of 11 September 2001. Mullah Mutawakil, in Kabul at the time, recalled contacting the Taliban leader upon hearing the news.]

At the time when that story [9/11] happened, I was in Kabul. I contacted Mullah Mohammad Omar in Kandahar immediately asking what should we do. He told me, 'Condemn it. Condemn this action as harshly and strongly as you can.' And I think the Taliban government was one of the first governments who condemned this action, and besides condemning it they also denied their involvement and they said that the killing of innocents wherever they are is not allowed (*haram*). Al-Qaeda at that time never said 'We did it.' If they did say something, then they said something like 'Whoever did that thing, we think it's a good thing.' They appreciated it. That's a big difference, that one side [the Taliban] condemned it, but the other side, al-Qaeda, appreciated it.

[In Islamabad, Mullah Zaeef received similar instructions, and dispatched a copy of the press release to the US Embassy.]

Bismillah ar-Rahman ar-Rahim

We strongly condemn the events that happened in the United States at the World Trade Center and the Pentagon. We share the grief of all those who have lost their nearest and dearest in these incidents. All those responsible must be brought to justice. We want them to be brought to justice, and we want America to be patient and careful in their actions.

61

RESOLUTION AND FATWA OF A BIG GATHERING OF CLERICS

[This was an initial fatwa issued by a group of clerics that proactively made the case for a defensive jihad. If America were to attack Afghanistan, they argued, this would open up exactly the same Islamic justification to fight back as had been the case with the Soviet Union.]

Anis, 23 September 2001

The Afghan nation has always referred to respected clerics for their crucial matters, and the clerics have made tireless efforts to solve the issues referred to them. The present weighty matter is that Afghanistan is at risk of probable attack by America. Based on their heavy responsibility, Afghan clerics took the following decision and issued a fatwa to solve the problems in the light of the holy religion of Islam:

When the territory of a Muslim country is attacked by any other country, jihad becomes mandatory for citizens of that country. Verses from the Qur'an and the hadith order all Muslims to jihad:

[Arabic text from the Qur'an ordering Muslims to jihad]

The translation of some of them runs as follows:

1. Fight until there is no vice and the entire religion is for Allah.
2. Those who were fighting were given permission, because they were being oppressed. Allah is very able to make them succeed.
3. You are to fight although it seems unpleasant to you. Sometimes you might dislike something while it is good for you, and sometimes you might like something while it is bad for you. Allah knows and you don't know.

[Hadith narrated by Anas bin Malik]

If infidels attack Muslim territory, if needed, Muslims can ask for assistance from Muslim and non-Muslim governments provided that the principles of Islam are held high. During the attack by America, if any Muslim—regardless of whether they are Afghan or non-Afghan—cooperates with the infidels, or if he helps and spies for them, then that person will be just like the foreign invaders and killing him becomes mandatory.

EXPANSION AND REVIVAL (2004–2010)

62

AN INTERVIEW WITH SATAN

[*Da Mujahed Zhagh was one of the first publications started by the Taliban following the collapse of their government in late 2001. Issues were more directly concerned with political matters and the flourishing insurgency. A Taliban overview of media publications in* al-Somood *magazine stated that the magazine was established on 6 August 2004 by 'brother Suleymankhil'. This article is a satirical interview with Satan.*]

Da Mujahed Zhagh *(web magazine), 18 July 2004*

We have been checking our phone records to find the mother of all deceptions and to prepare a properly conducted interview with him. An assignment was given to the staff of *Da Mujahed Zhagh* to make efforts to find this spirit-like creature and to arrange an [unclear] interview with him. But it wasn't within the possibilities of a man to find this unidentified and amorphous creature.

But after some time, by chance, the cursed person turned into an identifiable personality and gave us a call. His personality took on the features of various well-known people. Some of these signs were quite evident in his embodiment. We could observe the following visible signs of his physical presence: the eyes of Bush, the cap and gown of Karzai, the waistcoat of Mr Qanuni, the beard of Sayyaf and the nose and trousers of the Father of the Nation.[1] This hybrid personality was quite vociferous and he constantly claimed that he was the self-same Satan who played an important role in the deception of Adam. When our staff asked him for an interview, he promptly accepted it and was ready to answer our questions.

Q: Can you, the enemy of humanity and cursed by God, introduce yourself to us? What is your name and how old are you?

A: I am ready to brief you about my evilness and malevolence. I will also tell you my name and age. My name is Bushkarbani Fahsayaf Zahir Shah. I am centuries old. During my whole life I have never done anything virtuous. To the people of this world, the Qur'an has introduced me as an enemy of God. My duty is to deceive all

241

human beings. I have a large number of descendants. All of them are my partners in the enmity to God.

Q: What is your education level? How do you perform your official duties; and where are your headquarters located?

A: You have raised a very good question. I have no match in evil acts. God has shown only me all the ways and tricks of evil and sin. No one else has the right to use them. My descendants are my administrative staff. Besides this I have very efficient subordinates among human beings. Pharaoh, Haman, Nimrud, Shadad, Abu Jahl and all of their friends were my human descendants. At present, too, I have my administrative staff in every country. In the eyes of God, all these countries are the centres of ignorance. Bush in the United States, and Prime Minister Tony Blair of Britain are my main colleagues. My headquarters are in the White House of America where my evil flag waves in the air.

Q: Who are your most loyal servants in Afghanistan who serve you day and night?

A: Not only in Afghanistan, but around the whole world I have my allies. In Afghanistan I have very loyal friends. People know them as Pirs and Mullahs but in fact they are my people. They include Pir Sayyid Ahmad Gailani, Fazal Hadi Shinwari and Fayaz, the head of Kandahar's Ulema Shura. Besides this: Khalilzad, the current president Karzai and the ministers of his cabinet are my closest allies.

Q: As the enemy of God, tell us what you eat and how do you exist? Do others help you or do you do your own business?

A: I suck the blood of humans. I survive on bribery like Hadi Shinwari, the head of the Afghan Ulema Shura. Making people the enemies of God is the source of my nutrition. I lure Muslims from the Islamic [nations] to a world of infidelity and secularism and force them to swap their Islamic dress for Western trousers. This is the main source of my food.

Q: Where can you be reached and where do you live now? Do you live in your headquarters within the White House or outside?

A: Until a few years ago when the BBC and VOA still did not exist, mostly I lived in my own office.[2] Since the launching of these radio stations, I have been living in their offices and never go anywhere else, because it is through these radio networks that I can easily deceive many people. So far I have successfully deceived many of them. All of their programmes are organised as per my instructions. Their propaganda helps me a lot in the fight against God.

Q: Interestingly in the last few months the Voice of America has changed its name and now calls itself VOA Ashna radio. Did you tell them this trick too? If yes, then what was its benefit for you?

A: Yes, I changed the Voice of America into Ashna Radio Without Borders. It isn't only Afghans, but the Muslims of the whole world who hate the word 'America', and that is why I took this action in order to solve the problem.

AN INTERVIEW WITH SATAN

Q: May you perish! During the Loya Jirga, which was held for the ratification of the new constitution, why did you provoke Malalai Joya to disgrace all the mujahedeen and call them warlords?

A: By provoking Malalai Joya I wanted to identify those people who still mind if someone disgraces the mujahedeen. If still such people exist in Afghanistan I will bring them to the notice of the Americans. Exactly the same thing happened. Those who expressed their anger about Malalai Joya's accusations were arrested by the Americans and sent to Guantánamo.

Q: You claim that you have many friends in Afghanistan wearing the garb of Pirs, Hazrats and Mullahs among others. But you are still not in the position to bring peace and stability to Afghanistan. You construct a lot of rhetoric about the projects of reconstruction but so far no work has been done except the construction of the Kabul–Kandahar road.

A: I never work for the benefit of human beings, and especially not for Muslims. My duty is animosity towards God. I always want bloodshed. That is my benefit. I have not come here for the reconstruction of Afghanistan. Rather, I will carry on my efforts until the destruction of religion and the progress of infidelity across the whole Muslim world. My name is Satan and I just fulfil my evil deeds.

Q: Whose performance is the most satisfactory for you?

A: I am very satisfied with those labourers whom I stop from offering their prayers. They fully obey my orders. I am also extremely happy with Professor Rabbani. Because, when the Americans dropped daisy-cutter and cluster bombs over the Qur'anic students, he would tell the Americans that it was not enough and demanded more intense bombings.

Q: What do you think about the magazine Da Mujahed Zhagh?

A: When anybody reads the *DMZ* magazine or talks about it, I immediately criticise its quality by pointing to its various flaws.

Q: What is the reason for your propaganda against Da Mujahed Zhagh?

A: The name of my main enemy is again and again published in this magazine. I am very much afraid of his name. His name is Muhammad Omar. I am scared to death of this name. When I hear this name, in panic I think about Hazrat Omar.

63

SUGAR-COATED POISON

[*The online magazine took efforts to make the material they published engaging in a way that newspapers of the Islamic Emirate era often did not. This article brings in Pashtun proverbs, conversations with elders and crimes committed by foreigners. The style is common to this kind of publication: facts are not pushed on the reader, but thereby one learns about the local distrust of foreigners' motives...*]

Da Mujahed Zhagh, 18 July 2004

I have loved Pashto proverbs for a long time. During our childhood, our grandfather told us the importance of the proverbs. Our elders use the proverbs and other folkloric couplets in a very balanced manner. The Pashtun people often refer to proverbs in the course of their conversations. When a member of Pashtun society is able to use appropriate proverbs he is considered a clever man. When I was quite grown up I could comprehend many things and was quite advanced in my studies. At that stage I developed a special passion for proverbs. That is why the other villagers gave me the nickname 'clever boy'. I had an idea in my mind to collect the proverbs of the Pashto language and publish them in a book. For this purpose, my method was to have meetings with the elders of the village and gather the proverbs from them. It was during this research that I listened to many proverbs from the village elders.

One of these proverbs was the following: 'Your father's enemy cannot become your friend.' After hearing this proverb I was wondering how the enemy of one's father cannot become one's friend. On several occasions we have seen that people reconcile with their father's enemy. I made a lot of efforts to find out the real meaning of this proverb. For this purpose, on one holiday I went to a rural area. I found a group of people sitting in front of a mosque and enjoying the sun, which is called *lmar tsekai* by the Pashtuns. After greetings, I wanted to stay longer with them in order to reach my goal.

I had yet to commence the conversation when an elder, who seemed the village head, turned to another elder and resumed his conversation. He asked him, 'What

245

did they say?' The other replied that they wanted to build a clinic for us and for the surrounding villages. Then the elder turned to another villager, Shaista Gul, and asked about his knowledge regarding the work of the NGOs. The elder asked who they were. Shaista Gul told them that it was an organisation called [Médecins Sans Frontières]. They build clinics everywhere and provide medicine for people. The elder again asked what benefit they had by doing all this, and after all who they were themselves. Shaista Gul replied that in fact they were foreigners, and they took no benefit from that. This was humanitarian work and they called themselves the servants of humanity. This was the real purpose of their efforts.

On hearing this, many questions erupted in the mind of the elderly person. Then he addressed Shaista Gul and mentioned the following proverb: 'A stone can never rot, nor can an enemy ever become a friend.' These foreigners are the sons of the same foreigners who came to destroy our country some time ago. They tried to destroy our homeland and religion. But with the help of God, our gallant youth decisively defeated them. Our mountains and plains are still full of their forefathers' bones. Advise them to avenge and not to help us. It would be a kind of disloyalty on their part against their own forefathers. If they call themselves the servants of humanity, I think it is a kind of sugar-coated poison. Why do they believe that the enemies of their forefathers deserve their help? There are many other poor people who deserve it. I believe it is the same aggression which their ancestors also committed against our land. However, they lacked experience, while the modern-day foreigners are experienced.

Before Shaista Gul could say anything, all the other members of the meeting criticised the old man in a very harsh tone. They blamed him and told him that he was always against the prosperity of the villagers. They said that in the past another organisation wanted to build a school in the village. At that time he also prevented it from happening and said that they would train their children in infidelity. They said that he was then against the construction of the clinic. All of them laughed and asked ironically whether there was any infidelity mixed into the medicine.

He replied and said that he still believed it was the enemies' trick. Then he quoted their forefathers' saying, 'The enemy of one's father cannot become one's friend.' He told them that if all of them wanted it, he would agree with them, but that he personally remained reluctant.

It was the comments of this elder that made me comprehend the meaning of the proverb that the enemy of one's father cannot become one's friend, viz. an infidel can never be the friend of a Muslim. However, as the majority of the villagers did not agree with their elder, I was not fully sure about the meaning of the proverb. I thought that possibly the village elder had misinterpreted the proverb. Even though the foreigners are infidels, they are human beings and it is quite possible that they really want to provide humanitarian assistance to others. But when I recalled the elder's comment asking why they had selected only [that village] for their aid even though the world is full of poor people, I plunged into a myriad of questions. I thought too much about the role of the NGOs. The more I thought the about this question, the more difficult I found it.

On 6 March 2004 I visited the school office. While I was sitting with other visitors, they complained about the situation in the country. I asked them about whether something new had happened. One of the participants took up the newspaper of that day and told me that the Americans had given sexual arousal drugs to the young men and women of different areas of Kunar province which had caused various diseases. In the first stage, one of the patients had gone to a hospital in Jalalabad. After the completion of his inspections he was referred to the university hospital, and thus that news was also leaked. When I heard about it, I was very sad...

64

LAYEHA

A JIHADI CODE OF CONDUCT (2006 EDITION)

[*The* layeha *published some time in 2006 was the Taliban's first post-2001 attempt to codify the practices and standards by which commanders and fighters should seek to abide. It was in part an exercise in rebranding the movement publicly as a group that could both manage its own affairs and be accountable to the Afghan public it claimed to be representing.*]

[Printed document]¹, 2006

In the name of God, the compassionate and merciful.

The Islamic Emirate of Afghanistan: A Jihadi Code of Conduct²

Thanks be to God and may peace be upon his Prophet.

Jihad in the way of Almighty God is a such a great worship [*ebadat*] and a great obligation that fulfilling it will bring dignity and raise up God's testament of faith [*kalima*].It is clear that the goal will be achieved if it is worked towards in the light of God's orders [*ahkaam*] and in the framework of the appointed principles [i.e. this *layeha*], so every mujahed must abide by the following rules:

1) Any official can invite any Afghan who is in the infidels' ranks to accept true Islam.
2) We guarantee to any man who turns his back on the infidels security for himself and his possessions. But if he becomes involved in a personal dispute, or someone accuses him of something, he must submit to our judiciary.
3) Mujahedeen who would like to protect people inside the opposition must get permission from and inform their commander.
4) Whoever accepts the invitation and then breaks his promise and clearly abuses his commitments becomes a traitor and forfeits our protection. He will be given no second chance.

5) If a mujahed kills or harms a person who has left the opposition and whose security has been guaranteed by the mujahedeen, he will not be supported by the movement and will be dealt with according to Islamic law.

6) If a commander wants to move to another area, he is permitted to do so, but must get permission from the officials of the district and province which he is leaving and the district and the province he is going to join.

7) If mujahedeen capture a foreign infidel as a prisoner, they shall not release him for money or in an exchange deal without the leadership's permission.

8) A provincial, district or regional official may not sign a contract in return for money or other materials to work for a non-governmental organisation [NGO].

9) No official may use jihadi equipment or property for personal ends.

10) Every official is accountable to his superiors in matters of spending money and using equipment.

11) Mujahedeen may not sell equipment, unless the provincial official permits them to do so.

12) A group leader is not allowed to recruit members from another group in order to increase the size of his group. Of course, if a mujahed wants to join another group, he can do so, but all the equipment which the group leader has given him for the cause of jihad shall be returned to that group leader. If the mujahed has received booty and it is as a part share with other members of his group, that booty shall be left with the group.

13) Weapons and equipment taken from infidels or their allies must be fairly distributed among the mujahedeen according to holy shari'a.

14) If mujahedeen, for the good of jihad and Islam, establish contacts with those who are working with the infidels' administration, they shall introduce the person to the local official [to ensure his protection]. Killing him is outlawed. Whoever kills him must be punished according to shari'a law.

15) If an official or an ordinary person harms the common people in the name of the mujahedeen, his senior officer is responsible for reforming him. If he does not reform, the provincial officials shall introduce him to the leadership. The leadership will punish him accordingly or expel him from the ranks of the mujahedeen.

16) It is strictly forbidden to search houses and confiscate weapons without the permission of a senior official.

17) Mujahedeen have no right to confiscate the money or personal possessions of other people.

18) Mujahedeen should refrain from smoking cigarettes.

19) Mujahedeen are not allowed to take under-age boys with no facial hair onto the battlefield or into their military bases.

20) Officials of every province according to the province's situation have the authority to invite those who are in the ranks of the infidels [to switch sides]. If a per-

son surrenders, [fulfilling] particular conditions, they must give him a special guarantee for his safety [literally head] and possessions. Of course, this guarantee must first be discussed with the military commission.

21) Anyone with a bad reputation or who has killed Muslims while working with the infidel administration, who has searched the houses of the common people or recruited labourers for the infidels, will not be accepted into the ranks of the mujahedeen. If the highest leader has personally forgiven him, he will be placed at home in the future.

22) If a mujahed is found guilty of a crime and his commander has barred him from the group, no other group may take him in. If a group commander is found guilty and the senior official has barred him, no other official may take him in, as long as he does not repent.

23) If mujahedeen are faced with a challenge that is not described in this code, they must find a solution in consultation with local senior officials.

24) It is forbidden to work as a teacher under the current state—which is a state in name only—because this strengthens the system of the infidels. True Muslims should apply to study with a religiously trained teacher and study in a mosque or similar institution. Textbooks must come from the period of the mujahedeen period of the Emirate.

25) Anyone who works as a teacher or mullah under the current state—which is a state in name only—must be given a warning. If he nevertheless refuses to give up his job, he must be beaten. Of course, if a teacher or mullah continues to instruct, contrary to the principles of Islam, the district commander or group leader must kill him.

26) The organisations [NGOs] that come to the country are tools of the infidels. In the guise of serving, they are destroying Islam, so all of their activities are banned, whether it is roads or anything else, or clinics or schools or a madrassa or anything else. If a school fails to heed a warning to close, it must be burned. But all religious books, for the sake of respecting them, must be secured beforehand.

27) Except for the senior district official, no one has the authority to interfere in casting someone as a spy or punishing them. Witnesses who testify in a procedure must be in good psychological condition, possess an untarnished religious reputation and have not committed any major crime. Punishment may take place only after the conclusion of the trial.

28) No official has the authority to interfere in resolving disputes which have been brought to the mujahedeen. Of course, only a senior district official or the council of *mahaaz*es [military commission?] in very important cases can intervene. First they must solve the case through [ordinary] ulemaa or tribal elders, peacefully. If they do not agree on a peaceful solution, the decision must be made by well-known local ulemaa.

29) All mujahedeen must post a watch, day and night.

30) The above 29 rules are obligatory. Anyone who violates this code must be judged according to the laws of the Islamic Emirate.

This *layeha* is intended for the mujahedeen who dedicate their lives to Islam and almighty God. This is complete guidance for the progress of the jihad and every mujahed must keep these rules; it is the duty of every jihadi and true believer.

In peace [*wa salaam*]

65

CORRECTING SOME IDEAS

[*In September 2008,* al-Somood *magazine began printing a series of responses to an article published in* al-Furqan *magazine. In that original article, various criticisms of the Taliban movement were raised (concerning the present day as well as the past). These were apparently considered important enough to warrant a lengthy response in a multi-part essay written by Shahabuddin Ghaznawi. It is one of the few times that the Taliban are openly defensive about their actions, and the length of the response indicates the extent to which they seem to have felt challenged by the original article.*]

Shahabuddin Ghaznawi
Al-Somood magazine, 1 September 2008

His Eminence Doctor Bassam al-Shatti voiced several remarks or objections about the Taliban movement in *al-Furqan* magazine (issue number 46, which came out on Ramadan 5) in an article whose headline read: 'An overview of the Taliban's mistakes in Afghanistan'. We would like to mention all the remarks and criticisms of our honourable professor, His Eminence Doctor Bassam al-Shatti, one by one, to discuss them, answer them, comment on them and reveal the truth. We hope to convince firstly our dear professor, and then all those who were duped by the false rumours that were and are still being spread against the Islamic Emirate and are completely baseless. These remarks and our comments on them are as follows.

In his article, the Doctor mentioned:

'I have read the jurisprudence review books of the Gama'a al-Islamiyya, in which the group recanted its violent and erroneous opinions and tackled in certain parts the issue of the Taliban movement while the group was [ruling] in Afghanistan. I would like to write down the most important points that concern the movement. They did not unify the internal front (the specific demographic composition and ethnic, sectarian and racial divergence between the Pashtuns, the Uzbeks, the Hazaras and the Tajiks among others). Hence, instead of containing, integrating and giving them ministerial portfolios or ruling privileges in their regions in order to please them and guarantee their loyalty and belonging, they neglected them, dealt with them harshly and stood with the Pashtuns and none other.'

In his aforementioned remark, His Eminence the Doctor said that the Taliban sided with the Pashtun population and dealt with the others with harshness and stringency.

These remarks are not based on facts, because the Taliban was established and evolved in difficult circumstances, and includes the students of religious schools that have been present in the Indian subcontinent for a long time. The students of these, although they have reached the highest levels of belonging and loyalty to their religion and faith, do not know about politics, especially the political situation of our day and age that is governed by technology, which has altered most standards. This is due to the fact that the religious schools in the Indian subcontinent do not teach political subjects and were not the object of whichever intellectual invasion. In addition, as we have said, the movement was formed under specific circumstances, because the security situation in Afghanistan deteriorated and the people, their possessions and their honour were no longer safe. Indeed, wars and internal conflicts between the fighting parties reached their peak and their flames erupted across the Afghan provinces. At the time, the people needed security and the elimination of corruption and prohibited acts, and the movement was established to eradicate corruption and stabilise the situation, but also to implement the Islamic shari'a for which these persecuted people fought Russian colonialism for ten years, thus sacrificing their lives and possessions to reach their higher purpose and main goal. However, the internal conflicts and the heated battles led the country towards a predicament that caused political experts, analysts and intellectuals to become puzzled when thinking of ways to exit it. The movement was established to achieve the wishes of the martyrs and eliminate these difficulties. Its activities first began in the southern provinces because its founders were from the area, which is also the reason why the Pashtun tribes stood alongside it. This was only natural because, as we have said, the movement was established within their region and was subsequently joined by this region's tribesmen. But the more the movement's activities expanded to other regions, the more it was joined by non-Pashtun men, such as the Tajik, the Uzbek, the Turkmen and the Hazara among others. And they were given high positions in the government and had the upper hand in developing and expanding the movement's activities and in conquering the northern and north-western provinces, whose inhabitants are mostly non-Pashtun.

Among the key positions given to the non-Pashtun during the days of the Islamic Emirate are the following:

1. Minister of Higher Education, Qari Din Mohammad Hanif from Badakhshan province (Tajik)
2. Minister of Immigration, Mawlawi Abdul Raqib from Takhar province (Uzbek)

3. Minister of Labour and Social Affairs, Makhdum Abdussalam from Baghlan province (Tajik)
4. Minister of Hajj and Awqaf, Mawlawi Ghayyath al-Din Agha from Faryab province
5. Minister of Statistics, Mohammad Omar Faruqi from Paktika province (Tajik)
6. Ambassador to Pakistan, Mawlawi Saeed ar-Rahman from Laghman province (Pashayi)
7. Deputy Supreme Court Judge, Mawlawi Jalilullah Mawlawizadah from Herat province
8. Governor of Logar, Zia ur-Rahman Madani from the province of Takhar (Tajik)
9. Governor of Paktya, Mawlawi Shamsuddin Pahlavan from Badakhshan province
10. Governor of Bamyan, Mawlawi Mohammad Islam Mohammadi from Samangan province (Tatar)
11. Governor of Maidan Wardak, Makhdoum Abdul Haqq from Badakhshan province (Tajik)
12. Deputy Minister of Education, Abdussalam Hanafi from Faryab province (Uzbek)
13. Deputy Minister of Education Saeed Ahmad Shahidkhel from Ghazni province (Tajik)

This is not to mention the fact that all the [religious] students in Badakhshan province, the main stronghold and hometown of Mr [Burhanuddin] Rabbani, joined the Taliban movement and stood alongside it against the former President of Afghanistan, Mr Rabbani.

Even Mr Rabbani himself supports the movement. In his own words: 'The movement was able to eliminate corruption and spread security in the areas under its control.' But when it reached the outskirts of Kabul and the capital became threatened by the movement, he opposed the Taliban mujahedeen and called them the most horrific names through the media channels available to him at the time.

This is why we say that the Islamic Taliban movement was founded to gather together all the Muslims and eliminate ethnic segregation from which the Afghan people have suffered for a long time. As it is understood from its name, the movement is a religious Islamic movement that is opposed to racism and ethnic discrimination. We also say that the movement's foundations are based on solid rules and regulations that oppose all destructive, nationalistic and racist inclinations and are hostile to all parties who promote racism and nationalism. Moreover, it is opposed to all the organisations that violate the rules of Islam and is trying to bring together all Muslims, regardless of their gender, colour and race. It has offered the greatest examples of sacrifice in the defence of religion and faith, and all of this was done to implement the Islamic shari'a and remove the nationalistic and pre-Islamic slogans and calls that are based on racism and sectarianism. The biggest proof is that when it controlled the country, the people lived in peace and stability and there was no discrimination between the Pashtuns and others. Anyone could thus claim his right without fear, and no one could act unjustly or attack or offend another person based on colour, gender or any other specificity.

Despite all these positive points secured by the Islamic Emirate when it controlled the country, we do not claim to know everything that has happened. Hence, racist incidents might have occurred and racist practices might have affected some people, but they were not intentional and rather happened either by mistake or due to misunderstanding. Moreover, the occurrence of such horrific acts does not reside in the hands of the rulers. They are rather the actions of ordinary people or some [low-ranking] state employees. Despite our repeated efforts to restore our glory and implement our shari'a, we recognise our shortcomings in some issues which we did not know how to resolve the right way. Still, we are trying to make up for the mistakes that happened at the time, if there were any. For example, the Islamic Emirate's High Council currently includes all Afghan factions and sects. In addition, we are trying to eliminate all the obstacles standing between us and our original goals so that others no longer have any cause to criticise us. On the other hand, we call on all our Afghan brothers to join our ranks or at least abandon their loyalty to the Americans and the allies, as this is costing them this life and the afterlife and creating religious hostility between them and the mujahedeen. We believe that if brother Doctor Bassam al-Shatti reads our original goals that are drawn from the Qur'an and the sunna, and our positions against racism and nationalism, he will be convinced and will learn the current facts in Afghanistan. Indeed, His Eminence the Doctor cannot be held accountable at this level as he is distant from the arena and does not have exhaustive information about what is happening in Afghanistan. As such, he does not know who is defending the religion in the country and who is being loyal to the enemies. And we do not blame our brother the Doctor because the media and the press are controlled by our enemies who are spreading these groundless reports about the Taliban. If he travels to the field and meets with the movement's leaders, he will learn the truth and abandon his idea.

The second remark or criticism made by His Eminence Doctor Bassam al-Shatti surrounds women's [lack of access to] education. He thus said:

> 'The second mistake is: The prevention of women from acquiring an education, working and leaving their houses. It would have been better to teach women in order to support society's need for teachers, doctors and nurses among other jobs that are necessary at times and permitted at others.'

We recognise that the criticism of the honourable sheikh at this level is somewhat valid, but the issue is not as it was portrayed by His Eminence. Afghan society has always suffered from illiteracy and lack of education and this catastrophe escalated following the Red March and the internal conflicts that had a major and negative impact on this aspect of our life. Illiteracy thus spread, there were fewer schools, and the level of education dropped in general. Most of the schools and universities even closed their doors during the parties' wars, and when the Islamic Emirate gained control over most of the country, it tried hard to open schools and universities and took serious steps on this level. It thus reopened Kabul's main university, Herat University and Kandahar University among others, and opened many schools in the various Afghan provinces. In addition, it tried to secure university and school supplies as much as possible and the education level that had drastically dropped somewhat rose under the Islamic Emirate. For his part, the Minister of Higher Education visited many Islamic and Western states to bring in professors and specialised experts. He also made efforts to reorganise the regulations governing the acceptance of students at university and he was very successful in this task, as he reorganised them in a way so as to be in line with international standards.

[...]

Regarding women's education, one must say that despite the circumstances, they were many schools and colleges for the training of female nurses and doctors who are engaged in medical work at the hospitals and clinics. But in general, education for women was non-existent due to the difficult circumstances faced by the Emirate at the time. The internal conflicts and the heated battles that went on for many years caused the destruction of all the schools and university buildings, while the Emirate's economic situation did not allow it to rebuild and reorganise these facilities. His Eminence the Doctor may be aware of the fact that the Islamic Emirate was facing difficulties and crises on many levels, while the whole world stood against it and the United Nations imposed an economic blockade. This was another problem to be added to the other problems from which the Islamic Emirate was suffering and the situation was not suitable to ensure women's education. Moreover, Afghan experts and specialists left [the country] for other Islamic and European countries and no one was willing to return because of the economic blockade and the lack of basic livelihood conditions. We thus suffered from a low number of teachers, especially ones who could teach women, as there were no older male teachers or female teachers. This is another predicament faced by the Islamic Emirate back when it was controlling the country, and all of these factors and reasons prevented women's education.

With regard to the approach of the Islamic Emirate, it is completely clear, because as we have said it is drawn from the two main sources, i.e. the Qur'an and the sunna, both of which focus on education and learning. Even the first verse that was revealed to Muhammad (PBUH) pointed to the importance of education because it started by saying: 'Recite.' Moreover, this verse was revealed to him in a high place, i.e. Ghar Hira, which points to the high standing of education, teaching and learning. The Islamic Emirate was aware of the importance of education and learning ever since its establishment, which is why it always insisted on it and tried to spread it whether among men or women. For that purpose, it adopted positive steps and printed and published the curriculum that was drawn up by Afghan and Arab scholars during the days of the Soviet invasion of Afghanistan. It is a comprehensive scientific and Islamic curriculum and the Islamic Emirate chose it because of its exhaustiveness. Also, in light of these difficult circumstances, the Islamic Emirate is doing its best to open schools and universities in the areas under its control. And it has already managed to open some of these schools that teach the original and evolved Islamic curriculum. The foundations of the Islamic Emirate insist on education and give it a priority, provided it does not go against the shari'a rules and restrictions. This is why we say that our honourable Professor Doctor Bassam al-Shatti may not have read the Emirate's curriculum or was delivered his news by an unreliable source. Had he read what the movement has done and what it is currently trying to do in terms of the implementation of the true Islamic shari'a and its solid rules, he would have been convinced and he would have approved our Islamic foundations and restrictions, whose implementation we are seeking day and night. I finally say once again and confirm that the Islamic Emirate insists on education for women and men and is doing its best to raise the educational level of the devastated Afghan people, who have been suffering deprivation for many decades. Allah is the source of assistance and on Allah we rely.

[...]

The fifth mistake: [The movement] did not tend to the people's health, educational, social and economic needs among others, and did not pay any attention to development, to the point where Afghanistan became one of the poorest states with the highest unemployment rates. The people also suffered an intellectual siege [...] Muslims encountered many civilisations during their early conquests, but they always developed their inherited customs while upholding their faith, thus accepting whatever agreed with Islam and rejecting whatever opposed it.

It appears [that the Doctor] probably did not follow events in Afghanistan since the Soviet invasion, the heated battles and internal conflicts that went on for many years between the various parties and organisations, and what these destructive wars and bloody battles led to while burning everything on their way. During the Soviet invasion of Afghanistan and after the country's liberation, the Afghan people suffered poverty, unemployment and instability. And during the days of internal conflict and the divide between the various parties and leftist organisations among others, these problems and obstacles increased in the absence of educational or health centres. The hospitals and educational centres reached such a deteriorating state that their presence or absence became the same. Moreover, the education and health centres that existed under the Soviet invasion lacked medicine, specialists and necessary equipment. But due to the internal wars and the partisan and nationalistic conflicts, nothing remained of these centres. And despite all the suffering and fighting, the Northern Alliance took everything with it before leaving Kabul, to the point where the only thing left at the banks were useless papers.

The Islamic Emirate gained control over the capital Kabul and the remaining cities of Afghanistan under these circumstances, and at a time when the people were suffering educational, health, social, economic and cultural problems among others. The Emirate started rebuilding these centres from scratch. Hence, when it seized the capital Kabul, it focused on the rebuilding of new hospitals and clinics and renovating the hospitals and clinics that were destroyed in the heated battles. Moreover, it rebuilt and reopened the schools and universities that were destroyed or that closed their doors because of the bloody wars—namely Kabul, Kandahar and Herat universities among others—to which we have alluded in the previous section when we tackled corruption in the education administrations. Despite its difficult circumstances, the Islamic Emirate was able to improve the health and educational situation to a large extent, and managed to build hospitals and open universities and schools to provide health and educational services despite its limited financial capabilities and the international economic siege from which these persecuted people were suffering.

If we compare the efforts of the Emirate at this level to those of the previous and current governments, given the financial support they received from foreign sides, we can say that the work and efforts of the Emirate were far superior. For example, Karzai's government could not improve the health and education conditions despite the massive international financial support it is receiving, and the people are still lacking health, educational and economic services among others. Regarding the social and economic situation, I say: the social situation under the Emirate improved in an unprecedented way in the country's history. Indeed, society was cleansed of corruption, decadence, prohibitions, vice and obscenity among other things that lead to a society's collapse. Moreover, it put an end to all the problems and obstacles that provoked disputes and conflicts among the members and families of the community, issues that were dealt with by impartial religious courts. In addition, the Emirate spread security and stability, implemented the rulings of the shari'a and strengthened the relations between all the factions of Afghan society. Also, the mosques flourished when it controlled the country and became filled with worshippers, while the people became more inclined to learn about Islam and its solid rulings. Consequently, the people's morals improved, as they venerated the scholars, respected the sheikhs, had mercy on their children and had compassion towards women.

Today, however, all of these values have collapsed, since neither the old sheikh is respected, nor the scholar venerated, nor are children and women treated with mercy. And not one day goes by without dozens of elderly, women, children and scholars being killed, without women being assaulted, without the Qur'an and the Islamic sanctities being disparaged and without there being public consumption of alcohol. The incident of Abdul Rashid Dostum that occurred a month ago is the biggest proof of that, along with the rape by one of the soldiers of the government in Jowzjan province of a girl who had not yet reached puberty.

It is thus fair to ask: Who improved the social conditions? The previous and current governments or the Islamic Emirate? The economic situation also improved after the bloody wars that lasted twenty years and burned everything along the way, causing the people to suffer poverty, hunger, unemployment and other countless calamities. Indeed, when the Emirate gained control over the country, the situation stabilised, security spread and every member of the community could work and trade freely without any fear or terror. On the other hand, the Islamic Emirate restored the lands and government properties that were seized by the warlords by force, constructed many buildings and schools, renovated all the ministries, embassies and governmental departments that were destroyed or ruined by internal wars and partisan conflicts, and organised the customs authority and the state's imports and exports, which led to the improvement of the Afghan people's economic situation. In addition, transportation widely improved because the Islamic Emirate opened the country to dealers who imported cars, all types of transportation means and livelihood necessities from the United Arab Emirates and the remaining countries of the world. The Emirate used to help those merchants deliver their goods to the desired locations. At this level, security played a prominent role in allowing the merchants to import and export their products, and all these facilities and measures allowed for the improvement of the economic situation. The movement did all that at a time when the whole world was standing against it and when the United Nations was imposing an economic siege on it, which even prevented Afghan planes from carrying travellers to other states around the world, although this decision went against all the UN charters and regulations.

In conclusion, the Islamic Emirate did its best to develop the economic, political, social, intellectual, health and educational situations among others, although the difficult circumstances it faced did not allow it to achieve major progress. Still, its foundations required studying all the cultures around the world to benefit from them to the extent of their compatibility with our Islamic shari'a, but also looking into new and emerging problems and finding ways to solve them based on the rulings and stipulations of our religion. The problem does not reside in the Islamic Emirate and the foundation it has drawn from the Qur'an and the sunna, rather in the others that excluded it, besieged it and were unwilling to deal with it.

The sixth and final remark by His Eminence the Doctor was related to the fact that the Taliban movement linked the fate of Afghanistan to the Al-Qaeda organisation. He said:

> The sixth mistake: The Taliban leaders linked the fate of Afghanistan and that of their people to the fate of the al-Qaeda organisation. Throughout history, there has never been a state that linked its fate to and allied with an organisation in a way that led the

country towards confrontations it could not handle. The state must have ties and regional alliances with other states, not emotional ties that are void of thought ... Those who wrote about the Taliban among non-Muslims praised one thing it did, i.e. destroyed the poppy plantations and besieged the opium trade, thus relieving the world from this evil. But today, Afghanistan is considered the largest drug producing and exporting state in the world under Karzai's government and this is happening before the eyes and ears of the coalition states. Had they wanted to get rid of drugs, they would have done so.

It seems that His Eminence the Doctor did not get a chance to look at the approach and the fundamentals of the Islamic Emirate, but rather drew his information from the international media and especially the Western media that spread false rumours about the Islamic Emirate. The Islamic Emirate follows rules and regulations that are not linked to a particular organisation, party or faction, and it adopts its policies based on these rules and their stipulations, as is the case everywhere. Every state has a constitution and a law, and it allies with parties and other states based on this constitution and this law. The Islamic Emirate also has its own restrictions and regulations that are drawn from the Qur'an and the sunna and never linked itself or its people to the fate of whichever organisation. It also has a constitution that was printed in Pashto, Dari, Arabic and English, and the Doctor can read and review the Islamic Emirate constitution and not be duped by what is published by the media.

On the other hand, the positions of the Islamic Emirate towards the alliances and pacts with the remaining countries are clearer than the sun. Back when it controlled the country, it carried out numerous attempts to improve its relations with the world and especially the Islamic states, even called upon the world to sit around the negotiation table and solve all the disputes in a peaceful way. It insisted on that and said: The only solution to our predicament is through negotiations and talks, and called on America not to choose force. It also said: The only solution to all the issues of dispute is negotiations, but America was duped by its financial strength and its technological might, refused to listen to the Islamic Emirate and insisted on the use of force. Hence, the Islamic Emirate is respecting its methodology, its rules and decisions, is not linked to whichever side and deals with everyone based on its constitution and its regulations that are drawn from the two sources of Islam, i.e. the Qur'an and the sunna. Abandoning them to please others is out of the question and no one has ever abandoned them and gained anything, not even the satisfaction of the infidel states, God forbid.

With regard to what the Doctor said about the non-Muslims' singular praise of the Taliban's elimination of drugs, we wonder: Did the Islamic Emirate just eliminate drugs? Or did it protect its country's entity against the division plans and conspiracies concocted against it, reorganise it, spread security and stability in it, defeat the conflicting parties whose bloody wars caused the Afghan people to suffer, and implement the Islamic shari'a, for which these people resisted the Soviet invaders for around ten years and sacrificed their lives and money to reach this ultimate and essential Islamic goal? We have pointed to the remarks of His Eminence Doctor Bassam al-Shatti, may Allah protect him, with regard to the Taliban movement and its mistakes, and we have clarified and commented on them as per our principles and regulations in the hope that we have convinced the honourable professor and the venerated scholar. If not, we have provided him with more information about the Islamic Emirate, and we hope that the sheikh among others will review the fundamentals and the regulations of the Islamic Emirate to avoid being duped by the reports of the Western media, which is our enemy and that of Muslims around the world, and Allah knows what is right.

66

MESSAGE OF AMIR UL-MU'MINEEN TO THE NATIONS
OF AFGHANISTAN AND IRAQ

[*Not much had been heard from Mullah Mohammad Omar since the fall of the Taliban's government in 2001. There were occasional releases of Eid statements, though these only became lengthy and prominent from 2006 onwards as part of a renewed public relations push. In this source, the Afghan war is compared to the Iraqi conflict. Mullah Mohammad Omar counsels the Iraqi mujahedeen to stay united, 'because victory cannot be maintained without unity'. As we have already seen, disunity was one of the main concerns of the senior Taliban leadership in exile.*]

Al-Emera (website), 12 July 2007

Respected Muslim brothers and sisters! You know much better that today the Muslims in the world are faced with a lot of problems as the result of the cruel policies of America. If on the one hand the international colonialists invade Muslims and use different types of weapons, even biological weapons against the Muslims and have prisons like Guantánamo, Abu Ghraib and Bagram, on the other hand they are trying to create an atmosphere of mistrust and hypocrisy among Muslims. They make Muslims fight against each other in the name of tribes, language and religion. In the military field, self-defence is an obligation for all Muslims of the world, so it is necessary that Muslims stop all the trickeries of the enemy. They should not allow them to create hypocrisy among Muslims.

[...] I am sure that the regular resistance of the brave mujahedeen in Iraq and the resistance in Afghanistan under a unit leadership have caused the enemies to worry a lot. Now they are trying to get rid of the crisis, as sometimes they heavily bomb innocent people, and sometimes they create new conspiracies in the name of language and tribes among the people.

But what makes us pleased and assured is that most of their endeavours have failed and their puppet rulers have been rejected by the people. Despite all this, still more cleverness and cooperation is needed for national unity and brotherhood. Mostly, efforts should be made to persuade people not to cooperate with them. I have strongly instructed the mujahedeen of the Islamic Emirate to embarrass all Afghan groups and people of the different regions and tribes. They should be attracted by the IEA. The policy of the IEA is that a government should be established which can satisfy all tribes and different groups, a government which is not influenced by neighbouring countries and act cleverly based on all international and Islamic rules.

The Islamic Emirate never interferes in other countries' domestic affairs, nor can it tolerate the interference of other countries in our domestic affairs. We are making efforts to free our beloved Afghanistan with all our strength from the occupation of the invaders and to prepare free and liberal/liberated conditions for our people to live in. I strongly call on all the jihadi, national and political personalities to unite for the freedom of the country, and then for the establishment of an Islamic government in order to prevent the events of the early 1990s when the Russians left. This should not be repeated. In the future, endeavours should be taken that there should not be bloodshed in the name of any commander, mullah, mujahed or others.

This is our policy and we practise it. The international community and the people of the country should not term each comment to be those of the Islamic Emirate. The comments of the Islamic Emirate are those which are released by our official spokesmen and our Al-Emara web page. I thus ask the Iraqi brothers to avoid differences vis-à-vis Sunni and Shia, and to jointly resist the invaders, because victory cannot be maintained without unity.

67

OUR HEROIC MARTYRS

[Just as during the 1980s war, martyr profiles and biographies became an important part of how the Taliban defined themselves to a local and—in this case—foreign audience. Al-Somood was published in Arabic, though articles were also occasionally translated into Pashto, Dari and/or English. This issue contains two profiles that are emblematic of the broader genre; the value system that the Taliban construct through the biographical profile is clear to observe.]

Ikram Miyundi
Al-Somood *(online magazine), 19 March 2007*

'And when the believers saw the allies, they said: This is what Allah and His Messenger promised us and Allah and His Messenger spoke the truth; and it only increased them in faith and submission. Of the believers are men who are true to the covenant, which they made with Allah: So of them is he who accomplished his vow, and of them is he who yet waits and they have not changed in the least.'[1]

Martyr al-Hafiz Abdul Rahim

[He] has earned the highest degree of martyrdom our honourable companion, memoriser of the Qur'an, pious scholar, old sheikh and heroic leader Al-Hafiz Abdul Rahim, the son of the late Nassiruddin, the son of the late Mohammad Amin.

His birth: He was born in 1950 in the village of Kamali in the district of Spin Boldak in Kandahar province, which is located in south Afghanistan, is neighboured to the west by Helmand province, to the east by Zabul province, to the south by the state of Pakistan and to the north by Uruzgan province.

His family: Al-Hafiz, may Allah have mercy on his soul, came from the honourable clan of Noorzai, which is one of the famous Pashtun tribes. He was born to a middle-class family and his father and grandfather worked in agriculture. His father was a pious man and he loved knowledge and scholars, which is why he chose that path for his sons, Al-Mawlawi Abdul Wakil and Al-Hafiz Abdul Rahim.

His upbringing: The martyr, may Allah have mercy on his soul, grew up in an ordinary house with great qualities. He was raised on faith in Allah the Almighty and on jihad in his cause. He started his educational journey at a young age, memorised the holy Qur'an during his youth and pursued a shari'a education. He thus read to the sheikhs and moved from one mosque to another and one school to another until he earned, thanks to Allah the Almighty, a high degree in shari'a sciences. He thus graduated at the hands of prominent professors from the Jamia Binoria al-Alamia Islamic university in Karachi in 1971.

His biography: The martyr, may Allah have mercy on his soul, was skinny, tall, eloquent, ethical, an experienced commander, courageous, modest, a pious scholar, a worshipper of Allah, honest, loved whoever loved Allah and hated whoever hated Allah, and was free of any blame. He was a role model to the people, was heard and obeyed especially among his mujahedeen brothers, and had a pure belief that pushed him to fight superstitions, seek the elimination of innovations and reject customs that went against the shari'a. He, may Allah have mercy on his soul, was reliable at the level of his faith, his loyalty and his honesty, was good-tempered, intelligent and a good judge of character. In short, Allah the Almighty put in that man all the features of a Muslim leader, the characteristics of a pious scholar and the morals of a loyal soldier.

His dependants: He left behind a large family of three wives and fifteen children, including nine living in a house he rented for them in Dar al-Hijra. He left them little money, barely enough for them to survive for a few months, knowing that all his sons were studying in shari'a schools, that his oldest son Hamadullah is almost eighteen years old and his youngest Aminullah is three years old.

His jihad and his educational services: The martyr, may Allah have mercy on his soul, earned his high degree in shari'a sciences in 1979 and quickly joined the ranks of the mujahedeen, establishing a front dubbed the Faruqi Front in the Spin Boldak district during the Soviet occupation of Afghanistan. He was a prominent leader in the region with more than 250 mujahedeen under his command, did his best to defend Islam and the Muslims and tried to deter the soldiers of the occupation and the agents. When Allah the Almighty conquered the Spin Boldak district at the hands of the pious mujahedeen for the first time and cleansed it from the desecration of the atheists, martyr Al-Hafiz entered it as a believing conqueror and was appointed as commander of the district. But when the internal conflict started after the fall of the Communist rule, he fled the strife and returned home. But as a wise scholar, he tapped into another arena in the service of Allah by establishing a school called the Arab Islamic University for both young and old in the Spin Boldak district in the Watt region [name could not be found]. He tried hard to give the children of Muslims a sound Islamic education. He was the director of the school, a teacher and a preacher, thus trying hard to reform his community while carrying out other scholarly tasks. When Allah the Almighty sent to the Muslims the reformatory Taliban movement, he answered the call of Amir ul-Mu'mineen Mullah Mohammad Omar al-Mujahed and joined the ranks of the movement. At first, he was put in charge of equipping the mujahedeen, before earning many other positions, including police chief of Uruzgan province and Representative of Zabul province. He continued to serve Islam and the Muslims until Allah determined his fate. The enemies came from all sides, and fear and panic prevailed.

> 'There the believers were tried and they were shaken with severe shaking. And when the hypocrites and those in whose hearts was a disease began to say: Allah and His Messenger did not promise us (victory) but only to deceive.'[2]

Our friend martyr Al-Hafiz Abdul Rahim, may Allah have mercy on his soul and take him to heaven, was among those who did well, as he did not surrender to the enemy, did not abandon his post, grabbed his weapon and started calling on the people in his region to carry out jihad against the Americans. He used to disappear in daytime and carry out jihad at night. Some youths then responded to his calls, including his two cousins, martyr Abdul Bari and Al-Hafiz Abdul Ghani, the sons of Abdul Wassih, and he was also joined by his aide martyr Abdul Ghani ibn Maqr, may Allah have mercy on his soul. But then Allah the Almighty gave him his support by sending him believers, at which point his mujahedeen brothers became numerous. Allah the Almighty also provided him with equipment and ammunition and allowed him to defeat the enemies in many battles, until he reached a level that was used as an example of courage and steadfastness.

His jihadi heroics: He, may Allah have mercy on his soul, encountered the enemies of Allah among the Americans and their agents in the first battle in one of the villages of the Boldak district. He then encountered them in the second battle in the Adda mountains near the district, and in the third battle in the village of Nagar Moula Ali. In all three battles, the mujahedeen came out safe and sound and the enemies fled the region, knowing that merely imagining fighting with them at the time was very hard. In the fourth battle, he encountered them in Tor Ghar, another mountain near the district, and this constituted the battle of dignities. Indeed, the Americans participated in it with their agents, their tanks, their cannons and fighter jets, besieged the mountain from all sides and entered the battlefield to fight a maximum of fifty mujahedeen carrying light weapons. The battle lasted for two days, resulting in the death and injuring of a number of enemy soldiers and the martyrdom of his cousin Abdul Bari, the capturing of his other cousin Abdul Ghani and the injuring of Al-Hafiz in the shoulder. After their commander was injured, the others returned to their post. Following these battles, he became widely known and the zealous youths rallied around him. He thus sent a brigade to the Maruf district under the command of Mullah Abdul Wali (his nickname was Mullah Abdullah), and the latter was martyred with Mullah Mohammad Khan in the fighting that took place in the area. He, may Allah have mercy on his soul, then appointed Mawlawi Harun as the commander of this brigade. He, may Allah have mercy on his soul, also sent another brigade to

Zabul province and appointed Mullah Hidayatullah as its amir. After Al-Hafiz was martyred, Mawlawi Abdul Wakil, may Allah preserve him, i.e. Al-Hafiz' brother, was appointed as the amir of martyr Abdul Rahim's front. As for the amir of the afore-mentioned brigade, Mullah Hidayatullah, he was appointed as general commander of the front. When Mullah Hidayatullah was martyred, may Allah have mercy on his soul, Mawlawi Harun, may Allah preserve him, was appointed as general commander of the front.

His principles: He, may Allah have mercy on his soul, had unwavering principles, was harsh in dealing with the infidels, merciful in dealing with the pious and disin-terested in materialistic things. Some of his brothers blamed him for being ascetic, advising him to purchase a house or land. But he, may Allah have mercy on his soul, said: 'By Allah the Almighty, you will not hear that Al-Hafiz was martyred and left behind him a palace, this much money and this or that car.' His brother told us: 'A delegation from Karzai's government, including Haji Hashim and Mawlana Samizi, came to me and asked to meet with Al-Hafiz. I tried to find pretexts to avoid such a meeting, but when they strongly insisted, I helped them out. Al-Hafiz met them in my home and they said: "Stop opposing the government and calling on the people to carry out jihad, and we will give you guarantees and clean your slate with the govern-ment (in local terms, this meant he would be reconciled with the government). We will also give you cars, money and a prominent position, knowing that alone, you will not be able to achieve anything because the United Nations, the Americans, the European Union, NATO and the neighbouring states are all supporting the govern-ment. You and your friends will be killed and we have come for your sake to tell you what we think is best." But Al-Hafiz, may Allah have mercy on his soul, said: "Jihad in the cause of Allah is an obligation that should be performed by every Muslim. Allah the Almighty imposed jihad in his cause and we, thanks to Allah, are doing our best to serve that purpose. He did not impose results on us (Allah does not impose upon any soul a duty but to the extent of its ability). Martyrdom and victory lie in his hands and we can do without your assurances since Allah is the best guardian and guarantor. In regard to cleaning my slate, I, thanks to Allah, have a clean slate with God. I am sorry, but you will not clean my slate before Bush the infidel and the murderer. I pity you for you do not understand the following: We the mujahedeen have a clean slate with Allah, while you have a black slate with Allah the Almighty and the believers. As for the money and the position you mentioned among other things, faith is dearer to us and heaven is much more precious. Regarding our death, we pray to Allah the Almighty to honour us with martyrdom for his cause, for this is a great victory that is only achieved by a joyful believer. I ask Allah the Almighty that I be killed in his cause and dragged by my feet and so they would say: This is Al-Hafiz whom we have killed." O brothers in faith, what we have relayed is only the tip of the iceberg and these statements were made by Allah the Almighty through the words of a pious man, who is passionate about his faith and whose heart was entered by Islam.

His predicament: Al-Hafiz told us in person: 'On a very tough day at the beginning of the American occupation, my colleague and I left in the early morning and headed to a relative of mine in a village in the hope he would host us. When we reached his home he closed the door in our faces and apologised. We thus went to the desert and disappeared there without anything to drink or eat on a hot day. By nightfall, my friends and I were cleaning our clothes from the sand that was stuck to them and I found myself turning towards Allah the dear and the wise and praying to him by saying: "O Allah relieve my exhaustion, fix my situation and support me, O lord of both worlds." From that day forth, he supported me in every battle and backed me up with his help and with the believers.'

His martyrdom: Al-Hafiz earned his wish and Allah the Almighty accepted his prayer. He was thus martyred on 14 September 2003 in the Maruf district battle that was led by martyr Abdul Baki Mohammadi. Hafiz was martyred with his friends Mullah Samihullah and Mullah Abdullah, and they were buried in a village there. We belong to Allah and to Him we shall return. Three days later, the enemies of Allah the Almighty learned that Al-Hafiz had been killed. They thus dug out his grave, took his body out and roamed the country with it while saying: This is Al-Hafiz whom we have killed. They mocked him and then surrendered him to his relatives, and he was buried in his ancestors' graveyard. Allah replies to the prayers of the pious.

Martyr Mullah Ruzi Khan Akif

[He] has earned the highest degree of martyrdom our brother, the famous mujahed, the pious young man and heroic commander Mullah Ruzi Khan Akif, the son of Saleh Mohammad Salehi, the son of the late Mohammad Khan.

His birth: He was born in 1978 in the village of Mashizi in the district of Naw Bahar in Zabul province, which is located in south Afghanistan and is neighboured to the west by Kandahar province, to the east by Ghazni and Paktika provinces, to the south by the Pakistani border and the Maruf district that was annexed to Kandahar and to the north by Uruzgan province.

His family: Martyr Akif, may Allah have mercy on his soul, was from an honourable house of the Kishani family from the Tokhi clan, which is one of the famous Pashtun tribes. His father and grandfather were known and among the wealthy at regional level.

His upbringing: The martyr, may Allah have mercy on his soul, grew up in an honourable, pious and renowned house and was raised on the love of Allah the Almighty and on jihad in his cause. He started his educational journey at a young age, thus reading [the Qur'an] to the sheikhs and moving from one mosque to the other to acquire religious knowledge. At the peak of his youth (eighteen years old) he joined the ranks of holy jihad and could not continue his education. He proceeded down that path until he was martyred and joined his Merciful God.

His biography: The martyr, may Allah have mercy on his soul, was a big man, tall, with a smiling face, was good tempered and obedient to his parents. This reached the point where he did not talk much in their presence, was proud of his lineage, a brave and modest commander, calm and patient, and loving towards the people and his mujahedeen brothers.

His dependants: He left behind four young children, namely two girls and two boys, the oldest of which is Hikmatullah, who is five years old, and the youngest of which is Akifullah, who is three years old and was born three days after he was martyred. He also left behind his parents and four siblings, some of whom are studying the shari'a while others are fighting the attacking infidels. He also left behind many mujahedeen, who promised Allah to continue down the path drawn to them by the martyr, may Allah have mercy on his soul. After he was martyred, his father Sayyed Saleh Mohammad Salehi said to his sons: 'I ask you to fight in the cause of Allah, to adopt the same path as your martyred brother and to fight the aggressors and their men until the last drop of blood.' They thus rushed to the battlefields and the brother of the martyr, Ghazi Mohammad Akif (almost twenty-five years old) was appointed as commander of the front. Ghazi Mohammad said: 'Our front is continuing to fight the aggressors, and after the martyrdom of my brother, may Allah have mercy on his soul, the mujahedeen's determination grew stronger and their morale was lifted, and we will continue down that path until we achieve our goal with Allah's will.'

His principles: Martyr Akif, may Allah have mercy on his soul, joined the ranks of the Taliban movement at a young age (eighteen years old), but due to his honesty, his loyalty and his great heroism, he was a man among men. He was firstly appointed as commander of the Ghazni province brigade, and then as police chief of Uruzgan province. Later, the martyr was assigned to lead a jihadi division in the north, where there were more than 1,500 mujahedeen. He was injured twice and healed by Allah and remained in his post until the Crusader occupation in December 2001. When Amir ul-Mu'mineen, may Allah preserve him, wanted to attack the enemy, he, may Allah have mercy on his soul, was appointed as commander of the believing forces in Zabul province. He thus started his new jihadist round against the aggressors and led the mujahedeen in that province. He organised his ranks and gathered the weapons and equipment he had in Naw Bahar district, and fought the enemies of Allah among the occupiers and their Afghan agents. His jihad in the cause of Allah continued until he earned a high degree of martyrdom.

His jihadi heroics: We already mentioned that martyr Mullah Ruzi Khan Akif was patient and truthful. He was also a strong-hearted hero on the battlefield, which is why he was seen carrying out major acts of bravery, of which we mention:

1. He was caught alone in an enemy ambush in north Afghanistan during the days of the Emirate's government. He wouldn't surrender and was determined to fight. They thus dropped bombs on his car but Allah the Almighty protected him,

although his car was damaged. He attacked them with his light weapons, killed them and took their weapons with the permission of Allah the Almighty.

2. He, may Allah have mercy on his soul, was in another area riding in a car with six others. They had no weapons, were caught in an ambush led by two men, i.e. Nader and Sabin, in the district of Shamulzayi, and were asked to surrender. But he wouldn't and was smart and courageous enough to order his brothers to fight, asking them with a loud voice: 'Give me the hand grenade', although they had none. At that point, Allah the Almighty spread terror in the hearts of the enemies, who apologised and said to him: Proceed with your course. Allah the Almighty thus saved them from the injustice of the oppressors.

His predicament: He, may Allah have mercy on his soul, endured many predicaments in the cause of Allah. He was injured twice in the thigh and the head and saw with his own eyes many of his companions being martyred. I will thus mention some of these predicaments. He and his companions were besieged in Kunduz province for fourteen days, fighting day and night in one of the most difficult battles. But they never weakened or surrendered and they continued to fight with high morale until Allah the Almighty ensured their relief. He was also besieged by the American soldiers and their agents with their tanks and their fighter jets in Kishani village, among the annexes of Naw Bahar. But he was not saddened and did not show any fear, thus fighting as a hero until Allah found him a way out. He thus exited the siege, along with his martyred companion Shamseddin, safe and sound.

His martyrdom: Martyr Mullah Ruzi Khan Akif, may Allah have mercy on his soul, always hoped for one of two things: either a conquest, the implementation of Allah's shari'a and the defeat of the enemy, or martyrdom in the cause of Allah and earning eternal life. He thus got his wish and earned a high degree of martyrdom at 12 o'clock on 14 August 2004, at twenty-seven years of age. He, may Allah have mercy on his soul, was martyred in a fierce battle. He was alone as a guest in the village of Surkhukan in the Shah Joy district of Zabul and the enemies informed their spy (the filthiest of people) about his location. Suddenly, a fleet of helicopters (thirteen of them) filled with Americans and their agents besieged the village and were ready to fight. He wanted to go out and fight them, but the village's population would not let him, promising to protect and defend him. But he answered with deceit out of pity for the weak men, women and children of the village: 'It is impossible to fight with the latter and I wish to surrender to them.' The population was convinced with what he said and he went out to face the enemies of Allah the Almighty while raising his hands and carrying his guns (knowing that war is dupery). They thus started to race towards him, happy he had surrendered, as it was asked that he be brought alive. When they got close to him, he took them by surprise, killed four of them and injured others. He then shouted: 'There will be no surrender to the infidels as long as there is life!' He fought until he was martyred and surrendered to the Lord of both worlds.

After he was martyred, the aggressors did not dare come near him and resorted to some inhabitants to make sure he was dead. They then took him across the country for twelve days before they surrendered him to his relatives to be buried. We belong to Allah and to Him we shall return.

68

STATEMENT ON THE DEATH
OF MULLAH DADULLAH

[*Mullah Dadullah fought in the 1980s jihad against the Soviet Union and was an associate of Mullah Mohammad Omar himself. He lost his leg fighting in western Afghanistan in 1994 but went on to play significant roles in the Taliban's battles in central and northern Afghanistan pre-2001. He rose to further prominence in 2006 when he was seen beheading 'spies' in southern Afghanistan. He was killed by ISAF forces in May 2007. This profile is just one among a number of examples of 'martyr biographies', each of which praise the bravery, zeal and commitment of the individual.*]

Al-Emera (website), 15 May 2007

All the mujahedeen of the Islamic Emirate, and specifically the leadership council, express their condolences to [the] family [of Mullah Dadullah], the mujahed nation and to the painful and Islam-adoring Muslims of the world on hearing the heavily grievous news of the martyrdom of the great jihadi personality Al-Hajj Mullah Dadullah, and it wishes patience and rewards on the day of judgement from God.

The martyred hero Mullah Dadullah was on the one hand a resistant, patient and determined mujahed of the warm forts of the current jihad against illegitimacy, but on the other hand he was a real example of revolutionary activities and of unceasing combat, direction and bravery, not only for the mujahed nation of Afghanistan but for all the Muslims of the world. Today he is no longer among us.

If Mullah Dadullah was on the one hand a good trainer and leader for his respectful, intelligent and mujahed family, on the other hand he had captured the hearts of most Muslims of the world as a very clever hero and respectful personality about whom today most sorrowful Muslims of the world are painfully uttering painfully the words, '*inna lelah-e wa inna elaih-e rajeoon*'.[1]

Despite all this, we should say that the martyred hero Al-Hajj Mullah Dadullah has not hundreds but thousands of friends in his jihadi [']caravan[']. His ideas and jihadi policy will be accelerated hereafter. Thousands of his friends were confident in his existence. Today everyone will try to fill his gap and everyone will be like thorns in the eyes of the enemies, so as a result thousands of Ghazis will stand as mountains against the wild invaders and enemies. So courageously we can say that his bravery will strengthen and motivate our jihadi fighters more and more.

Wounds and martyrdom are not considered as defeat or injury in the culture of Islam. Such pains and events have been experienced in the great history of Islam, but the devotees of the [']caravan['] of Muhammad never had an opportunity to rest and be confident that if sometimes there was a gap, in very good order the Islamic Ghazis have filled it. Today also, the enemies of Islam and Afghanistan should be pleased about the death of Mullah Dadullah, but it is a time of grief and disappointment for now the enemies should pay heavily for the death of Mullah Dadullah. The enemies will cry in exchange for a slight happiness at the death of Dadullah and, God willing, soon the mujahedeen of the Islamic Emirate will take revenge for the wild action of the invaders based on Afghan culture and the instructions of the Islamic Emirate. We assure the entire sorrowful Muslims of the world, and especially the Muslim and mujahed nation, that the martyrdom of Mullah Dadullah will not affect the order and resistance of the mujahedeen negatively and our enemies will also not feel confident and comfortable.

Stay awake! The enemy should not be unaware of his revenge
The arrows of revenge still come out of the graves

69

ONE TALIB

I'M FED UP WITH JIHAD

[*This is not an official Taliban publication, but its level of interest and relevance is high, so we decided to include it here to give extra perspective. The account is of a well-known kidnapping of a number of bus passengers who were travelling from Herat towards Kandahar. The narrator tells of the conditions of their detention, his participation in their killing and his eventual remorse. Extra context and details around this account can be found in Anand Gopal's* No Good Men Among the Living: America, the Taliban, and the War through Afghan Eyes.]

Ghulam Sarwar

Full article originally published on larawbar.net, 23 October 2008[1]

For the past ten years I have been studying in Charu Bowri Madrassa in Quetta. Several of my friends had left this madrassa to go to Afghanistan, just as others were going from other Pakistani madrassas. In Quetta, the Pakistani and Afghan mullahs always gave speeches saying that the infidels [*kuffar*] are in Afghanistan and that they have occupied the country. Now the crusader wars are happening, they would say, everyone's obligation is to go to Afghanistan and fight. They made us ready to go and start jihad.

They were telling us: first kill the ANA and ANP. This is because they are supporting the *kuffar* and they are the eyes of foreigners.

In the month of *sunbula* this year I came to Afghanistan with several of my friends to start jihad. When we passed through Chaman, we separated into groups of two people. We gathered back together again in a specific place in Kandahar once we reached it. After one night in Kandahar we went to Panjwayi, Zheray, Sanzari and Maiwand districts. We four guys were all together, but when I got to Maiwand I had only one friend with me.

I stayed for a month in Maiwand, sometimes going to Gereshq bazaar. I sometimes stayed in Yakhtchaal, Mirmandaw, Nahr-i Seraj and other areas. We attacked several ISAF convoys in Maiwand and damaged their vehicles. But mostly we were killing ANP and ANA. After every event our friends in Quetta would call us and give congratulation to our leaders.

Aside from these things [convoy attacks], most of the time I saw innocents being arrested and brought [to the Taliban areas] by my friends. Some of these people were accused of spying, some of supporting the government, some of working with UN and NGO organisations, some of being teachers etc. etc.

I was two months in Kandahar, only participating in convoy attacks. I was never involved in the detention of people or bringing anyone accused of spying or of supporting the government or teachers etc.

For he who in his life has not even slaughtered a bird, killing a human is difficult for him. But when our friends stopped a bus in Maiwand district, around fifty of the passengers were taken away to a very remote area of this district. When I asked my friends about this issue, they said that they were all ANA guys.

We received such a report. When I went there, it was late evening and all the passengers were there. Their skin-colour was yellow [this denotes that they were pale/tawny with worry]. All the passengers were young boys. Our commander told them: 'When you were coming from Kabul to Kandahar we received a credible report that you are coming to join the ANA. We have good information/sources about what you came to Kandahar for.'

One of the passengers who had a yellow shawl asked, 'What did we come for?'

Our commander told him: 'Sons of Gulab Mangal! You have come here to join the ANA and then start fighting against us.'

The boys started swearing that they had never even seen Gulab Mangal and that they would never join the ANA. They were going to Herat, they said, and from there to Iran to find work.

The commander told them, 'We know what to do with you guys.' He turned his face towards his friends and told them that we will leave them/let them go.

I thought that they would let them go, but one of my friends told me that the commander would send them to another world. My heart hurt a lot. The young people were standing before my eyes at every moment. When evening came, they divided them into groups of four and five.

Two or three Talibs were allocated as guards to each house where the commander delivered the groups of boys. After evening prayer, many of the Talibs got together in this village and wanted to decide about these boys. I saw that there was doubt in the eyes of my commander as he was calling to Quetta and taking orders from someone there.

At first I didn't know who he was speaking with, but when I heard the names of Kuchlagh, Pashtunabad, Musa Kaluni Pashtunabad and Kachra road, then I knew that he was talking with someone in Quetta. He was taking orders from that side. The commander was telling [the whole story] that most of them are young boys; 'some of them have shaved their beards and they are like *angrezan*' [derogatory term for British dating back to the Anglo-Afghan wars]. He said, 'Don't worry, we'll do something to them so you will say "well done" to us.'

The commander said goodbye and switched his phone off. Then he spoke to us. 'Talibs! Only one phone call remains. When we get that call we will send these guys to hell.'

I became worried and thought to myself, 'We arrested these guys in Maiwand, and the people who are sitting in Quetta don't know anything about these people, who they are, where they're coming from and where they're going.' I was thinking to myself when the commander received another call and said, 'Don't worry, we'll do something to them so you will say "well done" to us. And none of them will remain alive.'

The commander swore on the Qur'an [that he would do this]. I wondered to myself: if the passengers were swearing to God that they were going to Iran to work, then how is it possible that the commander says he will kill all of them. I still didn't believe it; I thought that the commander would let them go.

Then the commander said to the Talibs, 'Go and help the other Talibs who are supervising the houses.' At the house where I was a guard, there were four other guests sleeping in a room. Even though they were guests, the door of [the guests' room] was locked, and sometimes we checked their room as well. At 2 a.m. we heard a sound at the door.

When I checked the door there was nobody there. When I got close to the door, two boys were looking out from the holes in the door; and two others were sitting and crying. I asked them, 'What are you doing?' They said, 'For God's sake, we are going to Iran for work. We have paid money to the smugglers, and they will take us to Iran.' I told them, 'Keep quiet. If they hear us, they will hit all of us.'

Then they became quiet. I talked to them through the holes in the door. One of the boys was heaving in his cries and said, 'My brother! I have one small brother and three sisters. My mother and father are old. If something happens to me, what will they do?'

I told him, 'I can't do anything. If the commander finds out, he won't let the matter rest.' I told them, 'Sleep now. In the morning I will see if I can do something.'

When morning came, we woke them up to pray. But none of them had slept and they looked worried. They prayed and took breakfast in the same houses. It was 7 a.m. when the commander called all of us at a specific time to come to a decision.

When we went to the place, the number of Talibs had doubled. The commander said that a decision had been taken and that they should all be shot. 'This is the decision of our ulemaa.' I said to the commander that the passengers swear to God that they were going to Iran for work and are neither with Gulab Mangal nor with ANP or ANA.

The commander then said to me, 'You are small now. You will learn about these issues only with time.' He added that we 'are only there to kill people. We cannot take decisions. Decisions are the duty of other scholars.'

The commander said that he had tried calling Mawlawi Sahib a lot, but that he wasn't picking up his phone. One of our friends said that one of his phones is always off. 'Call him on his Wared sim card [type of card in Pakistan] phone number instead.' The commander said that his Wared sim also wasn't working.

The commander said that he had three Wared numbers. The friend asked whether he had called all of them. 'No, I have just called one Wared number,' the commander said. The Talib gave him a second Wared number for Mawlawi Sahib.

When he called that number, the commander answered the phone. The commander said to Mawlawi Sahib, 'Your phones weren't working. I'm sure the other scholars have informed you about their decision, but I want to hear it from you with my own ears.'

This time the commander turned the phone on speaker-phone and we could hear as well. Mawlawi Sahib said to the commander that 'I was present with the other scholars when they took their decision as well. Just go and behead them.'

The commander said goodbye to Mawlawi Sahib. He looked at me. 'This is not my decision. It is the decision of all scholars,' he said. 'Do you agree with us now?'

I told the commander that the ulemaa are in Quetta. 'They are not here that they can see the situation and observe it here. How do they know? How do they know that these guys are not innocent?'

The commander spoke angrily to me. 'If they are not elders [if they don't know], well then they are the closest thing we have to elders [they are the only ones who would have a chance of knowing]. Keep quiet. Don't talk about this issue any more.'

The commander told the Talibs: 'Get all of these boys out of the village and be careful that all of their hands are tied behind their backs.' We used motorbikes to take all the boys out of the village.

When we reached a canal on the west of the village, we had allocated four or five guys to every group of prisoners. I was still thinking of a way to do something with the boy who had pleaded with me last night. When we took them off the bikes, the boy from last night said, 'Why did you bring us to this place? O God! I think it will be our final place.'

This boy was crying loudly, calling his mother and father and calling his brothers' and sisters' names. After a while, shooting started and crying started with the shooting. The boys were not far away from each other. They were all at a distance of 300 m.

One of the passengers' groups was with me. When crying/shooting started from the other side of the *kareez*, other passengers on my side started crying as well. And this time I saw the commander coming towards us on a bike and giving orders to every group of the Talibs to start firing on these guys.

I was with three other Talibs standing guard on these passengers on another side of the canal. When the commander came over he asked me, 'Why are you looking at the passengers? Get on with it ['start with a *bismillah*'].' My hands weren't working. Two Talibs with me started firing and their shots hit the heads of the prisoners.

The boy who was crying the night before and another were remaining. The commander asked, 'Why are you looking? Fire on them!' When he said this, I started misfiring on both sides of the boy [missing him] and the boy slithered down. The commander said, 'No, Talib! You can do it.' He took the gun and started firing on the boy.

In front of me the commander shot the boy in the feet. He was crying, shouting, and then he shot him in the head. Then the commander came close and fired two bullets in his head.

When the commander shot this boy, he said, 'All of you should go, but one person should remain here.'

When we started leaving, I saw four of five heads of the young boys on the side of the canal, while their bodies were lying in the canal [separate]. When I saw these heads, at this time my conscience got confused and I called jihad by the name of cruelty.

I took a decision there that after all this I am not a Talib. I should go home. The next day I came to the bank of the highway. I flagged down a passing bus. All the passengers were talking about the Talibs having killed forty boys. I was always thinking that the same thing was going on in Afghanistan that the scholars told us in Quetta.

But I know now that here is something else. In the name of jihad and killing of foreigners, here killing of my own Pashtuns and public people is going on. In my mind, the events are alive and usually hurt my heart. If they don't kill me, I will describe every event separately. If they kill me, I hope God forgives me. If someone can guarantee my life and can rescue me from the beastly Talibs, this is my email, they can email me there.

Ghulam...

I wrote these few lines with the help of my friend who can use computers. I don't know how to use them. I thank him for his help. One Talib who earlier wanted to do jihad.

70

DIALOGUE WITH AN OFFICIAL
FROM THE POLITICAL COMMITTEE

[*When this lengthy interview transcript was published, it was one of the first in-depth accounts of the political structures of the post-2001 Taliban. The individual being interviewed is believed to be Mutassim Agha Jan, former head of the Taliban's Political Committee who also worked on the Financial Committee. It is also one of the more extensive statements of the Taliban's position on a number of foreign policy issues.*]

Al-Emera (website), 24 February 2009

Q 1: When was the Political Committee established within the framework of the Islamic Emirate? What were the reasons behind that? In addition, according to its responsibilities, what are the duties to be performed?

Answer: In the name of Allah, the Most Merciful, the Most Compassionate. All praises and thanks be to Allah, the Lord of the 'Aalimeen. Peace and prayers be on His best creation, Muhammad, and on all his family and companions.

The Political Committee was established five years ago by the supreme command of the Islamic Emirate of Afghanistan when the attacks of the mujahedeen against the invaders increased tangibly. This was among the series of the administrative framework, which the supreme command set for the sake of organising and developing its affairs; and among them was the Political Committee. When the mujahedeen accomplished their major goals against the extorter American forces, other bodies became ready to establish bonds with the mujahedeen of the Islamic Emirate of Afghanistan. Thus, the supreme command saw the necessity to form the Political Committee to pursue such affairs. Consequently, the Commander of the Faithful gave an order to form such a committee to be able to organise matters in a reasonable way with well-organised planning.

As for its accomplishments in regard to its responsibilities, the committee has accomplished many things, and I say to you, we have been able to accomplish many positive results among which are: establishing mutual relationships with some countries and adopting mutual strategies to suppress the American plans which are based on widening its influence in Afghanistan and other neighbouring countries; and accordingly, we have been able to find the obstacles and consolidate our combats against their wicked goals, and many fruitful positive results have been accomplished.

In addition to that, the Political Committee of the Islamic Emirate of Afghanistan has been able to strengthen its relationship with the neighbouring countries, and has been able to reach high goals; and after the pattern of observing the political interests and remarks, we would prefer, for some time, not to shed light on how these goals have been accomplished, or to mention the names of those countries with whom we have strengthened our relationship.

The committee has also preserved its cordial relationship with the effective parties inside the country to resolve our common problem, and we have accomplished very important goals.

[...]

Q 4: Does the Islamic Emirate still believe in pursuing its old policy about Afghanistan and the issues dependent on it?

Answer: The policy of the Islamic Emirate, as it appears from its name, is based on Islam's solid bases and its pure historical origins, and at the same time putting in consideration the conditions and situations of the present time. It built its policy during its rule over the country, according to the issues related to the country on the principles of the pure historical Islamic origins and its intense bases, taking into account the political and national interests of the country, but there were some defects and points of weakness in several resources; this was according to the emergency unstable conditions; and we are now sparing no effort to redeem them and work on preventing them from happening again; and we are ready to attain mutual understanding with all bodies.

Thus, we are keen to adopt a mutual extensive Afghan strategy and negotiations with all Afghan groups to reach fruitful positive results and undertake the necessary changes, on condition that this does not contradict the jihadi strategy and still keeps the benefits of the Afghan people safe.

[...]

Q 7: We can see that the attitude of the Islamic Emirate in regard to resolving the Afghan crisis is the withdrawal of all the foreign troops with no conditions or prerequisites; and on the other hand we can see that those foreign forces stress holding talks with the Islamic Emirate and putting weapons aside; with regard to those contradictory positions, do you have a reasonable resolution to that crisis?

Answer: The Americans and their allies propose desperate solutions that are away from facts and applications to solve the Afghan crisis; moreover, they are not comprehensible to the human mind. They do not want to resolve the problem of Afghanistan, and they do not allow the Afghans to establish their genuine Islamic regime; also, they do not want the Muslim Afghan nation to choose for themselves the life of security, happiness and stability under a strong Islamic regime.

If the Americans are willing to resolve the crisis and put an end to the problem in a reasonable way, they should first show their readiness to withdraw their forces from this afflicted country without any conditions or prerequisites.

Then second, they should take an immediate decision to close all their detention camps inside and outside Afghanistan, whether secret or known ones, because they were built not only to punish and torment the mujahedeen, but rather to kill them under torture.

Then third, they should respect the mujahedeen and never mention their names inappropriately as eschewed names, and should cancel any lists of names that they have arranged to mock the mujahedeen and prosecute them. These conditions are built on facts to resolve the crisis of Afghanistan, and at the same time it is reasonable and logical; so the Islamic Emirate of Afghanistan is proposing these conditions to resolve this dilemma.

And as for what the Americans and their agent regime in Kabul say about the mujahedeen of the Islamic Emirate, that they have handed over their weapons to them, it is something that does not agree with reality and is rather impossible. To hand over someone's weapons to his enemy and at the same time proceed with the war is something unacceptable to the human mind; because this would lead him to dismount his power and destroy himself; Allah the Almighty has forbidden Muslims from doing so, as He says, 'Do not throw yourselves into destruction...'

The second issue is that the Islamic Emirate refused this proposition when it was living under the pressure of the Americans and their allies, when it was experiencing a critical situation. So how can it be convinced by it nowadays after Allah's blessings have caused them to gain many successes in the political and military fields?! The Emirate is now experiencing a powerful strong situation, not at all the kind of conditions that would make them ready to accept such a concession; they would never be contented to hand over their weapons in return for high positions in the traitor regime. The Islamic Emirate seeks to rule the country to establish a genuine Islamic regime, and not to occupy high positions in an agented rule.

Q 8: What is your analysis of the role of the Islamic Conference of the other Muslim countries with regard to Afghanistan?

Answer: We welcome all the peaceful attempts from whatever party, as far as it is for resolving the crisis of our case; yet, we would never allow anyone to interfere in our internal issues. We have said before, and we say now, 'The basic source of the Afghan crisis is the presence of foreign forces, and whoever wants to create security and improve the situation in Afghanistan has to put their efforts into convincing the aggressors to withdraw their forces without any conditions or prerequisites; we also say that securing stability and peace and improving the situation in the country when no foreign forces are present is the responsibility of the Afghans and it is their religious duty.

There is no doubt that the Afghan nation is capable of securing peace in the country and organising its affairs after the withdrawal of foreign forces. Securing peace in the country, defending our women and keeping our creed is the job of the Afghans and not that of the foreign forces. The Afghans were able to do so during the British war and during the Soviet invasion, and they are capable nowadays during the barbarian American attack on this country. All Afghans consider Afghanistan their real homeland and their real dwelling, and securing peace in it is a duty related to their belief.

Yes, what the Afghans need is to let their case and the pain of their cries reach the ears of the whole world; and what the Islamic Conference, the Muslim countries and the United Nations should do is to defame the barbarism and injustice caused by the Americans against the Afghans, to condemn America's attacks which result in horrible massacres and never choose to be silent on those savage deeds.

There is no doubt that what the Americans do in terms of horrid attacks and inhumane actions against the wronged Afghan nation are not acceptable by any human being or by any creature that has a little mind; accordingly, the Islamic Conference, the Muslim countries, the United Nations and all the free countries should perceive their responsibility and moral duty and do whatever they can to stop the American attacks and their unjust airstrikes against the wronged Afghan nation.

Everybody in our contemporary world knows that there are principled, international rules and positive regulations for the UN that are related to the life of human beings, their dignity and their companionship and defending their nobility of descent. These regulations require others to care for and respect them; besides, it is the responsibility of the whole world, including the Americans, to regard them as equals, without any discrimination.

The UN organisation, the Islamic Conference and all other human rights organisations are responsible for carrying out these regulations and caring for them, and they have to apply them across the whole world equally with no discrimination. They should not treat any differently those deemed weak and afflicted, as against the tyrant powerful forces of America and its likes.

The UN should not leave those powerful countries to do whatever they want towards those deemed weak and wronged nations.

The Islamic Emirate is capable, with the help of its nation, to secure stability and peace in Afghanistan, and the Emirate gave the most marvellous examples regarding this issue during its rule over the country, and the Americans acknowledged it as well. There is no need for forces belonging to the Islamic Conference, nor those of the UN, nor those of NATO to secure stability and peace in our country; on the contrary, we call upon the Islamic Conference and the UN to use their authority and power against the Americans to convince them to withdraw their forces from Afghanistan.

The Islamic Emirate assures that, for the sake of its Islamic Afghan interests, it is willing to agree and deal with all parties, whether the UN, the Islamic Conference, the neighbouring countries or with the other countries of the world or other independent institutions. From here, the Islamic Emirate reminds the UN that it has approved the massacre of those insane criminal savage animals under the aegis of its worldwide regulations and international law, according to its international competence.

We can see that the free world nations, including the Americans themselves, admit the ugliness of the wars of the assassin Bush and the danger of his multiple crimes, and there is plenty of evidence and documents to prove this issue. The UN should submit Bush—the war culprit—to the International Criminal Court to sue him in relation to his crimes against the wronged nations.

Q 9: It has been recently spread that there are negotiations to resolve the crisis of Afghanistan with the mediation of the Kingdom of Saudi Arabia; what is your opinion in relation to the role of the Saudi Kingdom about this case?

Answer: There is no doubt that the Kingdom of Saudi Arabia enjoys an unrivalled history and it has the honour among the Islamic world, because Prophet Muhammad (peace and prayers be upon him) established the unique Islamic community and the first Islamic country that has no like in the history of humanity; in addition to this, the *qibla* of the Muslims is there, which is considered the symbol of the unity of Muslims, and there is also the mosque of our prophet Muhammad (peace and prayers be upon him). Besides that, the Kingdom of Saudi Arabia, both as people and as a country, supported the mujahedeen with human and Islamic assistance during the Soviet invasion of Afghanistan. In addition, we are here looking forward to it supporting the mujahedeen and assisting them Islamically and morally. We call on the government of the Kingdom of Saudi Arabia and its zealous nation, and above them the servant of the two mosques, King Abdullah bin Abdul Aziz, may God keep him safe, to perform his Islamic duty towards the case of the Afghan nation and the rest of the nations of those deemed weak occupied Islamic lands. The Kingdom of Saudi Arabia should defend, with its good-heartedness, the cases of Afghanistan, Iraq, Palestine and other Muslim countries. It should stand by them and help those Muslims whose countries are being occupied both financially and politically; because Allah, the Almighty, has bestowed on them His open generous sources of livelihood and pure sound beliefs. Therefore, in order to give thanks for this Divine blessing, it should support those deemed weak Muslim nations worldwide. It is not a secret to anybody that the Arabs, with their power, have supported the Muslims from the dawn of Islam until now; and we also hope that they will stand by us and support us in all that we need in order to render our jihad victorious and to resolve our crisis.

Q 10: As you know, on Obama's gaining power, the Americans are willing to adopt new strategies towards international issues and towards Afghanistan in particular; in addition, Obama has presented a gift to the Islamic Emirate in Afghanistan, which is to decide to close down Guantánamo detainee camp; what is expected from the Islamic Emirate in return for Obama's decision?

Answer: Obama's decision to close down Guantánamo detainee camp is not considered a positive development, because we still see thousands of innocent Afghan detainees spending their gloomy days in prisons like Bagram, Kandahar, Pul-i Charkhi and others. We can consider closing down Guantánamo detainee camp as a turning point in American politics and a positive result if the detainees there are freed and sent home to their sons and homes. But the situation is not like this: the detainees are to be sent to other prisons, and this will never benefit the detainees nor relieve their sufferings. If a detainee still spends his days in dark prisons away from his family and relatives, then there will be no difference between Guantánamo and other prisons. Obama is talking of closing down Guantánamo detainee camp, but on the other hand announces he is pumping more forces into Afghanistan. Thus, Obama's adoption of these implausible strategies signals that he is planning a hot bloody war strategy, which will result in the destruction of many of his conceited forces, counter to the Holy Afghan jihad, God willing.

[...]

Q 12: All the parties sharing in the internal and external crisis in Afghanistan believe that it cannot be solved with the use of force, so it must be solved through entente; what is your proposition to find a way out of this crisis?

Answer: Yes, we told the Americans a long time ago that the use of force is not a suitable way to solve the problem, but the Americans were deceived at that time with their financial and technological power, and they were not ready to accept any peaceful solutions. They started their savage attack on Afghanistan, violating all the civil and international regulations. When they attacked Afghanistan with their force by waging war, the Islamic Emirate was forced to react in the same way to defend their honour. It sees resistance as the only way to defeat them, and it decided therefore to pursue resistance and jihad against those extorting forces, to compel them to withdraw from this afflicted country. It also sees that because these forces are localised in Afghanistan, there will be no other way to solve the problem except with jihad and resistance. It also sees that when it can force those transgressing forces to step back from the resistance of the mujahedeen, then the Islamic Emirate can carry out effective plans and programmes over the whole country. It will then propose this issue and will negotiate with the other Afghan parties about assigning the future political regime for Afghanistan; but now it sees that the only way to drive the Americans and their allies away is to pursue resistance and jihad against them. In addition to this, the Political Committee for resolving the Afghan crisis has invited the parties involved and negotiated with them, and has started to call upon people who have stood by the Americans, because they have been deceived by the false American slogans and their shining pretence to join the Political Committee of the Islamic Emirate; and our call has succeeded to a great extent, and it has had a great positive effect.

Q 13: If we searched for the historical cases that were in dispute and read through them with deep thought, we would perceive that those cases were not solved through political means and the parties involved did not reach the desired results: like the case of Palestine, Kashmir and others. What is your opinion in relation to such cases? Which one do you deem better: the political or the military solution?

Answer: Each case has several dimensions. If the case is related to the attack of an enemy on another country to overthrow its regime, then it is natural that the only reaction towards it is to react in the same way, which is the use of force against that enemy; in such a case, the military solution is the only preferable way to solve the problem. Allah (*subhanahu w ta'ala*) has guided His believing people to use this way and said, 'Then whoever transgresses the prohibition against you, you transgress likewise against him.'

Starting from this point, the Islamic Emirate of Afghanistan has preferred the military solution, because the country has experienced a situation where the transgressors attacked it, and because it has been facing war, battles and occupation. Accordingly, it has preferred such a solution, and in addition to military resistance, it is willing to solve the problem by negotiating with the Islamic Conference, the UN and other effective parties. It is willing to make those parties understand the fact that the Afghans did not go to houses and homelands of others to attack them, but it is the Americans who occupied their land and attacked their holy places until they forced them, to preserve their genuineness and their freedom to defend their creed and religion, to carry out military resistance and wage wars against the transgressors.

Q 14: According to historical facts, we can see that Muslims entered other countries through jihad and force; and that the centre of Islam, Mecca, has been entered by military force; we can also see that Islam ruling over other countries has been through military forces as well. Isn't the military solution a suitable way to preserve the sacred places of Muslims and their law, to restore the extorted lands and to defend their countries and their homelands? Isn't this solution better than the political one?!

Answer: Yes, this is a fact admitted by everybody, and everyone knows that the establishment of the roots of Islamic law came as a result of sacrifices and *fedayee* acts. It is undeniable as well that defending and preserving sacred Muslim places and their genuine legislations needs more sacrifices and *fedayee* acts. Muslims should consider the military solution preferable if they want to restore their extorted lands. They should make all necessary preparations to accomplish these honourable intentions and dearly loved goals.

The Islamic Emirate, according to Divine guidance and the study of historical incidents, believes that its religious responsibility and obligatory religious duty are to defend its country, establish Islamic law, and root it in the country, to throw out the invaders and strengthen its military force. Yet, in addition to this, it does not dismiss political agreement and peaceful negotiation, because people should not think that the Islamic Emirate focuses only on war and issues of military politics. In addition to our military attempts, we call upon others to sit around the table to negotiate a solution to the problem, and this should have positive, fruitful results.

Q 15: All Muslims, including those in Afghanistan, have been able to engage in wars against their enemies and have been able to obtain great victories on a military level; yet in the field of policy and dealing with others, they have been far beyond the victors; what is the reason for their delay in the political field from your point of view?

Answer: When the mujahedeen carry out holy jihad against blasphemers and invaders according to Divine instructions, and when they defend their creed and sacrifice themselves in return for preserving their religion, honour and money, then Allah with His great blessings and His ample mercy will render them victorious and will create defeat in the hearts of their enemies, and their fate will be destruction and death. Allah, the Most Sublime, when He ordered Muslims to jihad, He ordered them to unite and agree, as He says, 'And hold fast, all of you together, to the Rope of Allah and be not divided among yourselves.'

Thus, all Muslims should carry out this wise order in the same way they carry out other ones. There is no doubt that Muslims have been able to secure wonderful victories in the field of combat and jihad all through their history, but they have not been able to achieve worthy victories in the fields of policy, because of their disputes and their break-up into conflicting groups. In addition to this, the enemy is watching these cases and is wasting no effort in causing national, verbal and racial conflicts, and so carrying out its wicked plans among them. If Muslims want to achieve victory in all fields of life, they should discard controversy and choose to be on one side, because unity and agreement are the main reasons for victory and achievement of their goals, and at the same time for security of victory and perpetual honour. Allah, the Most Sublime, in relation to unifying the world of Muslims, says, 'Verily, Allah loves those who fight in His Cause in rows, as if they were a solid structure.' He also forbade internal conflicts and disagreements which might lead to their disunity and separation, as He, the Most Sublime, says, 'And do not dispute lest you lose courage and your strength depart, and be patient. Surely, Allah is with those who are As-Sabirin [i.e. patient].'

The reasons behind what Muslims face nowadays in the way of crises, hardships, calamities and disunity are their disagreements and disunity. Muslims should waste no effort in securing unity among them. Restoring their time-honoured glory and their late dignity is tied up with their Islamic unity. We call upon Allah to unite all Muslims in the whole world, amen.

[...]

Q 17: Most people think that the Islamic Emirate, during its rule over the country, was against modern education and especially educating women; to what extent is this true from your point of view?

Answer: I do not agree with this at all, and I say that the Islamic Emirate of Afghanistan was not against modern education, but on the contrary and in spite of its hard circumstances at that time, was caring for it; it opened all the schools and universities in the country and prepared all the curricula for them, bearing in mind that all learning institutions had been closed before the Islamic Emirate because of internal conflicts and sectarian wars. More than that, most of them were destroyed because of those wars; and so the sons and daughters of this afflicted country were deprived of education. As for educating women, the Islamic Emirate cared for it in accordance with the hard conditions of that time, and was able to secure the means for their medium and higher education in the biggest areas of Afghanistan, like the capital Kabul, Kandahar, Mazar, Herat, Jalalabad and others. Women were learning different sciences, especially medicine; and as for primary and preparatory schools, the Islamic Emirate managed to organise public and private ones in spite of all the hardships it was experiencing.

As for the obligation to educate women, it is as obligatory as that of men. Consequently, the Islamic Emirate believe that educating men and women is among the necessary duties of life and should be looked after according to the honourable Islamic shari'a. As to what you have mentioned about the world's criticism of the Islamic Emirate, I say, 'If one tenth of the current aid which the corrupted government pay for the corrupted administration in Kabul had been paid to the Islamic Emirate during its rule over the country, it would have been able to open all schools and universities for men and women in an organised way. It would have been able to accommodate them to worldwide standards. However, unfortunately, the world's aid, which they pay to the agent government, has fallen prey to embezzlement and corruption, without the people benefitting from it.

Q 18: It is understood from your speech that education is necessary for men and women, and you consider it one of the priorities of the Islamic Emirate, but we hear from some international mass communication that the mujahedeen of the Islamic Emirate of Afghanistan are closing down schools and educational institutions, even burn them down in some cases; what is your opinion about that?

Answer: This is not true. Spreading such rumours is one of the false allegations of the enemy, because most of the mujahedeen in the Islamic Emirate of Afghanistan are enthusiastic about learning; they know the importance of learning and culture; in addition to this, when the Islamic Emirate ruled over the country it dedicated a considerable budget every year to building learning institutions. So how could the mujahedeen destroy its science institutions, which were built with their own hands or by the foreign independent institutions?! We also say about those rumours, 'We have informed the mujahedeen and ordered them to detain and sue those who burn down those learning institutions; and they have achieved fruitful positive results on the basis of our commands. They arrested some people who did not belong to the mujahedeen and who were carrying out those corrupting acts; and they confessed during the interrogations that they were employed by some American systems to carry out those savage acts in return for major compensation.

On this basis we say, 'The main source of all calamities and afflictions are the Americans; they are not contented with destroying our schools, but rather they kill our afflicted people and shed their blood in a savage way; in addition to destroying their houses, they are destroying the whole country with their advanced rockets and deadly airplanes.'

Q 19: As you know, the Afghan nation belongs to many Islamic doctrines and schools, i.e. the Salafi, the Hanafi and the Muslim Brothers in addition to the Shi'i. What is the attitude of the Islamic Emirate towards those schools and doctrines?

Answer: Afghanistan is the homeland for all Afghans. They should choose their brother-like life and cooperation among them. The Islamic Emirate of Afghanistan acknowledges the rights and respects all those who belong to all the different Islamic schools and doctrines, without any discrimination. It sees that they are all equal on all rights, and it wishes for all the people in the country under the rule of a unified Islamic regime a respectable life with complete security and permanent stability.

[...]

Q 21: What is your message and advice to Muslims everywhere?

Answer: I direct my call to our nation and Muslims in general, to observe the Divine directives and the Prophet's hadith [sayings], to resist the colonial plans and paralyse their idolatrous goals, to protect the Muslims from their wicked conspiracies, as the conceited ones in this world wish to entrap Muslims in Hell with their satanic schemes; and they work day and night to entangle them in disunity and deprive them of mutual trust.

Muslims should consider these destructive conspiracies, and their rulers should depend completely on their Muslim people by using them only in defending their homeland, and to not to keep them away from them because of the tendentious schemes of the enemy; all Muslims should defend their homeland and should work to secure peace and security and respond to the commands of the responsible Muslims regarding defending the country, securing peace for it and saving its identity. They should keep away from the acts that force their rulers to seek the help of *kafirs* and thus help them with their schemes and conspiracies. The crises and problems in Muslim countries between rulers and their people and the current situation are paving the way for the enemy to have authority, and to wipe away Islamic identity and its powerful supremacy.

There is no doubt that American policy, which is based on enmity and which they present to their people under the cover of democracy and development, will destroy the whole world, especially the Islamic one. This policy carries with it a bitter chaotic message, as we have seen in Iraq and Afghanistan. Therefore, if Muslim countries are willing to secure peace, security and growth in their countries and the neighbouring ones, they should focus their efforts on saving their countries from chaos and corruption, on defeating the schemes and intrigues of the Americans and others, and on wasting no effort in spoiling their tactics.

Accordingly, they should support their brothers, the mujahedeen in Iraq and Afghanistan, who are carrying out jihad against the Americans and their allies, because the military jihad has been opened in Iraq and Afghanistan, and defending this jihadi frontline is considered as a defence for the Islamic umma in general and for the wronged oppressed nations in particular. Gaining victory on this frontline is considered as a victory for all the mujahedeen in the Muslim world against the savage American forces; and their failure in this trench, God forbid, would be a failure for the whole umma in front of the Americans. Jihad and resistance as found in Afghanistan and Iraq against the transgressor Americans and their allies have shaken the rule of America, and will lead to eradicating its sovereignty in the whole world, *Insha'allah*. Because of the mujahedeen's acts of sacrifice, they have been able to cause shameful defeat of the enemy and have given them an unforgettable lesson for centuries to come. They have been able with the power of their belief and the deep-rootedness of their creed to paralyse the Americans' modern technology and their developed military equipment. In general, we can say that the resistance of the mujahedeen has made the tyranny and conceit of America the subject to mockery and sarcasm; so, the rulers of the Islamic countries and those of the free independent ones should benefit from such a valuable occasion and support and defend the mujahedeen and their people everywhere to get rid of the evil of America and its master conspiracies. What deserves mentioning is that the Afghan mujahedeen, with the support of Allah the Almighty, are everyday taking steps forward to reach their sublime goals, which are the defeat of American territory and the establishment of a Muslim government over their country. Thus, the whole world should value their accomplishments, as they have the moral right to be respected, and should support them.

At last, we wish for the establishment of Allah's shari'a all over our countries. *Assalamu aleikum wa rahmatullah wa barakatuh.*

71

OPEN LETTER TO THE SHANGHAI SUMMIT

[*This source was issued prior to a meeting of the Shanghai Summit in 2009. It is included here not so much for the uniqueness of its message, but rather because it was frequently cited (exclusively so) by Taliban interlocutors at the time as being the best expression of the Taliban's policy towards Afghanistan and towards the international community.*]

Al-Emera (website), 14 October 2009

Those with a free conscience in the world know that America and NATO member countries have been shedding the blood of innocent Afghans for the past eight years under the pretext of terrorism. Tens of thousand of miserable Afghans, including women, children and old men, have become victims of this fatuous pretext. Still more, this spree of killing, prosecution and torture at the hand of the invaders has been continuing unabated.

Our parents are not able to send their children to school with peace of mind, fearing they might be killed because the invaders have frequently shelled seminaries and schools under the excuse of them being training centres of terrorists. Our ordinary public passengers fear they may get stuck between military convoys of the invaders and lose their life.

Many a time, it has happened that the so-called international security forces have run over ordinary people's vehicles. Afterwards, they claimed that the passengers had not paid attention to their signals. In other words, they considered passengers not heeding their signal a justification for killing them. Our businessmen are grappling with various problems in their daily commercial activities, being not able to perform their normal business routines. They fear their goods may be damaged by foreign troops while transporting them from one province to another. They also fear that some officials in uniform will loot their stock.

A few days ago, foreign forces set fire to 2,000 shops in Gandum Raiz bazaar, Zamindawar area, Kajaki district, Helmand province, burning them to ashes. Other bazaars of the district are under similar threat. Our farmers are not able to work peacefully in the fields because enemy helicopters and fighter planes are hovering over them. Sometimes they take peasants' farm equipment to be weapons and the farmers to be armed militants busy erecting outposts, so they open fire on them. Our ordinary people cannot go to sleep without fear, because the foreign troops often raid people's houses and kill the elders of the households or take them to Guantánamo, Bagram, Kandahar or other notorious jails. In fact, our nation is a hostage in the hands of the foreign forces in Afghanistan. They have been terrorising our people, ostensibly under the name of fighting terrorism.

Despite the atrocities that they have unleashed, still a great part of Afghanistan is under the control of the Islamic Emirate. The problem is that the American and NATO forces are in complete jitters and suffering from psychological diseases. They think every Afghan, child or a mature person, male or female, is going to attack them by blowing up him or herself. So they fear every rock and bush of Afghanistan, considering them to be their enemy, thinking that the Taliban might have planted a landmine under it. They open fire in every direction.

The invaders have turned our country into an inferno where the oppressed Afghans are burning. Therefore, we urge the participants of the Shanghai Summit to help liberate the people and land of the region from the claws of the colonialists and take a decisive stand regarding the West's invasion of Afghanistan.

The Islamic Emirate of Afghanistan, as a liberation movement, wants to play a positive role in the peace and stability of the region, besides its current mission of liberating the country.

The esteemed amir of the Islamic Emirate has touched upon this matter in his recent message as follows:

> The Islamic Emirate of Afghanistan wants to have good and positive relations with all neighbours based on mutual respect and open a new chapter of good neighbourliness of mutual cooperation and economic development.

We consider the whole region as a common home against colonialism and want to play our role in peace and stability of the region.

We remind the participants of the Shanghai Forum to be wary of being swayed by the bad propaganda launched against us by the colonialists. We do not have any intention of harming our neighbouring countries, but we want to gain the independence of our country, which is our natural right, and to establish an Islamic system as a panacea for all our economic and social problems, for which we have been suffering unremittingly tremendous sacrifices.

The Islamic Emirate of Afghanistan as per its peaceful policy wants to have constructive interactions with the Shanghai Summit member countries for permanent stability and economic development in the region, on the basis of mutual respect.

72

A GLANCE AT THE AMERICAN ELECTIONS DRAMA

[*The period of heightened foreign interest in Afghanistan—in 2009, it was the major issue discussed at conferences and diplomatic gatherings—was also the heyday of the Taliban's media machine. They churned out commentary article after commentary article, often accurately analysing the political dynamics at play at a particular moment prior to adding their own slant towards the end ('and that's why you should participate in the jihad against the Americans').*]

Al-Emera (website), 9 November 2009

On 2 November, the first episode of the American colonialist drama ended which had started two months before on 20 August. For the last four years, the American rulers have been blaming Hamid Karzai for the constant failures in the country.

They allege that corruption is rampant in government offices, that the people are alienated and that Hamid Karzai, as well as his immediate relatives, have secret links with drug traffickers. As evidence, they constantly refer to some well-known heroin smugglers being released from prison by Hamid Karzai. On the other hand, Hamid Karzai accuses them of disbursing financial assistance to Afghanistan through the channels of foreign NGOs which are involved in embezzlement and corruption, spending only 20 per cent of the assistance in Afghanistan and putting the remaining 80 per cent in their own pockets. While their bickering continues, the American rulers have brought forward a new pawn by the name of Abdullah, who agrees to all the legitimate and illegitimate wants of Washington.

People boycott the elections

People responded positively to the statement by the Islamic Emirate of Afghanistan calling for boycott of the election. Seeing that only a minuscule numbers of voters turned out on the day of polling, the followers of Karzai and Dr Abdullah in northern and southern Afghanistan resorted to stuffing the empty boxes with fraudulent ballots. The Election Complaints Commission received 2,800 complaints about fraud and rigging votes. American rulers, with the complicity of the United Nations, jointly handed over the complaints to the Complaints Commission which was headed by a foreigner, and its foreign members outnumbered the Afghan members. Even one Afghan member of the commission stepped down, accusing the foreigners of taking everything into their own hands and taking decisions by themselves without consultating their Afghan counterparts.

After two months, the Complaints Commission invalidated 30 per cent of Hamid Karzai's votes, pushing him below the 50 per cent threshold. By doing this, they gave Hamid Karzai a message that they knew his tactics, which would either strip him of power or induct him through legal means. As another instrument of pressure on Karzai and the Afghan people, the Americans suspended payment of all ongoing projects and stopped launching new ones.

Meanwhile John Kerry, American Democrat Senator and Chairman of the Foreign Relations Committee, visited Kabul to find out whether Karzai was ready to accept all the American demands or was still in bickering mode. After a few days of hot discussion, pressure and telephone calls from the White House, Karzai unconditionally accepted all American demands and the Americans announced that a run-off would be held. This was a political ploy to legitimise Karzai's victory.

John Kerry applauded Karzai for being a sagacious statesman, whereas Hillary Clinton said that Abdullah's pulling out of the second round of elections would not leave a negative impact on the legality of the elections. The Independent Elections Commission, after consultation and instruction from the American rulers, declared Karzai as next president of Afghanistan. Ironically, now the same Karzai who was shortly before responsible for all corruption and heroin trafficking was the legitimate president after bowing to American demands. The American and British rulers immediately congratulated him on his victory, and the UN General Secretary, visiting Kabul, congratulated Karzai as a further rubber-stamp on his victory.

Veracity of the stance of the Islamic Emirate

Our people surely remember that the Islamic Emirate always maintained that the real decision about the results of elections is made in Washington. The elections are held in order to throw dust in the eyes of the people and hide the colonialist agenda under the clout of elections. They want to keep the common people occupied in the election drama to distract their attention from the civilian casualties caused by the blind bombardment by the invaders, their poverty, unemployment and corruption. This is to ensure that people are not able to form a common front against these atrocities. Our people are aware that the Americans, as they so often do, left Dr Abdullah in the lurch after using him against Hamid Karzai to tame the latter.

They had given him substantial promises at the outset, but then left him standing. Still, the White House rulers will keep him as a spare piece in order to use him time and again for taming Karzai. No doubt they will always install the one who dances better to the tune of the Americans.

The Islamic Emirate as a force of the people

Events in our country in the last two months showed that the Islamic Emirate of Afghanistan is both a military and a public force. It is a public force because people responded positively to the call of the Islamic Emirate to boycott the elections and stood by it, and it is a military force because all the American, NATO and the stooge regime military and police force could not prevent the mujahedeen from carrying out attacks on polling day, 20 August. The mujahedeen made two hundred attacks throughout the country on that day, paralysing the whole elections process.

Observers believe that the military strength displayed by the mujahedeen of the Islamic Emirate on the polling day for the run-off elections caused the Americans great frustrations, while the audacious martyrdom-seeking attack on UNAMA guest-house in Kabul played out their last strength to hold the run-off.

Conclusion

These events show that the Islamic Emirate is an undeniable reality. The last eight years have proved that no one can obliterate this reality by dint of military force, political manoeuvring or propaganda campaigns. The invaders should understand and admit this reality today, rather than admitting it tomorrow. They should let the Afghans start a new life under the shade of a just Islamic system in an independent country. The colonialists' ambitious dreams of colonising as they did during the eighteenth and nineteenth centuries are not feasible in this twenty-first century. The people are awake now. They know that it is their natural right to have freedom and a government of their choice. The colonialists should grant them this right willingly; otherwise, they will surely grab the right away from them.

73

CAN WE CALL THIS RECONCILIATION?

[*The commentary pieces published on the Taliban's website were often directed at specific audiences. This item reflects on the so-called 'reconciliation process' which was one of the main ideas for finding a way out of the conflict at the time. The article is clearly pitched towards a foreign audience, while making sure to include enough that will appeal to an Afghan reader at the same time.*]

Al-Emera (website), 6 February 2010

After the London Conference, the Kabul surrogate administration farcically speaks of peace and reconciliation. Hamid Karzai, head of the stooge administration, visited Saudi Arabia to ask Saudi King Abdullah to mediate between the Islamic Emirate of Afghanistan and the Kabul regime, and by extension with the USA. However, if we ponder the whole process of reconciliation, we see that it is no more than eyewash, designed to show ostensibly to the public of these countries who are against the war, that the American powers-that-be want peace and an end to the current war. But contrarily, the Pentagon is at present making preparations for new military operations in Helmand province, south Afghanistan. Similarly, they put forward conditions that are tantamount to escalating the war, rather than ending it. For example, they want the mujahedeen to lay down arms, accept the constitution and renounce violence. Nobody can call this reconciliation.

Likewise, it is a condition that the Kabul stooge regime has no writ beyond the capital Kabul. Even in Kabul they are not safe. The audacious attack of mujahedeen on the buildings of some important ministries, near the presidential palace in Kabul, is an example of the military strength of the mujahedeen and the inability of the stooge regime to face the committed members of the Islamic Emirate.

According to the International Council for Development and Security, the Islamic Emirate has influence over 80 per cent of Afghanistan, and with the passage of time that influence is spreading. So the Kabul regime's effort to call on the Islamic Emirate to surrender under the pseudo-name of reconciliation is a futile effort.

This is not the first time that the Kabul regime and the invading countries want to throw dust in the eyes of the public of the world by announcing reconciliation in words, while in practice making preparations for war. Ironically, the Pentagon is trying to lure away the rank and file of the Islamic Emirate by offering them cash rather than making an honest effort for peace based on grounded realities and on the realisation of the natural rights of Afghans. No doubt, by resorting to the old British formula of *divide and rule*, the invading Americans will only prolong the war but will not end it.

The Islamic Emirate has certain goals to achieve. They are:

1. Complete independence of the country.
2. Establishment of an Islamic system representing the wants and aspirations of the Afghan people.
3. Progress and prosperity for the country and its people.

Our first priority is to achieve these goals through talks and negotiation. But if the invading powers in Afghanistan are not ready to give the Afghans their natural rights, which are the right of independence and to establish a government based on their aspirations and wants, then the mujahedeen of the Islamic Emirate are determined to carry on the fight until the realisation of these said goals.

74

AN IN-DEPTH INTERVIEW WITH HAJI AHMAD SAEED, HEAD OF OPERATIONS IN KANDAHAR CITY

[This article was much debated at the time of its release. It was an early attempt to lay to rest some of the criticisms of the movement around their causing so many civilians to be killed and wounded in the course of their operations, whether this meant in suicide bombings or attacks against buildings and government offices. The then-head of operations for Kandahar city is repeatedly asked to explain why this is happening. At the time, the Taliban were ramping up their targeted assassination campaign in Kandahar city, which would reach several assassinations a day at its peak.]

Al-Emera (website), 11 November 2010

The recent operations in the province of Kandahar by the enemy ISAF forces are viewed by the Western-orientated media as the last military push against the mujahedeen. The majority of them are of the opinion that should these operations fail as well, the Americans would have no option other than to leave Afghanistan.

The enemy admits that the essential objective of this operation is to prevent the collapse of Kandahar city (Afghanistan's second largest city) to the mujahedeen forces. To achieve this, the enemy, besides conducting operations in the districts surrounding Kandahar city, has now also started military operations in the city centre as well. To find out exactly what impact these operations have had on the mujahedeen forces, we talked to Haji Ahmad Saeed, who is in charge of mujahedeen military operations in Kandahar city. This detailed interview is presented below.

Al-Emera: First of all, please give us some general information about the recent operations of the invading forces: what are some of the activities the invaders have undertaken?

Haji Ahmad Saeed: All Praise is to Allah. Kandahar city, which has in the past many years borne witness to some of the mujahedeen's greatest operations and bravery, has seen sustained attacks by mujahedeen warriors. These attacks have caused our internal and external enemies to panic, to the point of admitting they could very well fall to the banner of the Islamic Emirate's soldiers. Since then, the enemy has completely revised its strategy, focusing almost exclusively on Kandahar city and its surrounding regions. In line with this strategy, the enemy has increased its presence in the region considerably.

This increase has been witnessed in the city centre as well, where the enemy has increased its infantry and motorised battalions. They have also carried out large-scale raids against the civilian population by surrounding entire districts, then carrying out house-to-house searches for weapons and mujahedeen. They have also started operations in regions that are under mujahedeen control. They have infested the city centre with numerous foreign and army outposts, besides the normal police stations. They have set up more and more checkpoints on the roads and increased their intelligence-gathering spy-rings. All this has given Kandahar city the appearance of a city under siege.

The enemy has caused all this commotion and carried out these measures to stop our activities in the region but, *alhamdulillah* and again *alhamdulillah*, as our recent operations in the heart of the city have shown, the enemy has utterly failed in this objective. Even the Westerners' own governmental and non-governmental agencies confirm our success by stating that mujahedeen activities in Kandahar, instead of decreasing, have increased by over 24 per cent.

Al-Emera: The enemy invaders claim that they have set up a belt round our Kandahar city to choke the movements of mujahedeen into and out of the city. What information do you have regarding this?

Haji Ahmad Saeed: It is true that the enemy has set up various checkpoints on the roads leading into the city and on the main highways and constructed some ten large army stations. One of these army posts is on the Panjwayi road near Kobai; another is on the way from Khanjakak towards Soop; another is on the Herat road near Silo; another is on the Arghandab road near Mir Ahmad Khan's Kalachi; one near Kotal; one on the Shah Wali Kote road; one on the Kabul road near Ayno Meena; one on the Boldak road from Shurandam towards the city. They have also set up two new army posts on the roads leading from Mahalajat. All these outposts have some of the most high-tech detection and identification tools available to the West.

Yet despite this they have never captured any of our mujahedeen, nor detected any explosives-laden vehicle. Everyday our explosives-filled vehicles pass through these army checkpoints and army posts without being detected or captured. This is all by the Grace of Allah who has favoured us in all opportunities. The enemy's so-called 'belt' has achieved no purpose other than harassing the local populace. As you can see, our attacks on the city have increased rather than decreased. Therefore this belt is no impediment to the mujahedeen operations, and its purpose has been inflated far beyond its capabilities.

Al-Emera: How are the mujahedeen's operations inside Kandahar city?

Haji Ahmad Saeed: In the city, as of old, as soon as darkness spreads the stooge government's rule comes to an end, our battalions start their patrols and our operations begin. At night, we set up our ambushes on all the major roads, sealing the enemy inside their outposts. Due to our ambushes, now the enemy has accepted that they cannot provide support to their other outposts if and when they get attacked. Similarly, the mujahedeen always watch their activities during daytime. Every day, enemy spies and soldiers are shot dead by our snipers. Several days ago, on the Kandahar bypass road, mujahedeen conducted searches of cargo trucks, finding and subsequently burning those trucks carrying supplies to enemy soldiers. All this proves that the mujahedeen have the capabilities and willingness to conduct operations in the city according to their own initiative, while the enemy has lost all morale and determination to fight.

Al-Emera: It is said that since this new operation was launched, many innocent residents have gone missing, some of whom have subsequently been found and have reported to have been kidnapped by American and puppet government officers. What information do you have regarding this?

Haji Ahmad Saeed: It is true that the enemy has arrested many innocent people, the majority of whom are still suffering in prisons. These people have been arrested by government intelligence services as well as by various local militias. Many of them have been arrested due to personal or tribal rivalries. These incidents require a thorough investigation, because many of these innocent arrestees have often been tortured to death without any legal process. These are all innocent Afghan civilians whose death should be investigated by all Afghan and global societies.

Al-Emera: The enemy has been announcing recently that they have captured a large cache of weapons, explosives and mines from the mujahedeen. What is your information regarding this?

Haji Ahmad Saeed: This is yet another of the enemy's baseless claims. We have not yet faced a situation where the mujahedeen's weapons or mines have been captured due to the enemy's intelligence-gathering. However, it has sometimes happened that some of our mines have failed to explode due to some technical or electronic failure. These have subsequently fallen into enemy hands, further inflating their egos.

Al-Emera: The issue of civilian casualties is hotly debated in Kandahar. The enemy propaganda claims that civilians are often killed in mujahedeen operations. What do you have to say about this?

Haji Ahmad Saeed: I, as head of Kandahar operations, feel very sensitive to this issue, first in front of Allah and then in front of our Afghan people. If we did not fear causing harm to our own people, then our operations in Kandahar would be ten times more than they are today. We have always tried our best to bring a complete end to any civilian casualties on our part. We have often had to cancel our operations when we feared the possibility of civilian casualties. On the other hand, the enemy always seeks to stay and move in our population centres, so that if the mujahedeen attack them, any resulting civilian damage would be blamed on the mujahedeen. As much as we want to attack the enemy, we know that they want to use our people as human shields for their protection, and therefore we abstain from confronting them in these areas.

Al-Emera: Partly as a result of the recent operations and partly due to the targeted killings of government workers, some people in Kandahar are beginning to think that these shootings and bombings are random and indiscriminate. For this reason, these people are very fearful of the present situation. What is your message to these people?

Haji Ahmad Saeed: I want to tell these people that if they are not government workers, then they should be completely calm and relaxed. The operations in Kandahar are not random and spirit-of-the moment operations; instead each step is thoroughly planed and meticulously executed. The mujahedeen of the Islamic Emirate first conduct thorough background research into their targets, and only when their relationship with the puppet government and their foreign paymasters is fully confirmed do they proceed to punish these collaborators. Only once during my term has one of our mujahedeen mistaken an innocent person (who fully resembled the intended target and was present in the same neighbourhood) for an intended target and killed him. On that occasion, we contacted the family of the deceased and resolved the matter under the law of shari'a.

Other than that, no innocent person has been killed in these targeted assassinations. I want to console my fellow countrymen that the valiant mujahedeen would never steep to randomly killing their own countrymen. It is quite possible that the puppet government and the foreign invaders have put some moles in the city who terrify the populace by defaming the name of the pious mujahedeen. We have provided a contact number for the people of Kandahar to seek our help if ever confronted by these stooge government bandits.

Al-Emera: How would you describe the Kandahar government?

Haji Ahmad Saeed: The government in Kandahar is barely capable of defending itself. We can see that the Kandahar government has no staff or functioning bureaucracy. Its only functioning organs are the police stations, which are run by the American invaders. On the other hand, the mujahedeen have set up various different committees which are always busy resolving the daily disputes of the local people in Kandahar.

Al-Emera: To conclude, if you would like to say something else or send a message, please feel free.

Haji Ahmad Saeed: I, as a mujahed and Muslim Afghan, would like to outline three issues which, if acted upon, will *Insha'allah* bring success in this world and the one to follow.

My first message is to the puppet government workers. I say to them as a Muslim Afghan to leave this government. The government they work for is neither lawful nor shari'i (which applies the rule of Allah) but is a slave institution set up by the

Americans to further their imperial goals. It does not befit a Muslim to work for the infidels in such an institution. They should hasten to leave this institution, and the mujahedeen will uphold all their rights.

My second message is to the various different contractors responsible for working for the Americans in exchange for money. I tell them that even if your collaboration with the foreigners brings you wealth, it also increases the misery of Afghanistan under foreign occupation. For this reason you must give up earning such unlawful wealth and give up your collaboration with the American invaders.

My third message is to the various militias around Kandahar that are set up and run by the American invaders. Most of the commanders and soldiers in these militias are those same bandits that infested Kandahar before the inception of the Islamic Emirate. These bandits were once disarmed after the invasion, but have once more been re-armed to serve as the shovels of Americans. I ask these men to consult their conscience: how the Americans used them at the start of the invasion and then denounced them as bandits and miscreants. Now that they are again knee-deep in the mud, they invoke you to do their dirty deeds. Is it not enough for you to learn from your previous mistakes? You should not involve yourself once again in this dangerous war.

75

ON THE SUDDEN DEATH OF HOLBROOKE

[A number of articles (not included as part of this volume) comment on the spate of ill-health among the US state apparatus. At the time, Petraeus had fainted during a senate hearing, then Holbrooke died, and then Hillary Clinton suffered concussion and was treated for a blood-clot in a vein in her head. This article considers Holbrooke's death, placing the blame for this at the feet of US foreign policy.]

Al-Emera (website), 14 December 2010

According to credible global news agencies, the American president's Special Envoy for Afghanistan and Pakistan, Richard Holbrooke, has died in George Washington's University hospital at the age of 69. He had been suffering from heart issues for the past few days.

Appointed on 22 January 2009 as special envoy for Afghanistan and Pakistan, Holbrooke was keeping an eye on the Afghan issue. Sometime ago, he told reporters that he had been passing through a difficult phase of his life, which exerted crippling and sapping pressure on him. He passed out in his office for Afghanistan and regional affairs on Friday last, following his above-mentioned revelations. His life of toil and fatigue ended after admission to hospital where yesterday he breathed his last.

The American rulers have not made any statement about the cause of his sudden death, in view of the sensitivity of the issue, but rumours have it that this giant of American politics and diplomacy became ill with heart disease when his previous fame and credibility came under question after the unremitting failure of the mission to Afghanistan and his dealing with the difficult task. The protracted Afghan war and the descending trajectory of the Americans' handling of warfare in the country had made a lethal dent in Holbrooke's health as a high-ranking American official. He was grappling with constant psychological stress.

The emergence of such an untoward phenomenon as an offshoot of the Afghan issue is now no strange thing. The same was the case with the former Soviet Union as the crisis reached its climax. Former Soviet leaders Brezhnev, Konstantin Chernenko and Yuri Andropov all had heart attacks a short time before Mikhail Gorbachev came on the scene. They relieved themselves of the hard task of the Afghan mission by retreating into the lap of death.

The recent symptoms indicate that an outbreak of the same epidemic diseases has started in the political and military echelons of America.

A few months ago, an American four-star general, General David Petraeus, fainted during a Senate hearing when he faced tough questions on the issue of Afghanistan. The end of Holbrooke, the fate of general McCrystal and the Defence Secretary Robert Gate's warning to step down show that the war in Afghanistan is heavily weighing down on the psyche of the American military and political high-ups. Some of them lighten their burden by simply going to the other world; and others, while still alive, choose to avoid shouldering the mission.

The sudden death of a high-ranking American diplomat happens at a time when American strategists under Obama's administration have been reviewing the issue of Afghanistan for the past few days. They are expected to announce their decision soon.

We believe Holbrooke's timely death could have a didactic effect on the American strategists, teaching them many things [they need] to learn. In view of the American entanglement in the aggravating swamp of Afghanistan, the Islamic Emirate of Afghanistan calls on the American powers-that-be to abandon their dream of military domination and colonial sway in Afghanistan. Their formulation of new military strategies will never change the imminent defeat into a victory in the country. Still, if they are bent on continuing with the status quo, they will face many unexpected events and imbroglios. Their political and military circles will have to grapple with constant crisis and untoward situations. They will achieve nothing more than that.

76

MULLAH MOHAMMAD OMAR'S
EID UL-ADHA STATEMENT

[*By 2010, the release of Mullah Mohammad Omar's two Eid speeches / statements had become an event of sorts among foreign policy circles, even if there was less attention paid to the specifics by the Afghan audience. The statements ballooned in size each year, with different sections addressing different audiences. The paucity of other statements from Mullah Mohammad Omar meant that they were often scrutinised as if reading tea leaves, and individual side-comments took on a significance that was perhaps unwarranted.*]

Al-Emera (website), 15 November 2010

Regarding the puppet Kabul regime:

The situation of the Afghan people and the beloved country is going from bad to worse during this reign of the surrogate Karzai regime. Hardship, starvation, poverty, homelessness, civilian casualties, various diseases, aberrations of the youth and cultural and social deviation in the name of democracy are reaching their climax. A few hoarders in high government slots have control over all items, including basics for daily consumption. This is being carried out under the name of the open market system. They determine the prices.

We witness this hard fact, that many miserable families in the country have been forced to resort to begging. Corruption is at its height. This is not just what we say, for the founders and masters of this regime admit that their puppet regime ranks second in the index of the most corrupt regimes of the world. This is because the rulers of the regime have been installed by others and they are not interested in the future and prosperity of the country. They are only hankering after filling their pockets with money and fleecing the masses. Many of them have foreign nationality and do not consider Afghanistan as their own country.

The Americans are intending to maintain in the country a regime installed under the leadership of some Westernised elements: a regime which is totally bereft of any resolve and determination; a surrogate relying only on foreign aid. Thus the invaders want to prolong their presence in the region and extend their occupation. Every Afghan in this corrupt regime has the obligation to desist from supporting the invaders because of the current ordeals and tribulations that the Afghan Muslim people are passing through. They should not help their enemies of faith to destroy their home.

There is no moral and religious justification to work in a regime which is a puppet and traitor to its people. If they are not able to join the ranks of jihad, at least they can desist from cooperating with them. Thus they should perform their patriotic and ideological obligation. They should take care lest they stand shameful before their people and history and Allah (SWT) on the Day of Resurrection.

The number of those who have left the ranks of the enemy has increased following our previous call to do so. This is a commendable phenomenon. We have instructed all mujahedeen to favour them with special incentives and acclamations.

Regarding the rumours of peace talks by the Americans

The Islamic Emirate still holds its previous stand regarding the current issue of the country. The Islamic Emirate believes that the solution to the issue lies in withdrawing the foreign invading troops and establishing a true Islamic and independent system in the country. The cunning enemy which has occupied our country is trying, on the one hand, to expand its military operations on the basis of its double standard policy; and on the other hand, it wants to throw dust in the eyes of the people by spreading rumours of negotiation. Claims about negotiation, flexibility in the stance of the Islamic Emirate, are mere baseless propaganda. The enemy wants to cover up its failure in Afghanistan by wrongfully raising hollow hopes in the hearts of their own people.

The open-minded people of Afghanistan and the public of the world should not trust any news report or rumour about the stance of the Islamic Emirate disseminated by anyone other than the leadership of the Islamic Emirate or designated spokesmen, because such news reports are spread by the intelligence agencies of the hostile countries. Then the media outlets affiliated with these espionage entities irresponsibly publish them with great fanfare. The aim is to play down the defeat (of the enemy) in the military field through media warfare. But these conspiracies will never prove effective against our brave people and mujahedeen, as these experiences have already been tested.

The former jihadi leaders and influential people based in Kabul should know that as the invading Americans already used you against the mujahedeen in the framework of the peace council, they will use you again for their illegitimate objectives beside the puppet regime of Kabul. We can't figure out why you are unilaterally trading with the invaders? Can the present regime reflect your objectives of former jihad? Was the aim behind your fourteen-year-old jihad to let the place of the Russians be occupied by the Americans?

MULLAH MOHAMMAD OMAR'S EID UL-ADHA STATEMENT

If you want to extricate yourself from this dilemma and lead life like a proud Muslim Afghan, the only way towards honour and dignity is the way of sacred jihad and independence for the country. Come and compensate for your mistakes of the previous years by embarking honestly on the path of struggle against the invaders. This does not mean that everyone has to join the stronghold, but everyone should utilise his capability in support of the current resistance. The Islamic Emirate of Afghanistan has a comprehensive policy for the efficiency of the future government of Afghanistan; for true security, Islamic justice, education, economic progress, national unity and a foreign policy based on norms to protect itself from the harms of others and convince the world that the future Afghanistan will not harm them.

Regarding the military situation

Our forthcoming military programmes will forge ahead on the basis of the climate of the country and the geographical locations as per the plans now at the disposal of the mujahedeen. The aim is to entangle the enemy in an exhausting war of attrition and wear it down like the former Soviet Union. This will force it to face disintegration after deal it a crushing and decisive blow, after which it could not survive.

To achieve this, we have hammered out short-term and long-term plans. We are optimistic about the results of these plans. Our strategy is to increase our operations step by step and spread them to all parts of the country to compel the enemy to come out from their hideouts and then crush them through tactical raids. This experiment was effective in Marja, Kandahar and some other areas. Therefore, the mujahedeen should focus on their jihadi efforts more than ever and expand their jihadi operations on the basis of the given plans. They should try their best to compel the moribund enemy to flee from our soil.

They should constantly and unremittingly remember Allah during the performance of their tasks and be sure that Allah is the ultimate creator and conductor of all affairs; they must have the conviction that their achievements are the result of the exclusive blessings and victory from Allah; they should increase their worship and recite their prayers during jihad, which the holy prophet (peace be upon him) usually recited. This will bestow on them solace and consolation and will strengthen in them the essence of trust, sincerity, humbleness and the desire to seek the pleasure of Allah (SWT). These characteristics of a believer are an asset which even in worse conditions lead to a blessing and victory from Almighty Allah. Similarly, do not forget the Islamic moral conduct, even for a while, during your journey on the path of the sacred jihad.

You should study the jihad-related affairs in the books of the Sayings of the Holy Prophet (peace be upon him) and in the laws of religious jurisprudence. Pay attention to the life and property of the civilians so that, may Allah (SWT) forbid, your jihadi activities will not become a cause for destruction of property and loss of life of people. Anything that is not permissible in Islam has no place in our military policy. Spread fraternity among yourselves and help each other during the time of distress and ordeal. Maintain close contact with the people, seek the advice of local influential figures and hear their constructive advice and consultation and put them into practice.

To the young educated generation and men of letters of the country and the students of universities

As a young educated generation and men of letters (writers) of our Islamic country, you are the leaders of tomorrow for our country. Our enemy is turning every stone to spread their cultural and ideological influence over the young generation of this Muslim country and thus jeopardise our history, religious values and our future. Our religious and historical enemy has cunningly launched a propaganda drive, spending huge amounts of money in order gradually to strip our young generation of their Afghan and Islamic identity. As a young generation of this Islamic country, you have an Islamic and Afghan responsibility to confront these hostile anti-Islamic and anti-Afghan endeavours of the enemy with all your capabilities of tongue and pen and indefatigable struggle. Do not let your historical, religious and cultural enemy succeed.

You should know that the cunning enemy both financially and extensively fund some Afghan circles who have sold out in a surreptitious manner, to enflame a domestic war on the basis of language and geographical locations. Thus they want to harm the identity and integrity of the country and take revenge on the Afghans. You, the young educated generation, should not become part of these negative movements. Instead, focus solely on serving the cause of dissemination of Islamic culture, the independence of the country and its unity. The honour of a Muslim lies in Islam and Islamic unity. It is you who are able to protect the pillars of Islamic culture and Afghan identity from crumbling down. The Islamic Emirate is your flank of battle and a stronghold.

The Islamic Emirate is proud of your support; your jihad of words and pen bestows on you high esteem and praise. This resistance will increasingly boost your scholarly and cultural efforts.

To the peoples and governments of the Islamic world

On this occasion of Eid ul-Adha and on behalf of the Islamic Emirate and as a member of the world Islamic family, I would like to remind the governments and peoples of the Islamic world to forget the issue of occupied Afghanistan and the miserable condition of the people of this country. You should remember that the Afghan people have played an impressive role for the defence of Islam and the Islamic world, offering numerous sacrifices in this way throughout different stages of their history. This nation stood as a wall of iron in front of the invasions of Genghis, the British and the Communist colonialists, saving the Islamic world.

Today, this nation is entangled in a complicated trial and a war imposed on them for having professed their (Islamic) ideology. Every day, men and women of this nation fall prey to bombardment by the invaders, and their children become orphans; miserable people are displaced internally due to the operations and fear of bombardment by the enemy. The people are grappling with hardship and poverty. But the Afghans have embraced all these sufferings out of commitment to the great cause of establishing the rules of the Holy Qur'an and defending the Islamic faith. So the Muslims of the world should share and feel (their pain) and have conduct with them on equal terms as pious Muslim. Perform your obligation of fraternity (towards them) in your material wealth. The countries of the Islamic world should not beholden to the issues of Afghanistan, Iraq and Palestine, and should not waste their efforts in this regard in framing their foreign policies. They should consider the pain and hardship of these suffering people as their own pain and problems, and play a positive role in the solution of their problems.

To the American and European peoples and to members of their parliaments

Afghanistan is an independent Islamic country. It has a proud history and freedom-loving people at the level of the region and world. This nation has not harmed the independence of other countries and, throughout its history, has not permitted anyone else to take their independence. Now, when your forces have invaded this territory for the achievement of some colonialist objectives and goals, so it is the religious and humane obligation of the Afghans to stand up to your forces. Think, if your country were invaded by someone else, would you remain indifferent in such circumstances? What do you think, should our people allow the invasion and aggression in their country and remain insouciant vis-à-vis the invaders? And should they not show some reaction towards the aggression against their honour, religious values, national dignity and independence?

If you are an impartial judge, you would yourself give us the right to maintain our path of resistance against the invaders, and even increase it more than ever.

Considering the limited resources at their disposal and their firm determination and conviction of being in the right, the Afghans have demonstrated to your military chiefs and political leaders, over the past nine years, that you the invaders are not able to force this nation to accept your occupation. Your surge in troops made no change in the status quo, and will never be able to turn the tide, God willing. Body counts from your troop's casualties have spiralled upwards, but still your political leaders and military chiefs stubbornly persist in their failed policies.

First of all, you should find for yourselves the realities on the ground and then study them. Ponder them impartially. How long will the governments and peoples of the world tolerate your tyrannical policies and your habit of taking our people hostage? To relieve yourselves and the Afghan people from the weariness of this unjustified war, you should put an end to the war as soon as possible. The more the war is prolonged, the more the casualties of your troops increase and the heavier the economic burden becomes. Nothing more than this will be achieved by you staying.

This is the country of the Afghans. The Afghans will not relinquish it. The resistance will continue as long as the invaders are stationed here. You should review the historical facts to learn some essential points from them. It is more rational to stop adding fuel to the flames of war by leaving this region. The presence of foreign forces on our soil can only cause intensification and aggravation of the war, from which you will face colossal financial costs and loss of life.

To the neighbouring countries in the region

As an independent country, Afghanistan has been forced to wage a sanguinary war for the attainment of its identity. The colonialist countries, led by America, want to turn our historical and independent country into a military base under various pretexts. It has persuaded some other countries to align with them, and has even compelled the international community of the United Nations to issue resolutions palatable to the USA. It has turned the international community, de facto, into the personal entity of America.

I urge you to define for yourselves the realities on the ground instead of listening to the futile propaganda of the colonialists. Do not forget your responsibilities for the independence of our oppressed country.

On the basis of its hypocritical policy, America wants to project our legitimate mission to defend our country and the current resistance as a threat to the world; whereas they have no convincing proof and evidence to hand in this regard.

Request

To this end, I urge all Muslims to remember the families of the mujahedeen, the prisoners, martyrs and IDPs in these day of sacrifice and selflessness; they have sacrificed themselves in the defence of this venerable religion (Islam) and the country. Remember their orphans and heirs and treat them as you treat your children; in particular, favour them with a share in the joy of Eid.

Once again, congratulations on the occasion of Eid and may Allah protect you from grief and anguish. Peace be on you all.

The servant of Islam, Amir ul-Mu'mineen
Mullah Mohammad Omar Mujahid

77

INTERVIEW WITH THE ISLAMIC EMIRATE WEBSITE
ADMINISTRATOR

[*This article, originally published in* al-Somood *magazine in Arabic but republished a few months later in a Pashto translation, describes the universe of the Taliban's media operations. These were, at the time, considerable. They ran a website simultaneously in Pashto, Dari, Arabic, Urdu and English, publishing dozens of news reports and commentary articles each week.*]

Al-Emera (website), 17 February 2011[1]

In our series of *al-Somood* interviews with officials of the Emirates, we present to you this time an exclusive interview about the jihadist media activities of the Islamic Emirate with esteemed brother Abdul Sattar Maiwand, who is responsible for the Al-Emera website on the global internet. We invite you to read it.

Al-Somood: To begin, we wish you to provide the readers of al-Somood with a summary of the media activities of the Islamic Emirate.

Maiwand: Praise be to Allah. Blessings and peace be upon the Messenger of Allah, and upon his family, his companions and all those who followed him.

Among other committees, the Islamic Emirates established a special Media Committee to spread (news) about jihadist activities in different fields and dispel the voice of the unjust enemy who, before the entire world, was distorting the image of the jihad in Afghanistan and was claiming false victories here and there over the mujahedeen. There was a need for a media agency to take responsibility for the mujahedeen in Afghanistan; to speak on behalf of the Islamic Emirate; to deliver news of its victories on the battlefield to its friends and to the world; to expose the falsehood of its enemies and their media; to respond to their claims and their daily changing deceptions; and to deliver to the world the voice of truth and jihad and its point of view about current jihadist events in the land of Afghanistan.

Wars today cannot be won without media. The media are directed at the heart, whereas weapons are directed at the body. If the media can defeat the heart, then the body is defeated too and the battle is won. In the beginning, with the fall of the Islamic Emirate, the enemy thought that the field was completely open before them, and they spread their lies and falsehoods: that they had destroyed the Islamic Emirate and its mujahedeen, and that their victory in the land of Afghanistan was complete. All of their resources, especially their media, were directed towards changing the ideas of Afghans and injecting defeatist thought into them and instilling in them a petrifying fear of the new occupiers. First through the grace of Allah, *subhanahu wa ta'ala*, then through the victories of the mujahedeen and their rightly guided leadership; and after defeats were inflicted on the enemy on the field of battle, a Media Committee was established to contest with the enemy in that field.

Therefore, the media ranks of the Islamic Emirate were re-formed under a special committee that reflects the tangible reality on the ground in Afghanistan. Among its most important accomplishments at the beginning was the inauguration of the Islamic Emirate website under the name 'Voice of Jihad'.

The website specialises in conveying field reports from the combat zones and publishing the statements of the Amir ul-Mu'mineen and the statements of the Command Shura Council about different issues pertaining to jihad, in addition to articles and official analysis. They have many sections: for example, there's an Islam page, a magazine page, and a page for films produced by official studios. We also print magazines and statements and distribute them to groups at home and abroad. Additionally, we produce different publications and regulations and distribute them among the mujahedeen. There is also a 'Voice of Shari'a' that broadcasts news and official statements day and night.

The Media Committee has also appointed two official spokesmen to speak in the name of the Islamic Emirate to local and global media regarding the course of affairs.

Al-Somood: How do you gather news and field reports from Afghanistan and publish them on the website?

Maiwand: Yes, through the grace of Allah *subhanahu wa ta'ala*, the committee employees correspondents in all the provinces of Afghanistan to cover news of events and prepare reports on them.

They make every effort to follow news of operations in detail and keep abreast of developing situations, and they send reliable and precise reports of ongoing operations immediately to the official spokesmen of the Emirate, Zabihullah Mujahid and Qari Yusuf, who review the news and then send it to the news department of the website after in-depth scrutiny and examination.

Al-Somood: News, official statements and analysis are published simultaneously or soon after in five different languages. How do you manage that?

Maiwand: Yes, as you were so kind as to mention, news and other items are published in five different languages almost simultaneously. These include local languages such as Pashto and Farsi as well as Urdu, Arabic and English. The website first publishes news and other media in Pashto, and after that it translates directly into these other languages and publishes in their special sections.

Al-Somood: Are there ways to publish the news other than through the Al-Emera website?

Maiwand: Yes, brother, we send the news to journalists and global news agencies immediately after it occurs and is posted on the website. We have many email lists to which we distribute news and official statements. These lists include journalists and others concerned with the issues of Afghanistan. We are also active on Facebook and Twitter, where we publish the news every day and reach thousands of people. We also send daily news via cellphone text messages to many people.

Al-Somood: Could you please clarify that last sentence? How do you use the cellphone to send news?

Maiwand: The news that is posted on the website is converted to SMS messages and sent to a number of people, who pass it on to other people. Each of them sends it to their acquaintances inside and outside Afghanistan, and so a chain of dissemination begins. Each one tries to spread the news further and further. We have seen many people requesting their friends and relatives to forward the news they receive to at least twenty other people, and so this news becomes widely circulated in popular circles. Through the grace of Allah, we have seen many among the general populace rejoice when news reaches them of the victories of the mujahedeen over their enemies.

Al-Somood: Could you please explain for us some of the other activities of the Media Committee beyond the Islamic Emirate website?

Maiwand: The Media Committee has other media pulpits, including the Jihadi Studio which publishes mujahedeen operations in live video. Through the grace of Allah Almighty, it has created some good products in this field.

In addition to publishing live images of jihad and battles, the Jihadi Studio also produces films to preach (*da'wa*) and reform, with the goal of illuminating the minds of the mujahedeen and making them ideologically aware. These films have so far had a good impact in mujahedeen circles.

There is also a Pashto-language radio broadcast called 'Voice of Shari'a', which is transmitted via the internet. It broadcasts daily news and reports, political commentary, Islamic and jihadi *nasheeds* which have a direct impact on raising the morale of the mujahedeen. The Voice of Shari'a programmes are broadcast during morning and evening slots. In addition to audio and video information, there is print information in Arabic, Pashto and Farsi languages. The print media are represented by the monthly magazine *al-Somood* (Steadfastness) in Arabic; and the *Shahamat* (Gallantry), *Sarrak* (Gleam of Light) and *Morchal* (The Trench) magazines in Pashto and Farsi languages, also published monthly. The *al-Somood* magazine, where you are a staff member, has for five years provided a true picture of the Islamic jihad and hot events occurring on the Afghan battlefield to the Islamic and Arab world. It is concerned with publishing articles, political analysis and news reports, in addition to comprehensive statistics of monthly mujahedeen operations and their impact, in addition to the series 'Our Heroic Martyrs' to introduce people to the mujahedeen military commanders who were killed *fi sabeel Allah ta'ala*.

As for the magazines, *Shahamat* and *Sharrak*, they have been published for seven years in the local languages of Pashto and Farsi. They have many readers in educated circles, especially among madrassa and university students. The jihadist articles published in those magazines have had a tangible impact within these circles.

As for the *Morchal* magazine, it is dedicated to publishing news of the battles, reports of enemy crimes, statistics of enemy losses in lives and equipment and related issues. Its annual archive is considered the most reliable jihadist source to determine enemy losses.

All of these media capabilities are presented via the Islamic Emirate website on the worldwide web and everyone can view them on the website.

Al-Somood: How do you find specialised staff to carry out these media activities?

Maiwand: The mujahedeen enjoy the presence of people among them who, first through the grace of Allah Almighty and then through their capability and military experience, have been able to defeat NATO generals of great experience and expertise, so it also is easy for them to conduct such media activities with their proficiency in the media field.

Since the media jihad has today become one of its most important responsibilities, the Islamic Emirate has not neglected to prepare specialised media cadres. Rather it has, in the field of jihad, prepared mujahedeen media workers who can resist the enemy in the media field just as their brother fighters resist them in the military field.

Yes, I say with full confidence that with our simple and limited means, we have, through the grace of Allah *subhanahu wa ta'ala*, defeated the enemy in the media field. The enemy has been unable to redress this defeat despite the existence of their advanced means and specialist cadre and their vast expenditure of funds in this field.

It is possible for everyone throughout the world to view all our publications on the internet. Indeed, all the workers in the Karzai government who have internet access in their offices, universities and government administrations and even those who work in the American military and political administration view our publications and are affected by them.

There are many residents of Kabul city who listen to the Voice of Shari'a programmes via the internet and inform us by email of how they were favourably impressed by those programmes. They tell us that hearing the *nasheed* 'la Allah ila Allah' recalls to their minds memories of the rule of the Islamic Emirate of Afghanistan.

Even though the Americans, NATO troops and the security forces of the lackey government all exert great efforts to impede the activities of the Islamic Emirate, it frequently occurs that members of families from the upper class in the Karzai admin-istration display their sympathy with the mujahedeen.

The Americans also admit that the Islamic Emirate has defeated them in the media field. This confession was made in an article published on 22 May last year in the well-known American magazine *Foreign Policy* entitled 'Losing the Media War to the Taliban'. The author of the article was the well-known American writer Robert Haddick, who mentioned details of Taliban media activities and their media superi-ority over the Americans. The author advised his people, saying 'In their media battle against the Taliban, the Americans must use more effective methods and tactics, because the Taliban have won the media war using existing methods.'

A report by the American Council of Foreign Relations corroborated Taliban media superiority over the Americans in the media field. The report mentioned one reason the Taliban have moved ahead of the Americans in the media field: because they do not wait for appointed dates to publish news of events, but publish them as soon as they occur.

The progress of the Islamic Emirate and its media superiority over the Americans has become today's news to the Western press, which has begun to write articles and commentary about it everywhere.

Regarding Taliban excellence in this field, Michael Doran, the former American deputy secretary of defence, said that 'The Taliban have great skill in directing their media activities and are very quick to publish news: if any attack is conducted against our forces, news is being published 26 minutes later on the global satellite networks, taking its place in the breaking news tickers for most of the global satellite networks like al-Jazeera, BBC and CNN.'

He added: 'The Taliban are not only quick to publish news, but they are also for-tunate in the precision and organisation of their media work. They translate news of all their military operations as soon as it comes in from Pashto and Farsi to Arabic and English, and it is immediately published on their websites and their online radio Voice of Shari'a.'

Michael Doran continues by advising the Americans, 'It is necessary for the Americans to increase the capabilities of their soldiers in blocking Taliban media activities by granting them more authorities and limiting Taliban media activities by strengthening their (own) media channels. They must also close down all Taliban websites on the internet.' [The Council of Foreign Relations, May 2009]

General Azimi, spokesman for the ministry of defence in the Karzai administra-tion, acknowledged in an interview with Radio Free Europe last year during the battle of Marja that the mujahedeen media activities were stronger and more successful than those of the government.

Al-Somood: How do you explain the media superiority of the mujahedeen?

Maiwand: The sole factor in the media superiority of the mujahedeen is that they perform this work as undertaking a jihadist responsibility, and not as a job performed in return for a salary as others do. According to the moral contract to which they have committed themselves, they make sacrifices to the point of death for the sake of the success of this jihadi work. They endure hardships and regard success in performing this responsibility as a goal of their worldly life. Because of the sincerity, sacrifice and zeal of the mujahedeen, Allah blesses their efforts and grants them success. This blessing and success granted by Allah is acknowledged by the enemy also, and this grace has been witnessed by the enemies.

Al-Somood: What are the problems you encounter in performing your media responsibilities?

Maiwand: The path of jihad is full of trials and difficulties, but the mujahed accepts them with good will to please Allah Almighty and elevate His Word. These hardships are born *fi sabeel Allah ta'ala* and are a source of pride and a sign of the righteousness of His path. We face many material problems: problems with media technology, security problems and a scarcity of material resources. But they are easy to bear for the sake of achieving a noble goal, and we are proud of this.

The means we possess are very paltry when compared to the means of the enemy. Moreover, we also face in this field a shameless enemy who is not by bound by any humane or moral obligations. They speak excessively about slogans of freedom of expression and speech, but they do not recognise freedom of speech which runs contrary to their colonialist interests. In addition to that, they lie prolifically in their media. If twenty of their soldiers are killed, they announce the death of only one, and only if they are unable to hide this news. If twenty of their people are wounded, they admit that only one was wounded and say the wounds are slight and that he returned to his job after his wounds were bandaged and treated. If one of their aircraft is shot down by the fire of mujahedeen or is set alight in the air, they hide the news if they can. If they can't hide the news, they state that it was an emergency landing. When they arrest local citizens during night raids they claim that they have seized armed mujahedeen. This is their custom in all their media publications.

As for our media, despite our commitment to publishing the truth, the enemy attacks our websites on the internet, and closes or sabotages them. They threaten the companies which host our websites and send them warnings.

'Their intention is to extinguish Allah's light (by blowing) with their mouths: But Allah will complete (the revelation of) His light, even though the Unbelievers may detest (it).'[2]

Even though they commit all these crimes, we are, through the grace of Allah Almighty, able to continue our jihadist publications. We present to the world the victories of the mujahedeen and the defeats of the enemy. We show the world documented evidence of the defeats of the Americans and their allies in Afghanistan. We have had good successes in this field despite the many problems we face. Praise be to Allah for that.

78

WHEN THE DEAD ARE LIVING
AND THE LIVING ARE DEAD

[*Articles published on the Taliban's websites tended to comment on the political or military developments of the day, rather than on issues that concerned religion or belief. This piece, translated from the Arabic original in* al-Somood, *examines the idea of martyrdom, death and sacrifice through a discussion of various well-known Muslim personalities.*]

Ahmad Bawadi
Al-Emera (website), 26 December 2010

The dead live by their words and by what their fingertips have written. They live by the truth of their words and the steadfastness of their attitudes, despite the demise of their bodies and the ascension of their souls. The words written by their white hands will endure and revive and awaken hope after they have sacrificed themselves, their wealth, their blood and their worldly life for the sake of what they wrote, which emanated from their firm values and deep-seated principles in the cause of the *deen*. On that day, although they are dead, Islam and the Muslims shall triumph through them. The people of faith will be glorified and the people of *shirk* and idolatry will be debased and life will be honourable and dignified. Their blood and their sacrifices are the fuel and the fire that will eliminate injustice and take away sorrow and pain. Justice will prevail and the oppressed will be victorious. The prisons will be emptied and the afflicted set free. There will be no loss of rights, and neither tax nor toll.

When the living are dead, although their bodies are still walking on the earth, they have no life. Their hearts are dead because they exist only for their own whims, comforts and cravings. They have collected the wages of their employment, the wages given for their sermons and fatwas, for their insolence against Islam and the defenders of the *deen*. They were abstemious and the price was cheap: a few dirham or fame mixed with the blood of the noble and the free. They fall before the Lord of all creation in their councils and on their satellite networks while they are drowning in error from the soles of their feet to the crowns of the heads. They remove (people from Islam), mislead them and make them *jahili*. From their own mouths all who oppose them are foolish-minded or young. They speak of the good qualities of those who demolish the *deen*, while maintaining silence over their wicked deeds and the tools used in their work of destruction. This is no surprise when they themselves are the subversive tools in the hands of those wreckers. Among them, the people of truth and conviction are people of deviation and clear error.

When the cowardly have left the land forsaken ... only discredit and conflict will be sought when they are the ones who speak of the condition of the umma and the state of the Muslims. Islam and the Muslims will be humiliated and life will be one of ignominy and abuse. It will become nothing but submission, subjection and servility.

Countries will be occupied and the Qur'an defiled. That which is sacred will be sullied, the pure maidens will be raped and honour will be ravaged in order to revive from death *Laka' Ibn Laka'* upon the skulls of the innocent, the blood of the noble and the deaths of the guiltless. At their hands will come the day in which Islam will be washed away as a garment is washed away, and neither fasting nor charity nor piety will be understood. But they (will) meet a poor fate and come to a bad end, with the permission of the One, the Benefactor, as their wages for what they have done to the umma, for the blood they have spilled with their fatwas, for their silence about the truth and for the assistance they have rendered to falsehood. Yet, they will think that they have done well: *'Is he, then, to whom the evil of his conduct is made alluring, so that he looks upon it as good...'* Ibn Abu Dawud (he of the *fitna* of the creation of the Qur'an) lived on the blood of al-Bawayti (a student of Imam al-Shafa'i, may Allah Almighty have mercy on him), and although he was famed for his learning, eloquence and munificence, he was nonetheless of wicked intention and corrupt creed so none of that benefited him and he came to a bad end because of how he criticised, harmed and slandered the people of truth and faith.

Sayyid Qutb was one of whom it was believed that his words would be killed and their letters erased from hearts and minds. Yet, his words have endured as if they were carved in rock and stone. The words of those who attempted to destroy his honour and his writings, however, have died, even though they were seduced by his writings and his books. They stole from them and pretended that they came from their own thoughts. Allah has exposed them, disgraced them and sullied their houses. They are dead even though they are still alive, while Sayyid Qutb lives even though he is dead.

Sayyid Qutb paid the price of his words with his own blood. As for those who received their wages for their speeches, books and articles criticising Sayyid, and those who stole his words and collected their salaries from the publishing houses, or promoted themselves and earned a reputation on the satellite networks by criticising him: Sayyid Qutb is living even though he is dead, and they have died even though some of them are still living.

Many of the sons of this *da'wa* lived, and their words lived with them, when they revived among people the glory of the *deen*, and it was accepted and resonated. The righteous and the truthful gathered about them and on that day purity was not mingled with the defects of this world and it was not polluted with disturbances caused by whims or fancies or patchwork fatwas of favouritism. The Word of Truth and sincerity in counsel were the intent of the faithful. They lived and their words lived as beacons of light and guidance, and the people of piety and faith followed in their footsteps.

Other followers of this *da'wa* lived, and they were held with affection and esteem in people's hearts. Then suddenly (this affection) declined and receded and was taken by death and they suffered and sighed the moans of death. Perhaps someone will rescue or pay attention to it. Suddenly it becomes nothing more than a memory killed by its masters after they chose the life of their bodies over the life of their words and after they chose to live by principles and ideas of the West, the logic of the mind and the pretext of rationalism. They claim to show favouritism for and to flatter the people of innovation and error, that they had changed their paths and turned their ideologies and ideas upside down. They shed their values and principles; and the secularists gathered around them. They became the boon companions of the secularists and the liberals and, by their words, became secularists themselves. Their pulpits were the MBC and IBC networks and they became jurists of beggary (*fuqaha' al-tasawwul*) so that the righteous and true abandoned them. None remain in their life except some of the duped, the seduced; the secularists, the liberals and the democrats. So they have died while they are still alive. Their fatwas are circulated by the soldiers of the marines, by the vulgar; the men of surrender and treachery, and the people of defeat. They meet on the satellite networks and criticise those whose field is the arena of jihad and martyrdom. Birds of a feather flock together.

Ahmed Ibn Hanbal (Imam of the *Ahlus Sunnah*) has died and the head of *fitna* Ibn Abu Dawud (of the *fitna* of the creation of the Qur'an) has died and Bishr Mirisi (a Mu'tazalite sheikh) has died. Yet, what Ahmed bin Hanbal wrote lives and is redeemed by the truth of what his fingertips wrote and his tongue spoke. His words have been redeemed by his body when he was flogged, imprisoned and tortured by the executioners and his memory lives.

Ibn Abu Dawud and those with him died after they spent their lives in the palace of the sultan living on the screams and pain of Ibn Hanbal while they themselves dwelt in comfort. Their ideas and beliefs died with them and they have no worth except begging, injustice, subjugation to slavery and love of passions. How can such a worth bear any remnant of the truth? Ibn Abu Dawud died imprisoned inside his own paralysed body which for four years did not possess the power to move.

As for Ibn Taymiyya, his memory is immortal, Allah permitting, until Allah inherits the earth and those upon it. He composed his message of *astightaha*, but the people of innovation and whim were not impressed, as is indeed the case with them always and everywhere. So Ali bin Yaqub al-Bakari attacked him; Ibn Taymiyya, declared him *kaffir* and demanded his death. But the rulers joined forces and incited the people, stirring them against (al-Bakari). He was reviled, cursed and imprisoned. They went to great lengths to harm him until they gathered with the mob against him. They struck him and did him harm until he was exposed and fled. When the earth pressed around him he could find none but Ibn Taymiyya, in whose house he hid. Allah has exalted the memory of Ibn Taymiyya and his message lives. His enemies have died and their ideas have died with them.

Those ones sacrificed for the sake of their words and their writings. They did not eat by them and they did not beg through the ink of their books. They avoided uncertain (*shibh*) and forbidden (*muharramat*) areas. They did not find their nourishment in the efforts of others or from reviling, harming or slandering them. They did not accept a price from the depravity and pleasures of this world. They threw all of that behind them, as opposed to their opponents who—because they cursed, reviled and criticised the people of truth, faith and jihad and because they favoured the people of falsehood, error and deviation—are consigned to oblivion.

79

CODE OF CONDUCT FOR THE MUJAHEDEEN
(2010 EDITION)

[*The second layeha rulebook was a significant update of the short document that listed only thirty short articles back in 2006. Not only did the number of articles increase and get split up in subsections, the second version of layeha was a complex document that could be read in several different ways. The layeha was as much a window into the growing administrative structures and processes of the Taliban at the time as it was an outline of central Taliban policies. It also provided a window into the organisational struggles and grievances held against the movement. The text goes into great detail outlining the ideal organisational structure, offices and responsibilities of the Taliban. Individual sections (such as the first section on surrender of the opposition) outlines the policy the Taliban adopted, explaining it in practice and detail to its own followers, as much as to the people they would have liked to surrender. In the third section that discusses the matter of spies among the Taliban ranks, we find already the listing of behaviour that is not permitted. Rather than considering this to be a pre-emptive directive of the Taliban anticipating misbehaviour (in this specific case concerning torture), the Taliban's rules, much like those in the 1990s, were mostly reactionary and therefore specific issues that are addressed in the rulebook can be considered lists of issues that occurred within the Taliban. Where in later sections of the rules we learn about the various commissions the Taliban established, specific comments point towards far more intricate internal arrangements. The articles concerned with 'martyrdom operations' (generally understood to refer to suicide bombings), for example, explicitly mention 'those mujahedeen who have been given permission and private programmes by the leadership' that one can speculate refers in part to the operations run by the Haqqanis, shedding light on some of the more precarious processes of running the insurgency on a day-to-day basis. Other sections list issues that had already been addressed during their time in power during the 1990s, such as the prohibition of 'youngsters whose beards are not visible' and their presence in 'residential or military centres.'*]

[Printed document],[1] 29 May 2010

In the name of God, the compassionate and merciful. Praise be to God and blessings be upon his honoured Prophet. For thus says the blessed and almighty God:

> O ye who believe! Obey Allah, and obey the messenger and those of you who are in authority; and if you have a dispute concerning any matter, refer it to Allah and the messenger if you are (in truth) believers in Allah and the Last Day. That is better and more seemly in the end. (4:58)

> Hast thou not seen those who pretend that they believe in that which is revealed unto thee and that which was revealed before thee, how they would go for judgement (in their disputes) to false deities when they have been ordered to abjure them? Satan would mislead them far astray. (4:59)[2]

> From 'an-Nisa' [Chapter 4 of the Qur'an, in Arabic in original]

Jihad in the path of Almighty God is such a great worship [*ebadat*][3] and a great obligation, and fulfilling it will bring dignity and raise up God's testament of faith [*kalima*]. Jihad for Muslims' success and prosperity is such a significant instrument that with its blessings, the *shamla* [pride, literally the tip of the turban which points upwards] of the Islamic umma [the global community of believers] can rise. Nations who have made jihad have achieved the blessings of living in independence and freedom. Whereas nations who sheathe their swords in their scabbards and quit the path of jihad have not achieved any benefits other than to put the chains of slavery and captivity on their own necks. Now, when the mujahedeen promote the testament of faith [*kalimat allah*] for the sake of their Muslim nation [i.e. Afghanistan], the Islamic umma and their pride, and give their holy bride in charity [*nazrana*], the need is felt more than ever in the light of the declared jihadi [principles] that jihadi affairs be organised and managed for the mujahedeen for their administrative training, education, rights and moral instructions. They need a code of conduct, so that in the light of its appointed shari'a rules, mujahedeen will be able to identify their target much better, and identify the qualities of the enemies of Islam and their helpers and supporters, and to deal with the suspicions and doubts which they come across in their jihadi environment. Then they can find an easy solution for these doubts and, according to divine guidance, responsibilities shall be given to those who have piety, courage and such a wisdom that they can carry the responsibilities well and neutralise the plots of the enemy.

With the support and assistance of almighty God, the leadership of the Islamic Emirate was able to respond to this important need with the help of the outstandingly knowledgeable ulemaa, muftis and in consultation with the wise men and experts; in the light of shari'a of the Prophet Muhammad [peace be upon him], it has prepared this code of conduct and book of principles in 14 sections and 85 articles.

CODE OF CONDUCT FOR THE MUJAHEDEEN (2010 EDITION)

With the second printed version,[4] with the consultation of the aforementioned persons, and taking into account the current conditions, there have been added some necessary details which provide further clarification and explanation to some articles. After the second printing, it is the duty and responsibility of every official and mujahed of the Islamic Emirate to obey and implement the articles of this code of conduct.

All military and administrative officials and the common mujahedeen of the Islamic Emirate are obliged to restrict themselves [i.e. follow] this code of conduct in their jihadi affairs and manage their daily jihadi affairs in its light.

In peace [*wa salaam*].

Explanatory notes

i. Where the imam is mentioned in the code of conduct, it refers to the esteemed Amir ul-Mu'mineen,[5] Mullah Muhammad Omar (Mujahed), may God protect him. Nayeb refers to his deputy.

ii. In the text of the code of conduct where the term *ta'zeer*[6] is used, it cannot be understood to refer to getting money [i.e. mujahedeen or judges cannot impose fines instead of other punishments].

iii. If in the text of the code of conduct *tazmin* [bail or surety] is mentioned, this refers to non-transportable properties or to persons only. It does not refer to cash or transportable goods.

iv. This code of conduct is printed for the second time and has been enforced since15 Jamada ul-Thani 1431, which is 29 May 2010, which is 8 Jawza 1389. All the Islamic Emirate's officials and mujahedeen are obliged to act in accordance with this code of conduct.

Section 1: The surrender of [those from] the opposition and issues concerning inviting[7] them [to leave the government / join the mujahedeen]

1. Any Muslim can invite enslaved workers and those in authority from the Kabul administration to stop working with this corrupt government and cut themselves off from it.

2. When someone accepts the invitation to leave this corrupt administration or does so because of his own faith, if he is an ordinary man, the [shadow] district governor shall give a letter of permission. [But] if he has harmed Muslims, the district governor in consultation with the provincial governor shall write a letter and must inform the mujahedeen about him. If a mujahed kills him or harms him, he will be punished in accordance with Islamic principles.

3. Those who have surrendered and are penitent, and when in power [had worked with the infidels or their enslaved administration and] had damaged someone's

property or harmed someone [i.e. killed], this person is obliged by God to give the damaged party their due rights. Otherwise he will be guilty. Of course, neither the court nor anyone else can forcefully get this compensation from him and neither shall he be forcibly punished. And if a person who has surrendered but when in power had looted the property of the people and still possesses it, the real owners of these properties can take them back. If he no longer has the property, compensation cannot be obtained by force. Of course, if when he was in power or before he was in power he borrowed something or bought or sold something with someone who had agreed [to that transaction], the debt is still owed and the other person can ask for it. If the court asks about these issues, the person who surrendered must present himself to the court. Of course, if a group of thieves or a tribe has attacked another tribe, village, house, shop or vehicle or anything else and killed or stolen property, in this case appearance in court and compensation are mandatory. Reference in book of Hadith, go to Al Hedaya 2 p. 340; and 5 p. 340; and 2 p. 284.

4. For those who have broken their promises and loyalty after having been invited over and accepted and who have clearly betrayed [the Emirate], the agreement [between the parties] is cancelled. If he surrenders and repents a second time and the mujahedeen are not sure about hits loyalties, they shall take a surety.

5. If someone from the current corrupt administration is accused of killing Muslims, and the Muslims hate him and he has left the ranks of the opposition, then the mujahedeen shall take a guarantee so that he will not harm anyone [in the future] nor return to opposition ranks. Such a person can continue a normal life. In addition, the district officer, to make sure, shall keep an eye on him. After the completion of an important task, such as killing a foreign occupier or a high-ranking governmental official or preparing the ground for capturing them, he shall be introduced to the leadership [for commendation] so that he can get more significant privileges.

6. Anyone who has left the puppet administration and surrenders to the mujahedeen, for the mujahedeen's own good, they must not put him in their ranks until they trust him. After trusting him fully, they shall obtain permission from the provincial authority before they allow him to fight alongside them.

7. It is not allowed to intend to kill an armed opposition soldier who has become separated from his comrades and has come to you in a place where he cannot defend himself, unless you are fully sure that he is not really surrendering but intends to attack and trick you.

8. If a person from the opposition asks the mujahedeen to serve them while staying on in the opposition front [i.e. while still apparently with the government], on the condition that you or your group of mujahedeen will not harm him, if you have such a relationship there is permission to give the person a secret security [guarantee]. This will not be a public guarantee, and if there were to be such a relation-

ship, the mujahed must obtain permission from the district officer and the district officer must ask permission from the provincial governor. Apart from the person and the group [which has provided the secret security for the person], any other mujahedeen who might kill him or give him trouble will not be held responsible [if they kill or harm him] because the person was given a secret guarantee.

Section 2: Concerning prisoners

1. When an enemy—whether foreign or national—is captured, he shall be immediately handed over to a provincial official; after that, the provincial governor has the authority to decide whether he wants to keep him with the mujahedeen [who captured him] or give him to others.
2. If a soldier, policeman or other official of the enslaved government is captured, it is up to the provincial governor to decide whether to conduct an exchange of prisoners, either as a goodwill gesture or for a strong guarantee. Releasing them for money is forbidden. Only the imam, *nayeb* or provincial judge has the authority to punish or order the execution of a prisoner. None except them are authorised. In a province where there is no provincial judge appointed, the judgement for execution and punishment shall be given to the provincial governor. [This formula is repeated so often that they are referred to as the 'three senior officials'.]
3. If contractors who provide oil or other materials or construct military bases for the puppet administration and foreign infidels, [also] low or high-ranking officials of private security companies, translators of the infidels or the drivers procuring [these materials] for the infidels, are captured and if they are proven guilty of any of the aforementioned activities by the provincial judge, he shall order them to be executed. Of course, where no judge has been appointed in a province, then the evidence and decision to execute shall be given to the provincial governor.
4. If an infidel fighter is captured, the decision to execute him, exchange him for [Taliban] prisoners or release him as a matter of expediency or—for the sake of Muslims' needs—for money shall lie with the imam or *nayeb*. No one else has the right to decide. If a captive converts to Islam, then the imam or *nayeb* is allowed to exchange him, provided there is no risk of him reverting to being an infidel.
5. If the mujahedeen capture an enemy prisoner and they have not yet transferred him to their base and they face danger and cannot transfer him to a safe place, if the prisoner is a member of the opposition [i.e. with the government] and was captured during fighting, or if he is a high-ranking official [literally authority], the mujahedeen who are present are permitted to kill him. If this is not the case, if the prisoner is only suspected [of these things] or [his identity] is not known, or [the case against him] is not proven or if he has been captured because of a legal issue,[8] it is not legitimate to execute him—even if he has to be left behind.

6. Soldiers or police who have surrendered to the mujahedeen and are repentant shall not be executed. Of course, if they have brought weapons or carry out a similar heroic act, the mujahedeen shall commend [literally spoil] them further.

7. Captives shall not be tortured, whether with hunger, thirst, cold or heat, even if they deserve execution. Rather, whatever verdict has been decided upon, according to shari'a law, shall be implemented.

8. Other than the imam, *nayeb* or the provincial judge, no one has the right to issue a verdict. If the district judge sentences someone to death, the permission of the provincial judge must be obtained. Of course, if in some provinces there is no provincial judge appointed, the authority to execute or issue a verdict shall be handed over to the provincial governor.

Section 3: Concerning spies

1. If there is any evidence to prove that a person is a spy, in the current situation [i.e. a time of jihad] he shall be known as *sayi' bi'l fisad* [one who strives to spread evil]. The provincial or district judge or, in the absence of a judge, the provincial official has the authority to issue a verdict. The authority to execute a spy lies with the imam, his *nayeb* or the provincial judge, or if no judge has been appointed, it lies with the authority of the provincial governor. No one else has the authority to order an execution.

2. Whenever a person is known to be attempting to spread evil, proving it in the following four ways are required:

First: He speaks voluntarily and without force, by himself, and confesses to the espionage.

Second: There must be statements from two witnesses whose testimony can be trusted by the judge.

Third: There are such indications [evidence] from which the suspicion arose, such as special espionage equipment whose purpose is spying and/or other evidence. Of course, not all evidence is clear-cut. In the presence of the court, the judge must examine the evidence. If there is no court, expert scholars or wise men or pious officials shall weigh the strength and weakness of the evidence. If the evidence is weak, then the sentence should be reduced. If the evidence is strong, then the sentence must be harsh. If the evidence is so clear-cut that they are fully convinced that the suspect is a spy and the imam, *nayeb* or judge considers an execution is necessary, then they can execute him.

Fourth: A note on the just man: he is one who is fair, is not prejudiced and protects himself from the major sins and is not continually committing minor sins.

3. Getting confession by force—meaning by beating, threats or abuse—has no credibility and neither can it be used to prove a crime. The interrogator shall be pious

and wise in order to avoid forced confessions, because in shari'a confessions made by force are unsafe and not credible. Mujahedeen must not promise anything to the prisoner in return for a confession which they do not intend to fulfil. Likewise, the testimony of a spy [accusing others or claiming to be a witness to others' spying] is insufficient [to convict others]. In this case, as per article 2 above, the four methods [of proving guilt] are applicable and in the light of these methods, a judgement shall be reached.

4. If someone is accused of spying and his crimes have not been proved in accordance with shari'a principles, but the mujahedeen remain concerned about him and suspicious of him, the district governor, in consultation with experienced and expert persons, shall expel the suspected spy to a place where he is no longer a danger. Or they will get such a strong guarantee—meaning that reliable people locally and his relatives provide a surety and/or non-transportable properties—that if the suspected person carries out espionage or other destructive actions and escapes from the region and does not present himself, his properties can be seized so that he can no longer use them.

5. If a criminal deserves to be executed according to shari'a, his execution—whether he is a spy or another criminal—shall be carried out by shooting. Filming or taking photographs of his execution is forbidden.

6. The death of a human being has many shari'a laws attached to it. Therefore, if the mujahedeen execute a condemned person in a way that his relatives are not informed, they must inform his relatives in any way that they consider appropriate of the date on which they executed that condemned person.

Section 4: Concerning those who provide logistical support or [carry out] construction for the enemy

1. The burning of private vehicles which are used to transport supplies to the infidels or provides other services is legitimate. Releasing vehicles for money or using them is forbidden.

2. Drivers who transport supplies for the infidels, and if the mujahedeen are well-informed that they are transporting [supplies] for the infidels or their enslaved administration, they shall be killed and their vehicles burned; or if they are captured and it is proved to the judge that they undertook such activities, they shall be executed. If there is no judge in a province, then the evidence and authority to deliver a death sentence shall be handed over to the provincial governor.

3. Contractors whom it is known for certain build bases or transport fuel or other materials for the infidels or their puppet administration, the mujahedeen shall burn their equipment [vehicles] and kill them. If they are taken alive and it is proved to the judge that they have committed these crimes, they shall be sentenced to death. If there is no judge in a province, then the evidence and authority to deliver a death sentence shall be handed over to the provincial governor.

4. If it is known for certain that a contractor provides labour or other workers or supervises their work for the enemy, he also shall be executed.

Section 5: Concerning booty

1. Booty is the property of infidels which has been seized during battle. In Afghanistan, the law orders that one-fifth of the booty shall be given to the provincial official and he, according to the leadership, will be paid a *khoms* tax (a 20 per cent share). Four-fifths [of the booty] shall be given to those mujahedeen who were on the frontline, and those who were sent by their *amir* [leader] to ambush or provide information for the fight and to those who were sent anywhere else for any good reason, if they are able to fulfil these two conditions:

    First: They should have been very close to the area of operations so that their support could be requested, and if it was requested they could have gone there and helped.

    Second: They had the intention to take part in the operation, they were prepared for it and were in communication with the mujahedeen fighters, for example the commander had deployed mujahedeen near the battle, so that if there was a need, he could ask them to participate.

    If one of these two conditions is not fulfilled, they cannot be considered partners in the sharing of booty.

2. Before the fight, mujahedeen commanders shall write down the names and identities of the mujahedeen so that during the sharing of booty or if the mujahedeen are captured or they are martyred or for other necessities, the information will be available.

3. If the mujahedeen fight the infidels in a village and the villagers take part in the fight, they shall share the booty. If they do not take part, they cannot share the booty.

4. If a mujahed is martyred before the end of the fight, he does not get shares in the booty. Of course it is important for his comrades out of sympathy to give him a share. But if he has been killed on the battlefield or after the end of the fighting, he will get a share the booty. [Original Pashto is unclear.] His share should be given to his heirs.

5. If money or belongings are seized from the foreign invaders at the end of the battle, this is booty. If it is seized without fighting, it is known as *fei* and *beit ul-mal* [public property].[10]

6. The leadership can permit the property of the enslaved administration which is seized by the mujahedeen during a fight to be shared as booty. If it is seized not in a fight, it becomes public property and will be spent on the mujahedeen's needs.

7. Money which has been withdrawn from the public treasury [bank] and is in the hands of the cashier and has not been distributed to the labourers and civil ser-

vants, if seized during the fight, it shall be distributed as booty. If it is seized not during a fight, it is public property. If the money has already been distributed to the labourers and civil servants, they own it. The imam, judge or the provincial official can punish them, but they cannot seize the money. Those working with NGOs also come under this rule.

Section 6: Concerning organisational structures [*tashkilat*]

1. Provincial officials are obliged to establish a commission at the provincial level with no fewer than five members, all of whom should be competent. This commission, with the agreement of the provincial official, should establish similar commissions also at the district level. The majority of the members of the district commissions and at least three members of the provincial commission should [normally] be present in the area where they work. Members of both commissions should be chosen from individuals who will not have any pretexts for not working in their areas.

2. A district governor should be appointed in any district where the mujahedeen of the Islamic Emirate have prominent and visible activities. The district governor, with the agreement of his senior officials, shall then appoint a deputy to look after people's affairs, [someone] who is not too busy with military matters. The deputy, to some extent, should have experience in dealing with the affairs of the people and must have a good manner in dealing with the public and be also easily accessible to the people.

3. The creation of new groups and sub-groups is forbidden except in emergency circumstances and must be requested by a provincial official, agreed to by the head of the zone (*tanzim rais*), and approved by the leadership. Unofficial and unregistered groups shall be combined with official and larger groups by the governor. If these unofficial groups do not obey, they shall be disarmed.

4. The spokesmen for the Islamic Emirate shall be appointed at the request of the relevant administration by the leadership. They represent the whole Islamic Emirate. No one has the right to talk to the media as a representative of a group, unit or individuals. Following this principle will avoid disunity and chaos.

5. Every province's official shall establish a shari'a-based court at the provincial level which shall have one judge and two knowledgeable ulemaa. The court shall address the cases province-wide that other ulemaa and officials have not been able to resolve in the districts and villages. The provincial governor shall introduce the judge and other members [of the court] to the leadership to be approved.

6. In terms of the organisational structure of the province, the head of the zone, in consultation with the governor and the governor in consultation with the district governors, can bring changes. If the governor and district governor do not agree regarding these changes, then the issue shall be referred to the head of the zone. If

the governor and the head of the zone do not agree with each other, then the issue shall be sent to the leadership. Provincial commissions can change the district governors after complete research and investigation and with the permission of the provincial official and the head of the zone.

Section 7: Internal issues for the mujahedeen

1. The mujahedeen must obey their group leader, group leaders must obey their district leaders, district leaders must obey their provincial leaders, provincial leaders must obey their head of the zone and regional commanders must obey the imam and *nayeb*. This is obligatory (*waajib*) to be in accordance with shari'a.
2. Persons who are given responsibilities shall have the following characteristics: wisdom, piety [*taqwa*], courage, mercy and generosity. If not all criteria are found [in a person], wisdom and piety are necessary.
3. The military commission for developing military affairs is responsible for planning, taking into account mujahedeen strength, geographic locations and using successful techniques and experience, and for getting plans to the mujahedeen. If enemy pressures mount on the mujahedeen in a province, the commission must prepare plans for mujahedeen in the neighbouring and other provinces to demolish the power of the enemy and reduce his pressure on the specific area which is coming under pressure (in the other) province. It must submit the plan to the leadership for consultation and approval and implement the plan thereafter in the target provinces.
4. The military commission shall keep itself informed of the situations of all mujahedeen in the different provinces and indentify those mujahedeen who are working well and shall introduce them to the leadership for further support and praise.
5. As the members of the military commission are all commanders, it would be difficult for them to come together at all times, so any number of the members could come together at the necessary time [for the meeting] to go ahead. Or, the head of the commission shall manage to deal and continue with those members who are available, to avoid any possible setbacks and obstacles [in the way of progress].
6. The military commission will continually ask for clarifications from the provincial officials and also will encourage the mujahedeen to improve their development of military affairs; and in support of the process, the commission will every now and then send representatives to collect reports from the provinces.
7. In order to solve the people's issues and legal issues, this last article of the code shall be applied. But if there are issues between the people and the mujahedeen or amongst the mujahedeen, these issues shall be resolved by the district or the provincial commissions, and the district commission should get the agreement of the district governor or his deputy; and the provincial commission should get the

agreement of the provincial governor. They should listen to the claims of the different sides, and if they cannot resolve the issue then it should be taken to the military commission to seek a peaceful solution. If the issue is still not resolved, then it will be taken to the leadership. The leadership will resolve the issue through the relevant administrations or ulemaa; whichever commission decides on the matter, the decision shall be announced in the presence of both sides.

8. The provincial and district commissions, in addition to their other work, will also check that bad people do not get into the mujahedeen fronts; and if they see such people, they shall report them to the governor. If there are internal differences between the mujahedeen or between the people and the mujahedeen, they [the commissions] will try to resolve such problems. They will also monitor the implementation of all the decrees of the Islamic Emirate and the Code of Conduct and ensure that [failing mujahedeen] pay heed to the code and are reformed. Those who do not reform will be brought before the governor.

9. If a member of the military, provincial or district commissions or their *andiwal* [comrades or friends] is involved in a dispute with the common people or other mujahedeen and the authority to resolve the conflict is given to the commission, when it comes to the sessions which are addressing and resolving [such a] dispute, the person who is partial to one side of the case shall not participate in the session.

10. The provincial commission is obliged to structure the membership in such a way that every month in that province they will give mujahedeen who are based in the houses and rooms [of bases] guidance on obedience, piety and morals; they will also monitor their attitudes.

11. If someone in the mujahedeen ranks commits a crime or repeatedly violates the code of conduct and the group commander or district official decides to remove him because he has committed a crime, then the issue shall be referred to the provincial commission. After an in-depth investigation if the sentence is expulsion, then the commission, in agreement with the provincial governor, will make the decision. No one will be allowed to arm or bring the expelled person back again. If the person repents, the provincial commission, with the agreement of the governor, will re-assign him. If the person was a unit leader, district governor or deputy district governor, then the issue will be referred through the governor or provincial council to the military commission. The military commission is authorised to try to reform him, [invite him to reform] and advise or punish him; and if he does not reform, then he shall be brought before the leadership for disarmament or dismissal. If he repents, the approval of the governor and military commission [to bring him back] is required.

12. The provincial official at the provincial level and the district governor, according to the conditions in each area at an appropriate time, will consult on conducting good operations; also outcomes, losses and other activities in order to prepare better plans for future successes and to save the mujahedeen from losses.

13. If the leader of a group of a province or a district wants to move to another district or province to do jihad for a while, this is allowed, but he can do so only with the permission of the senior provincial and district officials. The leader of the chosen district or province is considered to be his leader and he must obey him.

14. If a governor or another senior official who had an active group in the past in a different province introduces his mujahedeen to the current official of a province to follow the orders of the current provincial governor, they should follow the governor's orders when carrying out their duties and the logistics shall be provided by the officials of that province just like the other mujahedeen of the province. According to the Islamic Emirate's structure [*tashkil*], setting up *mahaaz* [i.e. large, semi-autonomous military groupings] is forbidden and will not be part of the Emirate's structure.

15. If the commander of a group of mujahedeen from one province wants to help the mujahedeen of another province and wants to remain there afterwards, officials of the new province will not give him a permanent place or let him accompany them until they have received complete information, assurances and agreement about him from his previous province. It should also be asked why he left the previous province and came to the current one. If the reasons were based on shari'a, then he shall be accepted.

16. A group leader is not allowed to recruit members from another group in order to increase the size of his group. Of course, if a mujahed wants to join another group, he can do so, but any equipment which the group leader gave him for the cause of jihad shall be returned to that group leader. If the mujahed has received booty and it is owned jointly, it must stay with the group; if it has been approved that the booty is not share, he can keep it.

17. Those fighter mujahedeen who enter as a group into an enemy's base to target the enemy shall remember a number of issues:
    1. They should be well-trained and every one must [be able to] identify their targets well.
    2. They should be fully supported and equipped so they can inflict severe damage on the enemy.
    3. Before any attack, they or their commanding officers must have complete information about the area and must identify the way towards the target.

18. Concerning martyrdom operations, the following four points must be observed:
    1. The martyr mujahed shall be well-trained before the attack.
    2. Martyrdom operations shall take place against important and major targets. The Islamic nation's sacrificing heroes shall not be used against minor and valueless targets.
    3. In carrying out martyrdom operations, take great efforts to avoid casualties among the common people.

4. Except those mujahedeen who have been given permission and private pro-grammes by the leadership, other mujahedeen are obliged to get their orders from the provincial officials to carry out martyrdom operations.

19. In order to make further improvements in their activities, the general commissions of the Islamic Emirate need to have consultative sessions from time to time.

Section 8: Education

All the activities regarding education in the structure [*tashkil*] of the Islamic Emirate shall be according to the principles and guidance of the Education Commission. Provincial and district officials carrying out their educational affairs shall follow the policy of the commission.

[NB The Code does not specify what Emirate policy on education is.]

Section 9: The control and arrangement of the affairs of [private] companies and [non-governmental] organisations

Concerning the affairs of organisations [NGOs] and [private] companies, provincial officials shall follow the guidance of the Commission for the Arrangement and Control of Companies and Organisations. Of course, if there is a disagreement while provincial officials and the Commission are consulting each other about something, the Commission shall request the guidance of the leadership. The provincial, district and group officials and the representatives of the Organisations and Companies Commission in their respective province do not have the right to make their own decisions about the affairs of organisations [NGOs] and [private] companies.

Section 10: Health

The Health Commission of the Islamic Emirate, in order to manage its affairs, has special a procedure for the treatment of mujahedeen which shall take place according to this procedure. Concerning health, the provincial officials are obliged to follow the principles of the commission, and the relevant authorities shall ensure that its instructions are followed.

Section 11: Issues concerning the people

1. If local residents with legal or other disputes come to the mujahedeen and hand in petitions, group commanders do not have the right to intervene in the people's issues. Only provincial officials, district governors and their deputies can consider petitions concerning a dispute and must then seek the help of relevant bodies and a legitimate jirga to resolve the dispute in a way which is not in conflict with holy shari'a. If the peace jirga could not solve the dispute, then it should be referred to

the court if it exists. If there are no courts, the decision should be made according to the views of prominent ulemaa.

2. The renewal and reviewing of cases which were resolved correctly during the rule of the Islamic Emirate of Afghanistan is forbidden. This is the case even if one side is not satisfied with the verdict, because more justice was possible then than now.

3. Mujahedeen commanders and the individuals are not allowed to intervene in public disputes. They are not allowed to recommend anyone to a judge, nor go to court with them. They cannot take sides in any disputes.

4. Provincial, district, group officials and all mujahedeen with all their power must be careful with regard to the lives of the common people [aam khalq] and their property, such as cars. Those who do not pay heed to the lives and belongings of the common people shall be held responsible, taking into account their prestige [rank], and will be punished accordingly.

5. If an official or an ordinary person in the name of the mujahedeen harms the common people [aam khalq], his senior officer is responsible for correcting him. If he is not reformed, the provincial officials shall introduce him to the leadership. The leadership will punish him accordingly or expel him from the mujahedeen's ranks.

Section 12: Concerning prohibitions

1. As there was a vigorous process to collect weapons from the beginning of the movement up until now, that process will no longer take place and people's weapons shall not be collected under the name of disarmament or public property.

2. According to the previous order, mujahedeen shall fiercely avoid smoking cigarettes.

3. Youngsters whose beards are not visible, because of their age, are not allowed to be kept in residential or military centre

4. According to shari'a, cutting off someone's nose, ears or lips is fiercely forbidden. Mujahedeen are fiercely forbidden from such actions. Mujahedeen shall fiercely forbid such actions.

5. The mujahedeen of the Islamic Emirate shall not collect ushr, zakat or donations from people by force and if they gain money by collecting ushr and zakat, they shall spend it on their lawful [shari'a] needs.

6. Mujahedeen shall not search people's houses, but if there is an urgent need to search a house, they shall get the permission of the district official and take the imam of the mosque and two elders of the area with them.

7. Kidnapping of people for ransom, under any pretext, is forbidden and the relevant local official must prevent it. If anyone does this in the name of the Islamic Emirate, the provincial official, with the approval of the leadership, shall disarm and severely punish him.

Section 13: Recommendations

1. Every group leader is obliged to dedicate different times for the jihadi training of their group members, their educating in religion and morality. Except during times of fighting and emergency, they shall not quit education.
2. If there is no danger, the mujahedeen shall pray together in a mosque, and if it is difficult to pray in a mosque, they shall pray together where they are. They shall pay special attention to the recitation and remembrance [of the Qur'an] through which confidence and strength will come to their hearts
3. Mujahedeen shall redirect their power of thinking to military matters. They shall protect themselves from local disputes and protect themselves from public issues. Looking into disputes is a waste of time and can also create suspicion and difference between the mujahedeen and the people. If there are significant issues, then Article 62 [of this Code] shall be applied
4. All the staff of the Islamic Emirate shall try their best to encourage the duped opposition to surrender and lay down their weapons. On the one hand, this will weaken the ranks of the enemy; on the other, the traps[11] established by Afghans [literally *dakhili* or internal people] will be reduced and, in some cases, mujahedeen will receive guns and ammunition.
5. Mujahedeen are obliged to adopt Islamic behaviour and good conduct with the people and try to win over the hearts of the common Muslims and as mujahedeen be such representatives of the Islamic Emirate that all compatriots shall welcome and give the hand of cooperation and help.
6. Mujahedeen shall protect themselves completely from any tribal, linguistic and regional prejudice. It has been narrated by Hazrat Abu Horaira[12] that [text in Arabic and then translation into Pashto]: if someone fights under an unknown flag and has not understood or someone gets angry for tribal reasons or encourages tribalism or helps someone for tribal reasons and if he dies, he is dead in ignorance [*jahil*],[13] as if he has not been a Muslim
7. Senior officials shall go through the accounts of jihadi equipment and financial expenses of junior officials, from time to time.
8. Mujahedeen shall, within a shari'a framework, match their appearances, such as their hair, clothes, boots and other things, to the people of an area. On the one hand, this will help the mujahedeen and the people in the area with security; and on the other, they will be able to move around easily.

Section 14: Recommendations with regard to this Code

1. Any changes in the articles of this Code shall [only] come from the Islamic Emirate's highest authority and leadership council of the Islamic Emirate. If anyone else tries to change any article of it, or act against it, his excuse will not be acceptable.

2. The central military commission and the provincial and district commissions have the responsibility to deliver this and other Codes to the mujahedeen and to follow up on its implementation.

3. If an issue comes up which has not been discussed in the Code, it shall be resolved by discussion between the mujahedeen and district officials. Of course, if it is still not resolved, it shall be referred to provincial officials; if it is still not resolved, the head of the zone shall be asked to make a decision; if the matter is still not resolved, the head of the zone shall ask the leadership to decide on the matter.

4. Operating according to the mentioned articles is recommended and necessary, and if anyone abuses them, they shall be prosecuted according to the principles of Islam.

Expecting victory with God's support!

NEW REALITIES (2011–2017)

80

THE ISLAMIC EMIRATE OF AFGHANISTAN AND ITS SUCCESSFUL ADMINISTRATIVE POLICY

[*This article outlines the political and governance structures that the Taliban considered to be the basis for their success. These had been stated in the* layeha *or rule book published in several editions previously, but this republication of an original* al-Somood *article was intended more for the publicity value than to serve as a guide for Taliban affiliates and fighters themselves.*]

Ikram Miyundi

Al-Somood (Arabic-language magazine), 26 January 2011

It is patently clear from the experiences of those who preceded us and firmly established from our own observations that the success of Islamic governments, as well as democratic and despotic governments, and the prosperity of religious, educational, governmental and other establishments lies in the superiority of its administrative regime in heeding its important elements (lofty aims, the abilities of its leader, having a righteous entourage around him, etc.). Complete victory in this field requires diligent efforts from those heading it to implement decisions issued, established regulations and fixed principles. Attention must also be paid to the impartiality of the administration through the good selection of personnel who are recruited to work there.

I do not intend to list the components of a successful administration or to declare the characteristics of an Islamic administration. What concerns me here is to shed light on the Islamic Emirate's policy in the realm of administration and coordination, despite the difficult circumstances surrounding it connected to its heavy involvement in the Holy Jihad and the bitter war against the Americans and their partners in their repulsive crimes. I also strive to place before you, as Allah enables me, simple information regarding the order of the Islamic Emirate, or the Taliban regime, as they call it, so that perhaps it will benefit the readers of our heroic magazine *al-Somood* to 'heal the breasts of the Believers' and 'Nor is that for Allah any great matter'.

The loftiness of the desired objective and the sanctity of the anticipated goal—combined with the firm anchoring of this sanctity within those who belong to this administration after they are made fully aware of it—are together a strong factor in successfully achieving the declared and sought-after goal. It is also the secret behind reviving the spirit of altruism, dedication and sacrifice in the spirit of the staff (members). When they are convinced of the importance of their jobs, they will compete in rushing to complete their assigned tasks and exert the utmost of their efforts for the sake of achieving the highest objective and sacred goal, because they will see the laudable results and great benefits behind their activities and above the ceiling of their own invaluable works. As Allah Almighty says in this regard: 'They are those who, if We establish them in this land, establish regular prayer and give regular charity, enjoin the right and forbid wrong: with Allah rests the end (and decision) of all affairs.'[1]

Moreover, concern must be paid to attracting trustworthy and competent individuals, and choosing specialised staff, contingent upon piety and impartiality. Specialisation without piety corrupts an administration; and piety without competence weakens it. In the event of a contradiction, the pious one is given preference, because he is like the shepherd whose legs are tied and is unable to benefit the flock or serve the people; but the corrupt one is a ravenous wolf spoiling the earth and harming others. Preventing damage takes priority among wise men, and in any event the selection of righteous people is a strong element of a successful administration. This is in accordance with the words of the Almighty: 'Allah doth command you to render back your Trusts to those to whom they are due'[2] and 'Verily the most honoured of you in the sight of Allah is (he who is) the most righteous of you.'[3]

The capacity of the personality of the leader who directs the people religiously, politically and ideologically is no less important than any of the above. Indeed, it is considered one of the most important elements of a successful administration. The leader is the axis around which matters pivot. He employs the community to achieve his goals and directs people to goodness and happiness. He warns them against evil and danger according to his lights. Among the duties of the leader, after trust in and reliance upon his Lord and Creator, is to make a diligent effort in directing the activities of all the employees and volunteers who assist him, in an atmosphere of cooperation towards the fixed goal. He is also responsible for creating strong feelings among the people to move quiet hearts and slumbering eyes, and energise the human power for self-sacrifice for the sake of achieving high and lofty goals. It is notable that among the qualities of the successful leader are that he is free; male; of sound mind and emotion; with knowledge; vision; strength; courage; wisdom; organisational skills and other qualities mentioned in the books of *fiqh* and *'aqidah*. So seek it where you would expect to find it.

1. After this pleasant introduction, I take you to the subject of this study by saying: throughout its entire organisation, the Islamic Emirate relies on the Book of Allah

Almighty and upon the Sunna of his Messenger (SAWS), the Sunna of the rightly guided caliphs and the sayings of the companions, may Allah be pleased with them all. It utilises the fatwas of the followers and the opinions of *mujtahid* scholars, may Allah Almighty have mercy on them. The Emirate borrows from the history of bygone nations, and its system consists of the components of a successful administration balanced with the sanctity of its goals, the vision of its leader, and the strength of its faith and the qualifications of its workers with regards to piety, devotion, trust, competence, etc.

2. Based on this, the administrative system of the Islamic Emirate is based upon the principles of the Islamic Caliphate from the era of the rightly guided caliphs, may Allah be pleased with them, in dividing the country into provinces, appointing pious and righteous governors, guiding workers to piety and justice, encouraging the establishment of a religious and worldly policy, tending to the needs of the people, instructing them in matters of religion and encouraging them to make the utmost effort in promoting virtue and preventing vice. Regulations have been drawn up for the guidance of the mujahedeen *fi sabeel Allah*. Messages are constantly sent for this purpose to guide them, direct their deeds, illuminate their thoughts and have them follow in the footsteps of the companions, may Allah be pleased with them. Umar ibn al-Khattab, may Allah be pleased with him, spoke to the people thus, saying:

'O people, by Allah I do not send you governors to flog you or take your wealth but I send them to teach you your Religion and the way you should follow (sunna). If anything other than this is done to anyone, he should refer the matter to me. By Him in whose hand is Umar's soul, I will provide justice for him.' (Dr Hasan Ibrahim, *History of Islam*, Part 1, p. 455)

Uthman ibn Affan, may Allah be pleased with him, wrote to his governors in the provinces, saying:

'Allah has decreed the imams to be shepherds; he did not ask them to be tax collectors. When this umma emerged, they were created as shepherds; they were not created as tax collectors. Your imams are on the verge of becoming tax collectors and not shepherds. If that happens, diffidence, fidelity and loyalty will be torn apart. The best course is to look to the affairs of Muslims and what is requested of them. Give to them what is their due and take from them what you ought.' (Ibid., Part 1, p. 455)

3. The area of our Muslim country of Afghanistan is approximately 650,000 square kilometres, with an estimated population of at least 33 million people. The country is divided into 34 administrative units, each named a province such as Kandahar, Helmand, Herat and Balkh province. Moreover, each province is divided into multiple directorates, big and small such as Marja in Helmand province, Arghandab in Kandahar province, etc. Each directorate contains beautiful

areas and numerous villages. There are a total of 400 provinces, while there are tens of thousands of villages.

4. In each village, there is a faithful leader (appointed) by the Emirate and who is responsible for civilian and military affairs. He has around him from 10 to 50 mujahedeen depending on the prevailing circumstances. A new leader is selected from among them if the previous leader is martyred or is unable to continue to lead for any reason. In case of a disagreement, the matter is elevated to the amirs above them. This battalion (called a front) is ready for combat and to fight against the enemy night and day. They are also the recourse to whom people raise their complaints, whether among themselves or between them and other villages. If the problems are small, they are referred to notables of the tribe for resolution. If the problems are big, then they are elevated to the senior officials in the directorate for a decision to be made in accordance with pure shari'a law.

5. Each directorate has a governor of known piety among the people. He has a deputy with experience in affairs of the region. Under their command work different committees such as: Committee for Arbitration and Settling Disputes; Committee for Education and Development; a Military Commission to manage war issues, etc. The governor is the commander of the whole village and area leaders in that directorate, and he is responsible for the application of Allah's shari'a there. The appointment and dismissal of the governor is in the hands of the Supreme Command after consultation with the provincial governor and the province-level Military Committee. He works under the command of the provincial governor and is directly responsible for the directorate.

6. Each province of the country is an independent unit with a commander called the governor. He has a deputy to assist him. The governor is directly responsible for the supreme command of that province and directs its military, civilian, financial and legal affairs. Usually this important post is entrusted to an experienced and capable man: a man of religion and morality who fears no one but Allah. He is true and trustworthy, and capable of directing matters. Among his duties are application of shari'a laws and statutes; supervision of directorate governors; execution of the war plan; supervision of financial resources and expenditures. Committees with appropriate authorities work with him at the province level, including legal, military and financial committees, an education committee, etc. The appointment and dismissal of the governor is the responsibility of the Supreme Commander after consultation with the High Shura Council.

7. Above that is the role of the main committees with authority at the level of the Islamic Emirate. Each committee is composed of a number of trustworthy and loyal individuals with experience in their assigned occupation. In the current structure of the Emirate, these replace the old ministries, as circumstances dictate. They are as follows:

A. *Military Committee:* This is equivalent of the ministry of defence and coordinates military affairs, including preparing young men for sacred jihad; arming the mujahedeen with weapons, ammunition and equipment; preparing war plans; issuing orders for battles and attacks on enemy bases, dens of lackeys, etc.

B. *Preaching and Guidance Committee:* This is composed of senior scholars and issues fatwas on important matters of *fiqh*. It also appoints and employs scholars and preachers and provides guidance to the mujahedeen and citizens and gives advice to the commanders and officials.

C. *Ministry of Culture and Information:* This broadcasts statements of the Amir ul-Mu'mineen, may Allah Almighty protect him, as well as the decisions of the Supreme Command, the judgements, statements and decisions of the High Shura Council, and publishes magazines and newspapers in different languages. It publishes news of the mujahedeen and their conquests and refutes the claims of the charlatan enemy; reveals his conspiracies and plots; and refutes his propaganda via important websites on the internet.

D. *Political Committee:* This is equivalent to the foreign ministry and is responsible for foreign relations. It makes great efforts to build, expand and develop foreign relations.

E. *Education Committee:* This committee builds different kinds of schools; prepares an educational curriculum; selects well-known leaders from the provinces; appoints teachers and the administrative apparatus for the schools; all for the purpose of spreading Islamic and contemporary learning, obliterating illiteracy, fighting ignorance in society and educating the developing generation.

F. *Financial Committee:* This undertakes the development of financial resources for the Emirate, organises expenditure, monitors banks, etc.

G. *Committee for Prisoners and Orphans:* This is concerned with affairs of prisoners and orphans: it works strenuously for the release of prisoners, to raise their children and the children of the martyrs, and to help with the living expenses of their families.

H. *Health Committee:* This is concerned with treating the wounded and sick mujahedeen, and helps them with their living expenses. It also works to prepare comfortable quarters for them during their convalescence.

I. *Committee for Foreign Establishments:* This directs them to affected areas and supervises their work and their men up close to ensure that they are not carrying out works that negatively impact our *'aqidah*.

J. *High Shura Council:* This is composed of high-ranking men in the Islamic Emirate. The appointment and removal of its members is carried out by the Amir ul-Mu'mineen. The duties assigned to the council include monitoring the situation in Afghanistan; searching for suitable solutions for internal and external problems; guiding the main committees at the level of the Islamic Emirate in their work; and issuing statements on international, regional and internal occasions and drafting regulations and laws in accordance with the Book and the sunna.

K. *Supreme Command:* This is represented by the Supreme Leader, the Amir ul-Mu'mineen, Mullah Mohammad Omar (Mujahid), may Allah Almighty protect him, who is the direct leader of the holy jihad. He is the primary caretaker for all of Afghanistan's military and civilian affairs and, in his capacity as Supreme Leader of the mujahedeen and Amir ul-Mu'mineen, he is zealous in the application of Allah's shari'a, starting with himself; his household; his family; soldiers and followers; reporting to his flock and all Muslims in the world, as is made patently clear in his sermons and speeches. He strives, following those pious leaders who preceded him, to rule with justice by assigning positions to trustworthy people; carefully selecting his entourage; and choosing the loyal and righteous to accompany him. He closely monitors the actions of his men in high positions and advises them to be pious before Allah in public and private, give their people their rights and avoid causing them any harm.

L. *His two trusted deputies:* They act to aid him with devotion and piety. They are his helpers in rolling out the carpet of Allah's heavenly shari'a upon the land of the country. They carry out the experienced leader's decisions with all faithfulness and honesty without adding or subtracting anything. They are responsible for keeping pace with matters of jhad and putting the responsible agencies in action. They are also responsible for convening the High Shura Council and consultative councils and organising all affairs of the Islamic Emirate.

The last word

The strong faith of the Leader of the Islamic Emirate in Allah the All-Wise and All-Powerful; in the sanctity of his goal; and its deep roots in the hearts of his workers; and the impartiality of the administration in selecting righteous men as a symbol of heroism; and the secret of the success of the holy jihad in the country. This is especially represented in the faith of the heroic leader Mullah Mohammad Omar (Mujahid), may Allah give him victory over his enemies, when he said 'No, No' to occupation, relying instead upon Allah Almighty and Omnipotent, despite the greed of the infidels and their attacks upon defenceless people. Rather he ordered jihad against them to defend the religion and honour, uttering the words of his predecessors: Allah is sufficient for us; He is the best disposer of affairs.

There is no doubt that the mujahedeen are the helpers of Allah. If a mujahed is not a supporter of Allah, then who is? This is especially true in our modern age when they are led by noble scholars and seekers of shari'a knowledge and the righteous from among Allah's servants. As for the desired goal and objective of the Islamic Emirate of Afghanistan, it is to elevate the word of Allah Almighty and establish an Islamic government by every meaning of the word, and to expel the enemies of Allah, the

Americans, from the country. It is for Allah to humble to the depths the word of those who are infidels, to justify the truth and prove falsehood false. It is for Allah to give honour to the holy jihad, Islam and the Muslims and to humiliate idolatry and the idolaters.

And for this, let those aspire who have aspirations.

81

AFGHAN WOMEN AND THE
AMERICAN LITERACY PROGRAMME

[*This commentary article attempts to set the American military agenda alongside what the author views as a wider social agenda to alter the minds of Afghan women. It is a good example of the way the war in Afghanistan is understood to be as much about culture and perception as it is about the day-to-day military engagements.*]

Al-Emera (website), 26 January 2011

Trent Hickman, a senior American marines commander in Afghanistan, has said that they want to launch a programme which is intended to inculcate the notion of progress and development in the minds of Afghan women and familiarise them with American initiatives and values. He said, to achieve this goal they would use some media outlets, particularly the New World, which will broadcast the programme for thirty minutes each day. Every Afghan woman with a pen and a notebook will learn Pashto alphabets while staying at home. Thus, they will become literate.

Talking at an American military base in the centre of Helmand province, the American commander expressed his concern over the lack of measures in the past decade to improve the condition of Afghan women and to raise their literacy level. According to the American commander, they will make this possible now as the American marines have already distributed thousands of Chinese-made radio sets in Afghan villages and localities. Now the Afghan women are able to tune in to the New World and get literacy education.

As far as the notion of the American marine commander is concerned, we do not think the Americans will ever be able to strip the honourable and religiously-committed Afghan society of its faith and national spirit; still less after the exposure of American debasement and clear defeat on every front. In particular, they will fail to get the people in far-flung localities to compromise on their sense of decency and honour, ostensibly under the name of modernism and progress, while foisting on them the anti-Islamic culture of America based on nakedness and lewdness.

In the past decade, Afghans were witness to various accounts of American sympathy and altruism with Afghan women, children, old men and youths—in the shape of salvoes of bullets and missiles which American aircraft, helicopters and tanks rained down on them! Thousands of Afghan households, women and old men have witnessed gruesome scenes during which the callous American troops shot their sons, brothers and relatives point-blank on the floor of their houses and before the eyes of their parents, or they put the devilish hoods on their heads before taking them to American open and secret prisons. They will never forget these agonising scenes. Is it possible for an enemy and a murderer to project himself as a sympathizer, all of sudden, just by handing out Chinese-made cranky radio sets—still more, hoping that people will come round to believing them to be sincere?

Only last week, a documented report appeared in the media with photos showing how America obliterated a whole village, along with orchards and green fields, in a one-hour-long aerial bombardment, turning it to debris. Was not the village inhabited by Afghan wives, women, old men and children? Could there be any clearer proof of American so-called sympathy with Afghan women than this horrendous event?

If America had ever harboured an iota of humanitarian sympathy with Afghan women, it would already have drawn up plans for improving Afghan women's hygienic and economic conditions. The surveys conducted and reports prepared by the World Health Organisation indicated a high mortality rate among Afghan children and women due to lack of health facilities in their respective localities and because of widespread malnourishment among them. Every one is aware of the fact that hundreds of thousands of Afghan women and children are suffering from the after-effects of the poisonous weapons used by the Americans. Furthermore, as every one knows, the Americans are not intending to raise the literacy level of Afghan women in the true sense of the word, so that they will become literate and solve their day-to-day life and economic problems; nor it is possible that they will attain this goal through the Chinese-made radio sets, presumably in a thirty-minute-long radio show. But the real aim is to eradicate the sense of Islamic decency through pernicious and blasphemous programmes, and bring them round to becoming indifferent to their religious and traditional values.

The American commander has to know that this very notion of yours is a failure in the offing, because not only the Talib mujahedeen know your open and secret crimes, but the common Afghans are aware of them. They are ready to counter America's every ploy and initiative and want to deal with them tit-for-tat—just as last week, a tribal chief of Helmand crushed the head of an American general with stones, causing him to die instantly; this, so to say, taught him an exemplary lesson!

82

RESPONSE OF THE ISLAMIC EMIRATE TO THE VICTORY OF THE POPULAR UPRISING IN EGYPT

[*This was the first official commentary issued by the Taliban following the outbreak of unrest in the Middle East—initially in Tunisia, then in Egypt by the time this article was written. The author(s) attempt to draw a line between the Egyptian case and what is going on in Afghanistan. Advice is offered for the people in their moment of revolution in which parallels are drawn with the 1996 conquest of Kabul.*]

Al-Emera (website), 14 February 2011

The more than two-week-long popular uprising in Egypt at last compelled Hosni Mubarak, ruler of that country, to step down by ceding to the basic conditions of the protesters. He was at the helm of affairs of the Egyptian government for the last thirty years and had been enjoying universal American and Israeli assistance in financial, political and intelligence fields. However, realities on the ground established (once more) that an arsenal of weapons, a huge army and foreign support are no guarantee of continuing power; nor they can prevent the caravan of aspirations of the people from forging ahead. Whenever the patience of the people overflows its brim, it is set to lead the way like a strong tide.

The Islamic Emirate of Afghanistan prays to Almighty Allah to grant further success to the Egyptian people, like the victory of the historical uprising which they have already attained, so that they will succeed in establishing a real, independent and Islamic government and foil the conspiracies of foreign enemies. Though the uprisings of the Egyptian people have reached their destination of victory, the real phase of trial has just began. The Egyptian people must use these crucial moments to their advantage and carve out a new political life and direction as a Muslim nation. The developments in Egypt have a clear message for the invading Americans and their surrogates in Afghanistan, unveiling that:

1. Your use of advanced weapons, destruction of orchards and houses and filling prisons with free people does not contribute to your continuation of authority.

The atrocities that you commit against the Afghan people today will soon usher in a revolution, and the vessel of your arrogance will surely drown after a popular uprising, if God wills.

2. You are intending to establish a colonialist system in this twenty-first century. This is a venture against both the aspirations of the people and against the time. You will never succeed in your wicked (ambitious) plan at this juncture of history. Both time and people are against you.

3. Two-faced America urges a peaceful transition of regime in Egypt; but in reaction to the self-same popular demands in Afghanistan, they bombard villages, turn wedding ceremonies and other festivities into scenes of mourning, and martyr innocent Afghans in the stillness of the night while fast asleep. All these crimes are committed (against them) because the Afghans demand their legitimate rights. What face and conscience remain to Americans to make a show of their democracy and liberty while they have themselves unleashed a river of blood in Afghanistan under the empty and fatuous slogan of democracy!

4. The stooge Kabul administration has now taken the shape of a mafia state. Government vehicles are used for drug trafficking, and wealth has been accumulated in the hands of a few pro-American sycophants. This inequity will pave the way for the start of a popular revolution, and will eradicate this tenure of tyranny and atrocity through a comprehensive revolutionary movement.

5. For almost the last decade, you have fought against the Afghan mujahed people with all your power, but you gained nothing except humiliation, financial crisis and a spine-breaking load of debts. Do you think you will be able to bring Afghanistan under your rule so smoothly? Or otherwise, you will be buried in this graveyard of empires after the rising tide of a popular uprising.

6. We ask the rulers of the White House and Pentagon how long they would be able to create obstacles in the way of the aspirations of the masses through launching fraudulent elections, meaningless conferences, hatching conspiracies and rearing qualmless surrogates and continuing their colonialist policy interminably? How long would they be able to hide their life and equipment losses from the eyes of their people? Have they forgotten the financial meltdown in America during the last year? Is the nearly $1.5 trillion budget deficit not a sign of their imminent downfall?

7. Scarcely had twenty-four hours passed after the resignation of Hosni Mubarak when some American rulers and *Time* magazine started pointing to him with insulting remarks. We remind the present rulers of the Kabul incumbent administration that American colonialism uses you against your people when today it pats you on the back; but tomorrow these same invaders will call you murderers of humanity and traitors. They will wipe their blood-stained and soiled hands on your clothes. Now it is high time: come to yourselves, abandon the slavery of foreigners and choose the way of your people.

8. All people of Afghanistan must be cautious in these crucial moments at the current juncture of time and be on guard against all the subversive plans and conspiracies of the enemies of Islam and the country. Join hands in brotherhood against Western colonialism, injustice, atrocities, brutality, corruption and the Western culture of nakedness; move forward like a solid-cemented wall in the direction of popular Islamic revolution!

The mujahedeen of the Islamic Emirate are at your service and your side. We believe the (final) victory is ours. The enemy will become debased and humiliated, God willing.

83

HISTORY AND THE INTERESTS OF THE SHARI'A

[*This was the second, longer and more interesting commentary released by the Taliban following the fall of the Mubarak government in Egypt. Bawadi, a long-standing commentator for the Taliban's online publications, cautions that the new freedoms will be questioned and threatened and concludes that jihad is the only sure-fire way to ensure that revolution will lead to the establishment of a proper Islamic system.*]

Ahmad Bawadi

Al-Emera (website), 17 September 2011

Mistaken are those who think that the establishment of shari'a will emerge from the womb of revolutions which are calling for freedom, and mistaken are those who believe that these revolutions are an alternative to the way of the Believers or the path to a sound *manhaj*. When the banners of truth are borne by those who are not of its people, then these banners become blind guides coloured by desires and caprice. Who said that truth could be championed by falsehood, the very argument used to refute it? Who claimed that the banner of truth is being raised by those gangs of falsehood who oppose it? Those proclaiming these revolutions must devote their banners to the *deen* of Allah in order to achieve their security and faith. The shari'a of Allah is sufficient to guarantee a good lifestyle and a secure life.

> 'Whoever works righteousness, man or woman, and has faith, verily to him will we give a new life, a life that is good and pure, and We will bestow on such their reward according to the best of their actions.'

> 'Those who believe and work righteousness, for them is forgiveness and sustenance most generous.'

A person may be oppressed in his person, dispossessed of his wealth, his family humiliated and his dignity wasted. This does not give him the right, if he triumphs over the one who wronged him, to become a regent over others and to set up for them regimes and constitutions that accord with his whims and desires. He who thanks Allah after being delivered from oppression should comply with the command of his Lord by establishing the rule of shari'a. The fortune of those might change after Allah aids them, but they will never arrive at the divine programme while raising partisan banners, calling for democracy and demanding freedoms.

The state of Islam will not be established by a revolution for a loaf of bread, if that revolution was not undertaken for the sake of the *deen* and shari'a of Allah. No one should think that a revolution over unemployment will close the wine shops and nightclubs. They will not prevent women from going outside wearing make-up and unveiled and will not prevent them from showing their nakedness at pools and on the beaches. The networks of singing, dancing, prostitution and shamelessness will not be shut down by these revolutions, if they are not indeed the catalyst and motivator for these sins, when freedom and democracy become the religion and constitution of the people and are an alternative to jihad. When people rebel and bring down despotic regimes for the sake of unemployment and a loaf of bread, and these revolutions are conducted by people from all walks of life who come to terms over (being governed by) other than the shari'a of Allah, we are back where we started. If the revolution is carried out by such as these, then undoubtedly the state would be like the Buyid state and require new Seljuqs to deal with them.

We must know and understand that what has occurred in Egypt and Tunisia comes from the promise of Allah to support His oppressed and defeated servants to aid them against their oppressors. Our merciful Lord aids even the infidel against those who oppress him, even if the oppressor is Muslim. How much more (will He do so) when the oppressed is a Muslim? This lesson is a warning and admonishment to the unjust ones so that they may turn away from their injustice and oppression, and it is assistance to the oppressed, so that he may thank Allah for His grace. This is what we must understand so that we do not make this aid into a way to attain empowerment on earth, while we call for foul constitutionalism without guidance from the *deen* and shari'a of Allah and neglect to aid *deen* and its partisans.

Read, if you will, the Book of your Lord:

'Allah has promised, to those among you who believe and work righteous deeds, that He will, of a surety, grant them the land and inheritance (of power) that He granted to those before them; that He will establish in authority their religion, the one which He has chosen for them; and that He will change (their state), after the fear in which they (lived), to one of security and peace: "They will worship Me (alone) and not associate aught with Me." If any do reject faith after this, they are rebellious and wicked.'

'O ye who believe! If ye will aid the cause of Allah, He will aid you, and plant your feet firmly.'

These revolutions and their people will not recover Palestine, nor will they take the place of jihad and the mujahedeen and expel the invaders and conspirators from Afghanistan, Iraq and Somalia. Their banners are a morsel of bread and eliminating unemployment, drowning in worldly desires and following whims and keeping a distance from *jihad fi sabeel allah*.

> '(They are) those who have been expelled from their homes in defiance of right, (for no cause) except they say, "our Lord is Allah". If Allah did not check one set of people by means of another, there would surely have been pulled down monasteries, churches, synagogues and mosques in which the name of Allah is commemorated in abundant measure. Allah will certainly aid those who aid His (cause), for verily Allah is full of strength, exalted in might (able to enforce His will).'

Events which change the face of history and watershed moments of change and transformation are rarely repeated. What is happening in Egypt and Tunisia and what might happen elsewhere is extraordinary and emanates from the aid Allah has given to these countries and peoples at this time. Were it not for the kindness of Allah towards them, tens of thousands of people would have been killed, even half the population would have been destroyed without the ruler being shaken in his reign. Look if you will at other Islamic countries and the oppression, domination and tyranny that occur there. They are as close as possible to those great historical events which may only be repeated after a long period of time, or may not be repeated at all, even those events which are (not) outside the control of the people.

Look at how many earthquakes occur, and yet we've had only one tsunami over a long period of time. And look at how many bombings have occurred, but we have only one 11 September.

The Battle of Badr changed the face of history and was a turning point between truth and falsehood. The battle changed the scales and confused the forces of falsehood and tyranny. Did matters stop there and were all the battles and issues then decided? Or did it act to change views, ideas and beliefs after striking fear into arrogant hearts while bringing aid to the broken-hearted, becoming the spark that lit the fire which engulfed the people of falsehood and served as a torch illuminating the darkness for the people of the truth so that they could proceed with firm steps and confident in the support of Allah.

He who defeated the hosts at Badr is capable of bringing down those who are weaker than they. He who brought down the towers of America as if they were the least of its structures, and he who removed Shain al-Abidin in all his wickedness and Hosni with his might, will not be unable to remove that which is more oppressive and powerful. But Allah laid low their prestige and humbled their state before the eyes of the people so that mankind may know the power of the truth of the Almighty and Sublime and remove from them the dust of disgrace and shame and work to aid His *deen* and its adherents after He had humiliated the people of falsehood and strengthened the people of truth to make use of these events for their own advantage. Events such as these do not allow us to stop and stand by them or await similar events. Rather we must exploit these events and their consequences in a sound and correct manner to use these opportunities and realise satisfactory results through sound and good methods.

Scholars and preachers must make use of these events and advise the umma to employ the situation in a way that serves Islam and the Muslims and alert them to their duty to raise the banner of Islam in these revolutions. The concern of preachers should not be merely issuing shari'a rulings or becoming occupied in disputes, because these revolutions are the offspring of a vast accumulation of injustice and oppression. The people are not waiting for a shari'a ruling, because they are acting spontaneously and not deliberately, due to the injustice and oppression inflicted upon them by those who have held dominion over them and starved them, (keeping them) ignorant, weak and backward.

The Islamic historian Mahmoud Shaker al-Dimashqi, discussing the crisis during the time of the dominion of the amirs, soldiers and commanders over the lands and the believers in the second Abbasid state and those that followed them, wrote:

'The danger and evil of military rule lies in relations among people. For when soldiers are one party, and a dispute arises between two opponents, one of whom is armed, then the mind is compelled into silence, freedom disappears, injustice occurs, thought is suppressed and people are humiliated. The people hate those in power and there is a separation between officials and citizens. But the population cannot reveal that and it is maintained in secret. The country then falls behind socially and economically when the tyrants seek to exploit their situation and amass what wealth they can, leaving aside the looting, plundering and transgressions committed by the military and their followers, whether this is directly or indirectly through their soldiers who imitate them. Production drops because the population neglects it so as not to be targeted by plundering, oppression and tyranny. Morale drops because the people cannot fight; in whose name should they fight? For whom should they wage war? Why should they march?' (al-Tarikh al-Islami, 6/15)

The duty incumbent upon scholars and preachers is, before issuing a shari'a ruling on a matter that is already over and done with, to work to correct mistakes and direct them in a direction that is consistent with and serves the interests of shari'a. They must not leave matters in the hands of the people of falsehood to plot against Islam, exploiting and stealing these revolutions in order to use them for their own schemes and purposes. They must speak the truth and raise the banner of *tawhid* and al-sunna and let the people hear their voices so that among them a loaf of bread is not held to be of greater importance than the *deen* of Allah and the rule of their Lord's shari'a, so that they will accept no substitute for it.

The courses of these revolutions must be diverted onto this path. Time must be invested and efforts must be made to respond to those calls which aid and support the choice of the people, no matter what it is, only in order to thrust them back, thwarted and defeated.

HISTORY AND THE INTERESTS OF THE SHARI'A

When our Muslim preachers and scholars speak about aiding the cause of their umma and the *deen* of their Lord, they must not flatter, be deferential, paper over (issues) or err when it is they who are the leaders of the umma, its guiding light and strong fortress. Let not their position be as the poet said:

'What am I but a Ghazia. If they are tempted...
I am tempted. If they follow the right course, I follow the right course.'

The umma has no alternative to jihad. It will continue until the Day of Judgement.

84

THE RED CROSS AND NON-DECAYING BODIES

[This article brings us back to the 1980s reports of miracles among the mujahedeen, albeit now citing a report supposedly written by the Red Cross. Articles like this were often much more popular than the political commentary (judging by the number of hits the articles received on the Taliban's website) and spoke to the desire of the Taliban to make a connection between the United States military and the soldiers of the Soviet Union.]

Doctor Muhammad Andar

Al-Emera (website), 21 December 2011

The committee of the American Red Cross has released a report on its webpage regarding the bodies of the martyred Taliban compared to those of the foreign forces. This committee, which had the duty of collecting and burying the dead in Mazar-i Sharif province of Afghanistan, showed its astonishment as to why the dead bodies of the Taliban had not decayed or given off a foul smell?!! The report said that investigators initially thought that the cold weather was the reason behind this phenomenon; however, this theory was later shattered because the bodies of the Northern Alliance fighters which were lying in the same area had decayed and were also giving off a nauseating smell.

The report further says that it now wants to conduct research on the type of food consumed by the Taliban fighters! The researchers also want to find out if there is a relationship between food and blood, because the blood of some Taliban members keeps its warm temperature even after their death! (Source: Al-Misryoon, Ana Muslim and several other websites)

It is the bounty of Allah that the enemies profess before friends to the miracles displayed by Taliban martyrs in the face of the crusader onslaught. It should be stated that if all the scientists and chemists of the entire planet were to gather and research for their whole lives, they would never be able to find the answer to this puzzling question. For all we know, maybe they have even tried to locate the blessed body of Ibrahim (PBUH) so they can make fire-resistant clothes for their soldiers by studying his biological make-up!!!

363

Here the speech by a renowned scholar (Ustaz Yasir) comes to mind, which he made on the occasion of the funeral of a prominent commander of the Islamic Emirate, Shaheed Mullah Abdul Manaan Ahmad (may Allah have mercy on him):

> 'Here I would like to give a simple example which can be understood by everyone and denied by no one about why the Taliban are on the side of truth and the Kabul regime on the side of falsehood; why is it that our dead do not decay while giving off a pleasant fragrance, whereas the dead of our opposition rot and give off a foul stench!?'

As the aroma from the body of the martyred Mullah Abdul Manaan kept emanating, the respected Ustaz added:

> 'I challenge everyone to come! Let's take one dead of ours and one from the opposition side which have been killed at the same time and with the same weapon. We will leave them in an identical physical and chemical state. Then let us observe as our dead beautifies and starts to give off a fragrance of musk, while the body of the other becomes inflated and starts to decay and smell bad! Now let the world's specialists in the field of science and chemistry investigate and figure out its reason???'

We should also not forget that one of the major causes of the rise in defection amongst the ranks of the army of Kabul is because of the miracles exhibited by the martyrs of the Taliban. One group of ANA soldiers in Nangarhar province's Ghani Khel district who abandoned their duties states the reason behind their defection as:

> 'One time we fought a hand to hand battle with the Taliban in Kandahar province during which the Taliban retreated while both of our dead men were left on the battlefield. We were then ordered to stay in the area for the night. As some time passed, our dead started to decay and emit a nauseating smell which cannot be described in words. Meanwhile, the dead Taliban had started to emit a strange and beautiful scent. So that was when our buddies left their dead and stood next to the bodies of the martyred Taliban... So at daybreak, I and my buddies packed our personal belongings and abandoned everything else, even though there were only two or three days left before our next pay cheque and headed home!!!'

A whole book about the miracles displayed by martyrs in jihad against the Soviets has been compiled by the prominent martyred scholar Sheikh Abdullah Azzam (may Allah have mercy on him) under the title of *Ayat ar Rahmaan fil Jihad al Afghan* in which hundreds of incidents have been described. So may Allah give the scholars of our time the resolve to roll up their sleeves and write about the miracles displayed on the battlefields and by the martyrs in the current jihad so that people can distinguish between truth and falsehood and consequently join the righteous side.

To end, I humbly request all readers to pray for me sincerely that I be able to perform jihad and in the end be blessed with martyrdom, the virtues of which were mentioned by the beloved Prophet Muhammad (SAWS) and for which he himself yearned.

85

ON THE MARTYRDOM OF THE GREAT MARTYR SHEIKH OSAMA BIN LADEN

[*This was one of three statements put out in the immediate aftermath of bin Laden's death on 2 May 2011. This biography hails him as a heroic martyr, suggesting that his death will spur the Afghan mujahedeen on with extra eagerness. It stops short, however, of drawing links between bin Laden's wider agenda and actions, particularly with reference to the 11 September attacks, which many Talibs believe had no connection to bin Laden.*]

Al-Emera (website), 6 May 2011

> Among the believers, there are men who have been true to their covenant with Allah. Some fulfilled their vow by death and some are still awaiting and they have not changed in the least. (S:33-V:23)

The Caller to Islamic Jihad against the invading infidels, Sheikh Osama bin Laden, embraced martyrdom as per the will of the Almighty Allah during an abrupt attack by the American invading soldiers. (We are the creation of Allah and return to Him.)

The Islamic Emirate of Afghanistan extends its deep condolence to the family of the martyr, to his followers and to fighter mujahedeen of the way of truth and to the Islamic umma on this occasion of great tragedy. We pray to the Almighty Allah to accept, in His sight, the sacrifice of the martyr. May the Almighty Allah salvage the Islamic umma from the current situation of crisis due to the impact of the blessing of the sacred jihad and martyrdom of the martyr.

The martyr took part in the jihad against the Soviet invasion with great honesty and bravery, shoulder to shoulder with the Afghans. He offered such sacrifices in this way that the history of the Islamic umma will for ever remain proud of them. Sheikh Osama bin Laden was an ardent advocate of the legitimate cause of the first *qibla* of the Muslims, the Aqsa Mosque and occupied Palestine. He was an indefatigable fighter against Christian and Jewish aggression in the Islamic world and spared no effort for this cause. The life of this mujahed, who bore the antagonism against Islam, was full of fatigue, sacrifice and hardship. The history of Islam will always keep their memory alive.

The way of jihad and the path of defence of Islam is a way fraught with sacrifice and martyrdom. Like any other follower of this way, Sheikh Osama had aspired to attain martyrdom in the cause of the Almighty Allah. He reached his ambition with bravery, dedication and commitment in the last moments of his life.

If the invading Americans and their allies wallow in the hope that the morale and ranks of the mujahedeen will weaken in Afghanistan and other occupied Islamic countries following the martyrdom of Sheikh Osama bin Laden, this only shows their lack of insight. The sapling of jihad has always grown, sprouted and reached maturity through the irrigation of pure blood. The martyrdom of a martyr leads to hundreds more heading to the field of martyrdom and sacrifice.

The current jihadic movement of Afghanistan sprouted from among the masses and is representative of the aspirations of this proud people. In this land of the brave, a strike by colonialists breeds sympathy and produces (an urge) to strike back. If the mujahed people were prone to submit to force and tyranny, then is there any evidence either in terms of military muscle or other devilish conspiracy of success for the Americans during the last decade? The reality on the ground is that the use of force brings opposite consequences here. This popular movement can be likened to a spring which, when you put pressure on it, bounces back with the same intensity.

The Islamic Emirate believes the martyrdom of Sheikh Osama bin Laden will give a new impetus to the current jihad against the invaders in this critical phase of jihad. The tides of jihad will gain strength and size. The forthcoming time will prove this both for our friends and foes, God willing.

86

ISLAMIC REVIVAL

[In this article, the author refutes the claim that the revolutions and unrest across the Middle East and North Africa have been a victory for Western values of democracy. Rather, he argues that they show instead the triumph of the Islamic system and values. Finally, he connects this all back to what he sees as the enlightened rule of Taliban leader Mullah Mohammad Omar.]

Hunzala Mujahid

Al-Emera (website), 29 March 2011

The start of 2011 has been an auspicious time for the Islamic world. Almost ten years since America and its eastern and western allies declared a crusade against the Islamic world to destroy the light of Islam once and for all, the tides of history have turned once again. When the Americans started their war of 'Infinite Justice', all parties knew that this clash of civilisations would have far-reaching consequences for the coming century.[1] But few could have guessed how unforeseen they were to be.

Today, the great might of America, the greatest Western power since the Roman Empire, has been brought to its knees. Its allies are abandoning the banner of falsehood from left and right. And everywhere, the dictators of Muslim countries, so complicit in these crimes against the Islamic umma, are facing the wrath of our Muslim populaces.

The rulers of the Muslim nations have proved to be the greatest enemies of Islam in this war against the Muslims. They have not only been complicit in all the atrocities and war crimes being perpetuated by the Westerners against Muslims, but have even out-classed their masters in killing and torturing Muslim citizens. They faithfully carried out the orders given to them by the White House in arresting, imprisoning, torturing and murdering tens of thousands of their citizens in the so-called 'war against terrorism'. It seems that the sole purpose of these governments is to suppress their own populace and advance the interests of America and Israel in these regions.

Most of these rulers came to power through force, and for them insuring the survival of their barbaric regimes has always been of paramount importance. To achieve this end, they were willing to subvert the interests and aspirations not only of their own nation, but also of the entire Islamic umma. They built ruthless security apparatuses and cruel intelligence services, not to defend their people and country from external threats, but rather to suppress their own citizens. They sold their faith and their people for the small price of ensuring a few more days in their empty palaces.

Alhamdulillah! Alhamdulillah![2] It is with great joy that we hear about our Muslim brothers and sisters in these distant lands rising to challenge these agents of the West, and seeking to replace them with leaders who will rule them with justice and Islamic principles. There are many in the West (and their followers in the East) who have given a twist to this narrative and claimed that these protests are a great victory for the West and a loss for quote Islamists unquote.

Nothing could be further from the truth than this distortion of reality. The Muslim populace of these countries rose against their rulers precisely because these leaders prioritised the wishes of their Western masters over the aspirations of their people. The laws implemented by these rulers over the past ten years, in the name of fighting terrorism (but in reality to suppress their people even further), were one of the main catalysts for these rebellions.

The Muslim people of Tunisia, Egypt and Libya not only sought to remove their corrupt leaders, but then elected in their place other equally corrupt leaders who will seek the same policies of neglecting their own nation, transferring all the wealth of their nation to foreign banks, and aligning their foreign policies according to directives from Washington and Langley.

No! The Islamic umma has spoken, and they have spoken overwhelmingly for independence and self-sufficiency from foreign powers. The martyrs of Tunis, Benghazi and Tahrir Square gave up their lives for their beliefs and their people. Their main demands were resonant throughout. They want their governments to work for the people, not against them. They want police, security forces and intelligence services to protect the people from external threats, not to suppress them for foreign interests. They want a just social order. They want their governments to provide basic education for their children, employment opportunities, a fair and Islamic justice system, accountability for corrupt officials, and some measure of equality and redress for the poor and the oppressed. They are tired of their governments forcing their people to flee their country and live a life of servitude and hardship in foreign lands so that their families at home do not die from starvation. They are tired of their governments implementing policies that benefit America, France and Israel, bringing only misery and privation for their own people.

By the Grace of Allah, the revival within the Islamic umma is manifesting itself more clearly every day. We, the Muslim people of Afghanistan, send our messages of felicitation and support to all our Muslim brothers throughout the Islamic world, in their efforts to free themselves from the shackles of slavery and corruption. Any Muslim nation that wishes to build their country into a strong and independent nation must first free themselves from their corrupt and too often drunk leaders, and replace them with pious, accessible and accountable leaders who will work hard to serve their people and establish the rule of Allah in their country.

The only way in which the Islamic nations can regain their rightful positions as the leading, most powerful and advanced nations of the world is to abandon their slavery to foreign notions such as dictatorship, democracy, nationalism, nation-state and other equally fallacious ideas. These are ideas that were transplanted to our nations to continue the slavery of Muslim nations to their colonial masters long after they had physically left these lands. One has only to look at the colonialist policies of Britain in India, Iraq, Palestine, Egypt, and of Italy in north Africa and France in west Africa, to understand how much they tried to focus on educating an elite class within these societies who were completely enslaved and brainwashed with these notions. It was this very same elite who were then left in charge of affairs when their colonial masters exited the countries. For over half a century, these elites have bombarded our children with ideas of democracy, human rights, separation of politics and religion, and secularism; all in the name of enlightenment and modernism. But the conduct of these leaders has been far from enlightened or modern. Their enslavement to these foreign notions has prevented them from seeking any original solution to the issues facing their nations, and all they have done is cling to the tails of their former masters and say: 'Take us to hell and back, and you will find us steadfast in your path.'

How can anyone expect to live a life of dignity and advancement with such leaders in charge?! The only option for Muslims is to throw these elite leaders from their positions of power and replace them with leaders who will resolve all issues in accordance with Islam. Islam is the fountain through which we will regain our dignity and honour. It is the only system of government that looks at the needs of its people and responds to those needs. It is better than dictatorship, because it does not protect the corrupt elites; and it is better than democracy, because it does not rule on behalf of the rich. It is the only system of law before which the powerful and the weak, the rich and the poor, the black and the white are all equal. It is the only system that takes from the rich what they have taken unlawfully and gives to the poor what is lawfully theirs. In short, it is the only system through which we can achieve dignity, glory and social justice.

Muslim people of the world, your Afghan brothers say to you, we have seen every system of government possible on the face of this earth, from kingship to dictatorship to communism to democracy to Islam. We can tell you that none of these can compare with Islam. Islam is the only system of government that works at the grass roots, in people's houses, local mosques and local shuras: it permeates all the way up to the Amir ul-Mu'mineen, who is always in contact with the people, responding to their needs and addressing their concerns. Anyone who doubts this has only to look at the lives of the Four Righteous Caliphs. The Arabs were the most backward people on the face of the earth until Allah blessed them with Islam, and then they became the vanguard of the most powerful and advanced umma on this earth. If Muslims want to find dignity, glory and social justice again, then the only option for them is to return to Islam.

As a final note, I would like to remind us of the quote of Omar, the second Righteous Caliph, who said: 'We are people whom Allah exalted by Islam. If we still seek exaltation in things other than Islam, Allah will humiliate us.'

87

THE PRISON BREAK STORY

HOW FICTION BECAME REALITY

[*The Taliban's repeated ability to break out prisoners from Kandahar prison was a permanent source of pleasure to their media relations team. Sometimes this involved attacks and suicide bombers, sometimes forged release letters or, in this case, subterranean subterfuge and a daring plan. Many articles were published on this topic following the escape in April 2011.*]

Abd al-Ra'uf Hikmat

Al-Somood (magazine), May–June 2011

Kandahar's main prison lies in the Sarpoza area, north of the Kandahar–Herat highway. It is considered the largest state prison in south Afghanistan with its capacity to hold thousands of prisoners. It comprises a main gate and multiple segments; it is also surrounded by high and impenetrable walls.

This prison has essentially been built professionally, including high surveillance and watch towers at its four corners. It is also surrounded by a number of underground walls, further to its high [overground] walls, to prevent digging tunnels to the outside.

Despite this impervious building and its tight security measures, this prison has become the scene of a fascinating story not only in the Afghan domain but internationally as well. Over the past eight years, political prisoners have managed to escape on three occasions. The first time, in June 2003, inmate mujahedeen of the political ward dug a tunnel from within the prison to the outside, thus freeing all of this ward's prisoners, totalling 45, via the tunnel. Then in June 2008, the Islamic Emirate launched militant martyrdom attacks on this prison, causing the death of all the prison's guards and releasing close to 1,200 inmate mujahedeen. Subsequently, Americans and Kandahar officials took over the maintenance of this prison;

Canadian forces trained special policemen to guard the prison; watch towers were increased and monitoring cameras installed; all the prison was encircled by a deep, wide trench. Despite all these measures, the mujahedeen were able for a third time to release 541 prisoners after long planning, on 25 April of this year, 2011.

Pure fantasy

One of the surprising mujahedeen squad in the city of Kandahar, who by his connections gained full knowledge of the inside and outside of the prison, pondered one day whether it could be possible to dig a tunnel from the inside of a house on the other side of the street to the prison as a means of releasing the prisoners. This fantasy and imagination seemed laughable at first, even to its owner; he dared not share his opinion with others. But after more time and continued thinking, he reached a conclusion. On one of these days, while he was riding a motorcycle with two of his comrades, he shared that view with them. They thought it impossible initially and deemed it a fruitless, dangerous attempt. Finally, they placed their trust in God and shared their opinion with the mujahedeen high command in Kandahar. With guidelines from the command, the aforementioned four revealed [to] their trusted comrades their decision to implement this plan regardless of its risks and even if it looked impossible.

Concrete workshop

Six months ago these committed mujahedeen rented a house opposite the south corner of Kandahar prison. The rooms of the old house were in disrepair. Initially they built a new room. Then they brought in all the necessary [equipment] and machines to make concrete, hiring a number of workers who worked during the day. But in the afternoon, when the workers left, the mujahedeen stayed under the pretence of guarding it. It was during this time that they proceeded to dig the tunnel from within the room they had just built.

Hard labour for four months

At first, just four mujahedeen were plodding through this operation. Their work method was the following: one hit with the pickaxe, digging the tunnel, while the other three moved the soil. The tunnel was so narrow that the soil could not be moved out by wheelbarrows, so some operation planners went to the market and bought some children's bicycles; they removed their small wheels and fixed barrows on them to suit their task. Now they filled these barrows with soil, then pulled them by rope to the tunnel opening and collected the soil there before moving it to a lorry. In the morning, when the soil lorries headed to the city to sell their loads, the mujahedeen brought out their soil-filled lorry to sell the load and thus get rid of it.

For two months, four mujahedeen were working in the tunnel digging. Then their number increased to eight mujahedeen. Now they were digging 4 metres every night. When their continued work reached 100 metres, they faced the issue of ventilation and lack of oxygen; nevertheless they carried on until they'd dug a distance of 150 metres. At this point it was terminally difficult to continue working, due to lack of oxygen, and work carried on no further. At first they tried a ground fan; it resolved the ventilation issue, but it was winter and the cold weather caused headaches. Then they made an air-pump machine, delivering air by a pipe from the outside to the inside of the tunnel. This was the best method to resolve the ventilation and lack of oxygen—the machine worked quietly by a charged battery. But they then realised the risk of digging the tunnel under the road that carried heavy enemy vehicles to the inside of the prison: there was a possibility of the tunnel collapsing under intense vehicle pressure. The question was how deep should the tunnel be dug to exclude that possibility. As an experiment, they parked a lorry above the tunnel; it suffered no damage, assuring them that it would not suffer from enemy vehicles. The tunnel was 2.5 metres deep between the house and the public road, but as a precaution they deepened it further. Four months passed and the tunnel stretched to 220 metres. They were surprised by an iron well pipe, before they realised it was not a prison pipe but a pipe to a village south of the prison. In fact, the tunnel diggers, having no map, had deviated from the correct path to the right, crossing the road and reaching a village close to the prison. Here they recognised that the target could only be reached with a proper map and measuring tools.

One and a half months of efficient work

The tunnel diggers who had lost their way, causing an extra 120 metres of digging, now downloaded a prison map off the internet so they could pinpoint the prison location. Using earth measuring tools they re-dug a distance of 100 metres of the tunnel directly towards the prison. However, as winter passed, nights were shorter. So they increased the number of labouring mujahedeen to twenty-one. Also, earth evaporates less in summer, so ventilation was less of an issue, and work went faster and more effectively. By digging 166 metres they reached the middle of the prison. (It should be added that the Islamic Emirate's site mentioned the distance dug by the mujahedeen, including the distance dug in error, to be a total of 360 metres; whereas the precise distance, excluding the additional distance, was 266 metres. It is worth adding that the tunnel's height was 70 cm and width was 60 cm.)

The imprisoned mujahedeen were in two separate locations within the prison: most were in the political ward, where they numbered 530, but a small number were in a room called 'Tawqif Khanah' [arrest room]. The tunnel was dug first towards the Tawqif Khanah room, as it held a mujahed who was aware of the operation. He used to hit the ground for a reason and no reason, in order for the tunnel diggers to hear whether they were ahead or behind or at the target. Thus they were able to pinpoint the location, but for verification they raised a blade to the room, until the prisoner assured them of hitting the target. They moved on to the political ward. Five days produced a further 23 metres, reaching the political ward where its room 7 held two prisoners aware of the operation. The aim was to take the tunnel to room 7. Here again the tunnel diggers wanted to raise a blade to make sure they avoided any error when opening the tunnel to the prison. The mujahedeen were hesitant: were they under room 6 or 7? To keep the matter secret when the blade was due to be raised, the two prisoners held a Qur'an completion [session]; all the rooms were vacant, and the two aforementioned prisoners left, one to room 6 and the other to room 7. When the blade was raised it came up in room 6, contrary to their expectation. So they dug a further 2 metres to reach room 7. Now they could not vacate the rooms with the excuse of Qur'an completion again, so the mujahedeen used the afternoon time when prisoners went to the wash rooms to prepare for noon prayers; the blade was raised and made it successfully to room 7. The opening spot was pinpointed for the escape operation day. It should be added that the blade raising operation was designed to a wise and interesting plan. The prison ground level was about 2.5 metres above the tunnel, with the tunnel's height being 70 cm, so how could a long blade fit through the tunnel and up to the prison ground? The mujahedeen cut several iron blades of 50 cm length and joined them together; once they had raised a blade 50cm with a car jack, they would fix to it another blade and raise it with the jack. Then they prepared for the dismantling of blades a machine that would be attached to each blade then hit by a hammer downwards. This was how they were able to pinpoint the location precisely.

Prison release plan

Once the tunnel had reached its desired target, those responsible for the digging had finished their work. They asked the Islamic Emirate's high command for guidelines on planning the prison release. Meetings were held between high-ranking officials of Kandahar province and the Islamic Emirate on the secure and successful delivery of the release operation. After the consultation, the following plan was adopted.

The brains behind the operation, the one who on his own had hit the pickaxe laboriously to dig 300 metres of the tunnel, would himself be the commander of the prison release operation. He would adopt ad hoc plans during the operation, as needed. The high command would tell him about whatever might happen. The operation would be kept secret until the last moment of execution. Links would be established with the particular brothers within the prison; they would be prepared inside the prison to take the responsibility of organising and moving out the prisoners according to the plan. All decisions were taken in the same way, delegating the operation command to the aforementioned person.

Release operation

To make sure the operation ran smoothly, precautionary measures were checked and preparatory processes were taken again to solve the ventilation problem inside the tunnel. They used a powerful air pumping machine, while the pipe laid inside the tunnel was punched in ten places to deliver air to all parts of the tunnel. Forty-five lamps were also switched on to light the tunnel. As a precautionary measure, a team of potential martyrs were sent to the areas neighbouring the prison to launch a militant attack if necessary.

To keep the operation concealed, and for fear of being exposed, the leader chose five mujahedeen out of the team of twenty-one for the operation day, so that he would not lose all his friends, God forbid, if something bad were to happen. In the end, the release operation team was six persons. These six informed the three mujahedeen within the prison at 9 a.m. (one of them in the Tawqif Khanah room and two in the political ward) to be prepared for the coming night to be the date for the operation, God willing. The two prisoners in room 7 of the political ward planned to tell the rest of prisoners about the case at an appropriate time by preparing some hospitality in their room and inviting one or two prisoners from each room.

The operation command was planned as follows: four brothers of the six would enter the tunnel, two would start working to open the tunnel to the Tawqif Khanah room and two would work to open a tunnel to the political ward; the remaining two would be outside the tunnel. The mujahedeen would extend a telephone wire inside the tunnel, establishing a connection between the brothers outside and the brothers inside and allowing an exchange of information, e.g. where the work had reached and what needed to be done, etc.

The four brothers entered the tunnel with car jacks and solid iron [poles]. They started opening the tunnel to the Tawqif Khanah room and the political ward. At about 10 o'clock they easily opened the Tawqif Khanah room floor with the jack. The prisoners exited. But it was discovered that they had among them two spies from the prison administration disguised as prisoners: one was made unconscious by the mujahedeen, and the other taken out via the tunnel handcuffed to prevent him from causing noise.

As for the floor of the political ward, its construction was heavy-duty and it took the mujahedeen a long time to make a hole through. The jack was raising the concrete floor, but because of blocked air in the tunnel it was difficult to make an actual hole. After many trials the mujahedeen were able to smash the floor. After cutting a huge hole in the ward's room 7, the brothers down the tunnel gave four pistols and four daggers to the linked brothers for use in the operation. They also gave them a telephone handset to establish a connection with the brothers outside the tunnel. Thus the prisoners carried on escaping until 1.30 a.m. (on 25 April 2011); approximately 250 prisoners got out this way. But the work team realised that if they carried on in the same way it would take until 2 o'clock, while the plan was for the prisoners not to wait long [outside] as waiting till dawn would be dangerous, leading possibly to a botched operation. Therefore, the team deferred the escape of prisoners for half an hour. They started letting prisoners out again at 2 a.m. By 3 a.m. no prisoner was left in this ward.

We would like to add that all prisoners were inspected at the entrance and exit of the tunnel. When entering, any luggage was confiscaed as carrying it would cause delay and risk re-arrest. When exiting, any money surplus to 3,000 rupees would be withheld and granted to those with no money.

The leaving procedure was properly organised. The brothers in the team would wake up the prisoners of each room in turn and guide them to the tunnel. At the exit they would ride in the lorries parked at the house; each lorry would carry 36 people. It was 3:10am when [all] the prisoners had left and the lorries were allowed to depart. The lorries left from the yard, but some brothers headed to the town suburbs on foot; they were instructed to cover a distance before returning to the Kandahar–Herat highway after daybreak and then leave the yard using taxis.

It should also be added that two of these lorries transporting the prisoners made two journeys to transport them. By 3.30 or 400 a.m. no prisoner was in the areaa neighbouring the prison. By God's favour and thanks to the mujahedeen's care and wisdom, the enemy noticed nothing of what was going on next to them—the house used in the operation was about 20 metres from the enemy's watch tower that could easily see into the middle of the house; and a surveillance camera was also installed facing the house door. Nevertheless, and thank God, they noticed nothing.

The operation's expenses

We must add that there was no loss of life and the mujahedeen shot no bullet. Furthermore, the financial expenses were much lower than expected. According to the person in charge of the operation and its planner, the expenses during the operation's five months reached about 900,000 Afghanis (i.e. US$ 20,000). This included the house fees, mujahedeen food, lorry charges and other equipment the mujahedeen left in the house after the operation.

On the last day of the operation, the person in charge who built the concrete workshop for the operation stated: We sold during the five months 150 concrete blocks, making much profit. He added: After the operation and the final exit, when the house gate was locked, we left the air pump machine, 45 lamps, 10 concrete blocks, a pole valued at 50,000 Afghanis, 2 power generators, 2 wheelbarrows, 2 car jacks and some building materials; but this historic house benefited us so much that these expenses seemed as nothing.

THE PRISON BREAK STORY

PART TWO
'I was the second person to exit': a prisoner tells his story

Story narrator: Muhammad Idris
Editor: Habib Mujahid

Muhammad Idris, a 23-year-old Kandahar resident, had for many years been launching surprise operations in Kandahar city under the Islamic Emirate's command. He was caught seven months ago by the enemy in Kandahar city and was sent to Kandahar prison. He said he had yet to be tried. Since his captivity, he lived in room 9 of the huge prison with fifteen other mujahedeen. He was the second, out of hundreds, to exit the prison via the tunnel dug from the house outside to the prison.

Let us allow Muhammad Idris to tell his story himself:

The Kandahar prison is arranged like this: in the middle of the political ward there is a vast yard; all room doors open onto this yard, so the ward's main gate is always locked while the internal room doors are always open. Thus, prisoners are able to enter other rooms with no difficulty; they gather for communal prayers as well.

The prisoners of the room that the tunnel reached hosted their friends on Monday night and invited from each room one or two persons. This ward's prayer imam, a scholar prisoner, was also invited, while I represented my room. So off to the supper we went.

We had our supper. Then Mawlawi, the prayer imam, started talking. After some beneficial advice, the sheikh [imam] started telling the persons present about the release operation plan. None of us knew anything about the subject until then. During his talk he told the prisoners sitting in the room: 'Tonight an operation to free and release us will be made; we had better be ready for it. Anyone of you exiting is ordered not to operate his mobile until tomorrow afternoon. If he talks on his mobile, he must be careful not to mention how he got out.' Following these guidelines, he told us: 'Keep mentioning God sincerely so he brings this operation to success.' We all started mentioning God. Within half an hour all the brothers were busy with praises and prayers.

Then the brothers who were aware of the plan came to the particular room. They cleared the items and mats in a particular part of the room. Moments later the cleared area was knocked from below, and the brothers in the tunnel under the area put a car jack underneath. They continued the pressure until they broke the concrete floor. As the tunnel was low, they brought with them many strong poles in order for the car jack to reach the concrete [ground]: they would place the poles on the jack and then raise them. They repeated this two or three times until a huge hole was opened in the middle of the room.

Thereafter, the brothers inside the tunnel gave the prisoners a number of pistols, daggers and knives. They also gave them a box containing a telephone headset, video camera and other devices that I did not recognise. I looked into the tunnel and saw two mujaheds: one who had given the box and another. Both retreated and headed to the other opening. At this point the prisoner release operation was delegated to the prisoner mujahedeen who were aware of the operation. They linked the telephone headset with the wire, establishing a connection with the mujahedeen on both ends of the tunnel: inside and outside of the prison.

Then these key prisoners distributed the arms among themselves, adding a number of trusted mujahedeen to them. This ward was holding two rooms of criminal prisoners [as well]. There were also a number of state spies among the prisoners. So the decision was made that if these spies were to cause trouble or attempt to tell the prison guards, we would kill them with these arms and knives. They said that such an operation would be difficult to grasp; if any brothers did not trust it and refused to leave, we would force them with these arms to exit.

Meanwhile, the key prisoners said to those present prior to going down the tunnel: 'When you get out at the end of the tunnel, you will meet a number of mujahedeen. They will take surplus money from you, mobiles and other items. They will allow you neither to talk nor to leave; listen to them and do whatever they say to you.' We all agreed.

Now I was the second in turn in the group sitting in the room to the tunnel. The first prisoner went down and I followed. The tunnel was wide, but not very much. I mean we could walk kneeling or crawl easily. But the mujahedeen had dug it fantastically well. Every 15 metres there was a lamp, so it was very bright. Similarly the mujahedeen had laid a 6″ diameter plastic pipeline along the tunnel for ventilation. At its start they operated a device for pumping air in, and made small holes in the tunnel. We thus felt no lack of air in the tunnel. Additionally two wires were laid in the tunnel: one was for the telephone, and I did not know whether the other was for electricity or otherwise. It took about 15 minutes inside the tunnel to reach the far end. There was one in front of me and a large number behind me.

Upon reaching the tunnel exit there were fifteen armed mujahedeen. They meticulously inspected all people exiting from the tunnel, taking from all their mobiles and sim cards. If anyone had money, they would leave him with 3,000 rupees and take the rest. There was a coat in which they put the money they took from us. As for prisoners with no money or less than 3,000 rupees, they gave them cash from the collection so that they had 3,000 rupees. This was the best method for everyone to have money to help with expenses until reaching their destination.

After exiting I saw three mujahedeen I knew, so I joined them in the operation execution. In the house were six transport cars. The brothers told us to make anyone exiting from the tunnel get in the cars after inspection and ordered them to say nothing but mention God discreetly, as close to the [house] yard was a prison tower; if disorder was to occur, the enemy could notice. This way the prisoners exited from the tunnel and we made them ride in the cars. Whenever a car was full, we covered it. When all the brothers were out, one friend said: 'Not much space is left in the cars.

Brothers who know the area and town alleys should go by foot to the town suburbs.' The house gate was facing the prison, while its back faced a residential area. We made a hole in the back wall through which the brothers who could not be taken by car could walk to the town suburbs.

But I and four of my friends who were residents of the city discussed it between us and agreed to go to the city. At this point the cars left the house and the five of us left minutes later into the street. We waited a little while on the pavement until a taxi came that was heading to the city. We got in. It was 4 a.m. While heading to the city the police stopped our car at Dand roundabout, then waved us on. The same inspection process was repeated at Madad roundabout, but the policeman said nothing. We reached the city and we had our rescue: salvation.

I should add that the prisoners in the political ward of Kandahar prison are all mujahedeen. Nearby there was another ward called Tawqif Khanah where a prison room also held mujahedeen. From the main tunnel the mujahedeen dug a secondary one to that room, allowing 10–15 mujahedeen prisoners to exit that room, thank God.

In the morning, while I walked about the town and was following the news, in my view until 8 a.m. the enemy had noticed nothing concerning the runaway mujahedeen from the prison, as I saw no mandatory checks being carried out in the city. After 8 a.m., the enemy started action. The prison guards used to count us twice: at 8 a.m. and in the afternoon. I think that when they arrived at the political ward at 8 a.m. to count the prisoners, they found none there. Then they started searching and looking for them.

To my knowledge, not a single mujahed remained in the prison's political ward; but there was a room for the mentally ill, and they remained inside the prison. As for the other wounded and sick prisoners, all were freed. There was even a wounded prisoner with two iron bars in his legs; during his escape through the tunnel the two bars were broken and he fainted from extreme pain. Nevertheless, the mujahedeen carried him in this condition, got him out of the tunnel and transported him by car.

88

ON SCHOOLS

[Arguably as part of a renewed diplomatic push, the Taliban released a series of state-ments (and an entirely rewritten policy) on education. The core audience for this paper is not entirely clear. Its contents potentially appealed to much of Afghan society, but could also be understood as a nod towards international interlocutors, demonstrating that the Taliban were indeed evolving and worth talking to.]

Al-Emera (website), 30 May 2012

The Islamic Emirate of Afghanistan has always made efforts as much as it can for the independence, prosperity and educational progress of the compatriots. A particular example in this regard is in the area of education. When the Islamic Emirate was in power, despite all the economic hardships, it paid more attention to education than to all military and civilian sectors, and about 20 per cent of its annual budget was allocated to education. This percentage would be considered a high percentage in any country if it is compared to their annual budget.

Despite the fact that the Islamic Emirate began everything from zero, it opened more than 1,100 schools by 2001, which were attended by more than a million students. All the expenses were paid from the Emirate's budget without any foreign assistance.

For all our friends and foes to be aware of our stance, the Islamic Emirate once again announces that it does not have any problem with those schools and educa-tional establishments where nothing harmful to our sacred religion of Islam and to our common national values are taught, and where Judaism, Christianity and anti-shari'a activities are not promoted. In this regard, the leadership of the Islamic Emirate has approved educational regulations which have been acted upon for a long time. The regulations say in part:

Article 9: The Islamic Emirate envisages the following educational establishments: schools, village-level day-time madrassas, religious boarding madrassas, *Dar ul-Hefaz*, universities and specialised establishments for religious sciences.

Article 10: From the above-mentioned educational establishments, priority is given to the village-level day-time madrassas and schools.

Article 27: Every Afghan national can take part in establishing, renovating and maintaining schools in those areas which are under the control of the Islamic Emirate. Of course, they have to contact and seek permission of the educational official of the province.

Article 38: The education and training high commission is duty bound to take serious steps, proportional to its resources, to set up and promote educational establishments and schools for modern sciences for the children of the mujahed Afghan nation and in order to provide them with the needs of modern life.

Article 39: The high commission is duty bound to encourage the Muslim and mujahed Afghan nation to establish, proportional to their financial ability, private educational establishments such as village-level madrassas, schools, religious boarding madrassas and *Dar ul-Hefaz*. They should also support those educational establishments that are already operational so that the nation becomes self-sufficient as far as education is concerned.

Article 40: The high commission is duty bound to maintain contact with and seek advice and assistance from religious dignitaries, political and vocational scholars and tribal leaders in order to encourage the nation in the field of education.

Article 52: The official in charge of provincial education is duty bound to dispatch a delegation of religious dignitaries and scholars to carry out publicity in those areas where educational programmes are implemented, in order to educate the nation about the importance of madrassas, schools and knowledge, as well as inviting wealthy individuals to establish private schools and madrassas. The official in charge of provincial education is duty bound to obey the high commission in performing its activities.

The Islamic Emirate will only allow itself to intervene in the affairs of educational establishments when children and youths of the country are taught un-Islamic ideas under the name of education, or they are being trained for other hostile objectives under the guise of regular education. The educational regulation of the Islamic Emirate says in this regard:

Article 26: In any area where there is a functioning school, its teachers and the textbooks they are using should be controlled and supervised. They should not be closed down, but should be maintained where resources permit.

Article 22: Unsuitable and inadmissible subjects should not be taught: subjects that oppose jihad, promote inadmissible freedom for Muslim women, promote inadmissible laws of the infidel powers, etc.

Emphasis on caution and attention here is because Afghanistan is such an Islamic country that has offered huge sacrifices throughout its history in defence of its beliefs and religious values, and where no other value can be more important than our religious beliefs.

We are in favour of such an educational system in our country which will teach our children religious issues as well as essential modern education. In order to achieve this objective, the relevant structures of the Islamic Emirate have been assigned the duty of supervising the educational process throughout the country and informing students, teachers and the public about the educational activities and programmes of the education and training commission of the Islamic Emirate from time to time through its officials and instructors without creating any problems in the day-to-day activities of the educational establishments.

As for the mercenary administration, the invaders and some unfair media outlets which accuse the Islamic Emirate of hostility towards education, the compatriots should know that it is these circles themselves which are the true enemies of education, because they use the education of children in this country as inadmissible propaganda for their political objectives, and always use such national issues as a tool of pressure and propaganda to defame the mujahedeen.

89

PROMOTION OF EDUCATION INSIDE THE COUNTRY IS ONE OF THE MAIN OBJECTIVES OF THE ISLAMIC EMIRATE

[*This commentary article makes the point that education is not just an abstract benefit to society but that it can be used for ideological indoctrination as well (by any party). By embracing education, the next generation will come under the influence of the Taliban, the author argues.*]

Al-Emera (website), 7 March 2012

The Islamic Emirate of Afghanistan, besides the promotion of the sanctified purpose of jihad for the sovereignty of the motherland and the implementation of the Islamic shari'a, is also focusing on the education and edification of the new generation.

Vigilant countrymen and the people of the world are fully aware that the invading forces in Afghanistan and their domestic stooges have inflicted heavy losses on the education system of the state and have misused this effect as negative propaganda against the Islamic Emirate. This ruthless enemy and those annexed to it have either reduced many schools to ashes or destroyed them up and down the country, and have always blamed the mujahedeen of the Islamic Emirate for it. This is still going on and they misuse it as an asset in their propaganda.

As the policy of the Islamic Emirate is based on the rules and regulations of shari'a, and the Holy Prophet of Islam says that seeking knowledge is the duty of every Muslim, so the Islamic Emirate in general does not resist education in the country. Of course the Islamic Emirate will not support that curriculum which is the filthy gift of the colonialists. It is a tool through which the transgressors and their in-house agents want to wipe away our Islamic and national values and replace them with Western culture. Obviously this does not mean we oppose education and educational institutions. We just ask for the replacement of their kind of curriculum.

Right now in many parts of the country, either by direct or indirect support and assistance from the Islamic Emirate of Afghanistan, thousands of schools are operating and millions of students are studying there. In fact without the support of the Islamic Emirate of Afghanistan, the running of these schools would not be possible.

But the invaders and their in-house stooges not only turn a blind eye to this knowledge-friendly policy of the Islamic Emirate, but also deliberately accuse the mujahedeen of the Islamic Emirate when the assigned stooges of the invaders destroy or set fire to the schools. There are incidents where the perpetrators have confessed that they have been supported financially and logistically in destroying and ruining these educational institutions.

Let us say that the Islamic Emirate considers education as a necessity for the new generation and claims the responsibility of spreading it throughout the country. But undeniably a curriculum which manifests our Islamic and national ideals and reflects the vital needs of the nation is also a thing to be wished and strived for. The Islamic Emirate considers the support and implementation of such a curriculum as its national obligation.

90

Q&A

EDUCATION AND WOMEN

[*This is an extract from the Taliban's 'Ask Zabiullah Mujahed a Question' page, which was extremely popular for a period of two years. Hundreds of individuals wrote in and received public answers to their queries. In this excerpt, questions are raised about the Taliban's attitudes towards education. The person asking the question is clearly sceptical about the movement's previous and current policies.*]

Taliban's Q&A section on Al-Emera, 28 March 2012

Q: I am happy you have given a chance to our compatriots to ask questions. I hope most of their questions will be answered. First question: You have mentioned that during its rule the Emirate did not have enough of a budget for girls' schools. But when foreign NGOs were ready to provide the required funds, why did you not agree to them?

A: Dear brother, I think you do not have accurate information about this. During its rule the Islamic Emirate, in accordance with Islamic principles, tried to contact many foreign NGOs for funds, but none were ready to provide actual assistance to the Islamic Emirate. They deliberately left the issue of girls' education unsolved in order to use it as a pressure tactic. I hope you will confirm this from other sources too. We still have evidence of promises made by foreign NGOs and the UN which were never fulfilled.

Q: You don't do anything against schools established in the areas of our Hazara brothers. But on the contrary you create problems for schools that exist in Pashtun areas; Ghazni province is a clear example. Do you have an agreement with Iran that you will not cause any trouble to the schools of Hazara areas?

A: We don't create any kind of problems for schools. There are some schools which are closed as a result of the ongoing turmoil. But in those areas where the situation is comparatively calm, the Islamic Emirate's mujaheden have never created any kind of problem. Right now there are tens of schools open in the areas of Ghazni province that are under our control. If we want we can create problems for the schools that exist in Andar, Qarabagh, Gelan, Muqur and other districts of the province where our mujahedeen have a presence. But the Islamic Emirate does not have any plan to create problems for educational institutions. Instead it works, according to its capacity, for the progress and development of education.

The following articles are part of our educational charter:

26) In all areas where there are schools, the teachers' and curriculum books should be scrutinised. They should not be closed down, but should be supported if possible.

27) Every Afghan can work to establish or repair a school in areas under the control of the Islamic Emirate's forces. However, prior contact with and permission of the Emirate's provincial educational representative is necessary.

38) The High Commission for Training and Education must take steps to provide modern education and establish schools for Afghan children.

41) The High Commission is also bound to protect and allow all seminaries (madrassas), schools, Qur'an-memorisation centres, universities and private institutions. There should not be any interference in their daily management. The founders and managers of these institutions should be protected.

44) The High Commission has to invite and encourage all children to get an education and avoid the use of any kind of force and compulsion. Our people have been misled by internal and external enemies. We should try to be kind and befriend them.

52) The provincial educational representative has to send a special delegation of ulemaa to areas where educational activities take place. The delegation will create awareness among locals about the importance of education and invite local influentials to take part in building schools and seminaries. The provincial education representative is obliged to follow the instructions of the delegation.

53) It is the duty of the provincial educational representative to visit the schools and seminaries at least once a month. However, once again I want to explain that there some areas where people are unable to go to school because of the ongoing fighting. For example, there is fighting and bombardment in various areas of Helmand province. The Hazara populated areas are not affected by fighting and foreign forces don't go there frequently. That is why the schools are not closed in the area.

The Islamic Emirate is currently at war against a global superpower and suffers many sacrifices. It is unable to make any considerable achievement in the field of education, nor should you expect it to do so. I hope you and those who have an opinion on the basis of Western propaganda will try and form a new view. Please come here and witness everything up close.

Q&A: EDUCATION AND WOMEN

Q: For the last several years a number of districts in Kandahar and Helmand were under your control, but you did nothing for the people there except for the legal system. For example, why you did not establish a school in Maruf district?

A: You must have heard the popular proverb about how sweets are not distributed among people during a fight. When we are present in any district of Kandahar and Helmand we are faced with fighting, search operations and counter attacks against the enemy. We are always on the alert and live in a state of constant combat. Most of our energy is consumed in fighting against the enemy. That is why it is impossible for us to participate in reconstruction work. If these areas were under our control in a normal and peaceful manner, then your question would be pertinent. Generally, we spend half the day fighting, and the rest in preparing for the next day's combat. It is not possible for us to provide social services while we are under attack.

91

THE CRUCIAL RESPONSIBILITY OF THE NATION
TOWARDS THE CHASTE AFGHAN WOMEN

[In contrast to many statements and edicts issued during the 1990s, the post-2001 Taliban output often sought to portray their concern for women as paternalistic in nature. This source thus frames the fighters associated with the movement as being the protectors of women.]

Al-Emera (website), 20 June 2012

Women are held in very high regard by Afghan society and family life. Not only are they compassionate mothers, beloved sisters, free-willed wives, treasured daughters, but they are also considered the tribes' honour and the nation's dignity because it is these women who breastfeed their children by reciting *bismillah* ('in the name of Allah') and teach them about protecting their religion, honour and country in the cradle. It is women who expound jihad, zeal and sacrifice for the defence of Islam and it is women who indoctrinate young men with the creed and present them for service to their religion, nation and country.

The honourable status of women in Afghan society in reality gets its origins from Islam. In the time of ignorance, women didn't even have the right to live; they were buried alive or were distributed and treated as property. When the divine religion of Islam first dawned, it foremost gave women the right to live, then rights of heritage, ownership, trade, marriage of choice, education, teaching, jihad in the path of Allah, judiciary, issuing fatwas, giving advice, worship, giving infidels security and all the other rights of life. The Prophet (SAWS) said: 'Those who have a girl, discipline her with the best discipline; educate her with the best of education and cover her with the blessings with which Allah has blessed him; then she shall become a shield between him and the fire', meaning he shall be protected from the fires of hell due to his daughter.

And for those who oppress women, they have been addressed with the harshest of terms in Islamic shari'a, for example the saying of Allah: 'When a female infant is buried alive, the question will be asked "For what sin was she murdered?"', meaning that question shall definitely be asked on the day of reckoning.

Islam has also brought with it some rulings for women which protect their chastity and dignity, for example the hijab; therefore it is stated at the end of the verse regarding covering: 'It would be better for them to be known [as free respectable women] so as not to be annoyed.'[1] The hijab in reality is a fortress for a woman in protecting her from immodest, unreligious and harmful people.

In this dark period of American occupation and in complete disagreement with our Islamic and national customs and culture, women are intentionally being pushed towards ignorance; are having to face inhumane conditions under the name of democracy; are being oppressed by unconstrained militias who work under the shadow of the invaders; are being kidnapped; are made to cry day and night due to barbarism and cruelty; they burn themselves up to a stage where their screams are heard throughout the world, which is being maliciously used by the media, but still no one bothers to ask about them. Surely to Allah we belong and to him is the return.

Therefore it is an obligation upon the mujahedeen and the entire nation to protect the rights of women in these sensitive times; regard it as their duty; make sacrifices in its defence; all means should be utilised to attain their due Islamic rights; they should not be left alone to the cruelty and abuse of oppressors; and they should protect this national honour with full determination and unshakable will.

92

ON THE WITHDRAWAL OF FOREIGN TROOPS, THE AFGHAN CASE AND RECONCILIATION

[*This speech, coupled with the next one made in Chantilly six months later (source 93), can be said to have driven the Taliban's political apparatus (of which the speaker, Adena Muhammad, was a part) closer to the possibility of engaging in serious discussions with the United States and (eventually) with the Afghan government. These attempts can be seen as having failed, but at the time the fact that they happened appeared to many a significant moment. The earlier part of the speech repeats arguments made many times previously in this book about the origin story of the Taliban and their role (or not) in the conflict.*]

Speaker: Adena Muhammad
Doshisha University, Kyoto, Japan, 27 June 2012

Stance of the Islamic Emirate regarding reconciliation

On 3 January, the Islamic Emirate of Afghanistan announced in an exclusive statement that we are ready to open a political office abroad in order to reach a peaceful solution of the Afghan issue and understanding with USA. It was reiterated that neither America nor its allies will ever solve the Afghan issue through the use of force or subjugate the Afghan Muslim people. Prior to that, a special envoy of the Islamic Emirate had reached understanding with an envoy of USA that the American side would implement a few confidence-building measures in order to bring about a conducive atmosphere of confidence. But despite the passage of several months following the issuance of the statement by the Islamic Emirate of Afghanistan, the American side not only did not implement the CBMs but linked the so-called strategic agreement with the Kabul administration, leaving the reconciliation process unfinished. This posturing by the US is in its own right contrary to CBMs and the reconciliation process. The Islamic Emirate has repeatedly said that the Afghan issue is two-dimensional with internal and external dimensions. The external dimension which should be dealt with, initially, concerns America and the Islamic Emirate; while the internal dimension of the issue is Afghan-related. It is the Afghans who have to pave the way for the establishment of an Islamic government in the country, through working out an acceptable mechanism reached as a result of understanding, display of selflessness and tolerance. The leader of the Islamic Emirate of Afghanistan, Mullah Mohammad Omar Mujahid (May Allah Protect him), has elucidated this point in his last year's message of Eid ul-Fitr as follows:

> 'Our manifesto is that Afghanistan should have a real Islamic regime, acceptable to all people of the country. All ethnicities will have participation in the regime and portfolios will be dispensed on the basis of merit; we will maintain good relations with regional and world countries on the basis of mutual respect, Islamic and national interests. Such dispensation will entirely focus on conduits to recover the spiritual and material losses that have been caused by the three decades-long war...

> Contrary to the propaganda launched by the enemies, the policy of the Islamic Emirate is not aimed at monopolising power. Since Afghanistan is the joint homeland of all Afghans, therefore, all Afghans have the right to perform their responsibility in the way of protection and running the country. The future transformations and developments would not resemble the developments following the collapse of communism, when everything in the country was plundered and the State Apparatus damaged entirely... Professional cadres and national businessmen will be further encouraged, without any discrimination, to serve their religion and country.'

It is to be said that the Islamic Emirate is still committed to the peaceful solution of the imbroglio of Afghanistan. But if America does not show honesty in its dealing and continues to resort to pretexts in order to prolong its occupation or deprive the people of Afghanistan of real independence under the name of strategic agreement, it will clearly indicate that America intentionally wants to create new hurdles in the way of a solution to the issue.

> The Islamic Emirate, on the basis of its policy, is ready to give assurance to all countries of the world, including America, that no harm will be done to any country from the soil of Afghanistan. We are ready to reach an acceptable mechanism in this regard with all relevant parties to the issue. This point has been referred to in a statement of the Islamic Emirate which was issued on 9 May 2012, a day before the opening of NATO Summit in Chicago. It says:

> 'The Islamic Emirate once again declares that it holds no agenda of harming any-one nor will it let anyone harm other countries from the soil of Afghanistan. Hence there is no reason for the occupying countries including America to continue the occupation of Afghanistan under the pretext of safeguarding its own security.'

ON THE WITHDRAWAL OF FOREIGN TROOPS

Request from the Islamic Emirate to nations and countries of the world

A brutal war has been continuing against our nation, ostensibly under the name of War on Terror. Every day, our children, women, old men and youth fall prey to the blind bombardment by America. Unfortunately, some media outlets of Western countries are trying to keep people ignorant in their respective countries with regard to the ground realities in Afghanistan. They spread baseless horror among people in the name of terrorism, so that people will have to continue their support of the war of Afghanistan. Therefore, we call on the media outlets of the said countries:

1. Do not participate in the current colonialist game which is continuing in Afghanistan under the name of War on Terror; put pressure on your rulers to put an end to the brutal war; spend your budgets on the uplift of the life of your people; follow the footsteps of the French people who took the laudable and rational initiative of withdrawing their troops from Afghanistan through the use of ballot boxes.

2. The existence of the Islamic Emirate is an undeniable reality. The international community should acknowledge this reality and should not ignore other realities existing in Afghanistan, just to please a few elements and to satiate their obsession and paranoia based on groundless biases.

3. Put an end to the unfounded allegations against the Islamic Emirate. In fact, the Islamic Emirate has no nexus with terrorism, and does not follow a policy of interference in the internal affairs of other countries.

4. The Islamic Emirate condemns the abhorrent action of destroying and burning boys' or girls' schools, particularly poisoning students. We call on all people of the world, particularly the media outlets, not to make a scapegoat of the Islamic Emirate through baseless propaganda for the sake of furthering the official policy of the invading countries.

5. One could not reach truth and reality without justice. We request all nations and countries to hear the voice of the Islamic Emirate throughout the world. Give it the opportunity to express its views so that it can convey them to the public of the world regarding the existing realities and facts about Afghanistan, like the opportunity that we were provided here to express our views. One-sided judgement against the Islamic Emirate should cease, because one-sided or partial judgement cannot solve issues, but has been the cause of atrocities and the continuation of war.

6. The civilian casualties are one of the main humanitarian issues. A complete impartial investigation should be carried out in this regard. It is [pathetic] that human rights organisations accuse only the Islamic Emirate of being involved in civilian casualties. Whereas, contrarily, America is the main factor of civilian casualties, intentionally and practically perpetrating such casualties. We have frequently proposed that a tripartite team should be constituted comprising the Islamic

Emirate, NATO and the international community to investigate the incidents. But America refused the idea forthwith. Even the human rights organisations did not show approval for the suggestion. Based on this, it is easy to determine who feels more responsibility as regards the civilian casualties. We repeat our proposal and hope the concerned parties may welcome it.

7. We urge all nations, countries and individuals who have free conscience not to spare their political and moral support for the Afghan nation in its struggle for the independence of Afghanistan. In fact, it is the nations that bring about governments. Therefore, governments should submit to the will of nations and take decisions about the war in Afghanistan as per the aspirations of their people. To that end, we thank the government of Japan, particularly Mr Masanori Naito, who provided us this opportunity to share with you our views and with the world through this forum.

93

CHANTILLY CONFERENCE STATEMENT

[*This speech may be seen as one of the moments of culmination for efforts made by the Taliban's political wing to have their voice recognised and for them to be taken seriously by the foreign policy establishment in Europe and the United States. Dilawar and Mohammad Naeem outline their understanding of the root causes of the conflict, as well as proposed solutions.*]

Speakers: Mawlawi Shahabuddin Dilawar and Dr Mohammad Naeem Speech text Chantilly, France, 20–21 December 2012

Balance of political power in the future government of Afghanistan

In the future Islamic government of the Islamic Emirate of Afghanistan, the balance of power or participation in government by all Afghan parties must be implemented in the constitution following the specifications below:

1. Codification of the constitution

Every power and system of government in the current world needs a complete and clear constitution to organise and coordinate its internal and foreign affairs in order to pave the way for advancement and prosperity of its citizens and so that every person properly grasps their role in the confines of law. The constitution is integral for every government because, without it, the affairs of development of its nation and country will face disorder and numerous obstacles. The personal, civil and political rights of all citizens of Afghanistan shall be regulated through the constitution; rights shall be given to all brother ethnicities without discrimination; will make clear relations between the government and people; will shed light on the balance of government's three structured powers; will determine government's type, administration and powers; in sum, will gain acceptance from the Afghan nation and the world regarding the internal and foreign policy of Afghanistan.

Therefore the Islamic Emirate, for the welfare, prosperity and advancement of its proud nation, considers such a constitution necessary, which is framed on the principles of noble Islam, national interests, historical achievements and social justice; abides by human rights and national values; guarantees the country's sovereignty and rights of all its citizens; and shall not contain any articles and clauses opposing Islamic principles, national interests and Afghan mores. With the blessing of the constitution, the way shall be paved for a political power balance and all Afghan parties to participate in the upcoming government.

We clearly state that the stipulations of the constitution shall be written by Afghan scholars in a free atmosphere and will then be presented to the nation for approval. The current constitution of Afghanistan is illegitimate because it is written under the shadow of B-52 aircraft.

[...]

3. Islamic Emirate

The Islamic Emirate of Afghanistan is an Islamic reality on the face of the planet, is the legitimate government of our beloved country, has every operational administration and has notable achievements in several areas. People in most parts of the country turn towards its courts, political activities in the shape of a Political Office known to everyone, an example of which is our presence here, and education is also forging ahead in many parts of the country with the Emirate's help. America with the help of over forty countries have invaded our country. The Islamic Emirate has carried out sacred jihad against the occupation for over eleven years and has put forward notable sacrifices for the independence of its country and defence of its religion and honour. The Islamic Emirate had brought security to over 95 per cent of the country before the invasion; had collected illegal weapons; had stopped narcotics; had secured borders of the beloved country; had provided education, work and open trade for the nation in complete security. We can even proudly state that in the previous reign of the Islamic Emirate, we achieved things which the Western world is unable to do even with its entire military and economic means.

It has repeatedly been expounded in the messages of Amir ul-Mu'mineen that we are not looking to monopolise power. We want an all-Afghan inclusive government. He has time and again urged his opposition for help in expelling the occupation. He respects his political rivals, expounds on realisation and understanding, and asks for help from them in defence of our nation and honour; this clearly displays his goodwill and political insight.

4. Sovereignty of Afghanistan

Allah Almighty has created humans free, and independence is a part of their nature. No human society can make advancements in economics, politics, culture and science without independence, or have control over its resources, talents and fruits of their work. Love with independence is naturally sown in the blood and body of the Afghans. History has shown that the Afghans have sacrificed their lives and everything dear for independence. All battles fought in the past decades against invasions have been for independence. No economic, military or political power has scared them in attaining their goal, and neither has the lack of means, men and hard conditions been a hurdle.

If we want to pave the way once again for the country's natural development and dignity, then the independence of Afghanistan must be restored and occupation ended so that the Afghans can make decisions in the best interests of its power and people for the benefit of its nation.

It is also a reality that every nation, after attaining independence, has a need to maintain its borders, security and sovereignty, and this need can only be accomplished through police and an army faithful to its people, religion and nation. Therefore it is incumbent that our security apparatus be trained on religious principles and national spirit; is cleansed from prejudice on lingual, ethnical and regional basis; and is bound to serving its people and securing its sovereignty. If it is not so, then such an army is not fit for maintaining its national and Islamic goals, and neither can it be called a national army. Instead of working for national interests, it will be used against its religion, country and people. Hence, as much as Afghanistan needs an army, its reforming and proper training is equally vital.

Afghanistan is an underdeveloped nation economically. It cannot maintain a highly paid army in the long term, due to its expenses being several times higher than the country's GDP. In such a condition, the government will be forced to abide by terms and sometimes unreasonable demands of lending nations, bringing the whole nation under the burden of interest and pushing them towards economic disaster. Due to this, it will be better for all Afghans to fulfil their obligation in securing the country.

It is also a reality that in the current world a country cannot feel secure and at peace without a powerful defensive system, or it will always have to feel in danger. Hence it is necessary that Afghanistan builds a strong air force alongside a strong ground force, in order to reassure its nation.

We must reiterate that independence is the key condition, because in the presence of an occupation, all this force will be used against its own people and for the goals of others. We observed in the past decade that an army built on political foundations gets used and is used against its people instead of for invasion and becomes the cause of many tragedies.

How can enduring peace be achieved in Afghanistan?

The Islamic Emirate came into being to bring peace to its people. Peace and tranquility are the natural desire of all creatures of Allah Almighty and especially humans, who are in need of peace more than any other being. Today humans have made much progress; for killing and destruction, it has created small, chemical and nuclear weapons, therefore it is in need of peace more than ever and efforts must be made for peace.

The Islamic Emirate, for peace and order, has made great sacrifices for this mutual goal, whereas it actually came into being to bring peace and security. The entire world is aware that the oppressed Afghan nation faced great difficulties before the Islamic Emirate came into being; corruption and insecurity had reached their peak; the life and property of the people were in constant danger and the country was standing on the brink of disintegration. The leaders of the Islamic Emirate, with the divine help of Allah Almighty and the backing of its nation, and as the result of many sacrifices, brought an end to all this anarchy, such that no one could have ever imagined, and transformed an atmosphere of insecurity and disorder into one of security and peace.

Taking away security from the Afghan nation under the guise of the September incident: the Islamic Emirate had brought security to 95 per cent of the country, and this displays the responsibility of the Islamic Emirate which it had and still has regarding the world, its region and specifically its own country and nation. However, with great regret, the invaders deprived the Afghan nation of this great blessing. They brought insecurity to the Afghan people in this eleven years of war and fighting, brought a culture of injustice and corruption, stirred up a habit of killing and murder, overflowed pools with blood, stuffed prisons with Afghan people, began oppressing children, women, old men and youngsters in villages and homes, created difficulties for the lives of women which is their most basic and important right, and planted seeds of enmity between Afghanistan and its neighbouring countries.

Some primary problems were created by this illegal and peace-shattering invasion:

1. Occupying Afghanistan and disturbing its atmosphere of peace.
2. Forcing an administration on Afghans embroiled in corruption and narcotics trade.
3. Working to divide the Afghan nation and country on the basis of regional, lingual, tribal, political and religious animosities.
4. Nurturing narcotics while the Islamic Emirate had brought it to a complete end.
5. Violating human rights, the most important issue of which is the life and destiny of women. According to well-established research, thousands of women are targets of repression every year, hundreds of whom have even died.

Invaders and their allies don't have a clear framework for peace. Foreigners and Kabul do not have an inclination towards peace, and neither are they ready to abide by the rules and goals of peace. If the invaders truly believe in peace, they would have listened to the legitimate demands of the Islamic Emirate in the initial phase. They should have tested peace before force; if it had failed to give results, then war was a last resort; however, they chose war as the first option.

Even now, they state one thing and do another. On the one hand they say that peace must be achieved; and on the other, they add new people to the blacklist; they say that they will leave Afghanistan, but sign strategic pacts in the false hope of prolonging their occupation. They are doing this despite being well informed that the Kabul administration can never represent the Afghan people; but they still bargain with them on the future of the Afghan nation.

The Kabul administration does not hold any jurisdiction or power, because the Afghan people, in their own land and through the medium of Kabul, are being imprisoned by the invaders! With their presence and their help, the homes of Afghans are being recklessly raided by the invaders at night against all laws and customs; children, women and old men peacefully asleep are being mercilessly killed, and they are still unable to take any steps against them.

The Kabul administration does not seem inclined towards peace due to some steps and because it does not have a clear framework for peace. On the one hand it says that it wants peace, and on the other it martyrs tens of mujahedeen every day or imprisons them or forces them to migrate. It shouts for peace, but then unjustly and brutally executes imprisoned mujahedeen against all international laws!

Sometimes it says it wants to talk with the Islamic Emirate, sometimes it says it wants to talk to Pakistan! Such ambiguous actions will never positively impact the peace process.

In reality, they want the surrender of mujahedeen under the title of peace; give up arms, abide by the constitution created under the shadow of invaders, bow your heads to our orders, and then we won't say anything to you! Is this peace? Do they think that the Afghan nation made colossal sacrifices for the past eleven years to surrender to the invaders? So that someone will assure their lives? This clearly shows that they do not have sincerity and a clear framework for peace.

Malicious propaganda against peace

Another factor damaging peace are those efforts made through poisonous propaganda deployed inside the country which tries to depict reality in another colour. Different types of propaganda are used against the ongoing jihad; sometimes it is labelled the work of neighbours, sometimes as against education and development, and sometimes is accused of causing civilian casualties; but they never seem to possess strong evidence and only reiterate repeated charges. Such black propaganda only prolongs the war and uproots any chances for peace.

Everyone is aware that members of the Islamic Emirate, for their independent Islamic and national policy, have not only tasted torture and martyrdom inside their internal prisons, but have also been victims of such behaviour in prisons outside the country. So can people of such determination and ideology ever become slaves of others?

The esteemed Amir ul-Mu'mineen (may Allah protect him) has given strong and clear guidelines to his mujahedeen, who are still practising them, in all his Eid messages regarding destruction of educational facilities, protection of civilian life and bombings in places of gatherings, which have also been published in the media. However, we can see that some intelligence agencies are reporting grotesque actions (blowing up bridges, throwing acid in students' faces and targeting civilian vehicles with roadside bombings) while the Kabul administration has never given thought to the guidance of Amir ul-Mu'mineen and is blindly using these incidents as raw material for its poisonous propaganda. Similarly, they never release findings of such incidents, which indicate that these have not been perpetrated by the mujahedeen but are the product of intelligence agencies. They either lack the courage to announce the reality, or believe that keeping silent is in their best interest.

They believe that through such actions they will alienate the Islamic Emirate from people and the world, and extend their power a few more days. Peace is being sacrificed in the long run through such unreasonable actions and poisonous propaganda. If this keeps on, it will only harm peace, the country and the people.

The Kabul administration and its backers must realise that such tactics did not bring security to the people, but threw them into a raging fire, violated their rights and prolonged the invasion, and will still fail to bring peace.

How can real peace be achieved?

The situation in Afghanistan has two facets: one foreign and the other internal. The foreign facet is tied to the foreigners, and the internal to the Afghans. How can they reach an understanding so that, in accordance with the aspirations of the nation, such an independent Islamic government can come into being as will guarantee justice, stability, development, economic growth and prosperity, wipe the tears of widows and treat the wounds of the people?

The Islamic Emirate, alongside all its efforts inside the country, is struggling for a true Islamic system and enduring peace; it considers this vital for human life, and regards the following few points important:

1. For enduring peace, importance must be placed on the aspirations of the people. The occupation must be ended as a first step, which is the want of the entire nation because this is the mother of all these tragedies. Invaders and their allies must realise that no international power can subdue the power of the people, and neither can the quandary end through irresponsible and unlawful agreements.

2. Islam is the religion of our people and the only guarantor of the country's economic growth, social justice and national unity. Without an independent Islamic government, no other system can solve our problems, because the Muslim Afghan nation will not accept any other system contradicting a pure independent Islamic

government, and they have presented countless sacrifices for this goal for the past thirty years and are still sacrificing.

3. Peace needs sincerity and good intention. Common and national interests must be favoured over personal interests. Peace can only be achieved under these circumstances and not through deceit and stratagems. We are seeing that every time the Islamic Emirate takes steps towards peace, the Kabul administration takes reactive tactical steps which (according to their own belief) have the potential to derail the peace process while at the same time not seeming counterproductive, i.e when the Islamic Emirate inaugurated its political office in Doha for peace talks, the Kabul administration, with the backing of America, recalled its ambassador to damage the peace process.

4. The leader of the Islamic Emirate, the esteemed Amir ul-Mu'mineen (may Allah protect him), clearly stated in his Eid message that we only have one channel for political efforts in the form of an office, and have made it known to everyone. But still the Kabul administration, under the title of the peace process but sabotaging peace, makes contact with people who have not been appointed by the Islamic Emirate for peace talks, and then accuses the Islamic Emirate of trying to derail peace. Peace is not a game of chess where every side is laying an ambush for the other; rather, peace is a joint responsibility and a means of giving rights to those entitled. Peace must be looked at with this vision, and ways must be paved for it.

5. The Islamic Emirate welcomes all civil societies that work for the benefit of the Afghan nation and abides by Afghan norms and humanity in the light of Islamic principles.

6. The policy of the Islamic Emirate is clear regarding the role of women. It will abide by all those rights given to women by the noble religion of Islam. Women in Islam have the right to choose husbands, to own property, the right to inheritance and the right to education and work. The Islamic Emirate will safeguard the rights of women such that their legitimate rights are not violated, and neither are their human dignity and Islamic requirements endangered under the guise of education and work.

7. In accordance with the rules and regulations of peace, such bodies should be utilised that believe in the sanctity of peace and are famously known in the country as righteous peace brokers. They must consider the establishment of peace as vital for the Afghans and must not look at it through the lens of a request made by foreigners.

8. For peace, talks must practically be given preference over war. At this very moment, the Kabul administration and its foreign allies are trying to put pressure on the mujahedeen so that they will make peace according to their conditions, but this truly increases the hurdles to peace.

9. As long as mujahedeen are imprisoned, where they spend nights in torture and persecution, true peace is cannot be achieved.

10. The Islamic Emirate wants to interact with the world and the region on the basis

of mutual respect and two-way cooperation. It did not harm anyone before, neither will it today or in the future, and neither will it let others use Afghan soil against others.

To end, a few appeals to the international community regarding the establishment of peace:

1. The whole impartial international community, be they countries or nations, associations or societies, especially the International Ulama Council, the Islamic Conference, Islamic governments and people, must lend all kinds of help to the Afghans in putting an end to the occupation, in order to remove this hurdle and pave the way for inter-Afghan understanding. We specifically ask the member states of the United Nations to stand next to the oppressed Afghan people, as they stood with the Palestinian people. Just as you did not care about force and pressure from others, adopt a similar and based-on-realities policy for the Afghan nation, so that on the one hand help is rendered to a persecuted nation; and on the other the tyrants realise that their oppression and cruelty will no longer be tolerated and they end their wrongdoings.

2. America and those who have allied with them under different names must answer the calls of the Afghans and their own nations, withdraw all their troops and put an end to the killing and oppression of the helpless Afghans. Instead, help them to create an atmosphere of peace between them. The step taken by France in this regard is worth respecting. All others should follow the footsteps of France and listen to the wants and interests of their people. Just as you do not desire killing, disorder, injustice, corruption and treachery for your own nations, do not desire it for others either.

3. We especially call on all those nations whose governments have sent their sons against their approval to kill the innocent Afghan people: take a page from the French nation and put pressure on your governments to withdraw their troops from our country.

4. The Islamic Emirate should be granted freedom of speech. It should be helped in reaching its voice to the world so that they are able to communicate directly their policy and demands. We also ask the international community to furnish all members of the Islamic Emirate with facilities, and exert efforts in removing all obstacles. We thank the government of Japan and officials of Doshisha University for giving the Islamic Emirate an opportunity to communicate its views and policies to the world, and now thank the officials of Foundation for Strategic Research and all other related sides in helping the Islamic Emirate in this regard. Other nations, in order to realise the realities, must also take similar steps.

5. We hope the international media will help the voice of the Afghan nation to reach the region and the world, and portray accurately the realities on the ground to the people, because this is their humanitarian responsibility and follows the ethics of journalism. And this is never hard for Allah Almighty.

94

Q&A

PEACE NEGOTIATIONS

[*By late 2012 to early 2013, the lower rank and file of the Taliban had started to speak out in confusion about the apparent turn-of-face by the Taliban. The newly-opened office in Doha, Qatar, and their announcement that they were going to negotiate with the United States, seemed a contradiction to many fighters.*]

Taliban's Q&A section on Al-Emera, 21 March 2012

Q: Peace be upon you! I am Muhammad Samim from Jalalabad. I want to ask why you are ready to hold peace negotiations with the invading crusaders instead of with the Afghan government. Let us make peace amongst ourselves and oust the invaders from our homeland and make it a prosperous country. How long will we continue to suffer bloodshed? If we reach a compromise amongst ourselves, there will be no need for the foreigners to stay in our country any more. If we are involved in internal fights, they will exploit our mutual differences and achieve their goals.

A: I must explain that this matter of the Kabul administration and Americans or Washington is so important. Some people object and say that the Taliban should ready themselves to hold a dialogue not with the Americans but with Afghans. In fact, this is a matter of independence and dependence. The people of Afghanistan and the whole world know very well that it is the US which is the true independent counterpart to the Taliban. Since the very beginning, the Americans have been utilising the Karzai administration as a tool for prolonging their occupation. So it is useless to hold a dialogue with such a government which has been appointed by the Americans, who have practically proved that for the time being everything in Afghanistan is in their hands. So there is no point in holding a direct or indirect dialogue with [the Afghan government], as it would be just a waste of time. Hopefully you will comprehend this point thoroughly: that today our actual counterpart is not the Kabul administration, but the invading United States of America.

95

Q&A

ON AMR BIL MAROUF

[*The fact that questions like this were publicly addressed and answered reflects the movement's desire to be seen as reflective and cognisant of their past difficulties, as a movement that could learn from their previous mistakes. The promise to 'completely review' the 'procedures and methods' of the Amr bil Marouf group would have been hard to imagine even a few years earlier.*]

Taliban's Q&A section on Al-Emera, 4 April 2012

Q: Dear Zabiullah Mujahed, peace be upon you! My question is the following: if the Islamic Emirate once again forms its government in Afghanistan, will it revive the department for the prevention of vice and the promotion of virtue? If yes, will it again implement its orders by force? Regards, and long live the mujahedeen of the Islamic Emirate!

A: Peace be upon you! The Islamic government will be formed with all its essential departments. The department for the prevention of vice and the promotion of virtue is an essential part of an Islamic government and it is obligatory on all Muslims to follow its instructions. However, this time its procedures and methods will be completely reviewed. The people will be persuaded towards the establishment of virtue in a softer manner and, likewise, they will be prevented from vice through wisdom. In this way, the use of unnecessary force will be avoided.

96

Q&A

MEDIA JIHAD

[*Quite a few of the questions directed towards Taliban spokesman Zabiullah Mujahed include offers of support and pledges to volunteer. This example is representative of others not included in this volume.*]

Taliban's Q&A section on Al-Emera, 25 March 2012

Q: Dear brother mujahed, may Allah give you rewards! Dear brother, I am unable to participate in practical jihad for some legal reasons. I cannot afford to stay for very long away from my home. Since I am unable to participate in practical jihad, I want to help you in the media jihad. Possibly Almighty Allah will give me a reward for my practical jihad. I know the Arabic language very well. You don't publish enough Arabic-language news. I can gather Arabic news on a daily basis and give it to you for publication. I always follow the Arabic-language media and keep myself informed about new developments. Please consider my request. Your mujahed brother, Muhammad Muhajir, hoping for your success.

A: Dear brother Muhammad Muhajir, peace be upon you! Many thanks for your offer of help within the field of media. I will forward your details to the Islamic Emirate's centre of the Cultural Commission. I hope they will contact you about the possibilities and ways of coordination. They will obtain your help in those areas which are easy for you. At the same time, you will be permanently in contact with the officials of the Media Department.

97

Q&A

A PERSONAL QUESTION

[*The types of questions that Zabiullah Mujahed answered on his Q&A page in 2012 and 2013 were highly varied, and he (or rather, his team) seems to have taken pains to address even small matters.*]

Taliban's Q&A section on Al-Emera, 13 April 2012

Question: Dear brother Mujahed, I want to ask you a quick question. If it isn't too difficult for you, could you tell me to which province you belong?

Answer: Due to security reasons, I cannot tell you my place of origin. Do please stop asking such questions in the present sensitive circumstances. Thanks.

98

WHO SHOULD BE EXECUTED

THE MUJAHEDEEN OR THE NATIONAL TRAITORS?

[*The closing months of 2012 saw a series of exchanges take place between former muja-hedeen figures (most prominently, Ustaz Sayyaf) in which the Taliban were challenged to provide a religious shari'a justification for the use of suicide bombing as a tactic. This was one of the first times that the Taliban had been forced into a defensive justification of a practice that had come to characterise how their attacks were often carried out. There are few details in this initial commentary piece, and it was the first of several such justi-fications issued.*]

Al-Emera (website), 14 September 2012

There is a great difference between suicide and martyrdom attacks, because suicide is self-killing, while martyrdom attack is the seeking of martyrdom willingly. The reason behind suicide is frustration with life, whereas the seeking of martyrdom is actually seeking the consent of Allah. It elevates the word of Allah and strengthens Muslims. The objective is to frighten the enemy, kill them and eventually defeat them.

There are frequent proofs in favour of martyrdom attacks in the Holy Qur'an, the traditions of the Holy Prophet (peace be upon him), the sayings and deeds of the holy companions. Various books have been written on this topic i.e. *al-amalyat al-istishhadia fit al-mezan al-fiqhi* written by Shaikh Nawwaf Al-Takrori and *al-adilla al-shar aiya fi jawaz al-amalyat al-istishhadia* written by Ali Bin Naif Al-Shahood.

A number of religious scholars have given verdicts in favour of martyrdom attacks. Some are as follows:

1. Al-Shaikh Nasir al-Omar
2. Al-Shaikh Ibn-i-Jabrin
3. Al-Shaikh Suleiman al-Alwan
4. Yusuf Bin Salih al-Ayiri

5. Abu Ishaq al-Hawini
6. Hamood Bin 'Uqla al-Shaiibi
7. Al-Shaikh Nasir-u-Din al-Albani
8. Dr Yusuf al-Qaradawi

On the other hand, the scholars have put strict conditions on martyrdom attacks. The first condition is the loftiness of target and abstaining from public casualties. Therefore in all the messages of Amir ul-Mu'mineen, it is repeatedly repeated to the mujahedeen to desist from public casualties and be cautious in choosing the target. But most of the time our sly enemy and their stooges blast bombs amid the masses and then blame the mujahedeen for it. They have done it in other countries as well.

It is a regret and even unjust that the people who call themselves mujahedeen do not talk about jihad in their meetings. They do not ponder the ways and means of ending the aggression. They do not say anything about the cruelties of the enemy over the masses. Instead they never give up backbiting the mujahedeen, who have taught an admonitory lesson to the enemy and whose cries have been heard worldwide.

99

A HISTORICAL TALE OF ATTRACTION TO JIHAD

[Allegory is a favoured way of communicating truths as practised by the Taliban through-out their front-facing media apparatus of magazines, videos and radio stations. This article was posted on the Taliban's sub-site devoted to jihad, and presents a traditional parallel for the contemporary world.]

Jabir Numani
Jihad sub-site, Al-Emera, 29 September 2013

The tale of Um Ibrahim al-Hashimiyya is one of the famous tales of jihad narrated by Abu Jaafar Ahmad bin Jaafar. There were a number of pious women in Basra. One of them was Um Ibrahim al Hashimiyya. An army of infidels attacked Muslim lands, and there was a need for fighters to deter the invaders. The governor of Basra was Abul Wahi bin Zaid Basri, who was also a renowned scholar. He encouraged people to go to jihad against the enemy. Um Ibrahim al-Ashmya, who was a pious woman, was also present on an occasion when the governor made his speech. During his speech Abdul Wahid talked about the heavenly virgins (Hoors), and also recited some poetry, hadiths and Qur'anic verses about their qualities. At the same time he invited Muslims to jihad and martyrdom.

When Um Ibrahim al-Hashimiyya heard his speech about heavenly virgins, she approached him and said, 'You know my son Ibrahim, who is a handsome young man. He is still unmarried and many wealthy people want him as their son-in-law. But the way you talked about the heavenly virgins has made an impression on me, and I want them for my son.'

Um Ibrahim al-Hashimiyya was a pious and rich lady. She granted 10,000 Dinars as a dowry of the heavenly virgins to Abdul Wahid and asked him to take her son Ibrahim to jihad. She prayed to Allah to grant her son martyrdom and bestow him with heavenly virgins. He would also advocate for his parents on the Day of Judgement.

Shaikh Abdul Wahid said, 'O, Um Ibrahim al-Hashimiyya, if you send your son to jihad and he is bestowed with martyrdom, he will be able to ask for forgiveness [on the Day of Judgement] not only for his parents but also for all members of the family.'

The woman summoned her son. He stood and told his mother that he was ready for jihad. She asked him whether he was ready to sacrifice his life for Allah and that he would marry the heavenly virgins. 'By Allah, I am ready to sacrifice my life for the sake of Allah,' he replied.

His mother pronounced, 'O Allah, as you are my witness, I want to sacrifice my son in your name so he can marry the heavenly virgins. He will not sin again. O Gracious Lord, please accept my sacrifice.' She offered 10,000 Dinars to Shaikh Abdul Wahid as dowry for the heavenly virgins. She told him to buy horses and weapons for himself and the mujahedeen, and she also gave a nice horse and weapon to her son.

When Shaikh Abdul Wahid and the other mujahedeen moved towards the frontline, they were joined by Ibrahim. On that occasion the reciters of the Holy Qur'an said the following verse: 'Indeed, Allah has purchased from the believers their lives and their properties [in exchange] for that they will have Paradise. They fight in the cause of Allah, so they kill and are killed. [It is] a true promise [binding] upon Him in the Torah and the Gospel and the Qur'an. And who is truer to his covenant than Allah? So rejoice in your transaction which you have contracted. And it is that which is the great attainment.'

Um Ibrahim al-Hashimiyya came out to bid farewell to the army of the mujahedeen. She gave a coffin and some perfume to her son. She instructed him to stay brave in the battle. Then she hugged him and kissed him on the forehead and said goodbye. 'My dear son, I pray that Allah will unite us on the day of judgement.'

According to Shaikh Abdul Wahid, when they arrived closer to the frontline, an advance party of mujahedeen went ahead. Ibrahim was part of the group. He killed many infidels and was martyred. When they returned to Basra, the Shaikh instructed his people not to inform Ibrahim's mother lest she lose heart. Many people had come out to receive the mujahedeen, Ibrahim's mother among them.

When she saw Abdul Wahid, she asked him, 'O, Abu Ubaida, if Almighty Allah has accepted my gift, then say congratulations to me. If He has returned my gift, then express your condolences.' He replied, 'By God, He accepted your gift. Your son has attained a true life and now he drinks and dines with other martyrs in Paradise.' When she heard this, she prostrated herself as a sign of thankfulness. She said, 'O Allah, I am thankful that you did not disappoint me and accepted my sacrifice.' Then she went back home.

The next day she came to Abdul Wahid and told him that she had seen her son in a dream. He was in gardens and palaces and seated on a throne of diamonds. He told her mother that the dowry she had offered was accepted and he was married to the heavenly virgins.

100

THE DIFFERENCE BETWEEN JIHAD AND FIGHTING

[The Taliban's sub-site devoted to jihad saw dozens of articles posted in the aftermath of the public challenges for them to declare their religious credentials in support of their jihad and the tactics they used in support of it. This article makes a distinction between jihad and merely fighting. Jihad is presented as the solution to many if not most problems.]

Muhammad
Jihad sub-site, Al-Emera, 15 May 2013

The main purpose of jihad is to end fighting. The forces and heroes of the Islamic army initiated jihad to bring peace. The ultimate aim of jihad is to stop the use of arms and weapons. When the Islamic system is faced with various challenges, Islam makes it obligatory upon faithful Muslims to take up arms and fight against trouble-makers until they surrender and put down their weapons, the fighting and excesses end and the way of preaching prevails. Armed jihad removes obstacles in the way of preaching, puts an end to the elements of violence and corruption and paves the way for the establishment of an Islamic system. Armed jihad also has a number of global aims. It has to fight against the forces of violence and corruption all over the world, liberate people from slavery and invite them to worship Allah, and establish the divine rule all over the world.

The reality of jihad in the light of the Qur'an: What kind of fighting and for what purpose? The Holy Qur'an says, 'In the way of Allah, fight against those who fight against you. Don't violate the appointed limits, Almighty Allah does not like the violators of limits. Kill them where you find them and expel them from where they have expelled you. Vice is worse than killing.'

In this verse Almighty Allah orders each Muslim and the entire Muslim nation not to be involved in any excesses, but He also orders them not to tolerate any atrocities. If others commit excesses and fight against you, then you should also fight against them and expel cruel people from the places, villages and country from where they had originally expelled you. You must kill them wherever you find them. You must understand that conversion of Muslims to polytheism and infidelity is worse than killing.

In the above-mentioned verse, Almighty Allah emphasises to Muslims to follow the principles of Islam and fight for the sake of Allah. Instead of following other principles, this fighting must be based on Islamic standards. This war must be for the protection of rights and gaining independence, and it must not cause atrocities of any kind or deprivation. This war must be for the enforcement of divine rule, not for the achievement of personal aid. This war is in fact a form of worship that will be rewarded in this world and the world hereafter. This is the war of the faithful, not the war of infidels. This war is just for the sake of Almighty Allah and has no other aim. Yes, this fight is in fact jihad for the sake of Almighty Allah and it is obligatory upon the Muslim nation.

On the basis of the above discussion we can say that jihad for the sake of Allah is in fact a practical and theoretical struggle against atrocities, oppression and imperialism. Jihad for the sake of Allah is the best guarantee of independence. Jihad for the sake of Allah is the best practical and theoretical defence for international peace, humanitarian security and sustainability. Jihad for the sake of Allah is the best way to the protection of rights and social justice. Jihad for the sake of Allah is a practical struggle for the enforcement of divine rule over human beings and the implementation of peaceful preaching. Jihad for the sake of Allah is an obligatory form of worship.

101

JIHAD IS A CLEAR AND ABSOLUTE OBLIGATION
OF ISLAM

[*In this overview of how the term jihad is used in the Qur'an, Jabir Numani collates the verses from Qur'anic suras and assembles a list of the various injunctions. This functions as a reference document on the Taliban's jihad sub-site.*]

Jabir Numani
Jihad sub-site, Al-Emera, 1 October 2013

According to reference, there are 484 verses about jihad in the Holy Qur'an. These chapters of the Holy Qur'an are about the concept of jihad: al-Baqarah, al-Imran, al-Mai'dah, al-Anfal, at-Tawbah, al-Hajj, al-Noor, Muhammad (al-Qitaal), al-Fath, al-Hujurat, al-Hadeed, al-Mujadilah, al-Hashr, al-Mumtahanah, as-Saff, at-Tahreem al-Adiyat, an-Nasr. (The concept of jihad has been explained in twenty chapters of the Qur'an.)

There are indications about jihad in the following Qur'anic chapters: Al-Baqarah, al-Imran, al-Mai'dah. In the Holy Qur'an, the concept of jihad has been discussed under the following ten themes:

1) The permission and obligation of jihad
2) The sanction of jihad
3) The tales of jihad
4) The importance of jihad, mujahedeen and martyrs
5) Rules and regulations of jihad
6) A call to jihad with the sacrifice of life and property
7) Consequences of negligence for the obligation of jihad
8) Hypocrites shirking jihad
9) Preparations for jihad
10) Special importance of the sale of property during jihad.

The jihadi battles mentioned in the Holy Qur'an:

1) The battle of Ibn Jahash
2) The battle of Badr
3) The battle of Banu Qaynuqa
4) The battle of Uhud
5) The battle of Hamra al-Asad
6) The (little) battle of Badr
7) The battle of Khandaq (Al-Ahzab)
8) The battle of Banu Qurayza
9) The battle of Hudaiyba
10) The conquest of Mecca
11) The battle of Khaybar
12) The battle of Tabouk
13) The battle of Hunayn
14) The battle of Ta'if
15) The battle of Banu Nazeer

The list of these fifteen battles proves that fighting is an Islamic obligation and form of worship. Fighting for the sake of Allah is the tradition of prophets. These battles also explain the concepts of jihad in accordance with the principles of shari'a.

The conditions of jihad:

A mujahed must be

1) a Muslim
2) male
3) a free man
4) sane
5) an adult
6) capable

The aims of jihad:

The Holy Qur'an has mentioned the following three aims of jihad:

1) The prevailing and protection of Islamic preaching
2) Helping weak Muslims
3) Countering a power that attacks Muslims

Jihad does not have an obvious allure like Ramadan, which is easily understood by Muslims as an obligation. However, jihad becomes attractive when the process of preaching faces challenges or an aggressive infidel power invades Muslim territory. In the former situation, jihad is optionally obligatory. If a particular group of Muslims is engaged in jihad, other Muslims don't have to join. But in the latter situation, jihad is obligatory for all men and women. Women can participate even without the permission of their husbands.

Reasons behind the obligation of jihad:

a) Almighty Allah elucidates the the obligatory status of jihad in verse 216 in chapter al-Baqarah of the Holy Qur'an: 'Fighting has been enjoined upon you while it is hateful to you. But perhaps you hate a thing and it is good for you; and perhaps you love a thing and it is bad for you. And Allah knows, while you know not.'

b) There are some verses that were revealed in Mecca about the non-obligatory status of armed jihad and insistence upon the regularity of prayers and *zakat*. As verse 77 of an-Nisa says:

'Have you not seen those who were told, "Restrain your hands [from fighting] and establish prayer and give *zakat*"?

But then when fighting was ordained for them, at once a party of them feared men as they fear Allah or with [even] greater fear. They said, "Our Lord, why have You decreed that we fight? If only You had postponed [it for] us for a short time." Say, the enjoyment of this world is little, and the Hereafter is better for he who fears Allah. And injustice will not be done to you, [even] as much as a thread [inside a date seed].'

c) There are verses that show that jihad is optionally obligatory for Muslims, i.e. all Muslims cannot go to jihad. As verse 122 of al-Tawbah states:

'And it is not for the believers to go forth [to battle] all at once. For they should separate from every division of them a group [remaining] to obtain understanding in the religion and warn their people when they return to them that they might be cautious.'

Al-Baqarah

The al-Baqarah chapter of the Qur'an, which has 286 verses, was revealed in Medina; 33 of its verses are about the concept of jihad. These verses explain four major areas:

1) the obligatory status of jihad
2) the philosophy of jihad
3) the importance of obedience to a commander and
4) suicidal attacks.

In this sacred chapter, the stories of the battles of Ibn Jahash, the peace [accord] of Hudaiyba and the martyrs of Badr are also mentioned. The following verses mention the concept of jihad: 109, 114, 153, 154, 157, 177, 190, 191, 191, 192, 193, 194, 195, 207, 216, 217, 218, 239, 243, 244, 245, 246, 247, 248, 249, 250, 251, 252, 261, 262, 273 and 286. There are five other verses that indicate jihad: 36, 58, 59, 89 and 214.

Al-Imran

In this chapter of the Qur'an, 58 of the 200 verses are about the concept of jihad. They explain many aspects of jihad, and we will discuss some of them.

1) The nature of relationships with infidels
2) Reorganising after suffering a defeat
3) In these verses the battles of Uhud, al Hamra, al Asad and Badr are mentioned. The verses about jihad are: 12, 13, 28, 110, 112, 118 to 129, 139 to 175, 195 to 200. These verses offer an indication towards the concept of jihad: 19, 52, 57, 71, 100, 101, 102, 104, 130, 131, 132 and 134.

An-Nisa'

This is among the chapters of the Holy Qur'an that were revealed in Medina. Of its 176 verses, 41 are about jihad. These verses elaborate on:

1) Jihad for the support of the oppressed
2) The superiority of the mujahedeen over those sitting at home
3) The inability and the eventual fate of those who refrain from joining jihad
4) Hypocrisy, escaping jihad and showing off
5) The divine way for preventing aggression or being besieged by infidels

In this chapter the battles of Hamra al-Asad and little Badr are also mentioned. These are the verses related to jihad: 29–84, 88–91, 94–104, 138–147.

Al-Mai'dah

Al-Mai'dah was revealed in Medina, and it has 120 verses, 20 of which are about jihad. These verses are particularly focused on:

1) The definition of the party of Allah
2) Categories of enemies.

This chapter also mentions the conquest of Mecca. These verses are about jihad: 2, 3, 11–26, 35, 51–56, 86. These verses point to the concept of jihad: 57, 58, 59, 60, 61, 26, 23, 27

Al-Anfaal

0/6Al-Anfaal was revealed in Medina and has 75 verses. These are entirely about the concept of jihad and are focused on two areas:
1) Offensive jihad
2) The matter of goods seized in war.

JIHAD IS A CLEAR AND ABSOLUTE OBLIGATION OF ISLAM

In this sacred chapter the battle of Badr is described in full. Al-Badr is the second name of this chapter, which describes twenty benefits of jihad, twenty-five merits of mujahedeen and fourteen principles of war.

Twenty benefits of jihad:

1) It leads people towards the righteous path (verse 5)
2) It leads to the prevalence of Islam (verse 8)
3) Humans meet the angels (verse 109)
4) Almighty Allah provides divine help (verse 11)
5) Achieving the love of and nearness to Allah (verse 17)
6) Gives life to human beings (verse 24)
7) Almighty Allah provides food and shelter because of jihad (verses 26 and 84)
8) Almighty Allah forgives one's sins (verse 29)
9) Almighty Allah grants a mujahed the power of decision-making and wisdom (verse 29)
10) Infidels suffer many financial losses (they become bankrupt) (verse 36)
11) Virtue is differentiated from vice (verse 37)
12) Infidels are weakened (verse 39)
13) Halal booty becomes achievable (verse 37)
14) Infidels receive a final warning (verse 42)
15) Almighty Allah gives various good omens to Muslims
16) Muslims develop and find success (verse 45)
17) Muslims maintain clout over infidels (verse 60)
18) Muslims establish unity among themselves (verse 63)
19) Almighty Allah grants them skills (verse 65)
20) Their faith is improved (verse 74)

Twenty-five merits of mujahedeen:

(1) Piety (verse 1)
(2) Mutual unity (verse 1)
(3) Obedience to Almighty Allah and His prophet (verse 1)
(4) Fear of Almighty Allah (verse 2)
(5) Relationship with the Holy Qur'an (verse 2)
(6) Boldness (verse 2)
(7) Regularity of prayers (verse 3)
(8) Unity for the sake of Allah (verse 3)
(9) Demanding help from Allah (verse 9)
(10) Resilience (verse 11)
(11) Immediate response to the call of jihad (verse 15)

(12) Obedience to the emir (if he does not violate the shari'a) (verse 20)
(13) Thankfulness (verse 26)
(14) Avoidance of the vices (verse 27)
(15) Sacrifice of offspring and property (verse 28)
(16) Making efforts to defeat the infidels' arrogance (verse 39)
(17) The distribution of collective properties in accordance to the principles of shari'a law (verse 41)
(18) Avoiding all types of disputes (verse 46)
(19) Being patient (verse 46)
(20) Avoiding arrogance and extravagance (verse 47)
(21) Consistently expanding the culture and power of jihad (verse 20)
(22) Keeping an eye on new developments (verses 21–26)
(23) Preaching the cause of jihad (verse 65)
(24) Avoiding worldly lust (verse 67)
(25) Avoiding ethnic, linguistic and territorial identities and giving preference to Islamic unity (verse 72)

Fourteen principles of war:

(1) Fight directly and don't attack from behind (verse 51)
(2) Always obey Almighty Allah and His prophet on the battlefield (verse 20)
(3) Obedience to the commander (verse 24)
(4) When a tactical idea comes to mind, implement it immediately (verse 24)
(5) Never commit corruption in matters of goods and property (verse 27)
(6) [Unintelligible]
(7) Always remember Almighty Allah (verse 45)
(8) Keep the army united (verse 46)
(9) Kill the infidels and don't backtrack (verse 57)
(10) Always keep the enemy under pressure (verse 65)
(11) Always have one group ready for jihad (verse 65)
(12) When you find the enemy, first shed their blood and then make them prisoners (verse 67)
(13) Do not delay when the oppressed and miserable demand your help (verse 72)
(14) When the infidels are united you should also remain united among yourselves (verse 72)

Al-Tawbah

Al-Tawbah was revealed in Medina, and has 192 verses, of which 29 are about jihad, focusing on:

1) Seven benefits and sanctions of fighting

2) Superiority of jihad
3) Reasons for jihad against the people of the book
4) Hypocrites evading jihad and their excuses

The conquest of Mecca and battles of Hunayn and Badr have also been mentioned in this chapter. These verses are about jihad: 1–20, 74, 74, 81–96, 106–112 and 117–123.

Al-Hajj

This chapter was revealed in Medina and has 178 verses. Jihad is discussed in 17 verses, which focus on the following:

1) The philosophy of jihad
2) Permission for jihad for the sake of the oppressed.

According to *tafseer*, the battle of Badr is also mentioned in this chapter. The relevant verses are: 19–24, 38–41, 55, 58–62, 78.

Al-Noor

This chapter was revealed in Medina and comprises 64 verses, of which four verses (53, 54, 55 and 26) discuss two themes:

1) The caliphate
2) Obedience to the emir

Al-Ahzab

Al-Ahzab was revealed in Medina. Of its 73 verses, 20 are about jihad, and they elaborate on:

1) The battle of Ahzaab and many jihad-related issues
2) The battle of Qurayza and the Almighty Allah's help
3) The punishment for blaspheming against the Prophet.

These are the relevant verses: 9–27, 20–62.

Muhammad

This chapter was revealed in Medina and comprises 38 verses, of which 32 verses (1–13 and 20–38) are about jihad and elaborate on:

1) Sanctions of prisoners
2) Hypocrites escaping jihad

3) A call for spending one's wealth for the sake of jihad.

Al-Fatah

0/6 This chapter was revealed in Medina and its 29 verses focus on the issues of jihad. The themes of allegiance, the Hudaiyba peace agreement and the conquests of Khaybar and Mecca are mentioned in the chapter.

Al-Hujurat

This chapter was revealed in Medina and has 18 verses, of which five verses (6, 9, 10, 14 and 15) discuss investigating the enemy and peace among Muslim fighters.

Al-Hadeed

This chapter was revealed in Medina, and four of its 29 verses are about jihad and mention the conquest of Mecca and the Hudaiyba peace agreement. The verses in question are 10, 11, 91 and 25.

Al-Mujadilah

This chapter was revealed in Medina and has 22 verses, of which three (20, 21 and 22) touch upon jihad. This chapter includes a description of Allah's party: Hizbullah.

Al-Hashar

This chapter was revealed in Medina and comprises 24 verses, 17 of which (numbers 1 through 17) focus on the infidels' methods of fighting and the technicalities of property. There are also references to the battles of Banu Nazeer and Banu Qaynuqa.

Al-Mumtahanah

This chapter was revealed in Medina. It explains espionage and other key laws governing war. It also cites the conquest of Mecca. Twelve of the thirteen verses of this chapter are about jihad: the relevant verses are 1 through 11, and verse 13.

Al-Saff

This chapter was revealed in Medina. Twelve of its fourteen verses discuss order in the ranks of jihad, the importance of unity among the mujahedeen, and jihad is described as a successful trade. These verses are 1 to 4, and 8 to 14.

JIHAD IS A CLEAR AND ABSOLUTE OBLIGATION OF ISLAM

At-Tahreem

This chapter was revealed in Medina and has nine verses. The last verse mentions how jihad is obligatory against infidels and hypocrites.

Al-Adiyat

This chapter was revealed in Medina. Six of its eleven verses (1–6) discuss rearing horses for battle.

An-Nasr

This three-verse chapter was revealed in Medina and describes the principles of conquests.

The list of jihad-related verses:

Chapter name	Jihad-related verses
Al-Baqarah	33
Al-Imran	57
An-Nisa'	41
Al-Mai'dah	20
Al-Anfal	75
Al-Baraa	92
Al-Hajj	17
Al-Noor	4
Al-Ahzab	22
Muhammad	32
Al-Fath	29
Al-Hujurat	5
Al-Hadeed	4
Al-Mujadilah	3
Al-Hashr	17
Al-Mumtahanah	12
Al-Saff	11
At-Tahreem	1
Al-Adiyat	6
An-Nasr	3
Total jihad-related verses:	424

If the verses of the chapter *al-Nahal* are added to this list, the number of verses increases to 485.

102

A NUMBER OF IMPORTANT FACTORS FOR JIHAD

[*In this commentary article published on the Taliban's jihad sub-site, Aziz warns against the enemy's attempts to win over the population to their cause. He argues that for the Taliban to be good at that would be an important part of their jihad.*]

Khalil Aziz
Jihad sub-site, Al-Emera, 16 November 2014

It is striking to note that despite all their abilities, barbarism and combat strategies, the US, NATO and their puppets could not succeed in harming the ongoing jihad of the mujahed people of Afghanistan.

They failed to discredit the mujahedeen and their sacred destiny. They couldn't forge a gulf between the mujahedeen and the common people of Afghanistan. They could not achieve the target of turning the people and the mujahedeen against each other.

I have pondered a lot over why the US, NATO and the puppet regime of Kabul failed to create misunderstandings between the mujahedeen and the people. I have found the following reasons:

On the one hand, the people of Afghanistan uphold their self-esteem and respect. Religion and bravery have a special place for them. The people of Afghanistan hate the measures taken by the US and its infidel allies over the last fourteen years. They consider these measures against their religion and honour. They are not ready to accept the dirty steps of foreign troops on their land.

On the other hand, the mujahedeen are aware of the enemy's conspiracies. They strive not to allow the oppressors to create any kind of distance between the mujahedeen and the people. In all official announcements of the Islamic Emirate and the statements of its leadership, it has been emphasised to the mujahedeen to deal with people in a kind manner and to avoid any kind of harsh treatment, and that they should develop a close relationship with people.

General Joseph Dunford, the former US commander, admitted in an interview that it is necessary to win people's hearts and minds in order to win the Afghan war.

He said that had they treated the people in accordance with their traditions, they would have won the war ten years ago. According to the general, if the Taliban treat people respectfully and win their hearts and minds, they will definitely win the war.

Dear mujahedeen brothers, let's discuss some important points in the interest of jihad and the mujahedeen. We will adopt these points practically if it is feasible.

Firstly, every phase of jihad needs understanding and comprehension. It is very important for the mujahedeen to understand the reasons and factors behind every phase of jihad. For example, the nature, expansion and capacity of the anti-NATO jihad is different from jihad against the Soviets. It is not possible to implement exactly the tactics which we implemented against the Soviets in fighting against NATO. During the anti-Soviet jihad, the whole world supported the mujahedeen. But in the current jihad against the US and NATO, no country is ready to support the mujahedeen because they are all afraid of the US. It is also difficult for people to support the mujahedeen openly as they did during the jihad against the Soviets. The people are also under the pressure of oppressive imperialists. Undoubtedly, their emotional support is with the mujahedeen. Without their support it would not be possible for the mujahedeen to continue the present jihad. They provide food and drink to the mujahedeen. They also provide them safe sanctuary and protect them from the enemy's raids and operations. They protect the mujahedeen at the cost of their lives. The mujahedeen should not make demands of people if they don't directly participate in jihad or are unable to give open support to our cause. If the mujahedeen resort to force and violence, they will most likely suffer disadvantages instead of benefits. God forbid that the mujahedeen lose the moral support of the people.

Secondly, orders must not be implemented in areas that are not under complete control. The mujahedeen should not hurriedly implement the Islamic Emirate's ordinances in those areas that are not under their complete control or where they only have partial control at night and where the enemy authorities return during the day. The enemy manipulates such a situation and spreads propaganda among the masses. They tell people that though the Taliban are unable to control the area, they still want to implement strict orders over them. If they gain complete control they will enforce an even stricter order.

The third point is about forcing people to give financial assistance and privileges. If the mujahedeen impose themselves as guests upon the local people or force them to give financial support, it will cause irrevocable damage. The people of Afghanistan are culturally hospitable and love their religion. They do all this voluntarily. But they will not do it by force. If they are forced, it will be their last time. So the mujahedeen must not force people towards hate. In this regard the Islamic Emirate's charter is very clear and all of us must follow it. It is also not allowed for the mujahedeen to organise attacks against the enemy from public places, because the enemy will then target people as part of its revenge. These kind of practices enrage people. It is better that the mujahedeen never organise this kind of attack.

Fourthly, the mujahedeen must adhere to the cultural traditions and customs of the local people. If the mujahedeen want to implement reforms, they should adhere to local traditions and customs. They should treat local people in the light of their religious rites and traditions. In every area the mujahedeen should adopt the locals' manner of dress. If they find something against the norms of shari'a, they should firstly consult with the local ulemaa and tribal elders and then take any measures. The locals will not mind this kind of treatment, and at the same time the possibility of negative propaganda will also be avoided. As once the Prophet addressed Aisha and said, 'If your nation were not newly converted to Islam, I would demolish the Kaaba and rebuild it according to the Abrahamic architectural design.' So if the Prophet can give up his wish to rebuild the Kaaba and compromise just to avoid the reaction of his people, then the mujahedeen, who consider themselves followers of the Prophet, should also accept compromises.

The fifth point is about treating people kindly. The mujahedeen must avoid harsh treatment and should not forcefully impose something upon people which they are not capable of doing. In other words the mujahedeen must not impose their will upon people by force. People who are unwilling to accept our demands should not be considered as enemies and must not be punished. As Ibn Abbas quotes, that once the Prophet on the occasion of Hajj asked me to bring some stones. He brought seven stones and handed them over to him. After receiving the stones, he said, 'You must avoid harshness and extremism in religion. The followers of the former religions faced destruction because they practised harshness and extremism.' Once an illiterate person urinated in the courtyard of an-Nabawi Mosque. When the companions of the Prophet wanted to stop him, the Prophet instructed them to let him be and pour water on that spot later. He explained that he was sent to spread the message with kindness, not with harshness.

Our mujahedeen brothers, we must adopt an approach of softness and kindness and build friendships with people. We must not compel them to become our enemies. In the battlefield our Prophet always adopted an approach of kindness and softness. We also must follow the same path. We must avoid revenge and being dictatorial. We have learnt from the experiences of the last thirteen years that we must practise ultimate restraint and caution. People must not be killed just on the basis of doubt and suspicion. The mujahedeen should also be very careful when they punish a tribal leader who has a large number of followers. If the mujahedeen punish such a person, his followers will definitely rise up against them and cause a lot of trouble. Hazrat Umar asked permission from the Prophet to sever the head of Abdullah bin Ubay bin Salool, the notorious hypocrite. But the Prophet did not allow him. On that occasion he said, 'Let him live, otherwise people will say that Muhammad kills his own companions.' Likewise once the Prophet prayed to Almighty Allah to convert one of the two Umars (Umar Farooq and Abu Jahl) to Islam. Both were powerful tribal elders. After that the light of Islam revealed in the heart of Hazrat Umar Farooq and he converted to Islam. Islam progressed rapidly after his conversion.

In summary, for the achievement of the goals of jihad (the establishment of a true Islamic system) close understanding and cooperation between the mujahedeen and our people is necessary. Without the cooperation of our people, all our success and conquests will be temporary. At present, a powerful imperialist power has prepared plans to take over our country. For this purpose it has established military bases and signed a security treaty with the puppet regime. I believe that the colonialists will no more engage in active warfare against the mujahedeen. Instead, they will use their technological prowess and the forces of the puppet regime as a shield. At the same time they will create misunderstandings between the people and the mujahedeen. So, my mujahedeen brothers, please be aware of the traps of the oppressors. You should be ready to bear all kinds of hardship, but always be tolerant towards your people and try to ignore their mistakes. Respect those who cooperate with you, and at the same time try to make friends with those who have joined the ranks of the enemy.

103

RESTRICTIONS AND CONSTRAINTS IN JIHAD (2014)

[This multi-part article covers a number of constraints and laws covering the practice of jihad as designated by prominent Islamic scholars. Extracts selected for this volume include advice about when fighting is permissible, which categories of individuals are to be protected on the battlefield and whether maiming or decapitation are permitted to be carried out by fighters of the mujahedeen.]

Mufti Abu Muhammad Haqqani
Jihad sub-site, Al-Emeram, 17 May 2014

We will discuss the restrictions and constraints to be practised in the process of divine jihad. For the better fulfilment of our duties, we will discuss the following contexts of restrictions and constraints:

A) The forbidden months:

Rajab al-Murajab, Dhu al-Qi'ada, Dhu al-Hija and Muharram al-Haram are the four months in which jihad is forbidden on the basis of the following Qur'anic verses: verse 36 of chapter al-Tawbah, and verse 217 of chapter al-Baqarah. Various scholars, including Imam Ahmad Hanbal, have expressed their opinions in this regard. But later on these Qur'anic verses about the forbidden months were nullified. The following verse permitted jihad in these months and at the same time nullified the previous verses that had forbidden it (verse 5, chapter al-Tawbah). Another proof is that the Prophet Muhammad participated in the battle of Ta'if in the month of Dhu al-Qi'ada. This means that jihad was forbidden during the sacred periods in the early days of Islam. But later on, specially after the battle of Ta'if, the verses that forbade jihad were nullified and jihad became permissible during all months. However, while jihad is not forbidden in these months, the launching or initiation of jihad is still not allowed in these months. With the reference of Hazrat Jabir, we know that Prophet Muhammad used to abstain from jihad during these months, with the exception of defensive fights. At the onset of the sacred month he would always stop fighting until the end of the month (Akhraja Iban Jarer Al-Tibri 300/4 Dar al-Maarif).

It was mentioned earlier that the ban on jihad during the four sacred months has been explained by various high-ranking scholars. They have proved that the ban originated in the initial period of Islam and was later annulled by Qur'anic verses. We do not give importance to the opinion of Imam al-Sarkhasi, who claims in his book *Al-Mabsoot* that the ban is still in place and valid. On the contrary, we give importance to the opinion of Mujahid who says that the ban has been nullified by Qur'anic verses and the practical participation by the Prophet in a battle during a sacred month. During these sacred months it was forbidden for the mujahedeen to initiate aggression. However, when the enemy launched an attack, then the mujahedeen were allowed to wage defensive jihad. This opinion is unequivocally supported by all scholars. For reference please see the following books: Al-Mabsoot, 10/3,2, Wa Nihayat al Muhtaj, 8/48, Rauzata Talibin, 204/10, Kashaf al Qinaa 37/3.

The battle of Ta'if was fought during one of the sacred months. The exact month is unknown, but it is generally believed that it was fought in the month of Dhu al-Qi'ada. But Imam al-Sarkhasi in his book *Al-Mabsoot* claims that it was fought in the months of Muharram and Safar. This matter needs further research. However, it is clear that the battle of Ta'if was fought during one of the four sacred months and it is suffice to support our claim that jihad is permissible in these months.

The killing which is forbidden during war

During the hours of jihad, the mujahedeen are not allowed to kill children, women, disabled people or those who are unable to fight against the mujahedeen. This is the unanimous decision of all scholars of jurisprudence. They are all of the opinion that the aforementioned people must not be killed during a jihad. This is also supported by the following hadith which has reached us with the reference of Hazrat Abdulla bin Umar: Once the Prophet came across a woman who was killed in the fighting. Afterwards he forbade the killing of children and women and those who were unable to fight. It is a unanimous decision that non-combatants, i.e. children and women, are not to be killed in jihad.

The majority of scholars are of the opinion that women, children and elderly persons who are unable to fight must not be killed during jihad. In his book *Al-Mosou'a al-Faqih*, Mr Mujahid quotes the following hadith: 'The Prophet says don't kill women, children and elderly people.' This hadith has also been quoted by Ibn Abbas, Umar Farooq and Abu Bakr Siddiq. The renowned scholar al-Tahawi, with reference to Ibn Buraida, writes that: 'When the Prophet would send a group of fighters to a battle, he would instruct them not to kill elderly people because, like women, they were unable to fight.' After the fight, when the Prophet found a woman who was killed, he said that women are not to be killed because they don't fight.

But Imam al-Shafi'i says that during fighting, elderly persons should also be killed. For this statement he gives the reference of the following tradition of the prophet:

'Abi Burda, with reference to Abi Moosa, says that after the battle of Hunayn the Prophet sent Abu Aamir as a commander of an army to Taus, where Duraid bin as-Simma came across and killed him. With the help of Allah he defeated the enemy. So some people prefer this tradition and say that during fighting the killing of elderly men is not forbidden.'

In his book *Sharh al-Ma'ani*, Imam al-Tahawi writes that an explanation of the two types of hadith of the Prophet is necessary. According to one hadith, the killing of an elderly man is forbidden; while according to the other tradition, it is permissible. Either of the two traditions must be implemented in the relevant and particular circumstance. The Prophet has forbidden the killing of those elderly men who are unable to fight or give advice about fighting to others. But those elderly men who give advice to the enemy should be killed. Duraid belonged to this category of elderly men, which is why he was killed, though he did not directly participate in the fighting. Advice is even more effective than actually fighting.

The Prophet similarly ordered that women would not be killed because they did not participate in the fighting. But when they fight, then they must be killed. Imam Jafar al-Tahawi says that they killed Duraid bin as-Simma on the basis of the aforementioned factors. So if an elderly man has special expertise in the affairs of combat and advises the enemy, then he must be killed. The same order is for those women who are able to participate in the fighting or give advice to the enemy.

Just as in the case of an elderly man, there are differences among scholars about those who are permanently disabled, paralysed, or those whose right foot or right hand has been chopped off. According to scholars, the priests of Christian churches and the rabbis of Jewish synagogues who don't mix with the common people are also exempted from being killed and the mujahedeen should avoid them.

In his book *Ma'ani al-Athar*, Imam al-Tahawi notes the following hadith with reference to Ibn Abbas:

'When the Prophet would send an army, he would instruct them not to kill religious leaders who run their places of worship when they remain away from other people and don't harm Muslims. Also those people will not be killed who are the dwellers of isolated mountainous areas and don't mix with the rest of the population. But those persons will be killed who are sometimes conscious and sometimes unconscious. They will be killed while they are conscious. According to the scholars of the Hanbali school, those people will also be killed who are ill at present, but will fight against the mujahedeen if they are healthy. But those permanent patients will be exempted who have no chance of healing again and are doomed to die.'

There are differences of opinion among the scholars of Shafi'i and Hanbali schools about the killing of farmers. According to Hanbali scholars, those farmers who don't participate in combat against the mujahedeen should not be killed. Imam Awza'i also supported them in this matter. They base their argument on the instruction of the second caliph Hazrat Umar, who would prohibit the killing of non-combatant farmers. On the other hand, Imam al-Shafi'i says that all polytheists deserve to be killed even if they are non-combatant farmers. If they pay *jizya* tax, then they would be exempted from the killing. *Al-Mughni wa al-Sharh al-Kabeer* are the two well-known books of the Hanbali school and they base their argument on the teachings of Caliph Umar, who would instruct the mujahedeen not to kill farmers when they would occupy a new territory, because they were non-combatants like the elderly men, children, women and priests. We searched other books of the Hanbali school but failed to find any considerable references. But the methods of Ashaab (the Prophet's companions) are enough for our guidance, and the Hanafi school does not contradict it. The killing of the infidels' ambassadors, diplomats, consuls or political envoys, when they possess recognised documents such as visas and passports, is also not allowed. In his book *Zad al-Ma'ad*, Allama Ibn Qayyim al-Jawziyya writes that infidels' envoys must not be killed. As Abu Sufyaan was an envoy of the infidels and Allah's Prophet did not kill him, because he was the representative of his nation. Imam Nawawi also writes that the killing of infidels' envoys is not allowed. All these arguments are based on the following hadith of the Abu Daud: 'When the envoys of Muslima, the liar, came up, the Prophet asked them what their message was. They said that their message was exactly like his message. The Prophet replied that by Allah if envoys were not exempted from killing, he would definitely have chopped off their heads.' The above-mentioned people are exempted from killing provided that they don't participate in combat operations against the mujahedeen. If they do participate, then they will also be killed; as in the case of Banu Qurayza, when a woman dropped the grinding stone of a flour mill upon Khaled bin Suwaid and killed him. When she was arrested she was killed. In his book, *Al-Mawsou'a*, Ibn Qudamah writes that if these persons participate in combat action, then their killing is permissible. Awza'i, Sufyan Sauri and Lais also support this statement. Likewise in the land of war (Dar al-Harb), all those people will be killed who have a free opinion, including a king. The *Mawsou'at al-Faqih* writes that all able infidels, including the deaf and lame (whose left hand or foot is cut off), will be killed. This is because these people have the potential to fight against the mujahedeen while riding. However, if a mujahed kills one of the aforementioned non-combatant people, he will only ask for a verbal pardon. He is not obliged to pay compensation, because the lives of infidels are guaranteed only after completing an agreement. In the battlefield the killing of close blood relatives is also not allowed. The Hanafi school says that the killing of close blood relatives (polytheist father, grandfather etc.) is not allowed; instead they should be kept busy in action. According to the scholars of the Shafi'i school, the killing of relatives is not good as the Prophet stopped Abu Bakr from killing his son Abdul Rahman during the battle of Uhud. But if they use abusive language against the Prophet, then killing them is permissible.

Deception, trickery and maiming

After deception and trickery, we reach the topic of maiming. Here we will explain maiming in the light of shari'a. Is there any restriction in this regard? Is it allowed to chop off the head of an infidel or blacken his face? What do the scholars of jurisprudence say in this regard? The chopping of someone's nose, ear, tongue, hands, feet and other parts of body and disfigurement is called maiming (Musla). In the Al-Jauhar Naira Sharha Mukhtasar Al-Qudri v. 7, p. 107 it has been defined as when prisoners' hands, feet, nose, ear, tongue and other parts are chopped off before killing or releasing them. Some scholars describe Musla as the following: prisoners' decapitation, tearing off their bellies or chopping off their private parts are not allowed. Musla is an undesirable act when the enemy is overwhelmed or taken as prisoner. However, it makes no difference before that. In his book *Al-Ghinayya*, Allama Al-Ghinayi writes that when someone's face is blackened with charcoal, or he is disfigured by chopping off his nose or other parts, it is called Musla. In *Al-Mawsou'at al-Faqih*, he explains that when someone initiates this act it is called Musla. If someone commits this kind of aggression against another nation, and afterwards the members of that nation chop off his parts of the body, then instead of Musla it is called revenge (*qisas*). The renowned books of Islamic jurisprudence state that Musla is forbidden against the living and dead. This matter has also been explained in the following books: Al-Mabsoot 10/5, Wa Tabyan al Haqayaq 244/3, Jawahir al Akleel 254/1. About the ban on Musla, the Islamic scholars have given the following references: Imran bin Hussain quotes, 'The Prophet would forbid us from Musla and persuade us to participate in charity.'

Similarly Safwan bin Assal quotes in the Sunan Ibn Majah, 'The Prophet (peace be upon him) sent us to Syria. He ordered us to fight against those who were infidels but to avoid Musla.' Hasham bin Zaid says: 'Once Anas and I visited Hakam bin Ayoob. Anas saw a youth who was shooting a chicken for the sake of practising. Anas told them that the Prophet had forbidden using animals for target practice.' Abdullah bin Umar says: 'The Prophet would curse those who committed an act of Musla against animals.' Hanafi scholars and the scholars of other schools say that when the infidels are taken as prisoners, their Musla is forbidden (*haram*). In Islamic shari'a, there is no legal permission for this act. But it make no difference if their head or some parts of their body are cut off in the battlefield before their defeat. Chopping off their hands, feet, fingers, tearing out their bellies and pulling out their eyes is all called Musla. These acts cause torture to the infidels and it is not allowed in shari'a. This has been explained in the following books: Haashya ibn Aabdeen, 3/224, wa Tabayan al-haqayaq, 224/3, Jawahir al-Akleel, 254/1.

Yes! In the initial period of Islam, the Areena incident happened which has been reported in detail in the hadith, when the people of the tribe killed and maimed the Prophet's shepherds and drove away the camels and cattle. In response the Prophet (peace be upon him) also chopped off the hands and feet of the tribe of Areena and then pulled their eyes out. According to scholars, the tradition was annulled after this incident and the Prophet forbade the act of amputation, as it has been explained in the al-Inaaya Sharh al-Hidaya, V. 7, p. 451 (the explanation is in Arabic). The same explanation is also given in the Sharh al-Ahkaam al-Ahkaa of Umdat ul Ahkam v. 3 p. 86. According to this hadith, the act of Musla is banned.

Removing the enemy's head

In the previous article we discussed the banning of Musla and insisted that Muslims should avoid it. We also discuss whether it is allowed for a Muslim to sever the head of an infidel and take it away to show his commander. Just as infidels are thirsty for their blood, Muslims also want to avenge the infidel armies who have occupied their land and inflicted many atrocities upon them. But it does not mean that they are allowed to cross the limits of shame and disrespect, just for the sake of revenge. Rather they are allowed to defend their right of property and honour. Chopping off and taking away the enemy's head to the commander is a controversial matter among scholars; according to some, it is permissible; while others say that it is not allowed. Scholars of the Shafi'i and Hanbali schools of thought say that severing the head of an infidel and taking it away is an impermissible act. They give the reference of Aqaba bin Amir which has been mentioned in the Sunan al-Kubra of Behaqi. According to Aqaba bin Amir, when Umarau bin al-Aasl and Sherjeel bin Hasan gave him the severed head of Denaaq to take to Hazrat Abu Bakar Siddiq. When he saw the head of Denaaq, Abu Bakr criticised this and refused to accept it. Aqaba told him that the infidels were also doing the same things to Muslims. In response the caliph said that he would never follow the traditions of the Romans and Persians. Just sending a written message to him would be enough. So this proves that taking away the severed head of an infidel is forbidden. According to the scholars of the Maliki school of jurisprudence, it is forbidden to take away the severed head of an infidel from the place of his killing to another place. Likewise taking it away for the sake of showing it to a commander is also forbidden because it is an act of Musla (Jawahir al-Akleel, v. 1, p. 254; al-Mughni, v. 8, p. 494). According to scholars of the Hanafi school, as it has been mentioned in the al-Dur al-Mukhtar, v. 3, p. 225, taking away the severed head of a commander is permissible if this act enrages his followers. To support this, scholars of the Hanafi school give reference to the battle of Badr when Ibn Masud brought the severed head of Abu Jahl and dropped it in front of the Prophet.

Face blackening

The majority of scholars agree that blackening someone's face as part of a punishment is not permissible. The face is the best and most beautiful part of a human body. It is the centre of all the senses. Almighty Allah created it and kindly bestowed it upon humans. Making any kind of changes will be considered an act of maiming which is forbidden. This matter has been explained in the following sources: al-Sarkhasi 16/145, Wa Tabayan al-Haqayaq, 3/170, Fasool al Istroshni fi al-taaziz, 30, Jawahir al-Akleel, 2/225, Wal Kharshi, 7/152, Kashaf al-Qina'a, 6/124, 125, Awn al-Ma'bood.

Different materials can be used for blackening someone's face, but generally the black material at the bottom of a cooking pot is used for this purpose. The *Mawsou'at al-Faqih*, v. 11, p. 353 mentions that the majority of scholars of the Hanafi and Maliki schools say that this is not permissible. However, scholars of the Shafi'I and Hanbali schools say that it is permissible in certain contexts. Imam al-Sarkhasi argues that the punishment of blackening someone's face is impermissible because it is an act of Musla (Al-Mabsoot Al-Sarkhasi, 16/145). Imam al-Sarkhasi argues that blackening someone's face with the black stuff from a cooking pot is impermissible because it is an act of maiming which is not allowed in Islam, and the Prophet of Islam has forbidden it. According to him, even the maiming by a biting dog is not allowed (Al-Mabsoot Al-Sarkhasi, 16/145, Akhraja al-Tibrani, 1/100, Al-Haisami fi Majma al-Zawayad, 6/249, Asnad al-munqata). Scholars of the Hanafi and Maliki schools insist that blackening faces of criminals is an impermissible act and the authorities must avoid it. While scholars of the Shafi'i and Hanbali schools believe that blackening the faces of criminals is allowed because the authorities can better judge the situation and status of the criminals as to when this kind of punishment is suitable (Nihayat al Muhtaj 8/16, Asni al-Matalib, 4/162, Hashya al Jama Alaa Sharha al Manhaj, 5/164, Mataalib Aula al-Nahya, 6/223, 110).

104

SEVEN THREATS TO JIHAD

[*In this commentary article on the Taliban's jihad sub-site, Numani outlines some of the challenges that jihad faces. Note that all the threats identified are internal struggles within the Muslim community. Many of them relate to differing conceptions of the purpose of jihad between different communities or individuals, but the author cautions readers to listen to 'the unanimous decision of the entire umma that jihad is an obligation.'*]

Jabir Numani
Jihad sub-site, Al-Emera, 3 September 2014

There are many threats against jihad for the sake of Allah. Only seven will be discussed here. The first three are theoretical, while the later four are practical threats.

1. Rejection of jihad

Some people call themselves Muslims but they vehemently reject the concept of jihad. They claim that jihad is not valid or possible any more. But it is the unanimous decision of the entire umma that jihad is an obligation like Salat (prayers), and those who reject it are infidels.

2. Rejection of offensive jihad (the real jihad)

These people apparently look very pious but are under the influence of the infidels. They reject an important obligation of Islam. They are apologetic about the glories and pride of Islam. In fact, they reject the concept of jihad. As they are cowards, they try to find different explanations and reject the concept of jihad that has been proved by the Holy Qur'an and hadith (the Prophet's traditions). The Prophet, his companions (Ashaab) and previous generations of Muslims have practically participated in jihad. But unfortunately the approach of some people towards Islam is limited and they have deprived themselves of the blessings of the rewards of jihad and also try to stop others from joining it. May Almighty Allah give them sanity and guide them towards the righteous path!

3. Changing the meaning of the concept of jihad

The Jews recited the verses of the Torah with correct meanings, but they explained it with additions as required. In exactly the same way today the verses of the Holy Qur'an about the concept of jihad are being recited with correct meanings. Some people are not ready to explain the concept of jihad as it was explained by Prophet Muhammad himself, and how his followers practised jihad. The concept of jihad used to be unequivocal. It was easily understood by small children and adults. In the time of Prophet Muhammad the meaning of jihad was fighting against the enemies of Islam.

These are the three theoretical threats to jihad. Dear reader, look around and see if these threats are stopping you from joining jihad. If you find these, immediately remove them. If a farmer does not clear the extra grass from the farm, his yield will reduce to zero. Jihad is the only way for Muslims to maintain their glory and success. There are some threats which destroy the very foundations of the concept of jihad. They want to defeat Islam and Muslims. These threats must be eliminated for the success, glory and victory of Islam.

These the four practical threats to the concept of jihad:

1. Lack of knowledge and piety

A large number of Muslims strive for a successful future but have forgotten about the afterlife. They have also forgotten their personal identity and faith. They are plunged into the dirt of worldly affairs. They are like mad dogs going after worldly gains and have no idea about jihad at all. They deliberately ignore the troubles of oppressed Muslims. They are not ready to listen to the complaints of their brothers and sisters. Should we bless or curse this kind of people? Should we invite them towards the right faith of Islam or leave them in the darkness of ignorance? They are removed from Islam. Let alone jihad, they give no importance to other principles of Islam. This is a common problem and many people have been affected by it. Many Muslims have no information about jihad. They are involved in bad practices and thus not ready to join the jihad. They pursue worldly gains and a joyful life and commit lots of sins.

2. Another group of people believe that they are unable to participate in jihad because their belief is not as strong as that of the Ashaab (the Prophet's companions) nor are they brave enough. They claim that the concept of jihad is irrelevant today. They have found a few alternatives to jihad. Some of them believe that organising demonstrations and public meetings and hunger strikes is enough. There are others who believe in preaching to the people. They pack up their luggage and wander around in the area. They should know that if we are free to make changes of our own choice, then we can also find alternatives to prayers, Ramadan, Hajj and zakat.

3. A struggle within the framework of the present democratic system

Democracy brings the rule of Karzai, Ashraf and Shukrya; it will never bring Islam in any country of the world, nor can it do so.[1] Especially in our country, democracy will only bring an Islamic system if angels descend from the heavens and cast their votes in ballot boxes. People cast their votes in favour of oppressors and wild people. It is important for Islamic movements and Muslims to hasten their efforts in this field. But they should understand that Islam will never be implemented through democracy. When we take these beliefs out of our mind, then we will give place to the belief that jihad is the only way through which the implementation of an Islamic system is possible.

4. Polemics and discussions over small issues

This problem has been imposed upon us by the English. They make Muslims involved in these issues and keep them unaware of the concept of jihad. The Holy Qur'an has 6,667 verses. Imam Bukhari knew 600,000 hadiths (traditions of the Prophet) by heart. Of these hadiths, 100,000 were correct [sahih]. But in his book, Saheeh Bukhari, he compiled just 7,500 of these hadiths. Imam Abu Hanifa has explained 1,200,000 issues of Islamic jurisprudence. Hundreds of thousands of pages have been written about the economic, judicial, social and defence issues of Islam. But some sell-out stooges have confined the vast religion of Islam to a few very limited issues. They consume too much energy over these issues. Research is conducted on issues such as raising hands, recitation of the al-Fatiha chapter of the Qur'an after the leader of prayers, eight sets of the Taraweeh prayers and repeating the word talaq (divorce) three times. They spend a lot of money on these issues. They train others and misinterpret the basic concepts. Special institutes with very large budgets have been established just for these issues. Experts and scholars are invited to take part in polemics and challenge one another's knowledge and the ulemaa's strength of belief. They give these polemics the status of jihad and forget about the real jihad against the infidels.

These are the four theoretical threats.

Dear reader, please pay some attention and look around yourself lest you are involved in one of them. If you are also trapped in one of them, please try to free yourself of it as soon as possible. Obtain self-control and don't follow the decisions of others. Be brave enough and fight against the evils. Try to understand the concept of jihad first and then come forward and join it yourself and also invite others. Encourage others and make them aware of the sacredness of jihad. If you spend your wealth on jihad, it will never be lost. Jihad is the only route to the glory and victory of Muslims.

105

JIHAD IS A SACRED AND HOLY ADORATION!

[*The Taliban's main website had traditionally shied away from fulsome explanations of the theology and religious support for the concept of jihad. The slow collapse of initial attempts at a peace process, coupled with a vigorous debate as to the strategy and direction that the movement should take, meant that articles like the following began to be published. Note that the author blends religious arguments with a political message directed at Afghans who maybe still continue to hedge their bets with regards to the Taliban and their jihad.*]

Al-Emera (website)
26 March 2014

Jihad is a consecrated adoration. Its objective is to safeguard the religion, honour and Islamic values and to emancipate the oppressed, helpless and weak people from the cruelty and barbarity of the brutal enemy. Its objective is neither to vex nor kill people, neither to destroy villages nor demolish towns. Therefore various agreements have been ratified with non-Muslims in the glorious history of Islam in which the life and property of the protégés of the Islamic State have been approved. From the times of the Holy Prophet of Islam (peace be upon him) and his guided caliphs (may Allah be pleased with them) throughout the brilliant history of Islam, the great leaders of jihad have constantly advised their followers never to kill women, children, aged people and monks during fighting.

The great leader of the holy jihad, the last Prophet of Allah (peace be upon him), had forbidden his followers to kill women, children, aged people and monks of even the hostile disbelievers, i.e. those infidels who are physically involved in fighting against the Muslims. Imam Bukhari writes in his book *Sahih Bukhari* that Abdullah the son of Omar (may Allah be pleased with all of them) narrated, 'Once a woman was found dead on a battlefield. When the Holy Prophet (peace be upon him) saw it, he disapproved of killing women and children and forbade his followers to repeat it.' There are several other traditions which corroborate the above-mentioned prohibition.

On the one side, killing women, children and older members of the hostile infidels is not allowed according to the rules and regulations of Islam, and the Islamic Emirate has not allowed anyone to do it either; but on the other side, the protection of Muslim women, children and old people is indubitably one of the foremost objectives of the holy jihad and the mujahedeen. Allah Almighty says in chapter 4, verse 75 of His Noble Qur'an:

> And what is wrong with you that you fight not in the Cause of Allah, and for those weak, ill-treated and oppressed among men, women and children whose cry is: 'Our Lord! Rescue us from this town whose people are oppressors; and raise for us from You one who will protect, and raise for us from You one who will help.'

It is an eminent fact that the esteemed leader of the Islamic Emirate, Mullah Mohammad Omar Mujahid, and his colleagues have constantly advised their follower mujahedeen quite explicitly to prevent civilian casualties to the best of their abilities. The Islamic Emirate has punished those who have been negligent. The mujahedeen have been so conscientious in this regard that they have established an independent commission for the prevention of civilian casualties. We have proposed the formation of a tripartite commission including UN representatives. But the enemy has not shown any interest yet, as they are mainly responsible for the civilian casualties.

In addition, specific objectives are set by the mujahedeen at the beginning of each jihadi year which are then pursued by them. Our noble and pious countrymen are solemnly requested to remain away from all those places where the enemies or their supporters reside, as well as their usual routes. The ordinary people are advised to refrain from these places so that they are not unnecessarily hurt.

Here once again, we ask our noble and pious countrymen to refrain from working with the foreign invaders as well as their stooges. They should also keep themselves away from all those places where the enemy lives. As has been proved, when attacked by the mujahedeen, the cowardly enemy open indiscriminate fire on civilians, targeting, wounding and killing them.

106

SUICIDE ATTACKS AND THE SHARI'A

[This article on the Taliban's jihad sub-site outlines the positions of various Muslim scholars on the tactic of suicide bombing. The author makes the claim that there is significant justification from the Qur'an as well as the hadith, and provides several examples to back up his case.]

Abu Abdullah Mukhlis
Jihad sub-site, Al-Emera, 1 October 2014

Ali bin Nayaf Al-Dimashqi has written a very good book on the topic of suicidal attacks, which has been translated by Abu Shaikh al-Mukhlis. Keeping in view the importance of the topic, we want to take some excerpts from this book and publish them in the *Mursal* magazine. As this subject is too long to accommodate in the magazine, it will suffice just to include the Pashto translation, which is the product of very hard work by translators. We hope this will be a precious asset for our readers who want to know about suicide attacks.

Regards, Admin

Before describing the sanctions, sayings and clarifying some doubts about suicidal attacks, it is necessary to give an account of the argument in accordance with shari'a law. All arguments prove that suicidal attacks are permissible.

These are the arguments:

1) Almighty Allah in the Holy Qur'an chapter Al Tawba, verse 111, says, 'Indeed, Allah has purchased from the believers their lives and their properties [in exchange] for them gaining Paradise. They fight in the cause of Allah, so they kill and are killed. [It is] a true promise [binding] upon Him in the Torah and the Gospel and the Qur'an. And who is truer to his covenant than Allah? So rejoice in your transaction which you have contracted. And it is that which is the great attainment.'

Explanation: The verse above says that there is a trade agreement between Allah and the mujahed. The Muslims are the sellers and receive the reward from Allah.

2) Almighty Allah in the Holy Qur'an chapter Al-Baqara, verse 249, says, 'And when Saul went forth with the soldiers, he said, "Indeed, Allah will be testing you with a river. So whoever drinks from it is not of me, and whoever does not taste it is indeed of me, excepting one who takes [from it] in the hollow of his hand." But they drank from it, except a [very] few of them. Then when he had crossed it along with those who believed with him, they said, "There is no power for us today against Goliath and his soldiers." But those who were certain that they would meet Allah said, "How many a small company has overcome a large company by permission of Allah. And Allah is with the patient."'

Explanation: The aforementioned verse of the Holy Qur'an proves that in many circumstances worldly material prowess is not essential for victory, but that in various situations victory can be achieved despite the lack of resources and small number of fighters.

3) Almighty Allah in the Holy Qur'an chapter Al-Baqara, verse 207, says, 'And of the people is he who sells himself, seeking means to the approval of Allah. And Allah is kind to [His] servants.'

Explanation: We will explain this point very soon with examples from the lives of the Prophet's companions (Ashaab) that one can sell his life to Allah. It means that if someone sells his life to Allah, he cannot be said to have committed suicide even if he, unarmed and unprotected, on his own infiltrates enemy ranks.

4) Muslim, with reference to Hazrat Suhaib, writes that the Prophet told his companions (Ashaab):

> Once upon a time there was a king who had a magician. When the magician grew older, he asked the king to send him a young boy to train in magic. The king appointed a young boy for this job. But whenever the boy went to the magician, he would also meet a Christian priest who lived on his way. He liked to talk to the priest very much and learnt about religion. Whenever he arrived late, the magician would hit the boy, and he would complain to the priest. The priest instructed the boy to tell the magician that he was late because he was busy at home with chores. He also told him that if he was afraid of his own family members, then he should tell them that he was busy with the magician. The boy followed his instructions.

> But one day the boy found out that there was a wild animal blocking the road of the people of a village. The boy decided that on that day he would try to find out whether the magician was true or the priest. So he took a rocket and asked God that if the priest was true, kill the wild brute. When he hurled the rocket he hit the animal and killed him, and thus the road opened. When he told the priest about the incident, he told him that he was upgraded to a higher status. At the same time he also warned him that he would face difficult tests. Then the priest requested him not to expose his identity if he faced any test.

The boy started to heal those born blind, albinos and other patients. A minister, who was blind, heard about the healing qualities of the boy and contacted him. The minister told him that if he treated him, he would give him many gifts and rewards. But the boy replied that he was not the healer, but in fact Almighty God gave health to his patients. He said that if the minister believed in Almighty God, he would request Him to heal his eyes. The minister immediately announced his belief in Almighty God and his eyes were healed.

When the minister returned to the royal court, the king asked him who had restored his eyesight. He replied, Almighty God. The king asked him whether he also had another lord than him. The minister confirmed yes, Almighty God who was the lord of both of them. The king tortured the minister till he exposed the identity of the boy. Afterwards, the boy was brought to the royal court where the king questioned him about his magic which had the quality of healing those born blind and albinos. The boy told him that he was not the healer, rather his Lord was the real healer of the people. The king also tortured him until he exposed the identity of the priest.

They brought the priest and demanded that he leave his religion. But the priest refused to do so. The king brought a saw and cut him into two halves. Then he called his minister and demanded him to give up his faith. The minister also refused. Once again the king took the saw up and slashed him into two halves. Finally, he made the same demand of the boy, who also refused to accept.

The king ordered his men to take the boy to a high mountain. If there he did not give up his faith, they should drop him from a high cliff and kill him. When they arrived at the peak of the mountain, the boy prayed to God to destroy all of them. The mountain moved and all the escorting men were killed. But the boy came back to the royal court, where the king asked him about the escorting men. He replied that Almighty God had rescued him from their harm.

The king ordered another group of men to take him in a boat and drown him in the middle of the sea. The boy once again prayed to God to protect him from them. The boat capsized and all of them drowned except the boy. He returned to the royal court where the king asked him about the escorting men. He told him that they were drowned and God rescued me from their harm. Then he told the king that he could not kill him, except in one way. The king asked what that method was. He told the king to crucify him on a cross and shoot him with one of his own arrows. Moreover, he also told the king that while shooting him he should say the name of his (the boy's) lord.

The king's men followed this method and succeeded in killing him. But soon after his martyrdom, all the spectators converted to the boy's religion. The news was immediately reported to the king. The king ordered for ditches to be dug around the town and all those who would not give up the new religion must be thrown into a fire. All the people refused to give up their new religion and voluntarily jumped into the fire. At the end a lady with a baby in her arms came. She was hesitant to jump into the fire. Her baby told her to be patient and jump into the fire because hers was the righteous path.

Explanation: This hadith proves that the boy let the king take his life because he was willing to sacrifice his life for the sake of his religion. It is a permissible act and cannot be called a suicide, even though he had not received any divine revelation in this regard. He already knew that he would be killed because of the selection of his choice. On the basis of these reasons, the Prophet appreciated his sacrifice.

5) Ibn Abbas says that the Prophet told them that on the night of his voyage to heaven, he noticed a strange fragrance. He asked the Archangel Gabriel about the nature of the fragrance. The Archangel told him that it was the fragrance of the beautician of the Pharaoh's daughter. When the Prophet asked the Archangel about the details of the story, he was told that one day a beautician was busy with the make-up of the Pharaoh's daughter and her comb suddenly fell on the floor. On that occasion the beautician immediately recited 'in the name of God'. The Pharaoh's daughter asked her whether she meant her father. The beautician said no, the Lord of both their fathers. The daughter of the Pharaoh said she would report this to her father. After receiving the report the Pharaoh called the beautician and asked her whether she believed in another God and Lord than him. She confirmed that she believed in Allah, the Lord of both of them.

The Pharaoh ordered a big pot to be boiled and the beautician along with her children thrown into it. Before that, the beautician requested the Pharaoh to bury their bones after their death. The Pharaoh accepted her plea. Her children were first thrown into the boiling pot, one after the other. When it was the turn of her infant boy, she was a little hesitant. But her baby boy told her to go forward because the torment of the world hereafter would be worse than the one in this world. With that she jumped into the boiling pot. According to Ibn Abbas, in history there are four babies who have talked. Mary's son Jesus Christ, the boy who has been mentioned in the story of Jareej, the witness of Prophet Joseph, and the baby son of the beautician of Pharaoh's daughter (Masnad Ahmad Al-Risala, 5/30, 2821).

Explanation: In this hadith it has been proved that Allah enabled the baby to speak and tell his mother to jump into the boiling pot. It is exactly like the episode of the story of the Ashaab al-Khudood, where a baby persuades his mother to jump into the fire. This act has been appreciated by all scholars as a sign of Allah.

6) Aslam Abu Imran says that they were once on a jihad mission from Medina to Constantinople and Abdul Rahman bin Khalid bin Waleed was their commander. The Romans had established positions around the city. One of the Muslims went forward alone to conduct an attack on the enemy. His comrades tried to stop him, but he recited the oath of belief in one God and went forward. Hazrat Ayub Ansari said that when the Ansar (the residents of Medina) assisted the Prophet and when Islam prevailed, they decided to stay at home and protected their properties. On that occasion Allah sent the following verse of the Holy Qur'an: 'Dedicate your properties for the sake of Allah and don't deliberately allow self-destruction.' If they were to stay

in Medina for the protection of their own properties, it meant a kind of self-destruction.

7) Asim, who is the grandson of Qatada and son of Umar, says that once Ma'az bin Ufra asked the Prophet about his favourite person. The Prophet replied it was the one who fights the enemy without any armour and helmet. Then he threw off his armour and helmet and penetrated into the enemy ranks and continued fighting until he was martyred. Ibn al-Nahas and Ibn Shabeeha have confirmed this tradition. But Ibn Ishaq writes that this man was Auf bin Ufra. Awaz and Mawaz were also his brothers. Their mother was Ufra and their father was Rafaa bin Haris of Banu Najar tribe. (Allah knows better.)

[...]

8) Omar bin Naeem narrates that once a man asked the Prophet about the qualities of the best of martyrs. The Prophet said, 'The best of martyrs are those who fight courageously and never turn their back on the enemy. These martyrs will stay in the highest ranks of Paradise and Almighty Allah will smile on them. When Allah smiles on someone, then he will not be answerable for his sins on the Day of Judgement.'

9) Abu Dardaa says that the Prophet said, 'Allah loves three kinds of people and gives them the ability for success. First, when someone's comrades flee the battle but he stays alone and continues to fight against the enemy, Allah will help and protect him from the enemy, or he will become a martyr. All will admire his patience. Second, if a man has a beautiful wife and a comfortable bed, but in the middle of the night he gets up and worships Allah and does not bother about lust and sleeping. And third is the man who travels with a group of other travellers; after covering a long distance they find a place and sleep, but while the rest are asleep he gets up and worships Allah in the later part of the night.

Explanation: The above-mentioned three points prove that the loss of life is the best part of jihad.

10) Abdullah bin Mas'ud says that the Prophet said, 'Allah loves two types of men very much. One, he who leaves the bed of his wife and gets up to worship Allah. Allah tells his angels that His worshipper left the bed of his wife for the sake of His paradise. And second is the man whose comrades flee the battlefield, but he prefers to stay and fight against the enemy till martyrdom. Once again Allah will tell the angels to look at His worshipper who is not afraid of losing his life and is ready to die as a martyr to achieve Paradise.'

Explanation: Ibn Al-Nahas says this particular hadith is enough for us to make a decision and infiltrate enemy ranks.

11) Zaid bin Zubyan, with reference to Abu Zar, says that the Prophet said, 'Allah loves three types of people. One, if someone comes to a village and asks for help but all the people refuse to help him; but one of the villagers secretly goes after him and

helps him without letting anyone else except Allah know. Second, when someone travels with a group of travellers, and after getting fatigued they retire and sleep, but he gets up and starts worshipping Allah and reciting verses of the Holy Qur'an. Third, when someone's comrades flee the battlefield but he stays firm and fights the enemy till victory or martyrdom.'

12) Abu Huraira says that the Prophet said, 'Allah likes two types of people. One, who always holds the reins of his horse and whenever and wherever he hears about something dreadful, he drives his horse there because he always ventures to dangerous places. And second, when someone lives in the highlands or valleys with his flocks of sheep, goats and pays *zakat* and *ushr* and worships Allah till the end of his life. These are the most favourite people for Allah. All of his works are for the welfare of others.'

These hadiths prove that the pursuit of martyrdom is the best deed in Islamic shari'a.

13) Hazrat Anas says, 'Once the Prophet sent Busaisa to get information about the trade caravan of Abu Sufyan. When he returned, only the Prophet and I were present in the room. He gave some information to the Prophet who immediately came out of the room and asked people whose riding animals were ready to join him. Some requested him to allow them to bring their horses from Awaali, an area in Medina. But he asked that only those of them should come whose horses were ready. The Prophet and his companions set off on their journey and arrived at Badr before the Quraysh of Mecca. Afterwards the polytheists also arrived there. The Prophet announced to his companions, "Come forward and jump into Paradise, which is wider than the distance between the earth and heavens." Umair bin Hamm asked him if it was wider than the distance between the earth and the sky. The Prophet told him, of course it is. Umair was extremely happy and enthralled. Afterwards he took some dates from his bag and started to eat. But very soon he said that eating the dates would delay him from joining Paradise. He left the eating and joined fighting. He fought until he was war martyred' (Muslim, 3/1510, 1901).

Explanation: The Prophet would generally instruct his companions to stand in orderly rows. But when Umair was enthralled about Paradise and decided to go ahead of other comrades to infiltrate the enemy ranks, the Prophet did not stop him even though he knew he would be killed.

14) Anas bin Malik says that his uncle, Anas bin Nazar, was not present in the battle of Badr. He once told the Prophet that he was not present in the battle of Badr, and added that if Allah gave him an opportunity to fight on the frontline against infidels, he would prove his bravery. During the battle of Uhud, the Muslims were forced to withdraw. But he said, 'O, Allah, I beg pardon for the action of other comrades and I curse the polytheism of the infidels.' Then he moved towards the enemy. On the way he came across Saad bin Ma'az. He told him, 'O, Saad, by Allah, I feel the fragrance of paradise in the vicinity of Mount Uhud.' Later on, Saad bin Ma'az

reported to the Prophet and said that Nazar demonstrated extreme bravery. According to Anas bin Malik, when Nazar was found, they saw more than eighty wounds of swords, knives, arrows and other weapons. The enemy had chopped off his ears, nose and lips. Nobody was able to recognise him except his sister, who recognised him by his fingers. They thought that the following verse of the Holy Qur'an was sent in the recognition of his bravery: 'Among the believers are men true to what they promised Allah. Among them is he who has fulfilled his vow [to the death], and among them is he who awaits [his chance]. And they did not alter [the terms of their commitment] by any alteration' (Bukhari 4/19, (2805) 16).

According to Imam Mujahid, the prophet had sent Abdullah bin Masud and Khubab bin al-Art alone to jihad (Al-Sunan Al-Behaqi 9/170, 18199), Sahih al-Mursal.

15) Huzaifa says that once the Prophet sent him alone to jihad (Al-Muajal al-Kabeer Li-Tibrani 3/162, 3003). Ibrahim bin Tamimi, with reference to his father, says that once they were with Huzaifa, one of their friends said that if he lived during the period of the Prophet, he would have participated in jihad in his company and proved his bravery in battle. After this, Huzaifa told him about his own bravery. He said on the occasion of the battle of Khandaq, the Prophet asked them if there was any volunteer to go to the enemy and bring information to him and be in his company in the world hereafter. But everybody was silent. The Prophet repeated this three times, but all of them remained silent. Then the Prophet asked Huzaifa to go to the enemy area and bring him the information but not to terrorise them. He had no other option but to go. He adds, 'After leaving the Prophet, my body felt a warmth. I moved swiftly and reached the enemy camp where I found Abu Sufyan, who was sitting near the fire and warming his back. I put an arrow in my bow and wanted to kill him. But immediately I remembered that the Prophet had told me not to terrorise them. I could shoot him but I did not and returned. When I came to the Prophet and reported to him, I calmed down. The Prophet covered me with his shawl on which he used to pray. I slept till morning. In the morning the Prophet came and woke me up (Muslim 3/1414, 99/1788).

Explanation: This tradition of the Prophet proves that when there is more risk in jihad, there are more rewards. There are no restrictions on jihad due to risks, but the more the risks, the greater the reward.

16) Abdullah bin Anan says that one day Prophet Muhammad sent him alone to jihad. Imam Shafi'i says that one of the members of the group of Bair Maawana remained behind and saw a pack of birds in the sky above the spot of the martyrdom of his comrades. He told Umraw bin Umaya that he would attack the enemy. He knew that the enemy would kill him, but he wanted to join his martyred comrades. He did attack them and got killed.

When Umraw bin Umaya reported the incident to the Prophet, he admired it and asked Umraw why he did not join them and attain martyrdom. Imam Shafi'i says that the Prophet had sent Umraw bin Umaya al-Zamiree and another person to jihad, and he had sent Abdullah bin Anis alone. Though the attacker would definitely be killed, the Prophet never forbade this act. On the contrary, he encouraged others to participate in these kinds of attacks and achieve martyrdom like their comrades.

Abu Huraira says that once the Prophet sent a group of ten people for spying and reconnaissance. Asim bin Sabit Ansari, the grandfather of Umbar bin Khatab's son Asim, was appointed as the commander of the group. They travelled and at last arrived at a spot which was called Hudaa, located between Mecca and Asfaan. After getting information about them, the people of Banu Lahyaan sent two hundred riders who were armed with bow and arrows after them. When Asim and his comrades saw the two hundred riders, they went to an elevated place. But they were soon surrounded by the enemy. Then they were told that if they came down and surrendered, they would not be killed. Their commander, Asim bin Sabit, said that by Allah he would never believe in the promise of the infidels and would neither come down nor surrender to them. Then he said, 'O, Allah, give our message to your Prophet.'

The infidels shot arrows towards them and Asim was martyred, along with seven other comrades. However, the remaining three, Khubaid Ansari, Ibn Dasna and another man, accepted their pledge and came down. Soon after their surrender, the infidels untied the strings of their bows and then with the same strings tied up all three of them. The third man protested and said that it was the first breach of the pledge. Then he said that by Allah he would not go with them and would follow his martyred comrades. They tried and dragged him to take him along with them. But he resisted and refused to go with them. Eventually they martyred him. They took Khubaib Ansari and Ibn Dasna and after the battle of Badr sold them in Mecca. Khubaib was bought by Banu Aamir, a clan of Banu Haris. Khubaib had killed Amir bin Haris in the battle of Badr. So he became a prisoner with them.

Ubaidullah bin Ayaz says that the daughter of Haris told him that once Khubaib borrowed a shaving blade from her to shave the private parts of his body. She gave him the blade. At the same time he also took her baby son with him. She was very afraid for her son's safety. But when she went there she found that her son was sitting on his thigh. After understanding her feelings, Khubaib asked her if she was afraid that he would kill her son. Then he assured her that he would never do that. Haris's daughter added, 'By God, I have never seen any prisoner better than Khubaib.'

She said that one day, when his hands were shackled, he ate a bunch of grapes, though it was not the season of fresh fruit in Arabia. Allah fed him. When they took him from the Haram to the area of Hull to kill him, Khubaib requested them to allow him to pray a set of prayers. They accepted his request. After offering a short set of prayers, he told them that he did not prolong his prayers because they would think he was afraid of death. He recited the following verses: 'I am being killed as a Muslim. It doesn't matter where I fell. I am being sacrificed for the sake of Allah. If Allah wills, he will bless every piece of my body.' The son of Haris martyred him. Khubaib left the tradition of offering the set of prayers for all those Muslims who face death penalty. Allah also accepted the wish of Aasim on the day of his martyrdom. The Prophet informed his companions about the incident and nature of their martyrdom. When the Quraysh infidels received information about the martyrdom of Aasim, they sent their men to collect some parts of his body because he had killed one of their leaders in the battle of Badr. But Allah appointed a pack of bees to protect his body from the mischief of Quraysh. They failed to chop off any part of his body (Bukhari 4/67).

107

Q&A

SUICIDE BOMBING

[*This question, submitted to Zabiullah Mujahed, shows how there was considerable uncertainty among non-affiliated individuals as to the legitimacy of suicide bombing as a tactic. The answer also replicates the experience many had when asking this question to the Taliban, in that all but the more qualified Islamic scholars would refuse to answer the question because they argued that they didn't know enough to be able to answer properly. This may perhaps explain the reticence to answer the question in full on their website until relatively recently.*]

Taliban's Q&A section on Al-Emera, 12 April 2012

Q: Peace and blessings be upon you! Dear Mujahed: the killing of any person without a legal reason is forbidden [haram] in Islam. I am not concerned about all the Taliban. My point is about those Taliban who carry out suicide attacks. Are they permitted to carry out such attacks? If so, please give me the reference for a Qur'anic verse and hadith and answer these questions which have come into my and other Muslims' minds. Regards, Asadullah Janbaz

A: In the present circumstances, this matter and the reasons relating to it have become quite clear. Please go to the ulemaa and ask them about this matter for a satisfactory answer. I am not a Mufti able to answer your questions. Thanks.

108

Q&A

EXPLOSIVES TRAINING AND CIVILIAN CASUALTIES

[*As part of the questions posed to Zabiullah Mujahed in the stand-alone Q&A section of the Taliban's website, this contains the suggestion of 'Ahmad', who suggests that if the Taliban were better trained, then they wouldn't need to detonate massive explosions to kill Afghan or foreign military soldiers.*]

Taliban's Q&A section on Al-Emera, 18 April 2012

Q: I have a suggestion. Sometimes explosions take place near a Ranger vehicle parked in a crowded area and kill or injure a large number of innocent believers. It is necessary for you (if really it is you who are organising these attacks) to train the mujahedeen to use assault rifles to attack the enemy instead of explosions. It will kill the enemy on the spot and also avoid the unnecessary casualties of innocent passers-by. Even if one mujahed loses his life, it wouldn't be a big loss. So in crowded places—instead of explosions—the methods of frontal attack would be more effective but without committing any sin. Regards, Ahmad

A: Brother, I have forwarded your advice and suggestion to the military commanders and other relevant authorities. We hope they will give it due consideration. It seems that you are also an experienced person. May Almighty Allah help you participate in the practical jihad which is obligatory on all of us! Our country has been occupied by infidels who commit barbarian and brutal crimes against our people. The country is in need of our sacrifices. Thanks.

109

INTERVIEW WITH MAWLAWI AHMAD BILAL, HEAD OF THE CONTROL AND CO-ORDINATION COMMISSION FOR NGOs AND COMPANIES

[*The Taliban reviewed policies and published interviews with relevant officials to explain new changes and developments. In this extract, the head of a new commission dealing with non-governmental organisations and companies explains the logic behind their activities and what people might expect from them.*]

Al-Emera (website), 20 March 2014

Q: What are the objectives behind forming this commission in the hierarchy of the Islamic Emirate, and what is its composition?

A: You know that after the American invasion of Afghanistan, a war situation prevails inside our beloved homeland. The Americans have imposed a type of government over Afghanistan which is the most corrupt regime in the world. Under the shadow of this corrupt regime, besides looting, usurpation and pillage, a great deal of injustice has been done in the field of human assistance.

On the one side, the war-stricken people of our country are facing numerous problems and issues in their day-to-day lives and they need help. On the other side, whatever comes to Afghanistan under the name of assistance, that is largely spent in paying the high salaries of the administrative personnel of foreign NGOs, paying the rents of luxurious and grand palaces, purchasing the latest model vehicles and other extravagant requirements of their officials. The remaining funds which are allocated for projects, most either goes into the pockets of influential figures inside these NGOs or into the pockets of corrupt officials of the stooge admin of Kabul. To deliver this support to eligible people and places and similarly to halt the selfish activities of the enemy in the disguise of assistance, the Islamic Emirate of Afghanistan decided to constitute a separate commission for the control of NGOs and companies and for the effective organisation and coordination of their activities and expenditures.

I would like to mention the second article of the 'Modus Operandi' of this commission, which encompasses the answer to the above question:

Article 2: The commission of control and coordination of NGOs and companies is established by the Islamic Emirate of Afghanistan, which will permit, organise and oversee the activities of NGOs and companies as needed.

As far as the structure of this commission is concerned, it is as follows:

A director at the top, a deputy director and two well-experienced members, admin and financial organs, organ for coordination of reconstruction, organ for coordination of wireless, public relations organ and branches in all provinces.

Q: What kinds of activities have been performed by your commission inside the country so far?

A: The NGOs and companies control and coordination commission has successfully prevented the waywardness which had become the order of the day by some irresponsible individuals misusing the name of Taliban or the Islamic Emirate. They used to make contacts with NGOs or telephone companies by various means and pressured them into fulfilling their illegal and unjustified demands. This practice had created impediments in executing public welfare activities. Human assistance could not easily be supplied to where it was really needed, and the poor and needy had no access to these facilities. On the other side, baseless propaganda was circulating that the Islamic Emirate was impeding development activities inside the country. By the grace of Allah Almighty, all these complaints and issues were settled by forming this commission. We managed to provide our programmes and rules of procedure through our well-organised set-up to our representative offices in all provinces. First, we wanted to stop the wilfulness of self-interested individuals; and second, we would like to get detailed information about the work and activities of all the human assistance organisations, private companies and wireless networks. They will be supervised so that the public welfare works are well organised and ordinary people benefit. We can say that a positive change is visible when compared to previous years.

Q: Do you supervise and control the activities of NGOs, or only remain in contact with them inside the country?

A: This commission has no specific agreements or contracts with NGOs and private companies; rather, we have our representative who remains in contact with them via telephone round the clock. He can easily be contacted by all the concerned sides and can convey their requirements and issues to us very easily.

Nevertheless, the working procedure is that whenever a project is implemented somewhere, after its approval, an application of permission is drafted by the local dignitaries to the jihadi in charge of the respective province. After the approval of the provincial representative of our commission, if the jihadi inc harge also agrees, then the subject is discussedin detail at a meeting of this commission. After thorough analysis, a permission letter is provided according to Article 8 of our working procedure. The implementation of the project is then supervised by the provincial representative of our commission, from the beginning to the end, so that any fraudulence can be prevented and the quality of the project is maintained throughout. When the project is completed, once again the commission is informed about it.

Q: What kind of activities are not allowed by your commission for NGOs, and what is eligible for them?

A: The Islamic Emirate has never opposed the reconstruction, rehabilitation and development of our beloved homeland. There is no hindrance for all those individuals or groups who want to rebuild and provide human assistance for the relief of our masses. They can openly go forward with their activities while observing the rules and regulations laid down for this purpose. Article 3 of the 'Modus Operandi' of this commission says as follows:

> The control and coordination commission of the Islamic Emirate for NGOs and companies bears the responsibility to allow all those public relief works like rehabilitation and human assistance carried out by NGOs and companies, in accordance with the principles laid down for them. This commission is also responsible for halting all those activities which are harmful for our religion and people and damage the ongoing jihadi process.

However, some foreign organisations are found to be involved in such activities which are against the sacred religion of Islam, under the disguise of human welfare NGOs. They want to convert our Muslim masses, especially the children and young ones, to Christianity and other null and void beliefs. It is the obligation of this commission to halt these kinds of illegal activities, as is mentioned in Article 4 of the working procedure of this commission, as follows:

> Those NGOs which invite people to un-Islamic ideologies like Judaism, Christianity etc. and are involved in activities against the mujahedeen, they are absolutely prohibited to work. The control and coordination commission for NGOs and companies will halt their activities with its full strength.

Q: You know that some of our countrymen are working with these NGOs. Now according to your policies, are these Afghans permitted to work with them or not? If the answer is yes, then what are the sectors in which they can work?

A: The Islamic Emirate finds no difficulty in working with those NGOs which are solely involved in public relief works on the basis of human sympathy. However, it is advisable for these Afghans working with foreign welfare NGOs that they should observe their Islamic and religious obligations and Afghan traditions as it is their Islamic and national responsibility for being a Muslim and an Afghan.

Q: If the demands or working procedures which are laid down for NGOs and companies are not observed by them, then how will you deal with them and can you close down their activities?

A: The NGOs and companies which violate the rules and regulations furnished by the control and coordination commission for them, or do not fulfil the accepted articles of an agreement for a specific project, these kinds of NGOs and companies are not given permission to work any more. The mujahedeen of the Islamic Emirate can halt these kinds of violators. But if they want to re-start their activities, then they should get work permits after providing a guarantee of no further negligence.

Q: Do you have the responsibility of control and coordination of telephone networks inside the country? We hear that the foreign invaders and their internal stooges are misusing these telephone networks against the mujahedeen and the masses in the country. What steps have been taken by you in this regard?

A: Yes. This commission is also responsible for supervising the telephone networks of the NGOs and companies. This commission has laid down different working procedures for these telephone networks, keeping in mind the prevailing circumstances of the respective province where these networks operate. In some provinces, these networks are allowed to operate for twenty-four hours; and in some areas, they work in the daytime and are closed at night-time; while in some other areas, they are allowed to operate for some specific hours. All these procedures depend on the demands of the masses and the mujahedeen. By implementing this strategy, we have successfully prevented the raids and indiscriminate bombing of the enemy in various parts of the country, which has inevitably resulted in the considerable decline of civilian casualties. On the other side, the Islamic Emirate has provided various kinds of facilities to these companies in the fields of security and the transportation of their personnel and equipment. I can say with full assurance that no one can threaten any more the employees of these telephone networks for fulfilling their illegitimate personal demands, nor can anyone seize their personal effects and vehicles. Overall, these networks are obliged to follow and observe the rules and regulations laid down for them.

Q: On behalf of the NGOs' control and coordination commission, if you have any message for them (i.e. for the continuation of their activities, what should they do and what should they refrain from), please do share it with us so that it is openly conveyed to them.

A: Afghanistan is a war-stricken country which has been facing various kinds of troubles for the last several years, therefore it desperately needs assistance and support in each and every walk of life. For keeping the door of human relief activities permanently open, our demand is that human welfare, rehabilitation works and health and education facilities should be provided to all citizens of our homeland without any discrimination. Favouritism and inequity between the inhabitants and areas should strictly be avoided.

Similarly, I would like to clarify to all assistance NGOs, societies and private companies that the control and coordination commission is formed in the administrative hierarchy of the Islamic Emirate so that the prevailing hindrances to the reconstruction and rehabilitation activities and the distribution of human relief should be removed. No one apart from the general representative of this commission has the right to be in contact with these NGOs and companies by adopting one name or the other. They are also advised to convey their issues and complaints directly to the above-mentioned commission via its representative.

My message to those mujahedeen who are fortified and living in the warm strongholds for defending Islam and their homeland is that they should be fully vigilant against all kinds of conspiracies of the enemy. They should continue their support of the local representatives of this commission and fully assist them when needed. They should also share their information with them and should not allow anyone to create an atmosphere of distrust under any disguise for the achievement of one's personal malicious interests.

The valiant Afghan masses should also realise that the control and coordination commission for NGOs and companies will not leave any stone unturned while enjoying your collaboration for the solution of all problems; so that, on the one side, the issues of our oppressed masses are tackled and they are provided a chance to leave a peaceful and prosperous life; and on the other side, the conspiracies of the foreign enemies and their internal stooges under the disguise of human relief are halted.

110

THE NULLIFICATION OF THE RECENT TALISMAN
OF THE INVADERS

[*The way the 2014 presidential elections process unfolded offered much by way of material to satirise or to enjoin readers to lose faith in the official political process. Corruption figured heavily and the denouement had to be mediated by non-Afghan third parties. For the Taliban's media operations unit, it was the perfect illustration of so much of what they had been writing about for years. This article is emblematic of this general line of criticism.*]

Al-Emera (website), 15 May 2014

The bitter enemy has executed various plans, trials and failed strategies for the subjugation and digestion of our beloved homeland during the previous thirteen years of American occupation. They used their full force and brutality. They tried their best to organise and strengthen the stooge admin of Kabul. They tested the conspiracy of the national police force and the national Arbaki militia who are mainly trained against basic Islamic and cultural values. They talked about reconstruction and economic revival. The issue of exploration of oil, gas and other mineral resources was raised. The insincere slogans of peace and reconciliation were chanted. The strategy of evacuation of Western forces from Afghanistan was put forward and so on and so forth.

By the grace of Allah Almighty, by the sincere sacrifices of mujahedeen and by the sagacity of the leadership of the Islamic Emirate of Afghanistan, all these conspiracies, deceptions and treacheries of the invading enemy were aborted. The enemy is not only defeated on the battlefield, but has also been confronted with a humiliation trounce on the diplomatic front. He has lost his military capability and supremacy. He is discredited internationally. His world role is under question. His inefficiency in tackling the world issues is disclosed to the extent that now most Americans are of the opinion that they have practically lost the war in Afghanistan.

The latest spell of foreign invaders was the futile and worthless process of recent elections which were held on 5 April 2014. The devious enemy has been beating the

467

drums for more than a year that these elections will be free and fair. After allocating a substantial amount of budget, this process was launched with great pomp and show. A programme was drafted, warmly discussed in the so-called councils and then ratified by Karzai. Members of the election commission were appointed and the programme was handed over to them. The candidates tried their best but the boxes were filled with counterfeit ballot papers and eventually the elections ended in such disgust and frustration that no one is satisfied except the invaders themselves.

Now that more than a week has gone by, the meticulous and reasonable counting of the bogus votes is on its way, as they say. But the tremendous number of complaints has not only exasperated the complaints commission, but has also driven the members of the election commission mad, as the cases of treachery are not in hundreds or thousands, but in hundreds of thousands. The candidates are themselves stunned. Everyone thinks that he is wronged as the votes reported to each do not account for even 50 per cent of the bogus papers. The question now is where have the remaining 50 per cent of votes gone which might have been cast for each by the nation?!!

The present scenario forecasts that this spell of foreign invaders will soon be nullified too. No change will emerge as a result of these counterfeit elections; rather it will be another humiliation for the occupiers and their internal stooges.

If the candidates succeed in reaching a compromise, or the elections enter a second phase: either way, a few well-known puppets will join a very fragile alliance, and the forthcoming administration will be even more pusillanimous than the previous one. It will have neither efficiency nor resolution to protect the lives, properties and honour of the people against the brutal foreign invaders. However, the outcome of these counterfeit elections will confirm the perception of Afghans that Americans are our sworn enemies and no good can be expected from them!!!

111

A LOOK AT THE US–AFGHAN SECURITY
AND DEFENCE COOPERATION AGREEMENT

[*This lengthy article examines the bilateral security agreement (BSA) signed between Afghanistan and the United States. It consists of a close reading of the text of the agreement, examining and explaining which articles are problematic from the Taliban's perspective. It is useful on account of the detail offered. Taliban statements often tend towards the general, but here there are specific responses that can be used to add to our understanding of the Taliban's perspective.*]

Al-Emera (website), 20 November 2014

Dear readers, as you may be aware, this year on 7 September 2014 the powerless new government of Ashraf Ghani signed the Security Agreement with the US and NATO states, thus giving an empty pretext to the continued foreign occupation of Afghanistan. This agreement had been signed after a fraudulent election which resulted in open US intervention in support of installing their candidate, Ashraf Ghani, who in return showed his loyalty to his American masters by signing the Agreement within twenty-four hours of being sworn in as the new president. The haste with which the Ghani regime signed this Agreement, despite the opposition of the masses, the religious scholars, the legal experts, and other influential and political figures betrays the loyalty of Ghani and his colleagues to the Americans over their own national interests. This haste also shows that the turbulence following the elections was engineered by the Americans so that they could compel the new government to sign the Agreement without demanding any changes to it. This Agreement, however, signed by a few American–Afghans under duress, and in opposition to the wishes of the Afghan people, holds no legal grounding. Not only is this Agreement null and void under Islamic law, but also it is so under international law.

In this brief article we will look at the various aspects of this Agreement, analysing their implications so that we can make our nation aware of the dangers that lie hidden within this contract.

The legal status of this Agreement under Islamic law:

This Agreement is in clear violation of Islamic law and therefore null and void under it. This Agreement is a long-term agreement of alliance and mutual assistance with the American infidels, which is in clear violation of Allah's commands which prohibit such relations with the Jews and Christians (refer to Surat Nisa' v. 122 and Surat Maida v. 51). This Agreement allows an unspecified number of US troops to stay in Afghanistan along with military weaponry, warplanes, helicopters, missiles and other military hardware. Under Islamic law there are very specific conditions under which non-believers can stay in an Islamic country. In Islamic law only those non-believers can stay in Islamic lands who are either *dhimmi* (those that are citizens of the Islamic state and consent to all the laws of the land) or *musta'min* (those non-believers who have come from a non-Islamic land and are given permission by the state to travel to Islamic lands without any weapons or without attempting to sabotage Islamic lands). Outside these two conditions, under no circumstances are non-believers allowed to stay in Islamic lands. Americans who invaded our country by force and now want to give legal cover to their continued occupation do not fall under either of these categories. Therefore their occupation of Afghanistan and the Agreement which purports to give them this right are null and void under Islamic law, placing a duty upon all Muslims to oppose their presence in the country.

Under Islamic law, in the field of battle, Muslims, keeping their interests in view, are allowed to sign ceasefire agreements with non-believer belligerent forces. They are then obliged to respect this agreement and adhere to it in good faith. Outside these circumstances, Islamic law does not allow for any agreements that enable non-believer forces to build military bases in Muslim lands, giving them exemption from Islamic laws and giving them free rein to kill and capture Muslims in the land. Such agreements have no grounding in Islamic law and are considered illegal and unenforceable. Allah Almighty states: 'And never will Allah allow infidels a way on the believers' (i.e. giving them supremacy over Muslims) (Surat Nisa', v. 161). From this maxim Islamic scholars hold that never can a Muslim become a slave to non-believers. If a single Muslim is not allowed to become the property of a non-believer, then how can it be allowed for a whole Muslim and independent nation to be enslaved to an infidel nation? The Prophet (peace be upon him) stated: 'Islam will be supreme and nothing will be superior over it' (Baihaqi). This also explains why non-believers can never be superior to believers.

On numerous occasions in the Qur'an, Allah Almighty has prohibited Muslims from allying with infidels or inclining towards them. Allah SWT states: 'O believers, do not ally with My enemies or your enemies; by allying with them you want to send them a message (of peace) while indeed they defy that truth sent upon you' (Surat al Mumtahinah, v. 1). He Almighty also states: 'And do not incline towards those who transgress or else the fire will be upon you, and none other than Allah will be your friends and none will be able to assist you' (Surat Hud, v. 113). He Almighty also states: 'Give glad tidings to the hypocrites that a painful torment awaits them. (They are) those who take infidels as their allies instead of believers. Do they look for glory with the infidels? Indeed all glory is with Allah' (Surat Nisa', v. 138–140).

Previously it has been stated that any Agreement of alliance with the non-believers is invalid under Islamic law. Even if we assume that such an agreement with the non-believers is valid, it cannot be valid at the hands of the Kabul regime. Any such agreement must be signed by the leaders of the Muslims, the Khalifa. Americans have not signed this Agreement with the mujahedeen. Instead it was signed by their puppet government, installed by them and surviving on American sustenance. As Imam Muhammad states, any agreement signed by non-believers with Muslims who are surrounded or imprisoned by them holds no validity. This is because any agreement signed under duress must surely be to the detriment of Muslims and the benefit of non-believers. Therefore any such agreement is null and void.

From the above arguments it can be deduced that any agreement of alliance with non-believers is invalid under Islamic law. Even if we assume it to be valid, because this Agreement is geared towards prohibited ends, therefore it (the Agreement) itself becomes prohibited. It is an Islamic maxim that any act which might by itself be allowed, but when it is geared towards prohibited acts or mixed with prohibited items, it becomes prohibited. This maxim states: the means towards what is obligatory are obligatory themselves, and the means towards what is prohibited are prohibited themselves (*Musallim al Suboot*). The military presence of Americans in Afghanistan has resulted in the ideological invasion of our country, illegal occupation, killing of Afghans, looting of property, bombing civilians and the spread of vice. Since all the above prohibited actions are the result of foreign occupation, and this Agreement enables the continuation of these illegal actions, therefore this Agreement itself is considered illegal in Islamic law.

Another Islamic maxim holds that if an item is collectively owned, and a group from within this collection (without the consent of the remaining members) sells this item or disposes of it in any way, then this transaction is considered invalid. All the land and airspace of Afghanistan is under the collective ownership of the Afghan people; if a person such as Ashraf Ghani or Hanif Atmar decides to give part of this land or airspace to the Americans for their use, then their agreement is invalid and the Afghan nation is under no compulsion to adhere to such an agreement. From the above arguments it has become clear that this Agreement is invalid and holds no weight under Islamic law.

The technical and legal defects of this Agreement:

This Agreement states that Americans are not allowed to conduct operations outside Afghanistan or against any foreign forces. However, we can all see that American forces conduct daily drone strikes in the tribal belt of Pakistan. This clearly proves that Americans pay no respect towards the legal clauses of this Agreement. Rather, they are only interested in the clause that gives them legal cover to continue their occupation of Afghanistan.

In this cleverly crafted Agreement, the Americans have managed to dupe the Kabul authorities completely. In many clauses Americans have avoided the wording 'America agrees' and 'America shall' and instead inserted 'America will seek to' or 'America will work to' or 'America may', thus avoiding any legal duty to fulfil its obligations.

In Article 4, clause 6, Afghanistan has been designated as 'a Major Non-NATO Ally'. Afghanistan has long pursued a policy of neutrality, so risks facing major challenges as a result of this designation. Aligning with the West in a military sense could prove disastrous for Afghanistan. On the one hand, the Shanghai Cooperation Organisation is trying to strengthen its presence in the Asian continent; on the other hand, Russia is now embroiled in a cold war with the West over the recent events in Ukraine and Syria. Moreover, resentment towards America is on the increase in Afghanistan's neighbouring states. In such a politically charged environment, Afghanistan's alignment with NATO could provoke hostility and embroil Afghanistan with the wider region.

Looking at the content of the Agreement, it becomes quite clear that this Agreement is not aimed at the security of Afghanistan, rather it enhances US's interests in the wider region. Article 6 stipulates: 'The United States shall regard with grave concern any external aggression or threat of external aggression against the sovereignty, independence, and territorial integrity of Afghanistan... In the event of external aggression or the threat of external aggression against Afghanistan, the Parties shall hold consultations on an urgent basis to develop and implement an appropriate response...'

If this Agreement was indeed aimed at the security of Afghanistan, then this Agreement should have clearly stipulated that United States would take all measures necessary to preserve the territorial integrity and sovereignty of Afghanistan. If America considers her obligation to be the mere expression of grave concern (in such an eventuality), then surely she can do so from American soil as well. Why does she need to station troops here in order to do so? Clearly the stationing of such troops serves no purpose other than advancing US interests in the region.

Article 13 of the Agreement stipulates that: 'Afghanistan agrees that the United States shall have exclusive right to exercise jurisdiction over such persons [i.e. members of the force and of the civilian component] in respect of any criminal or civil offences committed in the territory of Afghanistan... Members of the force and of the civilian component shall not be arrested or detained by Afghan authorities for any reason... Afghanistan and the United States agree that members of the force and of the civilian component may not be surrendered to, or otherwise transferred to, the custody of an international tribunal or any other entity or state...'

This Article in effect gives American military and civilian personnel complete immunity from crimes committed on Afghan soil. In effect they can do as they please, such as kill, steal, commit adultery, kidnap, spy, flaunt human rights, loot historical artefacts and other crimes, and the Afghan government is powerless to stop them. These personnel are responsible to US authorities only. In the past when American troops committed such crimes, the Afghan government at least had the right to protest. Now the Arg (Presidential Palace) authorities have accepted that US troops are exempt from any judicial oversight. What this Article means is that should American troops commit a repeat of the Azizabad massacre, or the barbarity of Zangiabad or the burning of Qur'ans (such as in Bagram), then the Afghan authorities have no right of protest, as they have granted them judicial exemption.

In addition to protecting their personnel, the Americans have also taken great care to protect their security contractors as well, under this Agreement. American security contractors are those non-military personnel who, acting as a militia or mercenary army, are utilised by the Americans for military purposes. Just as the local militias committed widespread killings, robbing, looting, kidnapping and smuggling, similarly these American contractors have reportedly committed all these crimes, albeit on a bigger scale. And the fact that they are American contractors means that they are never likely to be held accountable for their crimes.

Article 15 relating to 'Entry and Exit' stipulates that 'Members of the force and members of the civilian component may enter or exit Afghanistan at agreed facilities and areas at locations... Passports and visas shall not be required. Such personnel shall be exempt from Afghan law and regulations on registration and control of foreign nationals.' Therefore Afghan officials have retained no right to investigate or regulate their movement. Instead, these visitors are exempt from all controls and regulations regarding the movement of foreign personnel. Similarly, American military and civilian vehicles, ships and aircraft are exempt from any investigation or search regulations.

Under this Article, foreign troops and their civilian components have been given even more rights than the Afghans themselves. The Americans will be well poised to exploit these freedoms in order to steal historical artefacts, cultural valuables, chemical resources or other material from Afghanistan. Afghan natural resources are for the most part unexplored. One of the aims of the current invasion was to exploit our natural resources. America's prolonged presence in Afghanistan, coupled with the freedoms provided in the above Article, make it astoundingly easy for Americans to exploit Afghanistan's natural resources and transfer them out of here.

Article 16 of the Agreement provides that 'United States forces and United States contractors may import into, export out of, re-export out of and use in Afghanistan any equipment, supplies, material, technology, training or services. The importation, exportation, re-exportation, transportation and use of any articles brought into Afghanistan pursuant to paragraphs 1 and 2 of this Article shall not be subject to restrictions, such as licensing, inspection, or verification... or taxes and customs duties or other charges assessed by government authorities in Afghanistan.' Again we see Americans being exempted from all responsibilities that are usually exercised by governments over aliens or their own nationals. Afghanistan's greatest asset is its strategic location. It can capitalise on its location in international business, air transit and international transactions. It lies at the crossroads of the old Silk Road and is considered the gateway to Central Asia. Hence it can capitalise on its location to attract business and enhance its economy. Unfortunately, because Afghanistan has placed all its strategic embarkation and disembarkation ports at the disposal of the Americans, it has relinquished its right to capitalise on these gains. Moreover, not only has the Kabul regime relinquished this right for itself, it has also deprived the Afghan people of the ability to capitalise on their collective property.

Under this Agreement, Afghanistan has granted all its strategic transit points and airports for American services. Americans have access to military structures in Kabul, Bagram, Mazar Sharif, Herat, Kandahar, Helmand, Gardez, Jalalabad and Shindand, all being the most strategic locations in Afghanistan. In addition, all of Afghanistan's major air facilities, such as Kabul International Airport, Herat International Airport, Kandahar Airport, Shindand Airport, Mazar Sharif Airport and Helmand Airport, have all been officially granted to the Americans. To facilitate the transit of American military hardware, Afghanistan's border crossings at Torkham, Spin Boldak, Tor Ghondi, Sher Khan and Hairatan have also been made available for foreign troops, while the door has also been left open for them to use additional bases, border crossings and airports if needs arise.

The biggest financial resources of Afghanistan are the above-mentioned airports and border crossings, hence this is the biggest known felony in the history of our country that such facilities are furnished to the Americans without monetary charges, levy or rent. No one on this planet surrenders an empty room to another without compensation; however, the American stooges have handed over the control of the country's lifeline to their masters without charging a cent.

Publicly, the officials of Arg claim that in return for giving up bases and other facilities to the Americans, aid will be granted to the ruling regime. However, nowhere in the body of the Agreement has a clause been placed specifying the amount of aid (financial or other) to be given to the Afghan side monthly or yearly; a vague term has been deemed satisfactory: that America shall back and assist the Afghan government. If America solely works for its own interests within the framework of this Agreement and stops all aid to the Kabul government, the Arg officials will have no legal right to protest because the Americans, as aid givers, are not obliged to hand over anything specific as stated in the Agreement.

According to the Agreement, the Americans have the right to control a private frequency to air their programmes, and are granted communication channels and postal services which are exempt from being tracked or inspected by the Afghan side. With such provisions the Americans are able to change the location of their Intel bases inside Afghanistan, and similarly can launch a propaganda war against Afghanistan or its neighbouring states, which can only be detrimental to Afghanistan.

America had complete control of the communication spectrum inside Afghanistan long before this, and with their continued presence the violation of this Afghan sanctity will carry on unabated; and with it the Americans will blackmail and exploit anyone they wish for their interests.

American objectives attained through the Agreement:

America wants to stay inside Afghanistan for a prolonged period, until they are forced out. For their protracted presence, they needed such an Agreement with which they could deceive the Afghans and depict it as a legal document through the power of their propaganda machine. Therefore they conducted a several-year campaign for the signing of this Bilateral Security Agreement, set up a drama under the title of 'Loya Jirga', followed by getting the Agreement signed by those officials who were appointed and brought to power by their direct interference.

America could have prolonged its presence inside Afghanistan by invoking the International Security Council of the United Nations, but in order to fool the simple ordinary people and achieve superficial validity, it extended its presence in the form of a Security Agreement with the government in power, and there are many reasons why America hopes for a continued stay here.

Afghanistan from every angle is a place of hope and an impregnable fortress in face of the international *kufr*; its people are staunch believers and blessed with jihadi fervor; its location is extremely strategic, situated on Asia's high ground in mountainous terrain. Afghanistan is located in a sensitive area with access to the riches of Central Asia, the economic juggernaut of China, and nuclear-armed south Asia and Iran. Its second name is 'The Graveyard of Empires' and its history teaches its people and the world the meaning of jihad and freedom. America dreams of controlling the planet so cannot afford to let an Independent Islamic government rule here. Their main goal is to crush the spirit of Islamic rule, jihad and independence in this nation.

After the fall of Communism, the prime enemy of the Western infidels became political Islam, the adherents of which they refer to as 'Islamists'. The West, at the head of which is America, can never tolerate the formation of a true Islamic government in any corner of the world, or allow the rule of shari'a, the propagation of Islamic thought and other Islamic reform works to take place. To counter Islamic awakening, they not only install irreligious, tyrannical Westernised *coup d'état* regimes and anti-Islamic groups and individuals, but launch direct attacks on Muslim countries on top of intense propaganda wars; they build bases in Muslim lands to complete their occupation, in order to suppress the Muslims and Islamic thought completely. America's presence in Afghanistan not only aims to repress true Muslims and Islamic thought in this nation; rather, it wants to confront directly all Islamic awakening movements in the neighbouring countries and the broader region, for which America has already been waging military, propaganda and covert wars.

Following the fall of the Soviet Union, America considers itself the world's sole superpower. They label the twenty-first century as the American Century and are implementing their plan through the 'New World Order' project, which hopes to Americanise the planet through political, economic, military, cultural and various other means. The Muslim world must accept America's leadership; China and Russia must be controlled, their ground and influence sphere kept limited, and they must never be allowed to turn into a world power that poses a challenge to American supremacy. In order to achieve these goals, America has a need to set up military bases, intelligence and surveillance centres as well as airbases across the globe. Since Afghanistan has a geographically strategic position in the heart of Asia, America therefore wants to retain a robust prolonged presence here to meet any challenge presented by its deemed foes.

Petroleum and gas are critically important elements in today's world, powering the planet's vital lifeline. America has an eye on the untapped resources of Central Asia, as they foresee supplies dwindling in the Middle East; hence trying to monopolise this arena as well, and wanting to become its exporter worldwide, just as they currently are in the Gulf. To achieve this objective, America must maintain military bases in Afghanistan and have control over its land and airspace. If America were to reach this goal, then it will be another fundamental blow to the Islamic umma as the international infidelity once again strengthens itself physically and economically with the resources of Muslims, just like its ongoing looting in the Middle East.

To summarise the goals of the American military presence in Afghanistan then: America wants to force the Afghans to accept their international dominance, cultivate the system of Western democracy, 'Westernise' the Afghans by spreading irreligiosity, nudity, Western culture and other destructive behaviour so that the upcoming generation is apparently Afghan but with the creed, thoughts, behaviour and character of a pure American. On top of this, they want to loot the untapped resources of this nation, like the rare uranium and lithium chemical compounds, while forever keeping the country weak and dependent on assistance so it can be fully exploited.

We must accept that the prolonged presence of America inside Afghanistan is very dangerous. *Kufr* is absolute evil and the presence of disbelievers in the land of Islam under whatever pretext is detrimental to Muslims. The dream of an Islamic government in Afghanistan, the application of Islamic shari'a, the reform of future Afghan generations and other religious aspirations seem far-fetched during their existence. Their presence will lead to the spread of Western culture, Christianity, irreligiosity, nudity and other immoralities. They could possibly operate private media channels, educational institutes and other tools of recruitment from inside their bases, absorbing many Afghans. Since they are exempt from all inspections inside their bases, they could initiate deviatory programmes for future generations on a large-scale basis.

Their bases will be the recruitment and deployment centres for spies, while they operate their reconnaissance aircraft, including Reaper Drones, to target their opponents not only in Afghanistan but in south and central Asia as well as the border regions of Iran, which is a big threat for all Islamic and jihadi movements in the region. They will use these bases to project their power and intimidate Russia, China, Iran and even Pakistan; and since these facilities are based in Afghanistan and operated with its approval in the form of an Agreement, therefore these nations will view Afghanistan as an enemy and engage in destructive proxy wars. The Americans will use these bases as a hub for propaganda, intelligence, logistics and other things.

A tried and tested historical fact is that a pact between a weak and powerful party ties the hands of the weak and sharpens the sword of the mighty. The Agreement between the Arg and America can be viewed in the exact same light. America will never stick to their end of the Agreement, while the Afghan side will be forced to adhere to every condition and all their facilities will be fully exploited.

Afghanistan is the land of Islam, and the Americans are a transgressing infidel force which has invaded this soil and erected bases through a deceitful accord. When a land of Islam is invaded, then jihad becomes an individual duty for every Muslim nearby. If these Muslims are unable to repel this enemy, then jihad becomes obligatory on Muslims close to them; and if the effort of every Muslim is needed to drive back this enemy, then jihad becomes an individual obligation on everyone. With the invasion of Afghanistan by America, jihad has become an individual obligation on other Muslims as well, and not just the Afghans. Now that America has plans for a prolonged presence, Muslims must renew their pledge of jihad against the American infidels. If America is left peacefully alone in this land of Islam, it will have destructive repercussions. To combat America, a very comprehensive military, educational, cultural, propagation, academic and propaganda struggle needs to be put in motion. It is not wrong to assume that America cannot be pushed out once it has set foot here; rather this is just empty propaganda, part of the enemy psychological warfare, following the footsteps of its predecessor the Soviet Union which also pushed the notion and compared their involvement in a region to the foot of an elephant: once planted its removal is beyond human ability. We witnessed the Soviet elephant's feet chopped off in Afghanistan, disintegrated and never to be heard of again.

In reality no one has ever fought America, but [she] has been dealt a defeat each time she is resisted. Vietnam and Somalia are witnesses to these setbacks, and we also observed America suffering humiliating defeats on the battlefields of Iraq and Afghanistan.

Allah Almighty grants success to His slaves according to one's effort and will. The higher the ambition and the stronger the will, success and victory by Allah will be the same in proportion. If we have deep conviction that we can defeat the infidel America with our bare hands while solely relying on Allah Almighty alone, then He will surely grant us the same amount of strength and divine help.

One should never think that we will be able to live a life of honour and dignity with an American military presence and under the shade of an American elected government. If we want to know about life under the shadow of the Americans, then look no further than Japan, South Korea and their crimes in other countries where they have military presence. Just look at the oppression, transgression, embezzlement and other crimes of the American soldiers in countries where they abuse immunity from local law.

Look how America treats Japan: until recently Japan had the second strongest economy, and America desperately needed to maintain good ties, and yet they treated them in such an undignified and degrading manner. So how do you think they will treat Afghanistan, a country which functions on American rations and even pays the salaries of its employees from American aid?

In summary, just as jihad against America is religiously binding on every Muslim, similarly it is recommended for anyone who wants to live a free and dignified human life. We must understand that bliss, peace, brotherhood, security and advancement are not achievable so long as this evil is present here.

112

THE ARABIAN PENINSULA IS FRAUGHT
WITH DIVINE AUSPICIOUSNESS!

[The Taliban have for many years spoken of unity and obedience to legitimate rulers. This message followed in a similar vein, directed however at the conflict brewing among countries of the Gulf. The message is obsequiously cloaked and politely phrased. This is an example of the senior leadership trying to have an opinion on a particular topic but not wanting to offend donors and sometime supporters.]

Al-Emera (website), 20 March 2014

At the time when a black curtain of ignorance, cruelty and brutality was spreading the world over; humanity was chained in barbarism and despotism; people were drowning in their lusts and desires; there was fighting, injustice and insecurity; some people even buried their daughters alive; women were treated like animals; just then, a light sprang up inside the Arabian Peninsula which not only rescued the sinking boat of humanity but also guided mankind towards progress, security, justice, mercy, a prosperous life and all the blessings of this world and the world hereafter.

It was a great favour of Allah Almighty not only towards pious people but also towards the whole of mankind to bestow on them His last Prophet (peace be upon him) and his righteous companions (may Allah be pleased with them). Due to their sacrifices, political statesmanship and justice, it has been more than 1,400 years that Muslims are dwelling on a substantial part of the planet. It is an irrefutable fact that due to the blessings and benevolence of Allah Almighty, Islam is a stronger, more reasonable, authentic and more comprehensive system of life than any other system, which guarantees not only success in this world but also in the world hereafter.

The Muslim masses of the world have a high opinion of the Arabian Peninsula and people dwelling there because this holy land has special status in the heart of the Muslims due to the faithfulness, loyalty, gallantry, generosity of its people and their Islamic civilisation. They consider this area as not only bestowed with great blessings and favours, but also find themselves attached to the religious people of this area on the basis of ideological and cultural similarities. No matter how great the distances, how wide the oceans and how high the mountains, they share the same beliefs, the same divine laws and the same ideology.

It is also an irrefutable fact that even a minor difference or dissent among the Gulf countries causes great uneasiness and anxiety among the whole Muslim umma. This is the reason why the recent differences between these countries have negatively affected the minds of Muslim masses throughout the world and their aspirations for the unity and integrity of the Muslim umma will fade away if these differences are not solved as soon as possible.

We combine our voices with all other well-wishers and admirers of the Gulf countries and hope that their authorities and governments will be able to solve their grievances in a cordial atmosphere and find an opportunity to come forward and assist the needy and helpless Muslim masses for the sake of Allah's pleasure. They should unanimously support what is right and say no to the infidels and spurious and fictitious ones. They should neither care nor be afraid of the reproach of the reprehensible ones; rather they should unanimously fear Allah Almighty, who plainly says in His Holy Book:

O ye who believe! Fear Allah and be with the truthful.

We hope that they will follow the message delivered in the above verse of the Holy Qur'an and carry through their heavy responsibilities towards Islam and the Muslim umma!!

113

THE SECRET OF MUSLIMS' GLORY LIES IN THEIR UNITY!

[*This seems to have been a thinly-veiled criticism of the various conflicts in countries of the Middle East and perhaps also of the indirect conflict being played out there between Saudi Arabia and Iran. Note how the post does not specify any of this. They are sensitive to how donors and potential supporters read their statements, so this very generic statement has a layer of deniability to it.*]

Al-Emera (website), 13 July 2014

It is a great blessing of Allah Almighty that He has bestowed on us faith, the Holy Qur'an and the Holy Prophet (peace be upon him).

It is obvious that religion guides us onto the right path. All Muslims are brothers among themselves, and it is a manifestation of 'faith' to love one another for the sake of Allah Almighty. We should follow the teaching of the Holy Qur'an and the sayings of the Holy Prophet (peace be upon him). We should refer our differences and disputes to scholars and should obey their verdict with sincerity.

Muslims should help one another and share their joys and sorrows. The Holy Prophet (peace be upon him) has said: 'The believers are like one body in sympathy and benevolence among themselves; when one organ is in trouble, the whole body suffers from fever.'

We should work for the unification of Muslims; we should prefer the interests of the Muslim umma to our personal interests; we should bury the hatchet of disgust and not consider one's opinion superior to another; humility and love should be shown to one another. The Prophet (SAWS) and his companions used to be kind to each other and stern against their enemies. Love, kindness, brotherhood and care for one another bestow the help of Allah upon us, as Allah (SWT) says: 'Verily, Allah loves those who fight in His cause in rows (ranks) as if they were a solid structure' (Sura As-Saff, 4).

A Muslim must submit himself completely to the commands of Islamic shari'a, as Allah (SWT) says: 'But no, by your Lord, they can have no Faith, until they make you

(O Muhammad, SAWS) judge in all disputes between them, and find in themselves no resistance against your decisions, and accept (them) with full submission' (Sura An-Nisa, 65).

A Shura must be convened by all the leaders of the various jihadi groups, intellectuals and esteemed scholars in order for them to settle their disputes in its light; as Allah (SWT) says: 'and who (conduct) their affairs by mutual consultation' (Ash-Shura, 38).

Muslims must stay away from extremism in religion and desist from ruling on others. They should not have bad assumptions about their brothers and not believe baseless accusations and propaganda as Allah (SWT) says: 'O you who believe! If a rebellious evil person comes to you with news, verify it, lest you harm people in ignorance, and afterwards you become regretful of what you have done' (Al-Hujuraat, 6).

Difference of opinion about various issues is quite natural in human society. It is the duty of elders and wise people to find out solutions for those differences which can otherwise result in armed conflict. Our sacred religion has shown us clear guidance for solving our disputes. Allah Almighty says in His Holy Book: 'And if you differ in anything amongst yourselves, refer it to Allah and His Messenger (SAWS), if you believe in Allah and in the Last Day. That is better and more suitable for final determination' (An-Nisa, 59).

114

THE DEFINITION, AUTHORITY AND PURPOSE
OF AN AMIR ACCORDING TO THE SHARI'A

[This article, published on the Taliban's jihad sub-site, tackles the issue of how to distinguish between a legitimate and illegitimate leader according to Islamic teachings. The author of the piece would almost certainly not have been aware of this, but Mullah Mohammad Omar himself had most likely been dead for a year at the time of writing.]

Mawlawi Sailaab Omar

Al-Emera's stand-alone 'jihad' subdomain (website), 28 April 2014

The difference between a shari'a amir and a non-shari'a amir is found in the definitions given by great Muslim scholars. We have many great Muslim scholars who have always been considered the main source of knowledge throughout Islamic history. In particular, they had deep knowledge in the areas of political science and faith.

They define a shari'a amir in the following way: an amir is the heir of the Prophet in religious and worldly affairs.

The definition of imam and being an imam: imam is a word of the Arabic language and means a leader who is followed by the Muslim masses.

Imam and caliph:

The Muslim state, Emirate, sultanate and kingdom is called the caliphate.

The selection of an imam:

In his renowned book *Badaaya al-Sanaaya*, Aal ul-Deen al-Kasani writes that an imam is selected by a consensus vote of ulemaa (religious scholars). Hazrat Ibn Abbas quotes the Prophets saying: 'Islam and power (the sultan) are like two twin brothers. Both are inevitable for the reform of each other. Islam is the foundation, the sultan is the protector. If something is without a foundation, it is destined for destruction. Likewise, without a protector everything is destined for destruction.'

In his renowned book *al-Bab fil Uloom al-Kitaab*, Umar bin al-Damashqi writes that there will be no destruction until imams and kings follow the rules of shari'a. Hazrat Ibn Abbas quotes the Prophet saying, 'If rulers of a country follow the rules of shari'a and also instruct others to do the same, its people will not face decay despite committing sins and cruelties. On the contrary, if the rulers of a country commit sins and cruelties, its people will face destruction though they follow the rules of shari'a and also instruct others to do so. The most important duty of a caliphate is the implementation, empowerment and protection of shari'a. The main source of an Islamic state is the religion and its protection is necessary.'

According to Imam Mawardi's definition, the relation between religion and politics is even stronger. He says that without political support religion is doomed to decay and annihilation. If religion is removed, a political system will plunge into cruelty, treason and rebellion. It is not enough for a caliphate just to implement a shari'a system; rather it must also manage all worldly affairs of development. In fact, Imam Mawardi says that politics is an integral part of religion and there is no difference between religion and politics in Islam.

Conclusion

In the light of the above-mentioned explanations and statements of the great scholars, it has become clear that a legitimate amir's first duty is the implementation of the Islamic system, because an amir, sultan and caliph are the heir of the Prophet and it is their duty to follow the same system which was theoretically explained and practically implemented by the Prophet and his companions. According to Abu Hurraira, the Prophet said that the political affairs of the Israelites were run by their prophets. Imam Namvavi writes that the prophets of the Israelites managed all affairs just like the amirs and governors manage the affairs of their subjects. Abu Darda quoted the Prophet saying, 'The ulemaa (scholars) are the heirs of prophets'. According to Allama Ibn Najeem, when an amir makes efforts for reforms, it is called politics.

There are two types of politics. The first form is based on justice, which protects the oppressed from the atrocities of the cruel. The main source of this kind of politics is shari'a. Those who are not familiar with shari'a studies are unable to implement a just political system. Their second form, the politics of injustice, is forbidden by shari'a law.

Allama Ibn Khaldun defines shari'a law in the following words: All people should be encouraged to organise their lives in accordance with the laws of shari'a. These worldly affairs are only important when their goal is the achievement of welfare in the life after death. In fact the purpose of politics is the protection of religion and the pursuit of worldly affairs in accordance with the teachings of the Prophet. The first priority of the Prophet's politics was the protection of the belief system, and he then worked to manage the worldly affairs of the nation in accordance with divine laws.

The companions of the Prophet also followed his methods and gave first priority to the protection of the religion and faith, and then to running the worldly affairs of people according to the laws of shari'a.

The above-mentioned Prophet's sayings (hadith) prove that he (the Prophet) is the original leader and the ulemaa are his heirs. The Prophet has said that the ulemaa have the right to be his heir in Islamic politics, imamate, sultanate, caliphate and state affairs. For thirteen centuries the ulemaa controlled the reins of the state of Afghanistan and other Muslim states of the world. They protected all the Islamic traditions, beliefs, religion, sacred places and territorial integrity. They kept the whole Muslim nation united. When the Christian and Jewish devils destroyed the Muslim caliphate in Turkey, and the English, with the help of Mustafa Kamal Atatürk, introduced the system of democracy, they grabbed the right of power and authority from the ulemaa. After this nasty person came to power, the sacred religion of Islam was permanently severed from politics. Islam was banned in mosques and households. With the help of the evil Mustafa Kamal, the concept of democracy also appeared in various other Muslim countries of the world. Its ripples even reached our dear country of Afghanistan when King Amanullah Khan agreed with the English upon the system of democracy. Here too the infidels, in league with their trained stooges, grabbed the right of authority and power from the ulemaa. They removed the ulemaa from government offices and departments. After bearing many troubles, the ulemaa scarcely managed to maintain their control at least over the pulpit.

Gradually the sacred religion of Islam was replaced by the system of democracy; the titles of amir, sultan and king were replaced by non-shari'a republican titles. Emirate, sultanate and monarchy were replaced by republican structures. With the passage of time everything changed. Now even literate people are unable to differentiate between the two systems of Islam and infidelity, let alone the illiterate. With the help of their stooges, the infidels created many parties and groups in order to destroy the unity of the Muslim nation. This was the main target of the infidel democracy. They encouraged linguistic, ethnic and sectarian differences. They spread the habits and concepts of immorality, corruption, hatred, promiscuity, treason, violation of shari'a principles, religious blasphemy, dominance of infidel ideology and thoughts, lack of discipline, proposals of federal systems for the disintegration of the country, large-scale killings, cruelties and violation of rights in the country. The solution to all Muslim nations' problems and issues is the enforcement of an Islamic system. Other than an Islamic system, all other efforts are useless. It is the duty of the ulemaa to regain their right to be the heirs of prophets at all costs from the encroachers and oppressors. They should protect the prophetic heritage. Those who have been trained by the infidels are making a mockery of Islam. They use it as a tool for attaining power. The encroachers cannot differentiate between Islam and infidelity. They believe that they are the heirs of prophets. But this is neither right, nor do they deserve this status.

Islam is the complete code of conduct for the whole life of humanity. But they introduce it like the abrogated religions of Christianity and Judaism. The ulemaa must not be deceived by the false propaganda of the encroachers who pronounce that the ulemaa have no relationship with politics and should be confined to the affairs of mosque and pulpit. They claim that politics, the prophetic heritage, is not suitable for the ulemaa; and at the same time they are proud of their immoral politics. If the ulemaa fail to fulfil their duties, then definitely our religious values, beliefs, prayers, interactions, rights, traditions, sanctions, revenge penalties, morals and peace will be destroyed for ever. We will lose our future generations. There will be Muslims without Islam, believers without belief, ulemaa without knowledge, free people without freedom and rulers without power. The non-Islamic governments will be established for five-year terms on the basis of public polls for which the candidates will beg the voters. Corruption will spread and from rulers to the lowest ranking official all will indulge in stealing from the public exchequer. They will cause so many conflicts which will take the lives of millions of Muslims, and the religious ulemaa will be responsible for all that. For the sake of the establishment of the Islamic system, it is obligatory on all male and female Muslims to provide full and comprehensive support to the ulemaa. The consent of Almighty Allah, the salvation of the Muslim nation, the welfare of this world and the world hereafter and a prosperous life all are implicit in the establishment of a true Islamic system.

115

THE AFGHAN PEOPLE WANTS PEACE,
THEIR ENEMY WAR

[*Commentary pieces on the Taliban's website are still issued on a weekly basis (more if there are significant news developments), but the fervour that was present at the peak of the US troop surge is largely gone. This article is a representative summary of various positions that we might call 'the Taliban's positions', although that is a complicated phrase to use given numerous divisions and ongoing fragmentation within the movement.*]

Al-Emera (website), 20 November 2014

Peace is a great blessing of Allah and the accepted dire need of an Islamic society. Peace is a guarantor of security and stability. It removes hurdles in the way of development for a society and paves the way for a prosperous life. Peace is the demand and dream of every single Afghan, and it is the reason why intellectuals, elders and kind-hearted leaders have always prayed in the court of Allah the Almighty for peace to take shape, humbly asking Allah the Almighty to bestow this great blessing on the oppressed Afghan nation once again. 'Remember Allah's favour on you for He united your hearts when you were enemies, so that through His Grace, you became as brothers' (Surah 2, v. 103).

Peace is not a mystery that is impossible to understand or achieve; nor is it a high mountain that is impossible to climb. Peace has a clear meaning and is an obvious reality. Bringing peace to our society also has clear and simple methods. Whoever wants peace will search for ways leading to peace. If there are hurdles and obstacles, then he tries to remove them first and then take positive steps.

If there is sincerity and honesty, then peace like a light ahead will beckon those who crave it. If someone is trying to cash in on the name of peace, then that overloaded burden will not reach its destination.

If someone wants to provide his house with light, then there is no need to pay a visit to foreign counties, nor is there a need for the presence of American troops. Rather the house can easily be provided with light by simply cutting a window.

Obviously, peace has a different meaning in the view of the invaders if they think it can take place under pressure and force. In a speech to soldiers arriving back in UK from Afghanistan, the British Prime Minister David Cameron said: 'With your sacrifices you have saved the British [people].' Actually, the UK was safe even before the invasion of Afghanistan. In the view of David Cameron, peace means bombardment, massacre, displacement, harassment and oppression of innocent people, and they do not regret it. They think only the British people have the right to live a peaceful and comfortable life.

When Obama was initially elected president, he sent more troops to Afghanistan to put pressure on the mujahedeen of the Islamic Emirate of Afghanistan, because in his opinion this was the way to force the mujahedeen to submit to peace. According to them, peace is the superiority of one group over another, while in fact this is not peace but war.

Peace can be more easily achieved in our beloved country than in any other country or region, because we Afghans have five shared values:

– Afghanistan is an independent and sovereign state.
– Afghans have not accepted foreign invasions and invaders throughout their history.
– Afghans do not accept a life of subjugation nor stooge alien governments.
– The majority of people living in Afghanistan are Muslims.
– Afghans want an independent Islamic government.

Keeping in mind the aforementioned points, the following three-point agenda for peace should be seriously considered:

– All foreign troops should withdraw from our country.
– All agreements which contradict our sovereignty, integrity and the Islamic identity of Afghanistan, including the security agreements, should be declared null and void.
– An Islamic government should be established and Islamic shari'a fully implemented.

116

HALLMARKS OF THE ISLAMIC EMIRATE'S JIHADI MANAGEMENT

[*This article is perhaps best paired with text 80, 'The Islamic Emirate of Afghanistan and its successful administrative policy'. The author outlines some of the values and beliefs that he believes kept the Taliban afloat during this time, even when facing the combined armies of much of the Western world. As might be expected, Islam is at the core of his explanation, but so are the organisational principles that those associated with the Taliban have retained ever since the 1980s conflict.*]

Mawlawi Abdul Hadi (Mujahid)

Al-Emera (website), 2 February 2015

It appears that Allah (SWT) has destined Afghanistan to be an abode where contemporary infidel superpowers go to begin their natural decomposition. The decline of the British Empire began here, as did that of the Soviet Union and the entire world, in seeing that the crumbling of the unified military power of the West headed by America began with its foray into this land. Nearly all the major powers in this Western coalition, like America, Canada, Britain, France, Italy, Germany, Holland, Spain, Australia and others, have pulled out their troops from the battlefronts against the mujahedeen of the Islamic Emirate, resorting to a withdrawal approach instead of summoning the courage to admit defeat.

How did the Islamic Emirate manage to challenge this juggernaut of a military coalition throughout these thirteen years? How did it rally its nation and ranks to resist such a towering fighting force, made up of nearly 600,000 fully armed and equipped foreign and internal soldiers? How did it succeed in confronting international conspiracies, and prevent its ranks from flagging and sedition, instead encouraging them towards strength and solidarity? After the blessing and help of Allah (SWT), there is a committed and deliberate jihadi management process which has primed this resistance psychologically, militarily, economically, organisationally, politically and logistically at every stage, and propelled this lopsided war to favour a materialistically feeble and battered force in the face of a dominant world power.

The hallmarks of the management of the jihadi affairs of the Islamic Emirate can be summarised as follows:

1. Clinging to shari'a and relying solely on Islam

The true power source of the Taliban movement and management of the Islamic Emirate is derived from Islamic shari'a and conforming to its rules in every aspect of life, because the Taliban are not backed by any international military power and neither do they have a solid economic base; the movement and Emirate has not arisen or established itself as a result of long-tenured activism, nor does it have a nationalistic base or ideology to draw resources from a specific tribe or nation; it is not a member state of any international military coalition whose clout it could use for protection and to project power, and neither is it a highly trained military force equipped with an array of arms, that could employ its own manufactured weapons and might for its own survival and success. Rather, everyone witnessed its emergence and the stages it went through before its establishment with their own eyes, beginning as a self-conscious religious Afghan movement headed by former ulamaa (scholars) and commanders indoctrinated with a jihadi ideology whose soldiers were junior Taliban (students), who joined purely due to their strong religious fervour. It gained maturity ideologically, politically, socially and militarily during the different stages of its twenty-year struggle, and it confronted the formidable American-led international military coalition and compelled it to flee with exceptional insight, patience, courage and force.

The religious prestige of the Taliban made the Muslim nation stand behind it, supporting their devoted, volunteer and sincere army, and this religious standing motivated their confrontation both spiritually and psychologically.

Clinging onto shari'a during both hard and easy times, and building an Islamic government on this foundation, while ignoring all non-Islamic doctrines and rejecting any state law that opposed shari'a, these were the distinctive features that made the Taliban a pure Islamic symbol in the eyes of Muslims worldwide. It became a model for Islamic awakening, free from all influence of the contemporary infidel powers, an Islamic military and political blueprint of activism for all aspiring nations.

Many Islamic movements sprang up during the twentieth century throughout the Islamic world, but with the passage of time none of these movements retained their Islamic identities, due to misguidedly being intoxicated ideologically, politically, economically and militarily with a dangerous mix of ideas like communism, democracy, nationalism and others. They thus lost the trust of Muslims and sank deeper into the abyss, mutating into democrat, Western leaning, nationalist and deviant parties.

The source of Taliban power and salvation lies in their firmly clinging onto unadulterated Islam, rejecting all other beliefs and not retracting their Islamic principles and policies, for which they have created tens of thousands of martyrs in return for few political or worldly gains. If they do [presumably] take inspiration from other ideologies and political movements, then surely their fate will be no different from those parties which associate with Islam yet are in coalitions with secular parties in a democratic framework; they will be part of those governments which have declared open war against the mujahedeen throughout the Islamic world.

2. Belief in a jihadi solution, and refusing reconciliation with the enemy

Another hallmark of the Taliban movement and the Islamic Emirate is that it believes that the only solution to bringing about true change is the jihadi solution accompanied by education and *da'wa* (preaching), and for this lofty objective it has neither been lethargic nor has it offered concessions to the enemy.

The Taliban have learnt from the failed misadventures of contemporary Islamic movements and parties throughout the Islamic world; until and unless the reign of power is shifted to the hands of righteous people and governments founded on Islam, there can be no positive change. This reality can also be derived from studying the life of the Messenger of Allah, peace be upon him, and the famous leaders who delivered true change. Many movements and parties during the previous century renounced armed jihad in favour ideological, *da'wa*, political, educational and economic reform in the hope of bringing about change. They launched associations, dispatched millions of members, plunged into democracy, created coalitions with secularists, east and west leaning parties, wasted billions of dollars and precious years of their lives, but never were they able to change systems nor reform societies; contrarily they themselves were poisoned by secularism and democracy. They wanted to amend and improve tyrannical, despotic and foreign dictatorships by words and example, which contradict the logic of tyrants because the only language they understand is that of bullets and force.

Although the Taliban are not ideologically the inheritors of 'Sayed Qutb thought', yet essentially they have put into practice his idea that these corrupt ignorant governments can never be reformed through intermixing and activism in their established political framework; rather they must be uprooted and their remains discarded, so that upon the ruins new governments can be built on strong Islamic foundations and in the light of Islamic thought, because these systems will never accept reform or surrender to shari'a.

The Taliban also chose the natural and prophetic way of *da'wa* and jihad to bring about change, rejecting all endeavours of reconciliation with the internal corrupt secular parties and refusing to bow down to the arrogant US-led international crusader coalition. Neither did they compromise on their principles, nor did they reconcile with the enemy at the price of their principles and policies. And it was this stance by which Allah Almighty blessed their jihad and brought down a tyrannical enemy which cast terror into people's hearts through their hands. This political and military understanding of the Taliban proved that the policy of the sons of Madaris (religious seminaries), Minbar (pulpit) and Mihrab (altar) is far more evolved than the understanding of foreign-owned secular individuals and parties who consider themselves 'enlightened' but are in fact lost in the dark chasms of Western infidel thought, becoming alien to the true aspirations of the Muslim nation.

Adhering to the prophetic way of jihad and *da'wa* and inviting the Muslim youth to independence and Islamic revival is another hallmark of the Taliban and Islamic Emirate, which became an inspirational model for many jihadi movements. And abiding to this exact rhetoric in other Islamic countries is what essentially shook the pillars of power of the tyrant regimes.

3. A broad system and absence of individual/family control

Another hallmark of the Taliban movement and Islamic Emirate's management is that this movement is not tied to a specific race, tribe or region and neither does it orbit around a few individuals and families with others holding second-class status.

The Taliban movement and Islamic Emirate's management includes Pashtuns, Tajik, Baluch, Uzbek, Nuristani, Pashai and other ethnicities, and it is this pure natural characteristic that has propelled the current to all parts of Afghanistan.

The past few decades saw many organised Islamic movements arise throughout the Muslim countries, but as time went by their principles and Islamic thought were replaced in favour of power-sharing between individuals and families. This led to a loss of a popular base amongst the populace, turning these parties into family and individual franchises. A clear example of these events are our former jihadi parties and some of the other Islamic parties in our neighbouring countries.

However, the Taliban used extreme insight in their evolution and never restricted themselves to a specific ethnicity or a few particular families; rather they left the gates of opportunity open to everyone and swelled their ranks with qualified individuals committed to the cause of jihad. Therefore they never faced a shortage of human resources in any field throughout these fourteen years of dangerously long battle against America and Europe, and despite losing many mujahedeen and leaders to martyrdom and imprisonment, they were immediately replaced. Never did a feeling of vacuum occur in the fold, from Badakhshan to Helmand and from Herat to Nangarhar, because everyone felt that they truly belonged in their natural position and no one ever felt that a specific race or family was a pure breed and the rest secondary.

4. Absence of schism and dissent

Every movement and organisation that relies on individuals instead of ideological bonds, and its leadership leaches onto power at the price of the blood of the public, the results manifest themselves in forms of schism and dissent. However, it is rarely seen that a movement revolves around a set of beliefs and ideas while its leadership also accompanies its people into the arenas of sacrifice.

The rank and file of the Taliban remain motivated because its leadership is indeed always at the forefront of battlefields. This is why nearly 80 per cent of the leaders have either lost bodily limbs, or have lost their family members, or have suffered in the dungeons of prisons for many years. Naturally when the followers see their leadership in such a state, their trust in them becomes even firmer.

Becoming a leader in the Taliban hierarchy is not a proposition to acquire wealth and well-being, rather it is a grim invitation to the cradle of death and dark prisons. When the situation is thus, why would there be any quarrelling over leadership and positions?

The enemies of the Taliban plotted and schemed over the past twenty years to split the ranks of the Taliban, but none bore fruit. The unity of ranks has resulted in a materially and militarily weak side consisting of a few thousand mujahedeen overpowering an international coalition with an army of nearly 600,000 fully armed foreign soldiers and internal mercenaries.

The Talib ranks will only fracture and fissure if it indulges in tribal, religious and worldly incrimination, and begins leaning more on political favours than on jihadi spirit.

5. Consideration for Islam in all political and military affairs

Yet another hallmark of the Taliban is their deep consideration for Islam in all its military and political activities, meaning that just as their justice, legal, ethical and social works revolve around Islamic criteria, so do their military and political activities. They have continued their ongoing fight against the American Western coalition as a just religious war from start to finish. The Taliban did not label their fight a political struggle, nor did they cover it with the paint of nationalism; if they interacted politically, it was based on religious principles; and if they validated their war to their people and others, it was based on religious justifications.

Every reason provided by the Taliban for their jihadi endeavour in war, fighting spirit, political and ideological literature, interactions with the enemy and everything else have been based upon sound religious principles. It is with the blessing of this strong, practical relationship that they succeeded in winning over thousands of martyrdom-loving mujahedeen from the nation, and gained the prayers as well as material and spiritual assistance of the entire Muslim umma.

So long as the foundations of our jihad against Russia and Communism were based on Islam, the Muslims called it an Islamic jihad and rendered all kinds of assistance; but as soon as the jihadi leaders deviated due to their wrong political manoeuvres, decisions and steps, they lost their religious prestige and began relations with anti-Islam circles and government solely in pursuit of their personal agendas. In doing so, not only were they deprived by Allah Almighty from establishing an Islamic government, but these same leaders and their parties sided with anti-Islam forces working as mafias, militias, secular forces and West-leaning groups and shamelessly helped the crusader coalition against the mujahedeen and became tools in the hands of the West.

6. Assigning commissions during war for all civil and military duties

Another important hallmark of the Taliban and their jihadi work management is that they did not let the war conditions morph into anarchy and mayhem. Rather the war was kept orderly, and local fighting conditions were kept under tight control.

The Taliban did not allow anyone amongst the populace to form unauthorised groups or raise weapons that took advantage of the turmoil, but disciplined all civil and military conditions under a framework of methodical management while spreading the struggle countrywide. They assigned provincial and district governors, judicial authorities, military commanders, group leaders, and at the top assigned commissions for overseeing under the direct command of the leadership. In doing so, they not only kept the fight orderly, but also kept in check disorder, injustices and unauthorised groups and gunmen from prevailing among the populace.

That is why peace and justice are prevalent in the liberated areas, as compared to areas under the control of the American established regime; and that is why the ordinary people take all their legal and judicial cases to the Taliban courts. Even though the Taliban court systems are not exemplary, due to the various constraints, yet they are far superior to the stooge regime courts in every aspect.

The tidal wave that is the Taliban is a human manufactured current just like any other Islamic currents. It has its own distinctive advantages as well as faults, which we will mention in future posts. However, it is an accepted fact that the Taliban confronted an international superpower with extraordinary wisdom and courage, and in the process drew up a blueprint to follow for all nations combatting tyranny and injustice.

117

PUGWASH TALKS STATEMENT

[This statement follows in much the same tradition as the speeches delivered at Kyoto and Chantilly (sources 92 and 93 in this volume), offering a full outline of the background to the Taliban's emergence (not included as part of this excerpt) as well as a list of grievances and demands. This list is more specific than previous iterations, perhaps because the statement was delivered as a speech (though it was later published on the Taliban's website).]

Doha, Qatar, 2–3 May 2015

What do Afghans want?

Afghans are loyal to their country and religion. From Alexander to today's American invasion, whoever invaded their country, their Islamic and national values helped them resist their foe and guard their life and property. Still they are defending their homeland and values effectively, which is their universally accepted right. Afghans are never involved in damaging attacks against any nation or government in the world, but others come and devastate their homeland.

Afghans believe in the concept of mutual respect and demand cooperation in the areas of economy, education, health, culture and social affairs. They also demand that their leaders carry out joint efforts towards an independent, sovereign, united, peaceful Islamic Afghanistan: a regime that is the outcome of the sacrifices of the mujahedeen, where every man and woman has access to education, justice, economic prosperity and freedom of expression within the Islamic perspective. To bring about such an Islamic regime, where all ethnic groups are included, everyone should work for the development and rehabilitation of Afghanistan and finish off the imposed war. All the efforts of the Islamic Emirate are towards the above goals.

We regard the occupation of our homeland as the chief of our problems. The problems of our country cannot be solved through illegal and un-Islamic agreements, and such an agreement would create obstacles ahead of peace. We should prioritise our national interests over personal and party interests.

In our view, our nation wants their leaders to have a strong desire, intention and commitment towards peace. Stop any negative propaganda; our stance on peace must be clear, not the unclear and ambivalent approach of before.

Peace and national reconciliation

Peace is the basic need of every country, nation and individual. Without peace one cannot imagine achieving a comfortable life, or economic, educational, cultural, social and political development. It is obvious that those who want the development, prosperity and comfort of their nation will prefer peace. Peace cannot be achieved through mere slogans and statements, but needs a strong desire and practical measures. Before anything else, those obstacles need to be addressed that became the reasons for the elimination of peace.

In our country, occupation is the biggest single obstacle to peace. Also, injustice, the lack of a competent system, arresting innocent Afghans under different names and putting them in jail without proper trial, torture, night raids, putting the leadership of the Islamic Emirate on the international black list—these are among the obstacles to peace. By eliminating these obstacles, Afghans can come together on Islamic and national interests and values, and pave the way for permanent and lasting peace.

It is also important that the peace process is taken forward by those people who believe in the importance of peace, are notable for being truthful and honest, and can see the sustainability of peace as our basic need, and not a project based on the dictation by foreigners. Unfortunately in the past there were occasions when the peace process was viewed as a tactic. Peace can only be achieved when all the reasons for prolonging the war are eliminated.

We can see that there are foreign and domestic obstacles that are stalling the peace process. Among the foreign obstacles to peace are Americans and their allies respecting the opinion of Afghans, saying goodbye to the strategy of force, and withdrawing all their forces from Afghanistan.

The terrorism-related baseless allegations against the Islamic Emirate, and other such accusations, will only fuel the war. As a preliminary step towards peace, the Islamic Emirate should be given the chance to share its voice and opinion with the world and hear directly from the world.

About domestic factors, we would say that unfortunately whenever the Islamic Emirate took a step forward towards peace, the other side in the form of the BSA and Security Agreement tried to block those efforts. In one way or another, obstacles were created in the way of peace. The Kabul administration conducted efforts to make the peace process a failure, but in a way that no one could call them anti-peace.

Instead of talking to the Islamic Emirate, suggestions were made to talk to neighbouring countries; and when for the first time rumours were heard about the establishment of an office to discuss peace in Qatar, then the Kabul administration recalled their ambassador from Doha. And when the Islamic Emirate opened their office in Qatar, the Kabul administration expressed its opposition to it and intensified anti-peace negative propaganda.

The role of an office

To conduct talks, one needs for a neutral location and an office. Now, the Taliban don't have a specific address from which to conduct peace talks. One can only conduct peace-related negotiations from an office. An office is necessary to respond to public queries and eliminate their concerns.

We have seen that recently contradictory statements and rumours were spread about the beginning of peace talks that were far from reality. They added to the concerns of people, and such propaganda can only disrupt the peace process. If there was an office, then there would be a spokesman who could respond to such rumours and reports when needed, to avoid misunderstandings.

The dangers of the blacklist

There is a secret and baseless blacklist. There are people on the list who have no relation to the Islamic Emirate. Some are within the Kabul administration, and some are dead, but their names are still on the blacklist. The peace process and the blacklist are two opposing things, so there is a need to eliminate the blacklist.

It is also important that both sides take the peace process forward without pressure: not in a way that one side remains on the blacklist, is restricted in their movements and faces pursual, while the other side enjoys free movement and uses the blacklist as a tool to put pressure on their opponents at any time. Such an imbalanced process cannot be allowed, and will not have a desirable outcome.

Neighbouring countries, peace and the withdrawal of foreign forces

Peace in Afghanistan and the withdrawal of foreign forces are interlinked, because the withdrawal of foreign troops will pave the way for peace. Unfortunately until now the peace process has been used by the international community and regional players as a tactic. Peace has no place within the plans and policies of the Afghan government as a strategy; instead they are using it as a tool to fool the public.

Some parties believe that instead of achieving real peace, they would force the Islamic Emirate to surrender. They are trying their best to weaken the Islamic Emirate militarily, and then would force them to make peace from a superior position. Such efforts will prove useless and are far from reality. This is the old formula used by the Americans over the last fourteen years, but they weren't able to achieve anything. Thus we see that there is no tangible change in the policies of the Kabul administration.

In order to achieve peace, there is a need for clear intention and strategy that is based on reality. A statement made in the morning must not be different from an action done in the evening, as witnessed by our people in the last decade.

In addition to that, the international community and neighbouring countries must make honest efforts for peace and stability in Afghanistan. Like everyone on earth, Afghans also possess the right to have a sovereign and prosperous country and bring about a system based on its religious and national values. This will have positive results for the world and the neighbouring countries.

The role of the constitution

In this world, every government and regime needs a comprehensive law and constitution to maintain its domestic and foreign affairs, to pave the way for a peaceful and prosperous life for its inhabitants. A constitution is the basic need of every country, as without this important document major affairs of state will face problems and irregularities. Through a constitution, all the affairs of state, civil, political and social rights of Afghans will be organised and regulated and will guarantee equal rights for all citizens of the country. It will shed light on the separation of power between the three pillars of state, and will specify the form, authority and structure of the state. In general it will get the support and agreement of Afghans and the international community with regard to our domestic and foreign policies.

In line with this, the Islamic Emirate believes in a need for a constitution that is based on our holy religion of Islam, national interests, historical pride and achievements and social justice: that is responsive and committed to national values and human rights; that guarantees the territorial integrity and rights of all individuals; and will have no single clause or article against religious and Afghan values.

We clearly announce that the draft constitution will be prepared by Afghan intellectuals in the sovereign environment and then be presented to the people for approval. The present Afghan constitution is not acceptable, as it has been copied from the West and is prepared under the shadow of B-52 jet fighters. Articles are unclear and contradictory and are imposed on the Islamic society of Afghanistan.

The Islamic Emirate's political, social, economic and cultural vision

The members of the Islamic Emirate are of the local society and are living within the local society. They have always made sacrifices to achieve Islamic and national demands and objectives of the nation, so that we have an Islamic Afghanistan; the nation can exist in an independent and stable country and maintain our social, cultural, economic and political affairs according to Islamic principles.

In addition to that, the Islamic Emirate considers itself committed to all those rights of women that are granted to them by Islam. In Islam, women have the right to choose a husband, have the right to own property, have the right of inheritance, have the right to learn and work. The Islamic Emirate will safeguard these rights so that these rights are not violated, nor their Islamic and humanitarian values threatened.

The Islamic Emirate considers the construction and protection of the public welfare infrastructure as a basic need. Bridges, tunnels, hydropower dams, electricity transfer centres, mine excavation, oil refineries, educational institutions, madrassas, mosques, schools, universities, health centres, clinics, hospitals and other such public welfare institutions are considered the joint property of the nation, and their protection is a religious obligation. The Supreme Commander of the Islamic Emirate has always stressed the protection of lives, property and honour of the people, and has always instructed people to protect these public welfare installations and avoid civilian casualties. Despite propaganda from the enemy, the Islamic Emirate does not believe in the monopoly of power, but believes that Afghanistan is the home of every Afghan. Its protection is the obligation of everyone, so everyone has the right to take part in its development.

Peace reconciliation and the assistance of the international community

First of all, the international community must recognise all the legitimate rights of the Afghans, including the right to defend their country, nation and values—as is being practised right now by Afghans. They must put an end to the drama that is called terrorism. This will be in the interest and benefit of the International community if they play an impartial role in the Afghan peace process and do not victimise the Afghans for the sake of their colonialist objectives.

No one can kill the desire for independence in nations through force; rather, to the extent that a nation is oppressed, to that extent the desire and spirit to make sacrifices and their intention to resist intensifies. For the international community, the benefit of living in friendship and peace with Afghans is much greater than living in enmity.

The Islamic Emirate announces again, as a policy, that they don't want to cause harm to anyone, nor would they allow using Afghan soil against anyone. They want to cooperate with all countries, including their neighbours, for the sake of the prosperity of their nation; they welcome the honest efforts of 'everyone' in bringing peace to Afghanistan.

118

SPECIAL INSTRUCTIONS FROM THE ISLAMIC EMIRATE'S LEADERSHIP ON PRECAUTIONARY MEANS TO PREVENT CIVILIAN CASUALTIES IN THE ONGOING JIHAD

[*By 2015, the United Nations' regular reporting scorecard on civilian casualties (who had caused how many) had repeatedly provoked the ire of the Taliban's online commentators. Mullah Mohammad Omar (or whoever was writing his statements, given that he is said to have died in 2013) had started to insert more explicit language instructing Taliban fighters to be careful about causing civilian casualties. (Note that equivalent language had been present in the previous iterations of the* layeha *or rulebook.) This statement was a frank and de facto admission that not enough was being done. It is unclear to what extent the publication of this statement either stimulated any change in the behaviour of fighters or whether it was purely a public relations exercise designed to present a concerned face to the world.*]

Al-Emera (website), 4 January 2015

The Islamic Emirate's leadership imparts the following instructions to all mujahedeen regarding the ongoing jihad:

> Allah Almighty states: 'Whosoever killed a soul not to retaliate for a soul, nor for creating disorder in the land, then it is as if he killed all mankind.'[1]

Jihad is a holy obligation. Just as this struggle of jihad is obligatory, similarly, in all military campaigns and operations, it is obligatory on Muslims to follow the guidance of Allah Almighty, the instructions of His Messenger (SAWS) and the rights specified in Islamic law.

You have also received the instructions of the esteemed Amir ul-Mu'mineen through his messages regarding the importance of observing the rights and duties entailing our jihad in all your plans and operations. He has specifically emphasised that all mujahedeen operations should be executed with utmost care to avoid any civilian casualties.

Human life is priceless and a holy gift. You should thus exert all human efforts to avoid causing death of innocent lives and even those of animals, thus becoming a cause of usurping this priceless gift. In general human beings are considered as the creations and constructs of Allah Almighty. Therefore no one has the right to demolish these constructs of Allah Almighty except by His command and in accordance with His guidance.

In jihad the killing of enemies of Islam (infidels and those supposed Muslim lackeys who aid them) is made permissible according to the commands of Allah Almighty and in defence of His religion. In such circumstances the killings of such enemies of Islam becomes a cause of reward and Paradise by Allah Almighty. However, it is equally imperative that in carrying out this holy duty we do not cause the death of innocent or uninformed civilians.

Once an innocent life is taken, then it cannot be returned, even if we were to gather all the riches of this world. Such loss causes immeasurable sadness to the victim's family, relatives, children and those who know him, and this act is then described as cruelty and evokes the wrath and displeasure of Allah Almighty.

> The Messenger (peace and blessings be upon him) states: 'I swear by the One in Whose Hand is my soul, the killing of a Muslim is greater near Allah than the destruction of the Earth.'

In order to remind the mujahedeen that they must take even more care to avoid civilian casualties, by which they would become accountable for such a death in the Hereafter, or defame the name of the sacred mujahedeen, or allow such incidents to become propaganda tools for the enemies of Islam, we reiterate our command that you must take severe precautions to prevent civilian casualties in any operations that are undertaken. You must not carry out operations or bombings in any area where civilians could be harmed as a result of such actions.

If you cancel an operation against a high value target because you fear that civilians could be harmed as a result of this operation, then we are hopeful that Allah Almighty will provide an even easier opportunity for the mujahedeen to target this enemy and do so without risking the lives of civilians. When launching an operation against the enemy, the Messenger of Allah (SAWS) used to gather all the mujahedeen and forbid them to kill children, women or the elderly from amongst the enemy, and also he (SAWS) used to forbid them to destroy trees or farms.

Hence we also consider it obligatory that whenever mujahedeen commanders are launching military operations, they should gather their soldiers and remind them about not killing women, children or the elderly. Those people who do not stand shoulder to shoulder with the enemy forces and are not carrying out actions against jihad are to be considered as civilians, and no harm is to be caused to them.

INSTRUCTIONS TO PREVENT CIVILIAN CASUALTIES

If anyone fails to take precautions, plans negligent operations, causes civilian deaths or destroys civilian property, then such person will be answerable to Allah Almighty on the Day of Judgement and will be reprimanded in this life by the Islamic Emirate in accordance with the principles and commands of Islamic law.

119

COMMEMORATING THE NINETEENTH
ANNIVERSARY OF THE HISTORICAL GATHERING
AND SELECTION OF AMIR UL-MU'MINEEN
ON 4 APRIL 1996 IN KANDAHAR

[*This biography of Mullah Mohammad Omar was published to commemorate the application of the title Amir ul-Mu'mineen to the leader of the Taliban movement. It is one of the more detailed official accounts of the life and times of Mullah Mohammad Omar, even though there is reason to doubt some of the details.*]

Al-Emera (website), 4 April 201

4 April 1996 is a momentous day in the history of our Muslim people. Nearly two decades ago on this same faithful day, 1,500 scholars, dignitaries and jihadi leaders of Afghanistan approved Mullah Mohammad Omar 'Mujahed' as the leader of the Islamic Emirate, gave an oath of allegiance to him and conferred the title of Amir ul-Mu'mineen on him, i.e. leader of the pious believers.

In the official almanac of the Islamic Emirate, this day has its own significance due to that historical event, which subsequently is being commemorated by the Cultural Commission of the Islamic Emirate by publishing special articles and essays on this auspicious occasion.

As the publication of an inclusive biography of the leader of the Islamic Emirate was the urgent demand of our numerous colleagues, especially the writers and researchers, the Cultural Commission of the Islamic Emirate decided to commemorate that historical occasion by publishing a comprehensive biography of His Excellency, the Amir ul-Mu'mineen, Mullah Mohammad Omar 'Mujahed' (may Allah safeguard him).

For the prevention of false propaganda by a number of spurious writers, analysts and some biased circles, and to depict a clear picture for writers and ordinary people, we draw the life-sketch of His Excellency, the Amir ul-Mu'mineen, in the following lines.

His birth and early childhood

Mullah Mohammad Omar 'Mujahed', son of Mawlawi Ghulam Nabi, grandson of Mawlawi Mohammad Rasool and the great grandson of Mawlawi Baaz Mohammad, was born in 1339 AH (solar), i.e. 1960 AD, to a religious and learned family of Chah-i-Himmat village of Khakrez district in Kandahar province of Afghanistan. His father, Mawlawi Ghulam Nabi (late), was also born in Khakrez district and had received his early education in the traditional religious institutions and circles of this area. He was a well-known and respected erudite and social figure among the masses, due to his indefatigable efforts in educating and guiding people to the right path of Islam.

Two years after the birth of Mullah Mohammad Omar 'Mujahed', his father migrated from Khakrez district to Noday village of Dand district of this same province, and remained there till his last in spreading religious education among the local people. He died in 1965 in that area and was laid to rest in the old famous graveyard of Taliban in Kandahar city.

After the death of his father, Mullah Mohammad Omar 'Mujahed' moved at the age of five along with his family members from Dand district of Kandahar province to Deh Rawud district of Uruzgan province, where he started his early life under the supervision of his uncles Mawlawi Mohammad Anwar and Mawlawi Mohammad Jumma.

His early education

At the age of eight, Mullah Mohammad Omar 'Mujahed' joined the primary madrassa of Shar-i-Kohna area in Deh Rawud district to get religious education. This madrassa was supervised by his uncle, Mawlawi Mohammad Jumma, and Mullah Mohammad Omar 'Mujahed' also started his early education under him. Both of his uncles, particularly Mawlawi Mohammad Anwar, played a key role in his religious teaching and training.

Mullah Mohammad Omar 'Mujahed' successfully completed his primary and middle level education from this madrassa. When eighteen, he started acquiring the traditional higher religious studies in the region but could not complete them due to the malicious Communist *coup d'état* in 1978 in Afghanistan.

His family

Mullah Mohammad Omar 'Mujahed' belongs to the 'Tomzi' clan of the 'Hotak' tribe, which comprises many Pashtuns who have become eminent Islamic statesmen, national and jihadi heroes, like the legendary Islamic figure of 'Haji Mirwais Khan Hotak'.

Great Ghazi Haji Mirwais Khan Hotak (may Allah bless him), who is remembered with the venerated title of 'Mirwais Nika' (i.e. Mirwais, the grandfather) by Afghans, liberated Afghanistan from the tyranny of the Safavid dynasty in 1712 and laid down the foundation of a sovereign and independent Islamic state for Afghans.

Professionally, the family of Mullah Mohammad Omar 'Mujahed' comprises scholars and teachers of religious studies. They devoted their whole lives to serving the sacred religion of Allah Almighty, promoting religious knowledge and educating the Muslim masses ideologically. Therefore they were deeply admired in their area and spiritually were considered the most dignified and social figures in society.

The birth of Mullah Mohammad Omar 'Mujahed' in such a spiritual and learned family and his upbringing under the direct patronage of his well-educated and ideological patrons cultivated deeply in him the ability to grow as a sincere mujahed, a compassionate and vigilant Islamic and national figure who could emancipate Afghan society from tyranny, corruption and injustice and preserve our beloved homeland (Afghanistan) from the imminent danger of disintegration.

His brothers, uncles and all other family members are mujahedeen, and four of his family members have already sacrificed their lives as martyrs in the path of Allah Almighty. Mullah Mohammad Hanafia, the uncle of Mullah Mohammad Omar 'Mujahed', was the first to be martyred on 7 October 2001, the starting date of the brutal bombardment by American invaders.

His jihadi struggles

Mullah Mohammad Omar 'Mujahed' was in his early twenties when the Communists usurped control of Afghanistan through a bloody military *coup d'état*. It was a time when it became nearly impossible for Mullah Mohammad Omar 'Mujahed' like all other heedful students to continue their studies, as the atheist Communists were starting their encounter against scholars, Taliban, students and other Muslim intellectuals throughout the country. At that time, Mullah Mohammad Omar 'Mujahed' decided to leave his higher studies unfinished. He left the madrassa and turned towards the jihadi front to discharge his religious obligation.

He started his jihadi struggle under the well-known jihadi organisation of *Harakat-e Enqelab-e Islami* (Islamic Revolutionary Movement) in Deh Rawud district of Uruzgan province. After spending a while in this district, he earned a reputation for being a valiant jihadi figure who played an active role in several military operations against the Communists in various parts of that district. Due to his jihadi prominence and a successful role in various jihadi operations, he used to get the unanimous consent of all the mujahedeen of different parts and groups to be their commander in Deh Rawud district, for leading large-scale offensives against the enemy, and he executed exceptionally successful operations in which he was wounded several times. He participated in many confrontations for more than three years, along with his local mujahedeen, against the invading Russians and their internal Communist puppets.

The companions and commanders of his jihadi front say that Mullah Mohammad Omar 'Mujahed', in spite of being young, was efficient enough to discharge any responsibility or task, as he was bestowed with a strong physical composition and potency.

Later in 1983, he went to Maiwand district of Kandahar province along with his jihadi colleagues to improve the coordination of jihadi activities, and continued his armed struggle against the Russian invaders and their internal stooges under the leadership of the famous jihadi commander Faizullah Akhunzada, who belonged to *Harakat-e Enqelab-e Islami*, one of the seven well-known jihadi organisations of that time. Due to his successful role as a local jihadi commander in numerous jihadi operations and his efficiency and distinction in military tactics, he drew the attention of the then jihadi organisations, and eventually he was given the permanent responsibility of a jihadi front through *Harakat-e Enqelab-e Islami* headed by (the late) Mawlawi Mohammad Nabi Mohammadi.

From 1983 to 1991, Mullah Mohammad Omar 'Mujahed' executed very successful operations in the suburbs of Maiwand, Zheray, Panjwayi and Dand districts of Kandahar province, which were vital jihadi centres, and mujahedeen used to be involved in fighting the enemy on a daily basis. Similarly he personally and directly participated in several victorious operations against the Russian invaders on the main Kabul–Kandahar highway in the suburbs of Shahr-i-Safa and Qalat cities of Zabul province. His preferred weapon of choice was the RPG-7, which was simply called 'Rocket' among the local mujahedeen, as he was proficient and an expert in using this weapon. It is worth mentioning that Maiwand, Zheray and Panjwayi districts of Kandahar province were areas of intense fighting during the jihad against Communism, which turned the tide and brought about Russia's defeat and withdrawal. Such a large number of tanks and other military vehicles were destroyed on the main Kandahar–Herat highway that the enemy had erected walls made from these wreckages on both sides of the road to protect them from mujahedeen assaults.

Mullah Mohammad Omar 'Mujahed' was wounded four times in confrontational jihadi operations against the Russians, and in one of these operations he lost his right eye.

Mullah Mohammad Omar 'Mujahed' was known as a prominent and distinguished jihadi commander who played a crucial and decisive role in numerous jihadi operations against the Russian invaders and their internal Communist puppets in Kandahar and its neighbouring provinces. In the following lines, we will mention some events and anecdotes by his jihadi companions against the Russian invaders.

1. The enemy had a strong post inside Kandahar province which was known as 'Budwan' post. A military tank was stationed by the enemy at a strategic junction near the post which created a great hurdle for the mujahedeen as it could target any line-of-fire easily. The mujahedeen tried their best to destroy this tank but failed to succeed. Eventually Mullah Mohammad Omar 'Mujahed' was called in

for help from Sangisar area. He hit and destroyed this tank of 'Budwan' post with his RPG rocket launcher, which was a tremendous success for the mujahedeen at that time.

2. During the holy jihad against the Russians in the Mahalajat area of Kandahar province, Mullah Mohammad Omar 'Mujahed' was accompanied in a confrontation with the enemy by the martyred Mullah Obaidullah Akhund, who was later appointed Defence Minister of the Islamic Emirate and the Deputy of Amir ul-Mu'mineen after the American invasion. A large number of enemy tanks and other military vehicles were destroyed by them. The following day, visitors were bewildered and could not believe that the enemy was repelled. They thought that the enemy forces were still intact, even though a large number of their vehicles were burnt and the remaining ones were pushed back to their previous locations.

3. A convoy of Russian military tanks was passing through Sangisar area of Zheray district on the main Kandahar–Herat highway. Mullah Mohammad Omar 'Mujahed' was accompanied by Mullah Beradar Akhund, who later became the Deputy of the Islamic Emirate of Afghanistan, while they only had four RPG rounds. Unwaveringly they attacked the convoy and destroyed four military tanks with these rounds.

4. Mullah Beradar Akhund, a close friend of Mullah Mohammad Omar 'Mujahed' during the holy jihad era against the Russians, said that so many Russian tanks were destroyed by him that his friends are unsure of the exact number.

In 1992, after the collapse of Najib's Communist regime and with the eruption of factional fighting throughout the country, like all other righteous mujahedeen, Mullah Mohammad Omar 'Mujahed' laid down his arms, set up a religious madrassa next to the mosque of Haji Ibrahim in Gishaan village of Sangisar area in Maiwand district of Kandahar province, and settled there. He restarted his unfinished religious studies along with some other jihadi colleagues after a long and difficult fourteen-year struggle.

This was a time when deadly factional fighting had engulfed the entire country, including the capital city Kabul. Some factional warlords, purely for the sake of their personal interests, violated the objectives of the holy jihad against the Russians and brought humiliation to the aspirations of one and a half million Afghan martyrs who sacrificed their lives to defend Islam and establish an independent Islamic government in their beloved homeland.

Resistance against anarchy and founding the Islamic Emirate

Instead of establishing an Islamic system of life in order to fulfil the long-awaited aspirations of the whole mujahed nation of our country, internal factional fighting broke out. The fact was that the mujahedeen were weakened and sidelined through a pre-planned conspiracy. Some of the prominent Communist figures who should have been trialled were unfortunately given shelter by some former mujahedeen commanders, and some other warlords began looting, violating people and plundering the country in an organised fashion.

In this way, the whole nation and country was plunged into a state of anarchy and lawlessness which had not been experienced by the Afghans throughout their past history. The life, honour and property of all pious Muslims were endangered. Checkpoints and barriers self-made by stubborn, ignorant and brutal warlords were found on the main roads and thoroughfares of the country. Not only a disproportionate amount of money was demanded by these warlords from our poor countrymen, but the honour and chastity of our already oppressed people was also at stake at these barriers. The national assets of our country, the achievements of previous holy jihad and even the jungles and other natural and mineral resources were relentlessly exploited by those warlords, unprecedented in our history. Not only were the fruits of fourteen-year jihad against the Russians endangered, but the daily life of ordinary people was also at stake.

Social corruption, killing, looting and plunder, oppression, barbarism and the incessant sufferings of the Muslim masses were increasing daily due to the prevailing chaos and anarchy throughout the country. This situation deeply troubled the righteous mujahedeen who had fought for the freedom, dignity and prosperity of the Muslim Afghan masses.

Mullah Mohammad Omar 'Mujahed', who was living along with jihadi colleagues in Maiwand district of Kandahar province, was also deeply anxious about the prevailing anarchy, like all other true mujahedeen. He observed that numerous barriers were erected on the main Kandahar–Herat highway and the oppressed passengers, women and white-bearded elders were looted, disgraced and even killed in broad daylight by ruthless warlords. It is worth mentioning that the number of illegal barriers and checkpoints had increased to such an extent that the traders, bringing their merchandise from Herat province to the border town of Spin Boldak in Kandahar province, used to unload their goods in Maiwand district because of the unjustified demands of these barrier-holders. Then they would transfer their goods through little-known desert routes to their destination, which caused intolerable hardship.

Mullah Mohammad Omar 'Mujahed' and his colleagues were fully aware of the prevailing situation in Kandahar province, where the brutal warlords spread through each and every corner of the city. They were for ever grabbing both public and private property and selling them for huge amounts of money. They erected their private markets on government lands. Moreover, they often fought among themselves on minor issues, which caused great distress for the ordinary people.

These endless sufferings of the helpless and oppressed people of our country compelled the true and righteous mujahedeen to bond together and find a solution to protect the lives, honour and property of the Muslims. The mujahedeen started meetings and counselling amongst themselves.

Mullah Mohammad Omar 'Mujahed' and his companions arranged their first meeting in Zangiabad area of Panjwayi district in Kandahar province, involving the well-known and authentic local and regional ulamaa. This gathering of ulamaa headed by Mawlawi Said Mohammad (known as Mawlawi Pasanai Sahib), the arbitrator general of the mujahedeen in Kandahar province during the holy jihad against the Russians, told Mullah Mohammad Omar 'Mujahed' to stand and resist against this anarchy as he would be supported by all of them. This was the initial meeting of the Islamic Movement, and Mullah Mohammad Omar 'Mujahed' laid the first foundation of his struggle against chaos and corruption on 24–25 June 1994.

The Islamic Movement launched their struggle and fight against corruption and anarchy under the leadership of Mullah Mohammad Omar 'Mujahed', which was widely welcomed by the true and righteous mujahedeen and by the ordinary masses. First they liberated Kandahar province, and then other vast areas of Afghanistan from the corrupt and wicked warlords. At that time, when major parts of Afghanistan came under the control of the Islamic Movement of the Taliban, a large number of Afghan ulamaa, comprising more than 1,500 religious scholars, convened a meeting in Kandahar city on 4 April 1996. They approved the leadership of Mullah Mohammad Omar 'Mujahed' and conferred the title of Amir ul-Mu'mineen on him. On 27 September 1996, Kabul city, the capital of Afghanistan, also came under the control of the Islamic Emirate of Afghanistan, and subsequently the supremacy of the Islamic Emirate prevailed in 95 per cent of the territory of our beloved homeland, including all the central and northern parts of Afghanistan.

The Islamic Emirate of Afghanistan, under the leadership of Mullah Mohammad Omar 'Mujahed', established an Islamic system based on the sublime rules and principles of shari'a law. After a long interval, the world witnessed a practical model of an Islamic government once again. He saved the country from disintegration and disarmed the unruly warlords, which resulted in the restoration of exemplary peace and stability in the country, which had been deemed unattainable by the whole world, including the United Nations. But (and this is a huge 'but') the arrogant infidel powers of the world could not tolerate this shari'a system established by the Islamic Emirate, which became a thorn in their eyes. Therefore they adopted and initiated antagonistic behaviour towards it. They tried their best either to find or to create lame excuses to overthrow this system, and eventually they launched a joint military invasion against it.

His charismatic personality

As a leading personality, Mullah Mohammad Omar 'Mujahed' has a unique and charismatic personality. Contrary to high-ranking officials and leaders, he does not want to show off or boast. He is not eager or excited to speak if it is unnecessary to do so. And if needed, his words and sentences are keen, perceptive and logical. For instance in the early days, prior to the American invasion, wide-ranging propaganda was launched to demoralise the mujahedeen and oust the Islamic Emirate. The Americans left no stone unturned, and all the Western media outlets, their radio stations and popular television stations were fully devoted to promoting American malicious objectives.

But contrary to all these devious efforts and propaganda, he assured his own people in his simple, reasonable but self-confident mode and tone and delivered the following message:

'Allah is Almighty. Whether it is America or a tiny ant, it makes no difference to Him. America and her allies should listen carefully that the Islamic Emirate is not like one of the previous regimes whose Amir (head) would flee the country, as happened in the case of King Zahir Shah, the former monarch of Afghanistan, who sought asylum in Rome; nor will my soldiers (personnel) surrender to you. You should remember that these are well-organised jihadi fronts. If the capital and other cities of the country fall in your hands and the Islamic government is ousted, instead of surrendering our mujahedeen will spread through the countryside and go to the mountains. What will you do then? Inevitably, you will be caught and killed everywhere, just like the Russians.

You should realise that bringing chaos is very easy, but its eradication and the restoration of law and order is a huge and strenuous task. Death is inevitable and all living creatures will have to die one day. Instead of dying without faith and dignity while supporting the Americans, wouldn't it be better to die with faith and dignity in the service of Islam?'

Some people might not have understood these expressions of Mullah Mohammad Omar 'Mujahed' which were laced with firm belief, devotion and sincerity; but nearly fourteen years have elapsed since this huge one-sided battle was launched, and the American superpower, the NATO alliance and other allied forces are on the verge of defeat by the empty-handed but devotional and determined mujahedeen of Mullah Mohammad Omar 'Mujahed'. Those gentlemen might now understand the simple but historic expressions of our leader.

Similarly, at the beginning of the American invasion, he declared to the Afghan masses in a radio broadcast speech, while alluding to the foreign invaders and their internal stooges, that weapons can bring death but cannot defy it. This sentence might have been a meaningless and insignificant composition of words for some people, but in the previous thirteen years the implications of these simple words were practically observed when the brutal foreign invaders relentlessly killed a large number of innocent people with the help of their advanced technology and weapons of mass destruction; but they could not turn death away from their own soldiers, who have been incessantly killed, wounded and incarcerated for the last thirteen years by the heroic mujahedeen under the leadership of Mullah Mohammad Omar 'Mujahed'.

It is an important fact that even the arrogant foreign invaders, who are fully equipped with all kinds of modern weapons and other facilities, plainly admit that thousands of their soldiers were killed and wounded inside Afghanistan in this futile war.

According to Mullah Mohammad Omar 'Mujahed', it is better to speak less and do more as our religion emphasises deeds over words or ideas. His life is totally free from ceremony and unnecessary protocol. He has adopted a simple and plain style in all aspects of his life. Simple dress, simple food, simple talk, frankness and informality are his natural habits. He does not stand on ceremony and dislikes ceremonial people.

He considers determination, prudence and sincerity as the basis of all progress, and the more prudent, sincere and decisive he is among his colleagues, the more he is admired and loved by them. Similarly, he is used to facing hardship, suffering and the ups and downs of life. Whatever the magnitude and intensity of the tragedy or trouble might be, he remains tranquil and does not lose either his temper or his courage. During varying conditions of jubilation and jeopardy, triumph and failure, he remains serene and self-controlled.

He deeply respects scholars and other elders. Gravity of manner, dignity, modesty, reverence, reciprocal respect, sympathy, mercy and sincerity are his natural traits. Strong determination, trusting in only One Allah the Almighty and a strong belief in what is ordained by Him are the distinguishing features of his life. This is why Mullah Mohammad Omar 'Mujahed' is deeply loved and revered by his followers and the mujahedeen, which has nothing to do with his apparent worldly status. It has been nearly thirteen years since our beloved homeland Afghanistan was invaded and occupied by the brutal foreign invaders, but his devoted and sincere mujahedeen follow his verbal and written commands and decrees as reverently as they did in his presence and do not hesitate to sacrifice their lives to execute his orders.

His vigilance about international and Islamic issues

Mullah Mohammad Omar 'Mujahed', as the founder of the Islamic Movement of the Taliban and leader of the Muslims, is fully cautious and takes a keen interest in all the issues relating to the Muslim umma.

He has always defended the issue of the Al-Aqsa Mosque (the first *qibla* or prayer direction of early Muslims) and the vindicated claim of Palestinian Muslims. He has taken a clear stance and supported all issues of Muslims in all parts of the world. He considers it the duty and obligation of every Muslim to liberate the Al-Aqsa Mosque from the occupation of Zionist Jews.

Mullah Mohammad Omar 'Mujahed' feels pity and shares the sufferings of all Muslim people. His sincerity, sympathy, brotherhood and cooperation with the Muslim brothers of the world are not restricted to slogans, but rather he has proved them practically and in the real sense of all these terms.

His ideological association

Ideologically, Mullah Mohammad Omar 'Mujahed' belongs to the main *Ahl-i-Sunna wal Jama'a* (the believers in Qur'an, traditions of the Holy Prophet, peace be upon him, and the consensus of Muslim umma). He is an imitator of the Hanafi school of thought.

He is severely opposed to all heresy or heterodox opinions. He never likes sectional, ideological and factional differences among Muslims. He always recommends and insists on Islamic and ideological unity and cooperation with his followers and all other Muslims, as ideological unification among Muslims is the utmost demand at this crucial time. Following the path of our pious predecessors and leading scholars in the light of the Qur'an and hadith (i.e. the traditions of our Holy Prophet, peace be upon him) is considered the only path of salvation by him for the Muslim umma.

His personal life

Mullah Mohammad Omar 'Mujahed', who has spent the most part of his life in acquiring religious studies, jihad, invitation and guidance towards Islam, might be the poorest person who has taken no personal advantage from the *Bait ul-Mal* (i.e. the public treasury of the Muslim state) among the contemporary leaders of Afghanistan. He has not accumulated any wealth to spend on a luxurious life in the previous jihad era against the Russians by taking advantage of his personal influence, nor has he lived lavishly in the seven years' reign of his overall control during the Islamic Emirate of Afghanistan.

Mullah Mohammad Omar 'Mujahed' even now does not own an ordinary residence, nor has he any cash deposits in foreign bank accounts. In 1999, when unilateral and ruthless economic sanctions were imposed by the United Nations on the oppressed people of Afghanistan and all the foreign bank accounts of Taliban leadership were frozen, Mullah Mohammad Omar 'Mujahed', the highest-ranking official, being the head of the Islamic Emirate of Afghanistan, had no bank accounts either inside the country or outside, nor anywhere else with any assumed name.

During the reign of the Islamic Emirate, when his residence came under the deadly attack of the brutal enemy which resulted in the martyrdom of his family members along with several other innocent people, some officials of the Islamic Emirate decided to build another residence and an office for the leadership of the Islamic Emirate in the north-western part of Kandahar city, near the hill of Baba Sahib for his safety, as there was no residential area in the suburbs of this location. This residence was also administered by the *Bait ul-Mal* as one of its general properties, therefore it too was not considered the private ownership of his Excellency.

In 1996, when he was conferred with the title of Amir ul-Mu'mineen (i.e. head of the pious believers), instead of showing excitement or jubilation, he bitterly wept till his shoulder sheet was completely soaked with tears. At the end of that historical meeting, he told the ulamaa present:

> 'You are the inheritors of the Holy Prophet (peace be upon him) and you have thrown a heavy responsibility upon my shoulders. In reality, you will be held responsible for my steadfastness as well as any deviation from it.

> O our teachers and respected scholars! If I cannot discharge this huge responsibility of the Muslim masses in a proper way or deviate from it, you will have to guide me towards the right path in the light of your knowledge. If the Taliban make mistakes in the implementation of shari'a and you do not guide them knowingly, you will have to bear the responsibility on the Day of Judgement.

His nature and temperament

Besides the natural silence of Mullah Mohammad Omar 'Mujahed', he is affable and has a special sense of humour, as he never considers himself superior to his colleagues whatever their status might have been. He treats them cheerfully, cordially, compassionately and with reciprocal reverence. In most of his meetings, he usually speaks about jihad.

His daily activities in the present circumstances

In the present crucial conditions and regularly being tracked by the enemy, no major change and disruption has been observed in the routine works of Mullah Mohammad Omar 'Mujahed' in following and organising jihadi activities as the leader of the Islamic Emirate. He begins his working day with prayers to Allah Almighty and recitation of the Holy Qur'an. In his free time, he studies various commentaries of the Holy Qur'an and traditions of the Holy Prophet (peace be upon him). He keenly follows and inspects jihadi activities against the brutal infidel foreign invaders. In organising and reshuffling jihadi and military issues, he delivers his orders in a specific way to his jihadi commanders. He regularly follows jihadi publications and other international media resources to judge his victories, and likewise other issues against the foreign invaders. In this way, he remains in touch with the day-to-day happenings of his country as well as the outside world. These activities form his basic daily life in the present circumstances.

The Islamic Emirate under his leadership

The Islamic Emirate of Afghanistan was established as an Islamic Movement under the leadership of Mullah Mohammad Omar 'Mujahed' on 24 June 1994, which subsequently passed through several crucial stages while enjoying the support of thousands of scholars, mujahedeen and the pious masses of our country. It had the honour of implementing Islamic shari'a in 95 per cent of the land of our beloved homeland. It is still controlling vast areas of the country and is involved in armed resistance against the infidel Western invaders as a pure and lofty Islamic Emirate.

Mullah Mohammad Omar 'Mujahed' is still the leader in the present hierarchy of the Islamic Emirate of Afghanistan. His deputy, the leading council, judiciary, nine executive commissions and three other administration organs are active under his leadership, forming the warp and woof of the present set-up of the Islamic Emirate.

The deputy of the Islamic Emirate, besides inspecting and assessing all the subordinate organs, conveys their working reports to the Amir ul-Mu'mineen and communicates the orders and decrees of the leader to all the concerned organs and authorities. The leading council of the Islamic Emirate consists of twenty members who are appointed by the leadership and convene their meetings under the deputy of the Islamic Emirate. This council discusses and makes decisions about all political, military, social and other critical issues.

The judiciary of the Islamic Emirate has a separate and wide set-up which comprises primary courts, courts of appellation and courts of cassation which are busy discharging their own responsibilities.

To meet the needs of present circumstances, nine different commissions are set up in the present hierarchy of the Islamic Emirate. Due to ongoing jihadi requirements, the largest is the military commission, which consists of nine sub-circles. This commission is responsible for appointing governors or military in-charges for all 34 provinces of Afghanistan, military in-charges of all districts, setting up sub-commissions which are subsequently responsible for all military and civil affairs of their respective provinces and districts.

The remaining commissions are as following:

– Education and Training Commission
– Commission of Political Affairs
– Cultural Commission
– Economic Commission
– Health Commission
– Invitation, Guidance and Amalgamation Commission
– Commission of Prisoners' Affairs
– Commission for NGOs

The remaining organs of the Islamic Emirate are:

– Organ for the Prevention of Civilian Casualties
– Organ for Martyrs and Disabled People
– Organ for Collecting and Organising Special Revenues

The Islamic Emirate has controlled a major part of Afghanistan as a well-organised and working system for over two decades under the leadership of Mullah Mohammad

Omar 'Mujahed', which has sincerely implemented the Islamic system of life in all areas of its jurisdiction. Law and order is restored; the lives, honour and property of the Muslim masses are safeguarded.

During this whole period of time, the Islamic Emirate has faced several challenges and adversities as the only active Islamic system of governance, but it has successfully survived by the grace and benevolence of Allah Almighty through all these challenges and confrontations, as it has proved its determination and steadfastness to its lofty principles throughout these adversities.

May Allah Almighty protect and safeguard our leader!

120

9/11

AN INCIDENT AND A PRETEXT

[*The attacks of 11 September 2001, turned out to be a watershed moment for the Afghan Taliban movement. The key figures who planned and managed the plot were in Afghanistan prior to the attacks (some, like bin Laden, for years) and it was the proximate cause for the foreign intervention and the fall of their government. Despite all this, many within the movement (even senior figures) do not believe that bin Laden was involved. It has certainly always been an official position of the movement to cast doubt on any claims to the contrary. This commentary article, published fifteen years later, is representative of that position.*]

Al-Emera (website), 19 September 2016

If we look into the history of imperialism, we will find that illegitimate pretexts have always been crafted for the justification of invasions. The incident of the World Trade Center in New York on 11 September 2001 is a good example. Though the embassy of the Islamic Emirate in Islamabad immediately condemned this incident during a press conference following its happening and strongly denying any involvement of IEA in it, yet hardly an hour had passed before American officials started levelling accusations and used this incident as a pretext to invade our independent country.

If sabotage activities outside the country had been the policy of the Islamic Emirate, then it would have conducted many similar acts during the past decade and a half, because they have been practically fighting against invaders in the country. But the entire world has seen that the Islamic Emirate through its actions has proven wrong all the accusations made by the invaders in this regard.

Although many independent investigators shed doubt on the reality of this incident one and half decades ago, America invaded our beloved country under this pretext. So far they have martyred hundreds of thousands of our countrymen, and these so-called advocates of human rights have even harmed the tents of nomads, wedding ceremonies and funerals: for example, bombarding wedding ceremonies in Bala Baluk, Deh Rawud and Hisarak districts; bombarding funeral processions in Khost and Azizabad; bombarding a children's school in Kunar province and many other such examples which show the atrocities and inhumane actions of invaders. Unfortunately these incidents are still happening on a daily basis, while organisations calling themselves protectors of human rights in today's civilised world have neither raised their voices for these oppressed people in the past nor they are raising them now.

Keeping innocent people as prisoners in miserable conditions in Guantánamo and Bagram prisons, with no accusations substantiated against them, is another scar on the face of so-called Western civilisation, democracy and human rights. History will never forget it. Furthermore, the invaders installed a surrogate corrupt administration (in Kabul) under this pretext, which holds top position in the global corruption index.

They claimed that there were a few hundred terrorists, but ultimately ended up sending 150,000 troops to Afghanistan (to fight them). They used phosphorus bombs and daisy cutter bombs and chemical weapons against the Afghan people. In fact all these efforts were exerted to bring the brave mujahed people of Afghanistan under the yoke of imperialism. But the mujahed Afghan nation has once again revived the history of their Muslim mujahed forefathers. The brutalities of the invaders have not shaken their courage nor their terror; rather they have bravely confronted their conspiracies, money and weapons, leaving the Western generals in shock and awe.

We would once again like to remind the invaders that (our) nation can never be subjugated by your use of terror (tactics) and drones. Nor can you solve the issue of Afghanistan by use of force or false pretexts. The label of terrorism has lost its meaning. You should accept the reality. Independence and the establishment of an Islamic system are the legitimate rights of the Afghan Muslim nation. If you are going to come around to accepting this reality tomorrow, better accept it today. A wise choice if you prefer.

121

ISLAMIC EMIRATE

SOLUTION TO ALL PROBLEMS

[*The Taliban of 2016 is a different organisation to the group that took Kabul in 1996, or even the group that reconvened to fight in the early years following the fall of their government in 2001. Plagued by internal divisions and squabbles over resources, it probably doesn't make sense to talk in general terms about 'the Taliban's position' on a certain issue. This commentary article, as far as it is possible to judge from the outside, is sufficiently broad as to be shared by the majority of those affiliated with the movement.*]

Al-Emera (website), 7 May 2016

Many governments have been tested in our beloved homeland, but each has failed in delivering the demands of this strictly religious Muslim nation. Rather they toyed with their property, land, honour, pride, life and livelihood; but the only ruling entity which safeguarded their religious and national values and protected them from every harm was the Islamic Emirate.

The Afghans are a Muslim nation. They can only accept a government which gives them their due rights, like distribution and proper use of *Bait ul-Maal* (the public treasury), securing their lives, punishing the oppressor, helping the oppressed; in short, providing them with the opportunity to live peacefully under the shade of shari'a. And governments which endanger their lives and property, which fail to punish the oppressor but rather support them further, in which highways are dotted with robbers and businesses are ransacked, then this nation combats such regimes with all the might at its disposal, as one can see today with our own two eyes.

Today we are witnessing this exact type of rule being forced upon the throats of our religious countrymen, a regime enforced in the sky and on the land by the aircrafts and tanks of foreign powers. They feel no safety under this powerless regime which dances to the tunes of others, playing with their honour and lives and heaping oppression upon oppression. That is why they have been forced to unsheathe their swords and choose a life of hardship that only offers bitter food, destroyed livelihoods, imprisonment, injuries and martyrdom...

Today the property of this nation is looted, their villages bombed, their sons, wives and fathers martyred, tortured and maimed; today the honour of the noble chieftains, elders and religious scholars is played with by the vile regime soldiers and Arbaki militia, and not even our beliefs, Qur'an, madrassa and mosques are spared from their ridicule.

However, the Islamic Emirate—during its rule and in areas under its control today—has protected and respected all of their beliefs and religious sanctities. Today the people living in areas of the mujahedeen only fear the aircraft and helicopters of the two-headed regime. There is no fear of bandits of kidnappers, and neither do they have to worry about protecting their lives and property from thieves and strongmen.

During the Emirate, a thief never entered a home or kidnapped a child or violated the honour of anyone. Every oppressed person was given his due right and the oppressor was handed due punishment. And such peace of mind and happiness still reigns supreme in areas under the control of the mujahedeen today.

Even today, if there is ever a case of murder in areas under the control of the mujahedeen, the perpetrators are swiftly apprehended and punished accordingly; but by contrast today we witness the killing and bombing of our noble elders being responded to by the regime with eerie silence. Today we see our hospitals levelled to the ground along with all their doctors, patients and workers; yet the regime initially tries to justify the incident, and when the killers acquit themselves by playing the role of judge, jury and executioner, the regime welcomes their decision and encourages the perpetrators to continue their actions.

And similarly the term 'administrative corruption'—which was never heard of during the Islamic Emirate—became a household name and won our country second place in the world.

In conclusion, the Islamic Emirate is the solution to all the stated problems, just as it proved during its rule. It is the only entity which can provide this nation with a peaceful, serene and happy life; safeguard their religion, life, property, business and honour; and protect all of their religious and national values.

122

STATEMENT OF THE ISLAMIC EMIRATE
ON THE FIFTEENTH ANNIVERSARY
OF THE AMERICAN INVASION

[*The Taliban's media department have been issuing variations of this statement for months and years. As such, it can serve as a useful way to show the continuity in the Taliban's messaging, particularly in a time of upheaval amidst the leadership and fighting ranks.*]

Al-Emera (website), 6 October 2016

Tomorrow, 7 October, is also considered a black day in the history of Afghanistan, like the 6th of Marghumay.

Fifteen years ago on the same day, 7 October 2001, the US-led occupying forces launched a brutal military occupation of our sacred county in violation of all humanitarian laws and international norms.

American invaders apparently made the incident of 11 September an excuse for her savagery, which was not justified in any way and is not till this day, because the Afghan people neither had a hand in it nor were they aware of the plans.

But in spite of that, the then American rulers and her allies invaded Afghanistan against all international norms and without presenting any evidence.

To find some justification for their horror and to acquit from accountability to the oppressed Afghan people, they declared some other goals of their attack, which include:

1. To make Afghanistan self-sufficient.
2. To end narcotic production/trade in Afghanistan.
3. To form a government according to the will of the Afghan nation.
4. To establish peace, stability and security in the country.

But fifteen years have passed since the US occupation, and we can see that everything is going in reverse. Has Afghanistan stood on its own feet? They made it the poorest country in the world, and despite abundant resources no fundamental work has been done.

Before the US occupation, the Islamic Emirate was able to eradicate drug cultivation to zero, but now under the American occupation Afghanistan has shattered the world record for cultivation and export of the drugs.

Instead of building a government system according to the desire and will of the Afghan people, they have imposed the world's most corrupt set-up: a combination of thieves and gangs of evil and corruption with the force of airplanes and tanks, and are supporting them to this day.

The security and stability of the country are such that a senior US general declared that a thousand people are killed per month in Afghanistan. Bombardment of civilian houses and public facilities is the daily routine of the occupiers and their stooges.

Thus the Islamic Emirate condemns the barbaric invasion and the continuation of occupation by America and her allies in the strongest terms, and on the fifteenth anniversary of their horror once again calls upon the invaders to leave our country, to bring the brutal occupation to an end, to stop the bloodshed of innocent Afghan people in your heinous existence, and let the Afghan people decide about their own country and future.

This is the same sensible and reasonable solution to the dispute that the Islamic Emirate identified fifteen years ago, and has repeatedly declared it for you over time.

Otherwise the believing Afghan nation will continue their legitimate struggle under the leadership of the Islamic Emirate, until these invaders are expelled from the country like the previous ones; by which time you will have lost tens of thousands more troops and wasted hundreds of billions more dollars in exchange for a historical and humiliating defeat. That time is close, Allah willing, and the entire world is witnessing the signs of it.

123

INSTRUCTIONS TO THE MUJAHEDEEN
FROM THE COMMANDER OF THE FAITHFUL

[*The Taliban's current leader as of September 2017 is Hibatullah Akhundzada. He published a book in May 2017 entitled* Mujahedino ta de Amir ul-Mumenin Larshowene *(Instructions to the Mujahedeen from the Commander of the Faithful). It can be seen as a new take on the* layeha *or rule book which has been issued and revised in various forms over the past decade. This selection offers a sense of the style of the full 122-page book, the publication of whose translation is forthcoming by First Draft Publishing.*]

Published as a print edition in Afghanistan and Pakistan (Editors' digital copy), Summer 2017

Preface

All praise is due to Allah. We laud Him, we beseech Him for help and ask His protection; we confide in Him, we trust Him alone and we seek protection against the evils and mischief of our souls and from the bad results of our deeds. Whomsoever He guides on the right path, none can misguide him; and whomsoever He declares misled, none can guide him onto the right path. And we bear witness that none deserves to be worshipped except Allah. He is alone and has no partner. We bear witness that Muhammad is His servant and Messenger.

Allah says in the Qur'an (Al Ahzab, 56): 'Indeed, Allah confers blessing upon the Prophet, and His angels [ask Him to do so]. O you who have believed, ask [Allah to confer] blessing upon him and ask [Allah to grant him] peace.'

'O you who have believed, fear Allah and speak words of appropriate justice. He will [then] amend for you your deeds and forgive you your sins. And whoever obeys Allah and His Messenger has certainly attained a great attainment.' (Quran, Al Ahzab, 70–71).

'God Almighty speaks the truth.'

Respected Muslim brothers, and especially the mujahedeen of the Islamic Emirate:

It was the practice of the Prophet Muhammad (PBUH) to provide Islamic instruction including manners, permissible and non-permissible [elements] of jihad to the mujahedeen groups before sending them off to war. This was to ensure that the mujahedeen played their jihadi role according to the shari'a, not exceeding or deviating from the limits of the shari'a.

Regarding this, there is a hadith in the book Sahih Muslim: Hazrat Bareeda (RA) narrates that when Prophet Muhammad (PBUH) designated an amir for a jihad group of his companions, He ascribed piousness to the amir and other Muslims. He used to say, 'In the name of God and in Allah's path, fight with those who are infidels and disbelievers. Do jihad and do not steal goods seized in war, don't be unjust or betray, and do not kill children.' This hadith is very lengthy in which the Prophet Muhammad PBUH has mentioned essential instructions and manners to the mujahedeen, such that a mujahed needs.

From these sayings of the Prophet Muhammad, it is known that it is the duty of each Muslim's amir to issue instructions and guidance to the mujahedeen from time to time in order that the jihad of the mujahedeen is as per the shari'a, protected from deviations and exaggerations.

Jihad is not an unlimited action or audacious killing, but like every other religious practice the shari'a has set a special jurisprudence for jihad. Only by following that path and complying with those terms, orders and instructions is it possible to carry out actual jihad.

'Enough.'

As before starting other worship, it is compulsory to learn and understand the shari'a instructions and manners. Similarly, before anything else, a mujahed should understand the important instructions and manners of jihad.

All those important instructions that the mujahedeen need are published in general by the Islamic Emirate. From time to time through the Islamic Emirate head's messages, special instructions, military training lessons and during yearly training programmes, these instructions are described again and again.

This is so that the mujahedeen are more attentive to their character/role, their intentions and deeds are amended and their jihad finds acceptance with God. These instructions are presented to the mujahedeen from the leader of the Islamic Emirate, Amir ul-Mu'mineen Sheikh ul-Hadith Mullah Hibatullah Akhundzada. The mujahedeen should try to read these instructions, understand them and act accordingly. In case any mujahed cannot study, another mujahed who can read and write should read and make others understand these instructions.

We pray to Almighty God to make these instructions acceptable and effective, so that these become a reason for sincerity, piousness, renaissance, morality, brotherhood and unity among the mujahedeen. Similarly, for the Islamic Emirate shura member Mr Sheikh ul-Hadith Mullah Abdul Hakeem, we request ample rewards and privileges from God since he cooperated a lot in producing this booklet. May Allah accept his efforts.

INSTRUCTIONS TO THE MUJAHEDEEN

Amin, O Lord of the worlds.

On the importance of intention

Intention is an important order, not only for jihad but during all worship. Allah says: 'And they were not commanded except to worship Allah, [being] sincere to Him in religion, inclining to truth, and to establish prayer and to give zakat. And that is the correct religion.'

Meaning: When any work is done for a cause and there are no other demands or expectations, this is known as sincerity.

The word 'sincere' is used here to call attention to the fact that the task from the start until the end should have sincerity. A person who does good work is sincere because there is benefit and he goes to do obligatory work because it is compulsory. In this way he accomplishes every task for his God. His purpose is not to show off, for the law or anything else. Islamic scholars even say that the purpose of accomplishing good deeds shouldn't be in order to go to heaven or to save oneself from hell. There is no way out of it.

[...]

Obedience to the amir

Obedience to the shari'a amir is obligatory. As Allah says in the Qur'an:

Translation: 'O you who have believed, obey Allah and obey the Messenger and those in authority among you. And if you disagree over anything, refer it to Allah and the Messenger, if you should believe in Allah and the Last Day. That is the best [way] and best in result.' (Qur'an, 4:59)

First Allah orders a person to obey His commands, and secondly those of the Prophet Muhammad (PBUH), and after that Allah has ordered you to obey the commands of those vested with authority.

Sahl ibn Abdullah says: 'If a ruler orders an Islamic scholar not to issue a fatwa, then he has no right to issue a fatwa. If he issues a fatwa, he is a sinner. Even the ruler is cruel.'

Imam Qurtubi says: 'Then Allah has commanded that if there are any differences regarding issues among you, you should refer to the Qur'an and the sunna, and to how it is referred to in the Qur'an and sunna. This is best known by the ulemaa.' So it is clear from this that it is obligatory to ask the Islamic scholars, and their example is necessary.

Sahl ibn Abdullah says: 'People will be in goodness as long as they respect Islamic scholars and the ruler. If they respect them both, their lives in this world and the next will be pleasant; if they disgrace them, their lives will be ruined.'

Abu Bakr (May Allah be pleased with him) says: 'The one who respected the caliph of Allah, Allah will give respect to him on doomsday. The one who disgraces the caliph or ruler in the world, he will be disgraced on doomsday.' (Musanad Ahmad Hadith #20433)

Ziyad bin Kusaib Al-'Adawi said: 'I was with Abu Bakra under the Minbar of Ibn Amir while he was giving a Khutba wearing a fine garment.' Abu Bilal said: 'Look at our amir wearing clothes of wickedness!' So Abu Bakra said: 'Be quiet! I heard the Messenger of Allah (peace be upon him) saying: "Whoever insults Allah's Sultan on the earth, Allah disgraces him."' (Tirmidhi Hadith 2224)

As it is obligatory to respect the Khalifa or Muslims' leader, in a similar way it is obligatory to follow the orders and respect the amirs (sub-leaders). During the eleventh hijri year, the Prophet Muhammad (PBUH) organised a group for Ruum's war which included senior companions like Abu Bakr Siddiq, Umar Farooq, Saad Bin Abi Waqas, Abu Obeida bin Jarrah and others (May Allah be pleased with them). Osama bin Zaid was appointed as group leader, whose age at that time was not more than twenty. At this time an ailment of the Prophet Muhammad (PBUH) increased and the group delayed their departure. The Prophet Muhammad (PBUH) passed away because of this ailment. Later, Muslims pledged to Abu Bakr (May Allah be pleased with him). He sent the group and asked Osama bin Zaid to help him by leading Umar with him. He left Umar with Abu Bakr (May Allah be pleased with them). Later whenever Umar meet with Osama he used to say, 'Welcome, my Amir.' When someone was surprised by this respect that Umar gave to Osama (May Allah be pleased with them), he said, 'He was appointed as my amir by the Prophet Muhammad (PBUH).'

Here the respect of the amir is shown and it is clear that if an elder appoints an amir (even if he is younger), he should be followed.

Abu Huraira (RA) narrates from Prophet Muhammad (PBUH): 'Whoever obeyed me would have obeyed Allah, and whoever disobeyed me would have disobeyed Allah. And whoever obeyed the amir would have obeyed me, and whoever disobeyed the amir would have disobeyed me.' (Sahih Muslim, Hadith 1835)

Similarly, Abu Huraira (RA) narrates that Prophet Muhammad (PBUH) said: 'You should be obedient to the amir in every circumstance, whether there is woe or comfort, whether you like it or not, even if someone else is selected instead of you.' (Sahih Muslim)

In Fatah al-Muhalam's interpretation, it is written that 'Whenever more privileges or such are given more to others, the purpose is that it is not justifiable to stop obeying because of this, i.e. if the amir doesn't bring justice to the situation by providing privileges and resources to his subordinates by giving more to others.'

Abu Zar (May Allah be pleased with him) said: 'My friend the Prophet Muhammad (PBUH) advised me to obey my amir, whoever he is, even if he is from a lower tribe.'

Attention: Even if the leader of the mujahedeen is from a lower tribe, obedience to him is obligatory.

INSTRUCTIONS TO THE MUJAHEDEEN

[...]

In the case of disobedience towards Allah, there is no obedience to the amir

Ali (May Allah be pleased with him) narrated: 'The Prophet Muhammad (PBUH) said: 'There is no obedience to anyone if it comes to disobeying Allah. Verily, obedience is only for good conduct.'

One of the benefits of obedience is that it ensures unity among Muslims. If there is no unity among them, then everyone will indulge in vicious activities. The other benefit is that with this, Muslims can dominate their enemies.

You should have a positive perception of imams and officials

The general public and especially the mujahedeen should have a positive perception of imams and officials, and shouldn't interpret or compare their actions negatively (suspiciously). Rather, they should positively justify the actions of the amir / imam / officials to the best of their ability. Allah says in the Qur'an:

Translation: 'O you who have believed, avoid much [negative] assumption. Indeed, some assumption is sin. And do not spy or backbite each other. Would one of you like to eat the flesh of his brother when dead? You would detest it. And fear Allah; indeed, Allah is accepting of repentance and is merciful.' (Al Hujrat, 12)

Imam Qurtubi says: 'This means that if you see their deeds appear to be good, then don't be suspicious.'

Abu Huraira narrated: 'The Prophet said, "Beware of suspicion, for suspicion is the worst of false tales; and do not look for others' faults and do not spy, and do not be jealous of one another, and do not desert (cut your relation with) one another, and do not hate one another; and, O Allah's worshippers, be brothers (as Allah has ordered you)."' (Sahih Bukhari, 6064)

Qurtubi writes: 'Perception in this hadith and Qur'anic verse means "accusation", and it is forbidden to accuse someone without having a valid reason. For example, someone is accused of drinking alcohol or fornication and there is no sign of either of those. This is the reason that "doubt" here means accusation. Allah says: "If there is a suspicion in a man's heart, then he researches and investigates, tries to see and listen until the accusation is proved." The Prophet Muhammad (PBUH) has forbidden such kinds of accusation and that type of "doubt" is illicit. This is because you don't see the visible signs. If the one you are suspicious about has good deeds and has honesty, then this type of "accusation" is illicit and it's obligatory to stop it.'

Harms of misperception (suspicion)

Suspicion brings many harms, first given the Qur'anic verse stating that: 'Some doubts are punishable sins, like being suspicious about people and believers.' Secondly, suspicion creates hatred and establishes large distances between those who are close. Thirdly, if there is suspicion about amirs, this leads to disobedience.'

Values of Islamic government (Khilafa and Emirate)

Without the dominance of a caliph/ruler whose rule is based on Islam, shari'a orders cannot be completely implemented. The Qur'an is a complete system sent by Allah which covers people's interests, matters, belief, jihad, orders, education, limitations, direction, inviting good and stopping bad deeds, ethics and manners, and everything is present. To implement all of these, it is only possible to do so through an Islamic government having a caliph or ruler who implements Allah's transmitted law through his government.

When the implementation of obligatory orders is related to an Islamic system, then it is obligatory to have such an Islamic system. It is the supreme rule of principles and means that 'if an obligatory order is dismissed, whatever is dependent on that happening also becomes obligatory'. Allah says in the Qur'an: 'Indeed, I will put upon the earth a successive authority (caliph).'

Imam Qurtubi in interpretation of this verse says: 'This verse is sound evidence for having a leader and a caliph who is obeyed, so that he will be a focus for the cohesion of society. The rulings of the caliphate will be carried out. None of the imams of the community disagree about the obligatory nature of having such a leader, except for what is related by Abu Bakr Asim, who is from Muta'zillah.'

For us the evidence is what Allah has said (in the Qur'an): 'I am the One making a caliph on earth.' Allah says: 'O Dawood (AS), I am making you a caliph on the earth.' In another verse: 'Allah has promised those among you who believe and do righteous good deeds that He will certainly grant them succession (caliphate) to them on the earth.' Similarly, there are also other verses regarding the establishment of the caliphate.

Imam Qurtubi says: 'The companions agreed to make Abu Bakr caliph after the disagreement which took place between the muhajiroon [the ones who migrated from Mecca] and the Ansar [the people of Medina] as some of them said that one amir will be from you and one from us. Abu Bakr and Omar (May Allah be pleased with them) satisfied the muhajiroon and they took back their statement. If it had been a definite obligation that the ruler had to be from the Quraysh, there would have been no point in the argument and the debate which took place.'

Muhammad Omar an-Nasfi in his book *Beliefs* says: 'Muslims should have an imam (leader) who implements orders, sets limitations (limitations as per Islamic shari'a), protects the borders, prepares groups (army), receives Islamic taxes from Muslims, stops wrongdoers, usurpers, thieves and robbers. He sets up Friday and Eid prayers, stops conflicts between people, accepts witnesses related to rights, marries boys and girls without guardians, and divides the booty and more.

Ibn Khaldun says in his book, the *Muqaddima*: 'It is obligatory to choose an imam (leader) and as per the shari'a it is obligatory for the consensus of the Prophet's companions and their followers to be evident. Because when Prophet Muhammad

(PBUH) passed away, the Sahaba (companions of Prophet Muhammad, PBUH) prioritised selecting Abu Bakr (May Allah be pleased with him).' He adds that during every era Muslims selected their amir, and that they haven't been without an amir ever, and that this consensus is evidence in support of having an amir.

Islamic clerics say: 'The imam's role is among the most important obligations of the religion. The Prophet's companions (May Allah be pleased with them) selected the caliph before burying Prophet Muhammad (PBUH). Only later did they bury Him (PBUH). The importance of the caliphate and the Emirate is also obvious from this. There are many sayings of Islamic scholars regarding this, and no one can deny it.'

If there is no Islamic rule, then the shari'a commands of the Qur'an and hadith will remain suspended. These commands are for implementation and not for suspension, therefore the efforts of the mujahedeen for the establishment of the Islamic Emirate are the religion's most important obligation to be implemented.

NOTES

INTRODUCTION

1. Visit https://www.alexstrick.com/blog/2015/8/afp-covers-the-taliban-sources-project to read media coverage around when the British Library rejected the project.
2. Visit talibansourcesproject.com to learn more about the project and sign up to access the original materials.

PART 1: MUJAHEDEEN AND TOPAKIYAAN (1979–1994)

1. Contemporary scholars of the Taliban movement often make a distinction between small-t 'taliban' and large-T 'Taliban'. The former are those who were engaged in religious studies and also those involved in the fronts of the 1980s; the latter refers to those associated with the movement that took the name 'Taliban' in 1994.
2. *Otaq* means 'room' in Dari, and it was a word to denote the (small) group of people who fought together in a particular location during the 1980s jihad.

2. DESERT ATTACK

1. The Shindand military base is located in Herat province (western Afghanistan).
2. The word *kuchi* derives from the Dari *kuch kardan*, which means 'to be on the move' or 'moving'. *Kuchis* uproot their homes twice a year with the seasons and are found all over Afghanistan.

3. MIRACLES OF THE JIHAD

1. The group called *al-Amr bil Ma'rouf wa al-Nahi 'an al-Munkar* ('commanding right and forbidding wrong') was active in Taliban territories from the beginning in an informal sense, but was promoted to the level of a ministry in early 1996.

PART 2: ISLAMIC EMIRATE OF AFGHANISTAN (1994–2001)

1. This was a plan put together by southern (mainly Kandahari) mujahedeen who were frustrated by the dysfunctional nature of the interim government and planned to capture the territory spanning from Herat to Kabul.
2. Large-scale in terms of weapons and troop numbers deployed.

7. THE BEGINNING

1. Sura al-Baqara, 286.

32. SPEECH BY MULLAH MOHAMMAD OMAR

1. *Haram* is a religious term used to denote that which is not permitted by Islam. It is the opposite of *halal*, which literally translates as 'that which is permitted'.

33. THE GROUP

1. This means 'teacher' in Dari and Pashto, but sometimes is just used as an everyday honorific to convey respect.

40. YOUR LETTERS, OUR RESPONSES

1. 'Sisters' is used here to refer to fellow Muslim women.

46. MULLAH MOHAMMAD OMAR AND THE APPLE

1. Note that the story refers to Omar ibn al-Khattab (586–644), the second of the so-called Rashidun caliphs who ruled following the Prophet Muhammad's death. Omar succeeded Abu Bakr (see above) in 634 after the latter's death from an illness. He was a convert and a companion of the Prophet. He died in 644 at the hands of a Persian attacker.

47. THE RESPONSIBILITIES OF AN AMIR AND HIS OFFICIALS IN THE ISLAMIC SHARI'A

1. Abu Bakr (573–634) was the father-in-law of the Prophet Muhammad. He was the first Caliph (following the death of Muhammad) and ruled 632–4. He died of an illness in 634.

62. AN INTERVIEW WITH SATAN

1. 'Father of the Nation' or *baba-i mellat* is a reference to the former King, Zahir Shah.
2. The BBC and Voice of America (VOA) are prominent radio broadcasters operating in Afghanistan.

64. *LAYEHA*

1. This translation and the commentary were made by the Afghanistan Analysts Network, originally published on their website and reprinted here with their permission.
2. The 2006 *layeha* was first translated into German and English, with illustrations of the Pashto text in *Die Weltwoche*, 29 November 2006. The Editor noted that it was distributed initially to the 33 members of the shura, the highest Taliban council, at their meeting during Ramadan, September–October 2006. This is a fresh translation which is consistent with the translations for the 2009 and 2010 versions of the *layeha*.

67. OUR HEROIC MARTYRS

1. Al-Ahzab V.22–23.
2. Al-Ahzab V.11–12.

68. STATEMENT ON THE DEATH OF MULLAH DADULLAH

1. Qur'anic saying used when someone dies.

69. ONE TALIB: I'M FED UP WITH JIHAD

1. Reprinted with permission from larawbar.com (http://larawbar.net/6703.html).

77. INTERVIEW WITH THE ISLAMIC EMIRATE WEBSITE ADMINISTRATOR

1. The original date of the interview is 12 December 2010. Republished from *al-Somood* issue 55.
2. Al-Saff: 8.

79. CODE OF CONDUCT FOR THE MUJAHEDEEN (2010 EDITION)

1. This translation and commentary (in footnotes) was made by the Afghanistan Analysts Network, originally published on their website and reprinted here with their permission.
2. Translation by Marmaduke Pickthall, *The Meaning of the Glorious Qur'an*, originally published by A. A. Knopf, New York, 1930, accessed at http://www.islamicity.com/quransearch/
3. [ ] are used to indicate original Pashto words in the text or explanations of terms by the translators; ( ) are for brackets which are in the original text.
4. This is actually the 3rd edition. Earlier versions were published in 2006 and 2009.
5. Commander of the Faithful, Omar's official title according to the Emirate. In the Code of Conduct, the word 'imam' is used to refer to Omar; in Dari and Pashto, it is usually used for the cleric who leads Friday prayers and for notable Islamic scholars.
6. *Ta'zeer* punishments are those not fixed by divine law; those which are fixed (*hudood*) are restricted to crimes such as murder, adultery and blasphemy.
7. The word used for invite is *dawat*, which is an Islamic term used to invite people to join or renew the faith.
8. This refers to someone who has been arrested as part of a judicial case.
9. *Sayi' bi'l fisad* is a religious term dating back to early Islamic history and was used to describe spies and other fifth columnists.
10. *Fei* and *Beit ul-Maal* are both Arabic terms used in Islamic law to mean public property.
11. A *khand* is a hole or pit dug in the path of one's enemy in the hope that he will fall into it.
12. A companion of the Prophet Muhammad and one of the most important narrators of hadith.
13. The ignorance of pre-Islam or non-Muslims.

80. THE ISLAMIC EMIRATE OF AFGHANISTAN AND ITS SUCCESSFUL ADMINISTRATIVE POLICY

1. al-Hajj: 41 FN.
2. al-Nisa: 58.
3. al-Hujurat: 13.

86. ISLAMIC REVIVAL

1. This mission name was later changed to 'Enduring Freedom'.
2. Literally, 'praise be to God!'

91. THE CRUCIAL RESPONSIBILITY OF THE NATION TOWARDS THE CHASTE AFGHAN WOMEN

1. Qur'an al-Ahzab, 59.

104. SEVEN THREATS TO JIHAD

1. A reference to parliamentarian Shukria Barakzai.

118. SPECIAL INSTRUCTIONS FROM THE ISLAMIC EMIRATE'S LEADERSHIP ON PRECAUTIONARY MEANS TO PREVENT CIVILIAN CASUALTIES IN THE ONGOING JIHAD

1. Qur'an: al-Majida, 32.

GLOSSARY

alhamdulillah: praise be to God

(Allah), Azza wa Jal: Almighty and Most Great

(Allah), Ta'ala: The Most Glorified

AS: abbreviation of *'aleihi al-salaam* or 'peace be upon him' (see PBUH)

alim / ulemaa: singular/plural versions, literally 'one who has knowledge'; it refers to a religious scholar (primarily of the Sunni clergy) who has been educated in the religious sciences (the Qur'an, the sunna and the hadiths etc.)

Allah: God

Allahu Akbar: God is the Greatest

amir: literally translated as 'prince' or 'commander, the word amir has a specific meaning in the context of the Afghan conflict post-1979. The mujahedeen in southern Afghanistan, and indeed throughout most of the country, were organised into fronts and *otaqs* (literally, 'rooms') that had specific commanders associated with them, who would then be tied to a specific amir or chief, who would usually be fundraising across the border. The amir, in turn, would be affiliated with one of the seven mujahedeen parties officially sanctioned by the ISI, and therefore could gain access to funds, weapons and training.

Amir ul-Mu'mineen: an Arabic-language phrase literally translated as 'Com- mander/ Prince of the Faithful', first applied to the second of the Rashidun caliphs who succeeded the Prophet Muhammad, Omar ibn al-Khattab, and used by many who followed him. It fell out of use in the mid-thirteenth century but was invoked in 1996 by Mullah Mohammad Omar.

Amr bil Marouf wa Nahi an al-Munkar: 'the Promotion of Virtue and Suppression of Vice', a principle derived from the Qur'an and which the Taliban made into a fully-fledged ministry.

ANP / ANA: Afghan National Police / Afghan National Army

Arbaki: militia

GLOSSARY

Atan: a traditional Pashtun dance. Participants move in a circle while clapping their hands to the rhythm and spinning around. One person in the circle will be the leader and others will follow his moves. It is often performed at celebrations and weddings.

aya: term used to refer to each verse of the Qur'an

Beit ul-Maal: used to refer to the money that the Taliban group / movement had. It functioned as a sort of national treasury.

Bismillah ar-Rahman ar-Rahim: 'In the Name of God, the Most Gracious, the Most Merciful'

burqa: all-enveloping garment worn by the great majority of women in southern Afghanistan when they are in public. Famously imposed as obligatory dress by the Taliban in the 1990s, the burqa is most often referred to by Afghans as *chadari*. Sky-blue is its most common colour, but shades of brown, green and even red are to be found.

CBM: confidence-building measure

da'wa: literally 'invitation'; takes different meanings depending on context, but often it implies invitation to (convert to) Islam.

Dar al-Hijra: the country to which someone has fled; in the case of this text, Pakistan is sometimes referred to using this term

Dar al-Salaam / Dar al-Harb: the place (literally 'abode') of peace and the place of war. One series of Muslim perspectives on the world divides places geographically between *dar al-salaam* and *dar al-harb*. The Taliban would consider Afghanistan, as a place where Islam was respected, to be *dar al-salaam*.

Dar ul-Hefaz: literally 'house of memorisation'; refers to the educational institution commonly found in rural areas of Afghanistan and Pakistan in which the Qur'an is taught to students

Dari: one of the two national languages of Afghanistan; very similar to Farsi or Persian as spoken in Iran

Deoband(i): a small religious seminary in India (established in 1867) that has had a profound impact on the religious and ideological education/upbringing of generations of Muslims in south Asia. It is frequently cited as one of the major external influences on the Taliban's world view (since many were educated in Deobandi madrassas), but the precise extent of this has yet to be delineated.

deen: literally 'religion'

Eid: Afghans, and all Muslims, have two main religious days of celebration called Eid: Eid ul-Fitr and Eid ul-Adha, more or less equivalent to the Christian Christmas. The days of Eid are characterised by special prayers and sermons, as well as by an emphasis on family, friends and the giving of gifts.

GLOSSARY

fajr: the morning prayer performed at sunrise

fi sabeel Allah ta'ala: in the cause of Allah

fitna: an Arabic-language term that literally translates as 'sedition' or 'temp- tation', but with the various consequences also implied (e.g. disorder/chaos). It is often used as the antonym to a state of peace. As such, it takes on an Islamic context with the suggestion that dissent or conflict (e.g. within the umma) is un-Islamic.

Ghazi: literally translates as 'Islamic warrior' and is a loosely approximate alternative for the term mujahed

hadith: a report of the words and actions of the Prophet Muhammad as deter- mined and authenticated by a chain of evidence and proof (known as *asnad*). It is an impor- tant part of the oral tradition of Islam, and these reports survive in written form in collections codified by religious scholars.

Hafiz: an honorific or title conferred on those who have memorised the Qur'an by heart

Hajji: a title technically given only to those who have been on the Hajj, the Islamic pilgrimage to Mecca, which is one of the five pillars of the Muslim faith, but also a title which in Afghanistan (and throughout the Muslim world) is sometimes used merely as a term of respect for the middle-aged and elderly.

halal: a religious term used to denote that which is (legally) permitted by Islam. It is the opposite of *haram*, which literally translates as 'that which is not permitted'.

Hanafi: one of the four main Islamic schools of legal thought, it is predominant in Afghanistan (and also is the largest in terms of adherents globally). Named after the legal scholar Abu Hanifa (d.767), it advocates a more open approach to the Islamic law or shari'a.

Hanbali: one of the four main Islamic schools of legal thought or *fiqh*. Named after the legal scholar Ahmad ibn Hanbal (d.855), the so-called Sheikh ul-Islam, the Hanbali school is considered more conservative than other schools.

haram: a religious term used to denote that which is not permitted by Islam. It is the opposite of halal, which literally translates as 'that which is permitted'.

hijab: the veil often used by women to cover their hair and/or face

Hijra: literally 'emigration' or 'flight', referring to the Prophet's departure from Mecca to Medina in 622

hudud: literally 'limit' or 'boundary', this term refers to the punishments which are mandated by God as transmitted through the sources of Islamic knowledge. The *hudu* are Qur'anic offences, and so only apply to highway robbery, alcohol consump- tion, adultery/fornication, false accusation of adultery/fornication and theft.

GLOSSARY

IDP: internally displaced person / people

Insha'allah: literally 'if God wills it'; often used in a loose sense conversationally to mean 'maybe'

ISI: Inter-Services Intelligence is the main Pakistani military intelligence wing. Especially prominent in the funding and supplying of weapons to the Afghan mujahedeen, ISI has become synonymous with the strong involvement of Pakistan's military in political affairs.

Islam: Islam is a religion combining an ethical and philosophical system of belief with a set of prescribed rituals. It is, by implication, as useful or ethically 'good' a system as it is applied (i.e. by Muslims). Islam is found in multiple and varied forms around the world (a result of local cultural accretion and a natural evolving process).

Jahili: literally 'ignorant'; often used in an Islamic context to refer to the time before the Prophet Muhammad (and thus before Islam) as a time of 'ignorance'

Jalut: Goliath

jihad: the Arabic-language term is derived from an Arabic root meaning 'to struggle', 'to exert oneself', or 'to strive'. As such, the word can mean different things depending on the context: sometimes a struggle against evil inclinations (the so-called 'greater jihad'), or at other times a reference to legally-sanctioned (by the Islamic legal code) war. The term has a rich history of meanings (both theoretical and practical), some of which is explored in this book.

jirga: a Pashto-language term meaning 'council' or 'consultative gathering'. It is to be distinguished from the word shura, although the two are sometimes used indistinguishably in a loose sense.

jizya: an Arabic-language term referring to the taxes that non-Muslim subjects would pay to Muslim authorities / rulers in their territories. The tax requires the protection of the minority by the state with no obligation to defend the state militarily.

Kaaba: the building at the centre of Islam's most sacred mosque, the Al-Masjid Al-Ḥaram

kafir / kuffar: refers to a person believed to be in a state of *kufr* or 'unbelief'

kaldar: the national currency of Pakistan, rupees

Khalq: literally translated as 'people' or 'masses', the Khalq were a faction of the PDPA (People's Democratic Party of Afghanistan) headed by Noor Mohammad Taraki and Hafizullah Amin, and was opposed to the Parcham faction headed by Babrak Karmal.

Kuchi: Afghanistan's nomadic peoples. The word *kuchi* derives from the Dari *kuch kardan* which means 'to be on the move' or 'to be moving'. Kuchis uproot their homes twice a year with the seasons and are found all over Afghanistan. In Kandahar, there used to be many living in the Registan desert, but the 1980s war and the ensuing drought forced many to settle permanently in camps in Pakistan.

layeha: literally 'rules', this Pashto word refers to the Taliban's book of regulations that they started publishing in 2006

madrassa: religious school common in southern Afghanistan and Pakistan as the first choice for education (especially for the rural poor). Schools are by and large for boys only, although girls are educated in some, and the syllabus mainly constitutes a full outline of the religious sciences, often including the expectation that graduates will learn various holy books by heart (notably, the Qur'an itself).

Mawlawi: a title used by graduates of madrassas who have received further religious education as well. It is the equivalent of postgraduate study for scholars of Islam. A mawlawi is a member of the ulemaa, the Islamic clergy.

Mobashirat: 'glad-tidings', a form of direct guidance from God

mujahed / mujahedeen: the active participle *mujahed* (plural *mujahedeen*) is a term used to refer to someone who is or was engaged in jihad (this almost always implies combat). It is used both as a noun ('a mujahed was killed') and adjectivally (*haghe yaw mujahed saray wu* in Pashto: 'he was a mujahed-type of man'). The plural form is generally reserved for reference to those Afghans who fought in the 1980s against their government and the Soviet soldiers inside Afghanistan. This usage is inherited and common among scholars.

mullah: religious functionary or cleric extremely prevalent outside the cities in Afghanistan. They will usually be the single religious authority (having attended a madrassa during childhood, or maybe because they can read some Arabic and thus the language of the Qur'an) in a particular village. As such their authority is usually limited to religious matters.

nasheed: a chant of vocal music

naswar: a type of tobacco snuff consumed in Afghanistan and Pakistan. It carries a negative association for the Taliban, who often refer to those who perpetrated crimes during the early 1990s as *naswar*-users.

niqab: the veil that covers the face, leaving the eyes clear and visible

OIC: Organisation of Islamic Cooperation

Otaq: see amir

Parcham: literally translated as 'flag', the Parcham were a faction of the PDPA (People's Democratic Party of Afghanistan) headed by Babrak Karmal and opposed to the Khalq faction led by Noor Mohammad Taraki and Hafizullah Amin.

GLOSSARY

Pashto: one of the national languages of Afghanistan

PBUH: abbreviation of 'peace be upon him'

Qari: title used before people's names in Afghanistan. It refers to the practice/skill of being a Qari' (Arabic loan-word), which literally means someone who is able to recite the Qur'an.

Qazi: a judge. The word comes from the Arabic, and is used to denote the person who adjudicates, usually having studied in a madrassa or theological seminary.

qibla: an Arabic-language term that refers to the direction in which Muslims around the world pray (i.e. towards the Kaaba in Mecca, Saudi Arabia). The *qibla* was originally oriented towards Jerusalem, but this changed to the Kaaba in the year 623.

qisas: literally means equality, but has the shari'a meaning of retribution / retaliation. This legal principle, for example, is behind the Taliban's invitation for family members of those murdered to be the ones to administer a punishment to the guilty party.

Qunoot-e Nazila: refers to the specific prayer performed (usually during the Witr prayer) during times of difficulty in the Muslim world. It can be performed in any prayer, however.

Qur'an: the religious book of Muslims around the world, literally translated as 'recitation', since Muslims believe it is the result of the direct revelation of God to the Prophet Muhammad starting in 610.

RA: *rahimullah aleihi* (literally 'may God have mercy on him'), used when referring to someone who has died

Ramadan: also known as Ramazan, this is a month in the Islamic calendar during which all Muslims are obliged to fast during the hours of daylight. There are exceptions to this obligation though, for example for the sick and those who are travelling.

rupee: the national currency of Pakistan

saheb: a term of respect used after someone's title in southern Afghanistan. It is used for one's elders, the educated, those with high government positions and so on. Also known as *sahib*.

SAWS: an abbreviation of *sallallahu alayhi wa salaam*, which means 'may God's prayers and peace be with him'

Shaheed: an Arabic loan-word used in Dari and Pashto to mean 'martyred'. It carries religious connotations, fitting into the theology of jihad. Martyrs, in Islamic theology, go straight to heaven; they do not have to wait for the day of judgement. It is important to add that it is not only 'warriors' who are counted among the *shuhada'* (pl. term in Arabic for 'martyrs'); for instance, civilian victims of conflict in the

Muslim world are often described as *shuhada'*. Nor is this a modern corruption: classical Arabic sources, for instance, describe the victims of the Franks and the Mongols as martyrs, too.

shari'a: for shari'a this book follows Esposito's definition as 'ideal Islamic law'. There is a large body of thought which asks people to distinguish between shari'a and fiqh (human efforts to codify 'Islamic' law in the absence of a specific injunction in the Qur'an or the sunna), arguing that the former is 'ideal' and the latter is tainted and flawed. For this book, the term shari'a is generally used to refer not only to the prescriptions and proscriptions themselves, but also the system surrounding it—the scholars and clerics whose role it is to interpret the law, as well as the hadith and sunna repository. There are five prominent schools of Islamic law: Hanafi, Hanbali, Maliki, Shafi'i and Ja'fari.

Shi'i: distinguished from the Sunnis, the Shi'i are the so-called 'partisans of Ali' (coming from the Arabic phrase *shi'at 'Ali*). Shi'i Muslims identify the fourth of the Rashidun caliphs, Ali, as the head of a line of leadership that they consider legitimate over the Sunni clerics that followed.

shirk: the sin of practising idolatry

shura: an Arabic-language term meaning 'consultation', used extensively in the Afghan context to mean 'council' or 'consultative gathering'. It is to be distinguished from the word jirga, although the two are sometimes used indistinguishably in a loose sense.

sunna: The established custom or precedent established and based on the example of the Prophet Muhammad. It offers a separate set of principles of conduct and traditions which were recorded by the Prophet's companions. These customs complement the divinely revealed message of the Qur'an. A whole field of jurisprudence has grown up alongside the study of the sunna. The sunna is recorded in the ahadith (pl. of hadith), and represents the prophetic 'norm'.

Sunni: someone who follows the sunna; it is used to distinguish them from Shi'i Muslims.

sura: literally a 'chapter' of the Qur'an. Divided into 114 separate such suras, the Qur'an's chapters are ordered by descending length, rather than their chronological appearance or date of revelation.

SWT: an abbreviation of *subhanahu wa ta'ala*, literally meaning 'glorious and exalted is he'

tafsir / tafseer: an interpretation of the Qur'an

Takbir: Arabic phrase literally translated as 'God is the Greatest', although more approximate to 'God is Great'

GLOSSARY

Talib / Taliban: Dari/Pashto plural form of Talib. Used to refer to religious students, mainly those who are graduates of madrassas. The term became better known in the mid-1990s because of the movement that took the word as its name on account of its large number of madrassa student supporters.

Talut: Saul

Taraweeh: the special prayers each night during the month of Ramadan. During these prayers, long sections of the Qur'an are recited, and it is thus a way to gain exposure to the full text of the book during that month.

ulemaa: plural version of alim, literally 'those who have knowledge'. It refers to religious scholars (primarily used for the Sunni clergy) who have been educated in the religious 'sciences' (the Qur'an, the sunna and the hadiths etc).

umma: an Arabic-language term referring to the community of Muslims around the world. It is sometimes used in a secular form to mean 'nation' (as in the Arabic version of 'the United Nations', al-Umam al-Muttahida).

ushr: see *zakat*

zakat: one of the five 'pillars' of Islam, the practice of almsgiving or *zakat* is widespread and encouraged in southern Afghanistan. It is also—to a certain extent—systematised in such a way that it is in many instances a highly formalised type of charitable donation, whereby those with financial means must donate 2.5 per cent of their annual earnings and liquid assets for the needy. Apart from a nominal sum given to them by the government, the religious clergy—particularly in rural areas of the south—often have to rely on *zakat* and other donations from their fellow villagers. In Afghanistan this exists alongside the tradition of *ushr*, whereby 10 per cent of profits are shared out to fellow villagers.

zina: adultery or unlawful sexual intercourse

FURTHER READING

Agha, Sayyed Mohammad Akbar (2014), *I am Akbar Agha: Memories of the Afghan Jihad and the Taliban* (Berlin: First Draft Publishing).

Gumnam, Mohammad Tahir Aziz (2014), *Kandahar Assassins: Stories from the Afghan–Soviet War* (Berlin: First Draft Publishing).

Gumnam, Mohammad Tahir Aziz (forthcoming), *Kandahar Heroes* (Berlin: First Draft Publishing).

Ibn Mahmud, Husayn (2005), *Al-Rajul al-'Amlaaq: The Giant Man* (Online: At-Tibyaan Publications).

Mohabbat, M. Kabir and L. R. McInnis (2011), *Delivering Osama* (Online: Google Books).

Mutawakil, Wakil Ahmad (2007), *Afghanistan aw Taliban* [Afghanistan and the Taliban] (Kabul: Unknown publisher).

Muzhda, Wahid (2003), *Afghanistan va panj sal-i sultah-i taliban* [Afghanistan Under Five Years of Taliban Sovereignty] (Kabul: Unknown publisher).

Rasheed Ludhianvi, Mufti (2015), *Obedience to the Amir: An early text on the Afghan Taliban Movement* (Berlin: First Draft Publishing).

Strick van Linschoten, Alex and Felix Kuehn (2012), *Poetry of the Taliban* (London: Hurst & Co.).

Taliban Sources Project: see www.talibansourcesproject.com

Yousafzai, Sami (2009), The Taliban's Oral History of the Afghanistan War (New York: Newsweek), http://www.newsweek.com/talibans-oral-history-afghanistan-war-79553.

Zaeef, Abdul Salam (2010), *My Life with the Taliban* (London: Hurst & Co.).

ACKNOWLEDGEMENTS

Thanks to two anonymous reviewers of the manuscript. Your suggestions were useful in giving this book a wider appeal.

We appreciated having Anand Gopal and Michael Innes working with us on the hard slog of gathering and archiving the Taliban Sources Project materials. Our Advisory Board made useful suggestions and connections along the way. FFI, Thomas Hegghammer and Anne Stenersen must be thanked for their role in finding a final home for the archive, and we look forward to it being made available to a wider public. The Afghanistan Analysts Network stepped in at the last minute to help host the physical collection, and we thank their staff and Kate Clark for making that happen.

Both Asim Qureshi and Ed Hadley graciously volunteered their time for discussions of the minutiae of texts and their meaning. We are grateful for their friendship.

We thank M.M. for his help gathering sources for the Taliban Sources Project (and for much else). Authors putting together their memoirs for First Draft Publishing put a great deal of trust in us, without which there would be no manuscript or memoir. Mullah Abdul Salam Zaeef was one of our first introductions into the world of the Taliban movement, back when we first started working on *My Life With the Taliban*, and we want to acknowledge the importance of that relationship in developing our understanding. Many other Afghans worked with us on the translations and support for this book. The sensitivity of this project coupled with the ongoing conflict in Afghanistan make it unwise to list names. Needless to say, none of this would have been possible without their help and support.

Finally, we thank Michael Dwyer, Jon de Peyer, Rob Pinney and the rest of the team at Hurst for putting up with our delays.

INDEX

INDEX

INDEX

INDEX

INDEX

INDEX

INDEX

INDEX